Shakespeare's Lost Kingdom

Also by Charles Beauclerk:

Nell Gwyn: Mistress to a King

CHARLES BEAUCLERK

Shakespeare's Lost Kingdom

The True History of
Shakespeare and Elizabeth

Grove Press

New York

Published simultaneously in Canada
Printed in the United States of America

FIRST EDITION

ISBN-13: 978-0-8021-1940-7

Grove Press
an imprint of Grove/Atlantic, Inc.
841 Broadway
New York, NY 10003

Distributed by Publishers Group West

www.groveatlantic.com

10 11 12 13 14   10 9 8 7 6 5 4 3 2 1

For Lisa Marie

Contents

Every secret of a writer's soul, every experience of his life, every quality of his mind, is written large in his works, yet we require critics to explain the one and biographers to expound the other.

—Virginia Woolf

Preface

Methinks I see these things with parted eye,
When everything seems double.
(*A Midsummer Night's Dream,* IV.i.187–188)

IT IS ALWAYS DANGEROUS to take the Elizabethans at face value. The mentality that created their culture, evident as much in their politics as their art, was fantastical, ingenious, allegorical—witness Queen Elizabeth's mystical and mystifying statecraft, enduringly evoked in Spenser's *Faerie Queene*. The many portraits of Elizabeth that have survived bear witness to a deep and playful immersion in the world of symbolism and mythology; and what we might be tempted to call deceit in today's politics, Elizabethans would have called enchantment. The queen's extravagant courtship of foreign princes, for instance, though conducted in bad faith, was rehearsed and carried through with compelling diligence and betrayed a breathtaking belief in her own infallibility. But as with any production, a lot of unglamorous work went on behind the scenes. Polonius spying on Hamlet from behind the arras is a good example: hardly dignified employment for an exalted minister of state. Elizabeth's Lord Burghley was no different. Little wonder it is often difficult at this remove to determine what was real and what was not.

This mixture of the fantastic and the mundane led to a love of the grotesque and paradoxical, and encompassed a mischievous sense of humor. This was reflected both in the literature of the time (Bottom, Falstaff, Caliban), and in many of the paintings and portraits, nowhere more so than in the curious engraving by Martin Droeshout that appeared as the frontispiece to the First Folio of 1623 and has since become the iconic representation of the Bard, appearing on anything from bank cards to T-shirts. It is the most famous image of our most celebrated poet, and the first to be published. For those who never set eyes on the Bard during his lifetime, this would have been their first glimpse of the man.

It is illuminating to show such images to children, for rather than try to "make sense" of what they see, they let their intuition do the seeing. When I showed the Droeshout engraving to my eight-year-old son and asked him what he thought, he laughed and said it was a joke—which is exactly what it is. That absurd mask of a countenance (with the edge of a second face clearly visible behind it) hovering above the weird platter-like collar, not to mention the stiff sculpted hair framing the outsize egghead with its tablike ear and incongruous stubble—all contribute to a strong air of unreality. Nor does one have to look very carefully to see that the figure has two right eyes and two left arms. As an article in the *Gentleman's Tailor* of April 1911 put it: "The tunic, coat, or whatever the garment may have been called at the time is so strangely illustrated that the right-hand side of the forepart is obviously the left-hand side of the back part, and so gives a harlequin appearance to the figure."

There are many other anomalies in the portrait, but by no stretch of the imagination can these be labeled "errors" or the work of an inexperienced artist. The symbolism is clear: the face presented to the world is that of a left-handed (or spurious) author, while hidden behind him is the true or right-handed author. The two right eyes may be a pun on William of Stratford's motto "Non sans droict" ("Not without right"). Looked at as a whole, the sitter is indeed presented in the guise of Harlequin (from the Italian commedia dell'arte), a masked servant in patched costume, celebrated for his gluttony and slow-wittedness. Yet the collar and rich-looking doublet bespeak a man of social standing, reinforcing the impression that this is a dual figure. Far from bemoaning the artist's "errors," one is inclined to praise the skill of his carefully elaborated design.

The Droeshout portrait of Shakespeare is abnormally large, and because of its size lacks the allegorical figures, symbols, and other iconographic details that usually surround such a portrait.[1] The reason for the unusual scale is not hard to divine: the portrait needed to be sufficiently large for its anomalies to be detected and understood. In other words, the figure itself comprises the allegory. No further symbols were required.

What would wealthy, educated Jacobeans, the First Folio's original readership, have made of it? My guess is that their reaction would have been similar to that of Sir George Greenwood, lawyer and Member of Parliament, who, writing three centuries later, declared: "I can never understand how any unprejudiced person, with a sense of humor, can look upon [the print] without being tempted to irreverent laughter." This, surely, must have been the intention of those who sponsored and directed the publication, the Herbert brothers, Earls of Pembroke and Montgomery. They were part of the extended family of the true author, and knew that the only way to see the politically inflammatory works published was to conform to the official view of Shakespeare's identity. But their adherence did not need to be slavish and literal; they could thumb their noses while appearing to toe the party line. Hence the Droeshout's deliberate "blunders," and the many ambiguities in the First Folio's prefatory matter.

In an authoritarian age with little or no freedom of speech, writers resort to allegory as a means of disguising and revealing the truth. Mikhail Bulgakov's *The Master and Margarita* (1938) is a good example from the Soviet era. Allegory literally means "speaking otherwise," and its double meaning was beloved of the metaphorically-minded Elizabethans, addicted as they were to wordplay and visual puns. When Ben Jonson hailed Shakespeare as "Sweet Swan of Avon" in his prefatory verses to the First Folio, his readers would have picked up on the idea that the poet being praised was mute or had been silenced in some way—as in Sidney's fable of the swan in the old *Arcadia*—no doubt because of his criticism or satire of others.[2] "Art made tongue-tied by authority," as Shakespeare has it in Sonnet 66.

What then of the front man, the Harlequin who for four centuries has protected the identity of the true author?

On April 26, 1564, one Gulielmus Shakspere was baptized at Holy Trinity Church, Stratford-upon-Avon. Born to illiterate parents (his father, John, signed with a mark), he was the third of eight children, all strangers to literacy. Nothing is known of Gulielmus's childhood or possible schooling, though there is a legend that he was apprenticed to his father at age thirteen as a butcher and glover. No entry or attendance records survive for the Stratford grammar school, and no master there left an account of this budding literary genius. In November 1582, aged eighteen, he married Anne Hathaway, who was pregnant with their first child, Susanna, born the following May. Twins, Hamnet and Judith, named for their neighbors Hamnet and Judith Sadler, followed in 1585. As far as we know, his children were never taught to read or write. There are no further records of him until 1592, when it is recorded in London that "Willelmus Shackspere" made a loan of £7 to one John Clayton. Three years later, in March 1595, "William Shakespeare" together with William Kempe and Richard Burbage, "servants to the Lord Chamberlain," received £20 for theatrical performances at court the previous December. It is not certain that this "William Shakespeare" is the same "Willelmus Shackspere" who lent £7 to John Clayton. The following year his son Hamnet died in Stratford, aged eleven.

In 1597—and again in 1598 and 1599—"William Shackspere" is listed as a tax defaulter in Bishopsgate, possibly because he had already moved back to Stratford. Sure enough, that same year (1597) "Willielmin Shakespeare" purchases New Place, a large property in his hometown, and pursues his application for a coat of arms. Although various documents between 1599 and 1608 record the involvement of one William Shakespeare with the Globe, both as a shareholder and as a member of the King's Men, most of the records for the last twenty years of his life place William Shakspere as a landowner and dealer in bagged commodities in his native Stratford. He was also a litigant in several lawsuits to recover minor debts. When he died in April 1616, no books or manuscripts were listed in his will—an anomaly for an educated man of the time—and his death went unremarked even by his fellow writers. (We are told that when the Shakespearean actor Richard Burbage died in 1619, the whole of London was in mourning.) No letters, diaries, or memos in his hand have ever come to light; all that we have are six signatures, all spelled differently, three of which appear on his will. This in essence is the documented life of the man believed to be the greatest poet in the English language, perhaps in any language, who added more than 3,000 words to our vocabulary, left no corner of the human soul unillumined, and whom Jonson apostrophized as "the Soul of the Age."

As for the works he is supposed to have written, which were published from 1593 onward, they are sophisticated, politically explosive court dramas that evince a deep knowledge of the law, philosophy, languages (including Latin, Greek, French, and Italian),

European geography and culture, ancient and modern history, mathematics, cosmology, the fine arts, music, medicine, horticulture, heraldry, court manners, and aristocratic pastimes such as hunting, falconry, bowls, and royal tennis. Indeed, it is no exaggeration to say that Shakespeare was a polymath on the scale of Leonardo da Vinci. When *Venus and Adonis,* Shakespeare's first published work, appeared in 1593, it delighted the young men and women of the court with its polished Ovidian references and wittily salacious language, as well as its daring satire of Elizabeth (the mortal Venus). At the time, with the works appearing either anonymously or with the name "William Shake-speare" on the title page, no one would have associated the plays or poems with a man like William Shakspere of Stratford. After all, how did a country lad who lived four days' hard riding from London come to be obsessed with the throne and royal succession?

The educated elite who bought the plays from the London booksellers would have recognized them as court plays written by an insider, who was deeply versed in English history and European culture as well as the customs and manners of royal courts, both at home and on the Continent. For those at court, his identity was an open secret, which remained concealed from the public at large, rather like Roosevelt's polio during the war, which never leaked into the press but was common knowledge among White House staff. The people at court also knew that this was an author who did not scruple to speak of state affairs in his works; hence it was in their interest to protect the secret—that way, they shielded their insular world from the scrutiny of outsiders. Exposing the author would have meant exposing his satires of them and their queen.

King James I died within eighteen months of publication of the First Folio, and the issue of the author's identity remained off limits during the reign of his son Charles I. Not only were the offspring of statesmen lampooned in Shakespeare's plays now in positions of power and influence, but the works gave notice of Tudor heirs yet living. Moreover, the Puritans were rapidly gaining stature, and London was no longer the fertile ground for plays and masques it had once been. The Shakespeare taboo still held, as the anonymously published *Wit's Recreation* of 1640 boldly implied: "Shakes-speare, we must be silent in our praise,/'Cause our encomiums will but blast thy bays." Soon the Civil War was raging, and the theaters were closed altogether during the interregnum. The Restoration, when it finally came, saw a new type of court comedy in vogue, and Shakespeare, often poorly adapted, was dinned out by the heroic tragedies of Dryden and Sir Robert Howard. Though *The Winter's Tale* was played at court before Charles I in 1634, the next recorded performance was not until 1741, 107 years later.

Few realize that William of Stratford's authorship is an eighteenth-century phenomenon. Although John Aubrey had gathered some gossipy notes about the Stratford man in the early 1680s (first published in 1813 as part of his *Brief Lives*), it was not until Nicholas Rowe prefixed his 1709 edition of the Shakespeare works with a short biography of the Stratford man that a fledgling identity emerged. Nevertheless, there had been little advance on Aubrey in the intervening thirty years, and Rowe's life of Shakespeare, which according to Dr. Jonson was only "such as tradition, then almost expiring, could supply," is as flawed and hypothetical as its more florid predecessor.

Another sixty years would pass before the Stratford myth was well and truly launched, with the actor David Garrick's extravagant jubilee celebrations on the banks of the Avon in 1769, fully 155 years after the Stratford man's death. Both actor and playwright, Garrick saw his own reflection in the Shakespearean mirror and became an enthusiastic advocate of the putative actor-manager's authorship. Significantly, the eighteenth-century swing toward the cult of "Avonian Willy" coincided with an upsurge in English patriotism and imperialism, and Shakespeare was commissioned to do duty as the national poet of England. Yet the paucity of biographical detail for the great poet-dramatist, indeed his persistent and baffling anonymity, led to a spate of forgeries, first from William Henry Ireland in the 1790s, followed in the nineteenth century by the altogether more insidious and plausible fictions of the Shakespeare scholar John Payne Collier.[3] The desire to bring the Stratford grain dealer into some sort of harmony with the polymath of the plays was understandably pressing.

It was during this scramble to make sense of the curious disparity between the man and his works that the "Shakespeare authorship question" emerged full-fledged in the mid-nineteenth century. As if in anticipation of the coming inquisition, Charles Dickens had written to the lawyer and antiquarian William Sandys in 1847: "It is a great comfort, to my thinking, that so little is known concerning the poet. It is a fine mystery; and I tremble every day lest something should come out."

Although new lives of Shakespeare of Stratford continue to pour forth from the presses each year, one always comes away with a strong feeling that the man himself has eluded the best efforts of his biographers to capture him. There may be insightful passages about his works and whole chapters on the institutions and characters of Elizabethan London, including Shakespeare's hell-raising contemporaries Robert Greene, Thomas Nashe, and Ben Jonson, but the man himself is little more than an enigmatic smile melting into the horizon.

Still less do these biographies manage to connect the man to the body of literature associated with his name. In attempting to explain the dynamics of metaphor to a friend, the Russian poet Boris Pasternak took a box of matches and a pen from his desk and, placing them side by side, asked him to watch them interact. But the works of William Shake-speare have been placed side by side with the life of Gulielmus Shakspere of Stratford for nearly four centuries now, and no interaction has taken place; no dynamic current connects the two. In a letter to Nathaniel Holmes in 1866, Dr. W. H. Furness, editor of the *New Variorum Shakespeare,* wrote: "I am one of the many who have never been able to bring the life of William Shakespeare and the plays of Shakespeare within planetary distance of each other. Are there any two things in the world more incongruous?" This incongruity is the primary reason that biographies of Shakespeare fail as biographies, even if they succeed as engaging portraits of Elizabethan theater life or the age in general. Nothing in the life of William Shakspere of Stratford illuminates the works he is supposed to have written. Thus the plays themselves are reduced to works of fantasy rather than masterpieces of the imagination. As far as Shakespearean biography goes, we have reached a dead end.

Shakespeare's biographers fail to connect the life and the plays convincingly, not simply because they have the wrong man, but because they fail to recognize the identity crisis that is at the heart of Shakespeare's creativity. This omission keeps them sealed off from the core or creative soul of the author. As a result, Shakespeare remains to all intents and purposes anonymous, a mere cipher for the critical theories of the scholars. Like Banquo's ghost, he sits at the head of the table in awful silence.

Far better to acknowledge, indeed to celebrate, this crisis—this anonymity—as an intrinsic element of Shakespeare's greatness than to avoid it, for not only could it hold an important clue to the meaning of his works, but it may even have been part of his artistic method. What is certain is that Shakespeare's self-concealment kept him growing as an artist throughout his life, free from the limiting pressures of public opinion. (It is surely significant that the greatest of writers has the ghostliest of identities.) The little that we know of Shakspere of Stratford is probably all we shall ever know, for 200 years of the most intensive research has yielded almost nothing. Though a player in the Shakespeare controversy, he is not the author. In using him as the gateway to the works, we run the risk of restricting our understanding; but if we take the authorship question itself as our portal and see it as an outgrowth of the author's own identity crisis, we can enter an interpretative space that is both creative and illuminating.

Whatever view one takes of Shakespeare's true identity—and no fewer than sixty candidates have been advanced in the past 150 years, five in the last five years alone[4]—no one can deny that mistaken identity, concealed identity, loss of identity, and enforced anonymity are major themes in the works of this most celebrated poet-dramatist. Nor are these themes arbitrary or academic; rather, they bear the stamp and anxiety of actual experience. His contemporaries, too, were confronted with a mystery, and their cryptic accounts of him invite speculation about his identity.

If we allow Shakespeare to reveal himself to us through his principal themes, which build up a picture of his psychology, we see an author obsessed with his own frail sense of identity, which leads him from self-aggrandizing visions to outright renunciation; one who, in the end, subsumes himself in his works, the plays becoming the embodiment of his identity: his corpus.

Shakespeare himself, it seems, wanted to engage us in the question of his identity; in other words, he helped create what has come to be known as the Shakespeare authorship question. If we ignore this reality, we miss many of the essential elements of his art, leaving his message buried in the sands of time.

Part One

Child of State

~ *1* ~

Truth's Authentic Author

O God, Horatio, what a wounded name,
Things standing thus unknown, shall live behind me!
If thou didst ever hold me in thy heart,
Absent thee from felicity awhile,
And in this harsh world draw thy breath in pain
To tell my story.

(Hamlet, V.ii.349–354)

IN HAMLET'S DYING APPEAL to his friend Horatio, it is difficult not
to hear the voice of Shakespeare himself speaking to us across the
centuries. Such is the urgency of his entreaty that we feel impelled
to find out more about the author and his story—i.e., those things
"standing thus unknown"—and to tell that story to the world. Only
by discovering and telling the author's true story can we hope to heal
his wounded name. In its own way, this book is an attempt to do
just that.

It may be objected that Hamlet is merely a character in a play,
one of dozens that Shakespeare created in the course of his life. Closer
examination of the canon reveals that he appears in a variety of guises
throughout the Shakespeare plays. Whether writing for Berowne,
Romeo, Henry VI, Richard II, Prince Hal, Jaques, Brutus, Edgar,
Vincentio, Antonio, Posthumus, or Prospero (to name but a dozen),
Shakespeare is forever slipping into what Frank Harris described as
"the Hamlet vein," thus confirming our suspicion that the author
and the Prince of Denmark are one. This is not consciously contrived (indeed, it could be argued that it is an artistic fault), but is an

inevitable expression of the author's individuality. In identifying with a given character Shakespeare reverts, quite naturally, to his own voice—the Hamlet voice.

Macbeth is a good example. So unlike Hamlet on the surface, he is a valiant and decisive general, whose sword in battle "smok[es] with bloody execution." Yet no one can deny that, as Shakespeare paints him, he is also the sensitive, melancholy, irresolute philosopher so familiar to us from the pages of *Hamlet*. As Harris tellingly observes: "Let us take the first appearance of Macbeth, and we are forced to remark at once that he acts and speaks exactly as Hamlet in like circumstances would act and speak. The honest but slow Banquo is amazed when *Macbeth* starts and seems to fear the fair promises of the witches; he does not see what the nimble Hamlet-intellect has seen in a flash—the dread means by which alone the promises can be brought to fulfilment."[5] Even the Sonnets bear the stamp of Hamlet's personality.

Shakespeare's works derive much of their power from the curiously personal manner in which they speak to us, as vivid and subjective dramatizations of an individual struggle. In this regard they are unique in Elizabethan literature. Moreover, that struggle seems bound up with the question of the author's identity. Hamlet is one among a host of characters who must feign madness or assume a new identity in order to survive the rigors of the state. A prince by blood, he is prevented not only from inheriting the throne but from exercising any form of political power, turning instead to the theater as a means of influencing the ruling elite.

Hamlet is no ordinary character. His sincerity and individuality are such that he seems to break free of his literary existence, coming before us with all the sudden drama of his appearance in Ophelia's closet. The vivid realism of his portrayal is startling even today; at the time it must have seemed a truly shocking innovation. More than any other Shakespearean hero, Hamlet steps outside the boundaries of the play to appeal directly to his audience, as if Shakespeare wishes to express more than the restrictions of his art will allow. Hamlet is not interested in convincing the other characters of the justice of his cause (indeed, with the exception of Horatio, we get the feeling he has given up on them): rather it is to us—to posterity—that he addresses himself.

In his desire to "catch the conscience" of King Claudius, Hamlet stages a play called *The Mousetrap,* depicting the murder of which his uncle is guilty. The play, then, is used to present an alternative version of history, one that so nettles Claudius and his chief minister that the latter stops the performance. Through this device Shakespeare alerts us to the use to which he puts his own plays. *Hamlet* itself is an Elizabethan *Mousetrap* designed to hold the mirror up to Shakespeare's queen, Elizabeth I. Through its tale of a disinherited prince asserting his royal right by means of the theater, Shakespeare tells his own story. With this realization we find ourselves caught up in a political intrigue that seems to demand our participation even today. Suddenly the play becomes thrillingly real. Denmark is England, and we return to the theater again and again to listen to the agonized promptings of a royal poet, as if aware on some dim level of consciousness that our history has been tampered with.

In putting on *The Mousetrap* before the King and Queen, Hamlet is opposing his truth and artistic vision to the political propaganda peddled by Denmark's chief minister, Polonius, whom Claudius dubs "the father of good news." In this he is doing more than redressing a personal wrong; he is rewriting history for the benefit of the nation. As the Ghost of his father points out, "the whole ear of Denmark" has been "rankly abus'd" by the official story put out by the government—namely that he, old King Hamlet, died by accident. Through drama Hamlet discloses the unrecorded history of his age; that is why he is able to describe the players as "the abstract and brief chronicles of the time."

Polonius is a ruthless spin doctor who sets himself the task of protecting the lie on which the new reign is founded. In him Shakespeare coined the political doublespeak that holds our modern-day culture in thrall: circuitous, guarded, uncommitted, and ultimately inconsequential. We hear it day in day out from politicians of every stripe; it is the tangled web spun forth from the belly of deceit. Let us not forget that in priming Reynaldo to spy on his son in Paris, Polonius says, "And there put on him what forgeries you please." This is not a man who respects the truth.

It is not enough to study the historical records as they've been handed down to us by the Poloniuses of this world, for they represent a skewed perspective—if not of a single man, then of a powerful family or faction. As George Orwell commented wryly, "History is written by the winners." Queen Elizabeth's chief minister and self-appointed historiographer, William Cecil, Lord Burghley, who is widely recognized as the original of Polonius, and his son Robert Cecil, later earl of Salisbury, are the men according to whose word Elizabethan history has been, and continues to be, shaped. The official records, which are often little more than propaganda, have to be studied in conjunction with the literature of the time. Together they are the warp and weft of the nation's story. It would be impossible to understand the history of the Soviet Union, to take a more recent example, by confining oneself to a study of the Kremlin records. A deeply distorted picture would emerge. To gain a less biased view of the age, one would have to read the dissident poets and novelists, such as Mandelstam, Akhmatova, Zabolotsky, Bulgakov, and Solzhenitsyn, for, like Shakespeare, their works reveal the hidden or missing story: *history as written by the losers.* If autocratic regimes have taught us one thing, it is that fiction is simply a deeper, more elaborate way of telling the truth.

Ultimately, Hamlet's petition to Horatio to tell his story is Shakespeare's injunction to play the play, for his story is embedded in the text. Polonius, of course, stops the play, as authoritarian governments have been doing for centuries. Powerless to combat the sincerity and magic of Hamlet's art with a valid message of his own, he censors it. If we can imagine Shakespeare in the same position vis-à-vis Lord Burghley and Elizabeth's government, then the plays are revealed as more than simple fictions: they become precious historical and political documents.

When serious and persistent doubts over the identity of Shakespeare began to appear in print in the mid-nineteenth century, the search was on for the man whose life and learning matched the high culture of the Shakespeare canon. The Victorians promoted Francis Bacon, who held the field for over sixty years. Baconians, as they are now called, were the first to realize the significance of the royal theme in Shakespeare, but their reliance on fantastically complex ciphers, as witness Minnesota congressman Ignatius Donnelly's *The Great Cryptogram* (1888), stretched credulity. Then, in November 1918, a sealed envelope was entrusted to Sir Frederick Kenyon, head librarian at the British Museum, by an English schoolmaster with the provocative name of J. Thomas Looney (1870–1944). Inside was a statement of his discovery of the true identity of the man who wrote under the pen name William Shakespeare.

Those who discover startling new truths, whether in science or letters, tend to be dismissed as mad by colleagues clinging to the old paradigm. It seems appropriate, therefore, that the man who eventually solved the Shakespeare authorship mystery should have borne the name of Looney. After all, it is the fools and madmen who are the truth tellers in Shakespeare's plays.

Looney's thesis, which was the first attempt at an objective and logical quest for the author of the Shakespeare canon, was published by Cecil Palmer in 1920.[6] Looney wasn't pursuing a hunch; he didn't have one. His faith in the traditional author had been shaken, and he decided to make a systematic search to discover the man behind the mask, whomever he might prove to be. Looney had been a bona fide Stratfordian all his life, teaching Shakespeare to grammar school children, and in the preface to his work confesses that he had a deep-rooted prejudice in favor of the Stratford man's authorship, which he found hard to abandon, even in the face of strong rational doubts.

As Looney relates it, successive years of reading *The Merchant of Venice* with his pupils induced in him "a peculiar sense of intimacy with the mind and disposition of its author and his outlook upon life," which he found at total variance with the life and career of the reputed playwright. For one thing, it was obvious to him that the author knew Venice like the back of his hand: not only the topography of the city-state, but its customs, culture, legal system, and linguistic idiosyncrasies. The Stratford man, on the other hand, had never left the shores of England. In the absence of contemporary documents relating to Shakespeare the man, Looney realized that the evidence gathered by his investigations would be circumstantial rather than documentary and that the Shakespeare works themselves would provide the most fundamental evidence as to the character, station, and mentality of the author.

Acting like a profiler in search of an unknown criminal, Looney's first step was to examine the works and draw up two sets of characteristics that the author evidently possessed, one general and one special.[7] Totaling eighteen, they included the playwright's doubtful attitude toward women, his erudition, love of music, familiarity with Italy, feudal and court connections, Catholic sympathies, and improvidence in money matters. Looney also surmised that the author must have appeared eccentric and mysterious to contemporaries, as his secret Shakespearean life would not have been known to them. From the eighteen, Looney chose one predominant identifying characteristic: that the author was "a lyric poet of recognized talent." In particular he used as a key the stanza form employed by Shakespeare in his first published poem, *Venus and Adonis*. Combing through anthologies of the time, he found that the form—ABABCC—was less common than he had anticipated, and before long he was down to two candidates. One was anonymous; the other was a man Looney had never heard of: E. O., or Earle of Oxenforde, known to posterity as Edward de Vere, seventeenth Earl of Oxford.

Next Looney reversed the process, working back from the man to the works to ascertain whether Oxford matched all eighteen characteristics, and thus whether the plays and poems could be reflections of his life experiences. To Looney's astonishment, this obscure nobleman with an illustrious name fitted the Shakespeare profile perfectly. Moreover, all the characteristics Looney listed had at one time or another been identified by scholars as important components of the author's life and psyche. The remarkable thing about Looney's approach, however, was that he was the first person to gather these characteristics, and out of them construct the skeleton of an actual man. For the first time Shakespeare appeared human.

Once Looney began to explore Oxford's biography in depth, the accumulation of apparent coincidences between events in his life and incidents described in the Shakespeare plays was rapid and impressive. But even more important was the fact that Oxford's early poetry provided Shakespeare with his missing juvenilia, and a sense of a whole body of work, with all its stylistic and emotional developments, emerged.

The anomalies between Shakespeare's life and art that had originally prompted Looney to take up his search disappeared when he substituted Oxford as author. Moreover, Oxford's own fractured life became complete and intelligible when his secret Shakespearean existence was revealed. While acknowledging his high poetic gifts and close connections with the theater, historians had tended to dis-

miss Oxford as one who, because of his fickle head and violent temper, failed to live up to his early promise. After a brilliant start in the
world of letters, he had lapsed into permanent obscurity. As the Victorian literary editor Alexander Grosart wrote, "An unlifted shadow
lies across his memory."

Thus Looney's thesis solved the mystery not only of Shakespeare,
but of Oxford as well.

Looney, who was ridiculed more for his name than his ideas,
could soon count Sigmund Freud among the many adherents of his
theory. Freud, who had been profoundly influenced by Shakespeare,
now found the psychology of the plays illuminated by Oxford's life.
Another convert, the novelist John Galsworthy, described Looney's
book *Shakespeare Identified* as "the greatest detective story of all time."
In telling Shakespeare's true story, Looney had rewritten history
forever. As the poet and scholar Warren Hope puts it, "Looney's work
renders a world figure a nonentity and transforms a forgotten courtier into a leading light of humanity's intellectual life."[8]

Looney was correct in his belief that the plays and poems themselves
are the best evidence for determining the authorship of the Shakespeare canon. An author's works are bound to constitute primary
evidence of his preoccupations, both mental and emotional. Even
if Shakespeare had not deliberately depicted his life story in his works
to compensate for his enforced anonymity, his psychology—the
peculiar law of his soul—would necessarily be revealed through his
principal themes. This is true of any author, be it Homer or J. K.
Rowling. The unconscious never lies: there is no hiding the landscape of the soul the moment the pen creates its trail of ink on parchment. All such trails, however convoluted, lead back to the truth.

Truth is an obsessive theme in Shakespeare. In *Troilus and Cressida,*
Troilus is "truth's authentic author" and the phrase "as true as Troilus"
will, we are told, both "crown and sanctify" the author's verse. Given
that the Earl of Oxford's family name, Vere, meant "truth," the author's
persistent assertion of his truth can be interpreted as an assertion of
identity. Troilus even puns on Oxford's motto "Vero nihil verius"
("Nothing truer than truth"—or "a Vere") when he exclaims, "And
what truth can speak truest, not truer than Troilus." If nothing else,

this fixation on truth should convince us that in the works of Shakespeare we have a priceless dossier on the man himself. All the deepest secrets of his soul are there. "Alas!" cries Troilus of his addiction to truth, "it is my vice, my fault."

But Shakespeare's plays and poems reveal more than just the secret map of the author's soul, or his hidden identity; they are highly political documents—the concealed history of the time, no less—with the power to overturn the assumptions of centuries. The idea that the works contain political secrets might go a long way to explain the extraordinary silence surrounding the author, both during his lifetime and after, and thus shed light on why there is a Shakespeare authorship question at all.

It also makes us realize that Shakespeare's works are autobiographical in a very special manner, a consequence both of the environment in which he worked and of the extraordinary nature of the things he had to say. He lived in a society, for instance, in which it was a capital offense to criticize the government in print; and the court (which his works reveal to have been his natural milieu) consisted of a social and political elite that jealously guarded its privileges. Anyone who broke ranks and attempted to expose the vice and folly of his peers risked being ostracized, and would have to use considerable subterfuge. As for the monarchy, it was the deepest mystery of state, presided over and uniquely embodied by a virgin goddess made flesh, Queen Elizabeth I, whose own mythology was unquestionable.

Elizabeth's myth, the myth that buttressed the age to which she gave her name, was that of the Virgin Queen, a selfless sovereign who abjured the delights of the flesh and the comforts of matrimony to dedicate herself to the interests of her country. In her first speech to Parliament in February 1559, in response to a petition from members requesting that she marry, Elizabeth pointed to her coronation ring and declared: "I am already bound unto an husband, which is the kingdom of England, and that may suffice you." The notion that she was married to her people was a powerful factor in fostering a sense of national unity among Englishmen at a time when Europe bristled with threats to the security of her kingdom. (France and Spain supported the claim to the throne of Elizabeth's cousin, Mary Queen of Scots, and Spain's presence in the Netherlands, together with her suborning of English Catholics, made the danger of a coup ever present.) Queen Elizabeth's official chastity put her beyond the pale of sexual scandal (at least, that was the intention), helped create valuable Continental alliances through the promise of marriage, and enlarged her reputation at home. Her virginity, a metaphor for the impregnability of England, became a sort of national talisman protecting the country from invasion. England under Elizabeth was perceived as an island fortress, a promised land—"this blessed plot," as Shakespeare's John of Gaunt calls it—whose destiny was guided by the wisdom of the goddess.

The version of Elizabethan history that has come down to posterity and is still the basis of most of our assumptions about Elizabeth's reign is that of William Cecil, Lord Burghley, the queen's most trusted minister for forty years. As Burghley's biographer Martin Hume reminds us, "Everything passed through his hands," and much was transformed—or eradicated—in the process. It was Burghley who provided the primary material for the historian William Camden's *Annals,* in the form of state papers and his own private archives. Camden's work was finally completed in 1617, with a dedication to Prince Charles, in which the author declares:

> William Cecil, Baron of Burghley, Lord High Treasurer of England . . . opened unto me (far from my thought) first, some memorials of State of his own: afterwards, those of the Kingdom; and from them willed me to compile a History of Queen Elizabeth's Reign from the beginning. I know not to what intent, unless whilst he providing for the propagation of the Queen's honor, meant to take a taste of my abilities of this kind.

"The Queen's honor" meant the queen's virginity. Yet all the propaganda in the world could not disguise the crisis of succession that Elizabeth's official virginity inevitably engendered. If she were to live and die a virgin, as she proudly predicted in her first speech to Parliament, then there would be no heir of her body to succeed her, and England would be plunged into civil strife, with factions gathering around the various contenders for the crown. The very ideal that seemed to secure her throne undermined it. But what if her virginity were just that, an ideal, with no basis in reality: a political front, rather than a biological fact?

Unfortunately for Elizabeth, among those at court who knew the private reality behind the public icon was a man calling himself William Shakespeare. For him, she was as much strumpet royal as virgin queen, hence his skillful and trenchant exposures of her through such characters as Gertrude, Olivia, Titania, Cressida, and Cleopatra. Elizabeth the private woman, passionate, headstrong, licentious, was at complete odds with the public persona. Lord Burghley was given the task of keeping the lid on this can of worms, and he did a thorough job. Elizabeth's personal honor and integrity were at stake, as well as the honor and integrity of the church and nation she embodied.

In the traditional view of the Elizabethan age, Elizabeth and Shakespeare, the preeminent geniuses of the era, have been kept in separate worlds. Shakespeare inhabits the busy, rough-edged professional world of the public theaters south of the Thames, acting, directing, writing, then crossing the river to quaff with his bohemian friends at the Mermaid; Elizabeth, on the other hand, abides in the ivory-tower world of the court, whether at Whitehall, Richmond, or Greenwich, surrounded by her chaste ladies and amorous courtiers in a sort of dream of queenship—and never the twain shall meet. Yet even a superficial reading of the plays should convince us that Elizabeth's milieu and Shakespeare's are one—that the queen is the center of the poet's world. Shakespeare is not tucked away somewhere on Bankside, but is to be found at the very heart of the Elizabethan age.

If we separate the two Shakespeares—the citizen of Stratford and the man who emerges from the works—the incongruity between them is clear. On the one hand, we have a successful man of business who, beginning life as a glover's son and butcher's apprentice, made a small fortune out of real estate, play broking, shareholding, and dealing in bagged commodities. He bought the second biggest house in his native Stratford, to which he retired before the age of forty. When, several years after his death, a monument was erected to his memory in the Holy Trinity Church at Stratford, it depicted him holding a sack of wool or grain, the quill being an eighteenth-century addition. His strongly mercenary and uncharitable nature is well attested; he was guilty, among other things, of hoarding grain in times of famine and charging a visiting preacher for the wine he served him. This wholly conventional man is the author bequeathed to us by history, or, more properly speaking, legend. On the other hand, there is the man who stems from a study of the themes, prejudices, outlook, and philosophy of the works themselves. This is the cultured, well-traveled aristocrat, whose fluent wit and easy erudition are reflected in the facetious exchanges of his court characters with their puns and multilingual jokes, and whose contempt for money and the social ambitions incident to it is everywhere apparent.

Although the citizen of Stratford might proudly display his working class and proto-capitalist credentials, the author himself reveals a very different disposition, one that is more nearly feudal in outlook and has been frequently noted by commentators on both sides of the debate. Ernest Crosby, the social reformer and anti-imperialist author of *Captain Jinks, Hero* (1902), wrote: "Is there anything in his plays that is in the least inconsistent with all that is reactionary? A glance at Shakespeare's lists of *dramatis personae* is sufficient to show that he was unable to conceive of any situation rising to the dignity of tragedy in other than royal and ducal circles." Referring to *The Tempest,* he observes that "Shakespeare can not imagine even a desert island without a king!" One should also note that Shakespeare is peculiarly sensitive to the pressures and anxieties of court life. His kings dream of being shepherds, not the other way around.

Having enumerated many instances of the lower orders' being treated with obvious disdain, Crosby concludes that "it is hard to believe that Shakespeare would have so frequently allowed his characters to express their contempt for members of the lower orders of society if he had not had some sympathy with their opinions." Shakespeare, moreover, is suspicious of the new meritocratic spirit with its suggestion of greater freedom and democracy for society as a whole. "Despising the masses," Crosby writes, "[Shakespeare] had no sympathy with the idea of improving their condition or increasing their power. He saw the signs of the times with foreboding, as did his hero Hamlet: 'By the Lord, Horatio, these three years I have taken note of it; the age has grown so picked, that the toe of the peasant comes so near the heel of the courtier, he galls his kibe.'"[9]

Crosby was echoing Walt Whitman, the so-called poet of democracy, who wrote of the plays, "Common blood is but wash— the hero is always of high lineage. Doubtless in so rendering humanity Shakespeare strictly rendered what was to him the truth." Whitman also boldly declared that Shakespeare's plays were "unacceptable to democracy." The British playwright and socialist George Bernard Shaw thought that Shakespeare "conceived himself as belonging to the upper class . . ." Crosby's mentor, Count Leo Tolstoy, was of the same mind. "The fundamental inner cause of Shakespeare's fame," opined the author of *War and Peace,* "was and is this: that his dramas were 'pro captu lectoris,' i.e., they corresponded to the irreligious and immoral frame of mind of the upper classes of his time." Tolstoy condemned Shakespeare as an artist and vilified his works. Indeed, so fierce and irrational was his hatred of the Bard that one can't help feeling there was something deeply personal at work. George Orwell thought so, and in his essay "Lear, Tolstoy and the Fool" he explores the roots of the Russian novelist's revulsion.

Orwell comes to the conclusion that Tolstoy saw himself in Shakespeare, especially in *King Lear,* the play for which Tolstoy reserved his special scorn and which mirrors his own story with eerie precision. Tolstoy himself was an aristocrat, yet in his old age he renounced his title, estates, and all copyrights in order to live the life of a peasant. He hoped that his renunciation would bring him true happiness, a sort of heaven on earth, but he was sorely disappointed. Not only did his high-handed, violent character remain unaltered, but he was driven to the verge of madness by the peasants who took advantage of his diminished status. Having given up his throne, as it were, he expected everyone to continue treating him like a king. With his carefully planned salvation doomed, Tolstoy fled across the country in despair. He died in a remote railway station, attended by his youngest daughter. Shakespeare, then, held the mirror up to Tolstoy, who, instead of facing what he saw, took the glass and—like Richard II—smashed it into a thousand pieces. Shakespeare was the nobleman Tolstoy had come to detest in himself.

Despite the upward mobility of Mr. Shakspere of Stratford, the Shakespearean hero finds himself through loss of status, not the reverse. This supports Freud's intuition that Shakespeare was a "déclassé nobleman." Certainly, his heroes, far from being on the make like Marlowe's, are downwardly mobile. Prince Hal, for instance, is as much at home in the tavern as at court. The man of low estate who hauls himself up by means of the nascent capitalist system has no place in Shakespeare's works; nor does such a man provide a paradigm for

social cohesion. Instead, it is through the fallen king that the conscience of society is awakened. As Lear cries out on the heath:

> Poor naked wretches, whereso'er you are,
> That bide the pelting of this pitiless storm,
> How shall your houseless heads and unfed sides,
> Your loop'd and window'd raggedness, defend you
> From seasons such as these? O! I have ta'en
> Too little care of this. Take physic, Pomp;
> Expose thyself to feel what wretches feel,
> That thou mayst shake the superflux to them,
> And show the Heavens more just.
>
> (III.iv.28–36)

It seems all the more extraordinary, given the testimony of such
witnesses as Crosby, Shaw, Whitman, and Tolstoy, a social range if
ever there was one, that Shakespeare has been appropriated as an icon
of Everyman, and that this perception should sit side by side with
Shakespeare the poet of empire, an idea that first emerged around
1760, which, according to Professor Gary Taylor, editor of *The Oxford
Shakespeare,* is the year of Shakespeare's apotheosis as England's premier bard. "It would not be entirely perverse to suggest," writes
Taylor, "that in 1760 William Shakespeare and George III together
simultaneously ascended the English throne."[10] The concept of the
Everyman Shakespeare was an inevitable consequence of the Stratfordian mythology, though it could also have been a cynical ploy on
the part of empire to keep all estates of men on board the imperial
ship. Whatever the case, it is one more indication that what we are
dealing with here are *two* Shakespeares: the true author and his front.
Sensing the complex and tragic figure that emerges from the works,
the author and critic Frank Harris is forced to deny the Shakespeare
of tradition: "Without a single exception the commentators have all
missed the man and the story; they have turned the poet into a
tradesman, and the unimaginable tragedy of his life into the com-
monplace record of a successful tradesman's career."[11] Yet even
Harris, unwilling to abandon the Stratfordian paradigm, ends up with
a hybrid Shakespeare, half tradesman, half poet.

The more deeply one studies Shakespeare, the wider becomes
the division and the more disturbing the incongruity between the

author of legend and the author evinced by the works. In his *Shake-speare: The "Lost Years"* (1985), Ernest Honigmann, unlike Harris, made a virtue of laying bare what he called William Shakespeare the businessman (the Stratford Shakespeare), while insisting that William Shakespeare the poet (the London Shakespeare) was the same man. It is amusing to watch Shakespeare scholars struggling to square the circle. Professor Stephen Greenblatt of Harvard, whose *Will in the World* (2004) is an engaging if doomed attempt to imagine connections between the Stratford citizen and the works he is supposed to have written, appears to face the problem head-on by giving the contradiction a fancy name:

> Shakespeare was a master of double consciousness. He was a man who spent his money on a coat of arms but who mocked the pretentiousness of such a claim; a man who invested in real estate but who ridiculed in *Hamlet* precisely such an entrepreneur as he himself was; a man who spent his life and his deepest energies on the theater but who laughed at the theater and regretted making himself a show. Though Shakespeare seems to have recycled every word he ever encountered, every person he ever met, every experience he ever had . . . he contrived at the same time to hide himself from view.[12]

"Double consciousness." Such a phrase has the slippery virtue of making Shakespeare sound doubly conscious—or twice as intelligent —but in reality it is a poor way of saying that what we have here are two separate consciousnesses, two quite different human beings: Gulielmus Shakspere and William Shake-speare.

Why does it matter? Answer: if you get Shakespeare wrong, you get the Elizabethan age wrong—its literature, its culture, its politics. If you believe, for instance, that a man from the Stratford man's humble background, with no contacts at court, could lampoon the queen and her chief minister on the public stage with impunity, or chastise the Earl of Southampton in print (again with impunity) for growing common,[13] you are predicating a classless society in Elizabethan England, which is very wide of the mark. Even more to the point, if you get Shakespeare wrong, you get his plays wrong and so miss some of the richest layers of humor, pathos, and meaning.

It comes as a shock to most people to learn that William Shakespeare, the "Soul of the Age," was invisible in the society of his time. No one in London, a mere town by today's standards, claimed to know him while he was alive; nor are there accounts of him in the professional world of the theater. Not even his fellow playwrights acknowledge him as an acquaintance. No one said, "I saw Shakespeare last night at one of his plays" or "I had a drink with him at the Mermaid Tavern" or "I saw him presented at court." He was, to all intents and purposes, a nonentity. Nor was he any more conspicuous in the field of literature. His plays first appeared anonymously, and when finally ascribed to him there is no evidence that he was paid for them. Many were pirated, the author remaining mute, and not a single one is dedicated to a friend or patron. In a non-electronic age, when everything was written down, he left no paper trail, not even a letter to a friend or colleague. Even his death was met with silence.

How could the Soul of the Age be Mr. Nobody?

The most obvious reason for Shakespeare's anonymity is that he was having to conceal his identity and write under a pen name. He straight out tells us so in Sonnet 76 (emphasis mine):

> Why write I still all one, ever the same,
> And keep invention in a noted weed,
> *That every word doth almost tell my name,*
> Showing their birth, and where they did proceed?
>
> (lines 5–8)

Given that the name "Shake-speare" appeared on the 1609 title page of the Sonnets, the obvious inference to be drawn from the italicized line above is that the author's real name was not Shakespeare. The reference to "birth," although ostensibly about the ideas that determine his choice of words, is a suggestive glance at the author's own high birth; in other words, his writing cannot help but betray his nobility. Ben Jonson echoed this idea in his 1623 eulogy:

> Look how the father's face
> Lives in his issue, even so the race
> Of Shakespeare's mind and manners brightly shines
> In his well turned, and true-filed lines.
>
> (lines 65–68)

In Sonnet 55 Shakespeare leaves us in no doubt that he knows the worth of his own work ("Not marble nor the gilded monuments / Of princes shall outlive this powerful rhyme"), yet in Sonnet 81 he writes, "I once gone to all the world must die," which begs the question, why should the author's name not enjoy the same immortality as his works? After all, he remains the most celebrated writer of any age. This paradox makes sense only if Shakespeare is not the author's real name, in which case he is lamenting that his true identity is fated to die with him. Sonnet 72 provides a strong clue as to why Shakespeare's name might be lost to posterity:

> My name be buried where my body is,
> And live no more to shame nor me nor you;
> For I am shamed by that which I bring forth,
> And so should you, to love things nothing worth.

In aristocratic circles at that time, there was a stigma attached to writing professionally, particularly for the theaters, which were often in the red-light districts of town, as well as to having one's works, especially fiction, printed for public consumption. (A playwright was ranked as a popular entertainer, his status barely more respectable than that of a tumbler or balladeer.) This restriction extended to all court circles, so that even a knight like Philip Sidney never published his works in his lifetime. Many authorial names that we take at face value, such as John Lyly, Thomas Watson, and John Webster, may have been the pseudonyms of court writers who used front men. As Robert Greene wrote in his *Farewell to Folly* (1591):

> Others, if they come to write or publish anything in print, which
> for their calling and gravity being loath to have any profane pam-
> phlets pass under their hand, get some other to set his name to
> their verses. Thus is the ass made proud by this underhand brokery.

The feeling of shame that Shakespeare expresses toward his works in Sonnet 72 is perfectly consistent with this aristocratic code. If Shakespeare was a nobleman, the silence surrounding his life as a writer becomes natural and explicable.

It would also make sense of his strange designation of his works as "things nothing worth," for this again was the aristocratic manner, a sort of studied negligence toward intellectual accomplishment that Castiglione termed *sprezzatura*. In the first of two dedicatory epistles to the First Folio (1623), addressed to the Earls of Pembroke and Montgomery, Shakespeare's works are referred to three times as "trifles," and in the second epistle "to the great variety of readers," we are told that "what he [Shakespeare] thought, he uttered with that easiness, that we have scarce received from him a blot in his papers." It was acceptable for a nobleman to write verses on a rainy afternoon and circulate them privately among his friends (Francis Meres, in his *Palladis Tamia* of 1598, mentions Shakespeare's "sugared sonnets among his private friends"), but to write professionally, for money, and have one's works published and read by men of inferior class, as if one had written for their amusement, was considered beyond the pale. In 1589, four years before the name "Shakespeare" burst onto the scene, George Puttenham alerted cultured society to a layer of hidden authors whose works were privately circulated:

> And in her Maiesties time that now is are sprong up an other crew of Courtly makers [i.e., poets] Noble men and Gentlemen of her Maiesties own servauntes, who have written excellently well as it would appeare if their doings could be found out and made publicke with the rest, of which number is first that noble gentleman Edward Earl of Oxford.[14]

If the two dedicatory epistles to the First Folio acknowledge Shakespeare's *sprezzatura* or courtly dissimulation, Jonson's great elegy in praise of "my beloved, the author William Shakespeare," turns the courtly convention on its head, and in a dam-burst of heartfelt adulation for his fellow poet elevates both Shakespeare and his professional art to a place of national honor and renown ("Triumph, my *Britaine*! thou hast one to showe, / To whom all scenes of *Europe* homage owe"). Jonson's thrust throughout the eighty-line tribute is that Shakespeare's dedication to his art has made playwriting an honorable profession, one capable of bringing prestige to the nation. From the start, however, Jonson maintains the dual or two-faced stance toward the Bard's identity that is so marked a feature of contemporary commentary. In the opening lines he writes,

To draw no envy (*Shakespeare*) on thy name,
Am I thus ample to thy Booke, and Fame.

That Jonson fences off the word "Shakespeare" from "thy name," putting it in parentheses, is highly significant, suggesting a distinction between the two—as if the name Shakespeare is a mask, behind which lies the author's true name. Moreover, these lines are incomprehensible if Jonson is writing a straightforward eulogy to a celebrated author called William Shakespeare, who wrote under his own name and whose identity was not in doubt. If we take Jonson's words literally, they are nonsensical. If one wants to create envy toward someone, then the extravagant praise Jonson bestows upon Shakespeare (comparing him to the greats of antiquity) is a good way to do it. If, however, Jonson is addressing a man of high station, for whom writing plays was considered infra dig and a dishonor to his family name, then his words can be meaningfully construed as, "I am praising you in this profuse fashion so that the magnitude of your achievement will overshadow any prejudice or dishonor ('envy') that public knowledge of your playwriting might bring down upon your name." In other words, Jonson says that Shakespeare, through his art, has transcended the traditional taboo associated with literature as a profession and made something noble and heroic out of it. Nevertheless, there must have been a heavy price to pay within his own social caste.

Not only is Shakespeare's sense of shame and alienation from his class a prominent feature of his Sonnets, but it is alluded to by his contemporaries. In Thomas Edwards's *Narcissus* (1595), in which authors are identified by characters in their works, Shakespeare is presented under the guise of Adonis. In the second of two stanzas dedicated to the Bard, Edwards refers to him wearing "purple robes destain'd" (i.e., stained), suggesting that Shakespeare was tarnishing his royal or noble status by writing for the public stage, and maybe even acting on it. John Davies of Hereford, in his *Microcosmos* (1603), harps on this point with direct praise of "W.S.": "And though the stage doth stain pure gentle blood, / Yet generous ye are in mind and mood." Several years later, addressing Shakespeare as "our English Terence," he berates the poet good-humouredly for "playing some kingly parts in sport"—presumably on the public stage—and thus forsaking the opportunity to be "a companion for a king," i.e., to wield political power. (The Latin playwright Terence was a former African slave thought to be a front for the aristocratic Roman authors Scipio and Laelius.)

Jonson satirized the Stratford citizen as "poor poet-ape,"[15] but without suggesting who was the true author of the work he was stealing. In 1598 John Marston, in his *Scourge of Villanie,* while maintaining the secret, addressed this great concealed poet with unfeigned emotion:

> Far fly thy fame,
> Most, most of me beloved, whose silent name
> One letter bounds. Thy true judicial style
> I ever honour, and if my love beguile
> Not much my hopes, then thy unvalu'd worth
> Shall mount fair place when Apes are turned forth.

During my lectures on the Shakespeare authorship question at schools in the United States, I would put the name "Shake-speare" up on the board and ask the students, "What does it suggest to you?" Without exception, a hand would go up with the reply, "It sounds like the person made it up." Occasionally some bright spark would add, "It sounds like the name of a warrior." Correct on both counts. Then I would inform the class that the name Shakespeare was frequently hyphenated when it appeared on the quarto editions of the plays, including those of *Richard II* (1598), *Hamlet* (1603), and *King Lear* (1608). William Shake-speare, like the name Martin Mar-prelate,[16] the Puritan author who wrote pamphlets attacking the bishops and the Church of England, is indeed a made-up name, and its erroneous ascription to the man from Stratford-upon-Avon has led us all astray. With or without a hyphen, the Stratford man's name was *not* Shake-speare, but Shaksper(e) or Shaxper(e), pronounced *Shax-pair.* His personal records and those of his family are consistent in this.

He and the author were two separate men, and the playwright makes this apparent in a tantalizing passage in *As You Like It,* where Touchstone, the jester who has been a courtier and who compares himself to the Roman poet Ovid, berates the poor country fellow, William, for presuming to seek the hand of Audrey (emphasis mine):

> TOUCHSTONE: Give me your hand. Art thou learned?
> WILLIAM: No sir.
> TOUCHSTONE: Then learn this of me. To have is to have: for it
>   is a figure in rhetoric that drink, being poured out of a cup into
>   a glass, by filling the one doth empty the other. *For all your writers*
>   *do consent that* ipse *is he. Now you are not* ipse, *for I am he.*
> WILLIAM: Which he sir?
> TOUCHSTONE: He sir that must marry this woman [i.e., Audrey].
>   (V.i.37–45)

Audrey, meaning "noble might," stands for the works, and Touchstone—Shakespeare himself—is staking his claim to them. The highly suggestive name of the curate who is to marry them, Sir Oliver Martext, lends credence to this hypothesis. As so often with the truly revealing passages in Shakespeare, this little scene at the beginning of Act V is not germane to the plot of the play, and is frequently omitted in productions. Another example is the passage in *Henry IV, Part 2,* where Davy beseeches Justice Shallow to countenance William Visor of Woncot or Wilmcote. Though he demurs at first, saying "that Visor is an arrant knave," Shallow finally relents. William Visor would seem to be William the Mask or William the Frontman, and Wilmcote is the village near Stratford-upon-Avon from which Shakspere's mother Mary Arden came. The exchange is irrelevant to the plot, but clearly important to the author.

Ben Jonson, one of the few people who we can be sure was personally acquainted with Shakespeare, and who loved him "this side idolatry," wrote of him in his 1623 eulogy that "he seems to shake a Lance, / As brandish't at the eyes of Ignorance," clearly punning on the pseudonym "Shake-spear(e)." Three other tributes accompany Jonson's in the prefatory matter to the First Folio—those of Hugh Holland, Leonard Digges and I.M.—and in four of the five instances when the author's name appears, it is hyphenated: "Shake-speare." So what does the name William Shakespeare mean?

William, from the German Wilhelm, means "will" and "helmet" (or "protection"), perhaps with a glance at "helm" as "front," and is frequently glossed to mean "resolute guardian." The Belgian version Guildhelm means, simply, "gilded helmet." William the Conqueror was of course the first Norman king of England, so for the English the name had strong royal connotations. Shake-speare appears to be a clear reference to the Greek goddess of wisdom and warfare, Pallas Athena, to whom the epithet *hasti-vibrans*—"spear-shaker"— was sometimes applied.[17] The name Pallas is cognate with the Greek word παλλω (*pallo*), which means to brandish or shake, and the goddess is usually portrayed holding a spear in one hand and a goatskin shield in the other. Unlike Ares, a brutal and decidedly blunt god of war, Pallas was the divinity of the more tactical side of fighting. She was no bloodthirsty warrior but a strategist. To this end she possessed a golden helmet, a gift from her uncle Hades, which rendered her invisible. As the guardian deity of the hero Ulysses in Homer's *Odyssey,* Pallas shows herself a mistress of disguise. She presided over the arts, including literature; and Athens, birthplace of the modern theater, came under her protection. She was born fully armed from the brow of her father, Zeus, just as Shake-speare appeared out of the blue as a fully formed artist in 1593. Pallas was also the virgin goddess (Athena Parthenos) and was strongly identified with Queen Elizabeth.

The spear and helmet feature in an extraordinary reference to Shakespeare in John Marston's play *Histriomastix* (1599). The players are putting on a private performance for noblemen and gentlemen, in which the characters of Troilus and Cressida are introduced with startling incongruity. Troilus, described in Shakespeare's play as "truth's authentic author," is the very pattern of constancy in love, Cressida the archetype of faithlessness. Here is their only exchange in Marston's play (emphasis mine):

TROILUS:
Thy knight his valiant elbow wears,
That when he *shakes his furious Speare*
The foe in shivering fearful sort
May lay him down in death to snort.

CRESSIDA:
O knight, with valour in thy face,
Here take my skreene, wear it for grace,

Within thy helmet put the same,
Therewith to make thine enemies lame.
(II.i.272–279)

If Troilus is Shakespeare, then Cressida is Elizabeth, who gives him her "screen"—that of the spear-shaking goddess of disguise—to put in his helmet. In this way he can lame his enemies without being seen.

The spear Athena carries, which is a fundamental element of the name Shake-speare, is noted above all for its aim, for hitting the target, and suggests an author who writes with a very specific purpose. His spear becomes his pen, and vice versa. Implicit in this imagery is the notion of an exchange or metamorphosis—a sacrifice even—whereby the warrior sublimates his martial energies to become an artist, albeit one who uses his steel-tipped pen to defend or protect some vital principle. Champion jousters in Elizabethan times were sometimes known as "spear-shakers"; thus proficiency in the joust could also be suggested. On a metaphorical level, it could refer to an author who scores many "hits" (satirical gibes).

The spear is also strongly associated with redemption and restoration. The spear of the Grail King both wounds and heals; with it he was pierced and with it redeemed. Shakespeare performs the same alchemy with his satirical pen (as Jaques says in *As You Like It,* "And they that are most galled with my folly, / They most must laugh"). In *Henry VI, Part 2,* the Duke of York reminds us that the spear of Achilles was imbued with this same power of wounding and healing:

That gold must round engirt these brows of mine,
Whose smile and frown, like to Achilles' spear,
Is able with the change to kill and cure.
(V.i. 99–101)

Significantly, Shakespeare compares the crown to a spear, and it is the crown that quickly becomes the intention or target of his works. This finds an echo in the Anglo-Saxon invasions of Britain, when the spear served the Britons in exile as a symbol of guardianship and the restoration of their kingdom. The spear is also the primary attribute of England's patron saint, George of Lydda, who used it to slay the dragon. All these ideas reverberate in the name Shakespeare.

Drawing together the various strands of symbolism, and combining the ideas contained in the two names, we arrive at the notion of a hidden guardian of England—a national champion even—whose literary intent is closely bound up with the mortal Pallas, Queen Elizabeth, and the crown she wears. There is also something cocky about the name, as if the author is bragging of a special power and position.

If the First Folio of Shakespeare's works had been discovered for the first time in the present century, with no name on the title page and without the equivocal prefatory matter composed by Ben Jonson, it would be clear that these were pointed and erudite court dramas written by a court insider, who was satirizing a ruthless and venal political culture that had in some way prejudiced his status. It would be clear, too, that Shakespeare was an Elizabethan—not a Jacobean —author, though some of his plays were revived for the Jacobean court. After all, Jonson chose to mention only three of Shakespeare's "peers" in his 1623 eulogy—Lyly, Kyd, and Marlowe—all playwrights who stopped writing in the early 1590s. Shakespeare, as Jonson well knew, created the golden age of Elizabethan literature, which began in the 1570s.

In the preface to the 1609 quarto of *Troilus and Cressida*, we are told that Shakespeare's comedies "seeme (for their height of pleasure) to be borne in that sea that brought forth Venus." The "height of pleasure" refers to the refined art of courtly culture, and Venus, the goddess of love, as so often in the literature of the time, represents Queen Elizabeth. The sea is the genealogical pool from which she emerged. The hint being dropped is that Shakespeare himself was of noble, even royal, blood.

The plays themselves provide unequivocal evidence that Shakespeare's dramatic world was not that of Bankside and the public theaters, but one of private performance, whether at the Inns of Court, the great houses of the nobility, or the English court. Hamlet doesn't put on *The Mousetrap* at Denmark's equivalent of the Globe, for what would be the point? He puts it on at the royal court, its purpose being to expose the guilt of the King and goad the conscience of the Queen, his mother. These royal trappings are not simply the backdrop to Shakespeare's art; they provide its deepest subject matter—the rise and fall of kings, the mystery of the crown, the birth pangs of a new chivalry, the death and resurrection of sovereignty itself. As the English literary critic G. Wilson Knight wrote, "Shakespeare has throughout sounded, as has no other great poet or dramatist on record, the note of royalty. His is a royal world."[18]

The court of Gloriana was a perpetual theater, the actors and actresses forever "on" or waiting in the wings, some show or other playing night and day for forty-five years. It was the theater of England, the nation's public face, not only for foreign dignitaries and visitors but for the English people who came in the hope of glimpsing its star, their sovereign, Queen Elizabeth. The chief actors were the courtiers, whose task it was to court their royal mistress through all the weathers of the reign, professing their undying love, even to the bitter mark of her black teeth and sour temper. Elizabeth had always known how to play the role of queen—for her courtiers, for her people, for Europe, for posterity—moving from one mythic persona to the next with the lightning dexterity of a quick-change artist.

The effect of separating Shakespeare and Elizabeth, the poet and the queen, is to divorce the artistic life of Elizabethan England from the political, thus neutralizing Shakespeare in affairs of state—depoliticizing him, in other words. Shakespeare becomes a brilliant noodle, a hydrocephalic egg living its own solipsistic life on the South Bank, and Elizabeth an aloof politician, blind to the superb artistic flowering she inspired. Neither will do. Statecraft and stagecraft were virtually synonymous at the time. For all its sophistication, the theater was still a way of petitioning the queen and influencing policy. From the early years of the reign, when Robert Dudley, Earl of Leicester, used his company of players to sue for the queen's hand in marriage, both at court and in the great country houses, through to the glory days of the Rose, Swan, and Globe, Elizabethan theater was one long dialogue between poet and queen.

Shakespeare's dialogue with the queen, as we shall discover, was about the succession to the throne, and included his own contentious birthright. Elizabeth knew that she was the target of his gibes. When

the Earl of Essex arranged to have *Richard II*, a play depicting the depo-
sition of a reigning monarch, performed at the Globe in February 1601,
on the eve of his ill-fated rebellion, the manager of the company and
some of the actors were arrested and questioned. Although the play
was a direct threat to the queen's authority, the author himself was
not troubled. About six months after the uprising, in a conversation
with the antiquary William Lambard, Elizabeth broke out with, "I am
Richard II, know ye not that?"

Whatever his indiscretions or Hamlet-like pranks, Elizabeth was
usually able to protect her court playwright. Indeed, their relationship was the alchemical reaction that spawned the English Renaissance, though their true roles in its creation have been obscured by
the myths that grew up around them and whose purpose was funda-
mentally the same: to keep the queen's reputation clean. But dive
down beneath the surface, and how can one think of one without
the other? As the author and theater critic Hermann Sinsheimer
wrote:

> At a distance of four centuries, Elizabeth Tudor and William
> Shakespeare look like sister and brother. He too had a unique re-
> ceptivity, so unbounded indeed that nothing of consequence and
> significance about him as an individual now matters. He too as-
> sembled a thousand years around his throne. He is, as it were, a
> woman-man, just as his sister Elizabeth is a man-woman. . . . He is
> *the* Elizabethan poet, . . . she is *the* Shakespearian Queen.[19]

Ultimately, writers write about themselves because everything
they put on paper comes from within themselves—if not from their
souls, then from their minds. One should not have to state the
blindingly obvious in this way, but decade after decade of soul-
deadening literary theory has divorced art from life, warping our
perception of creativity. The poet Wallace Stevens wrote that a
man's work is autobiographical "in spite of every subterfuge," adding, "it cannot be otherwise."

If Shakespeare is to remain just a name, without an identifiable
human being behind it, we, his readers and spectators, will continue
to lose out. Whatever the art form—music, painting, or literature—
knowledge of the artist's life and psyche enriches our appreciation
and understanding of his or her works. An awareness of Mozart's

complex relationship with his father illuminates the terrible encounter between the statue of the Commendatore and the Don in *Don Giovanni;* the insights into Van Gogh's spiritual crisis that the letters to his brother Theo yield add a religious dimension to a picture like *The Potato Eaters;* and knowledge of Dostoyevsky's early life and the effect on him of his father's murder expands the emotional framework of *The Brothers Karamazov.* Just to feel the presence of Dickens in a character like David Copperfield makes the novel more intense, more real.

With William of Stratford as author, the plays of Shakespeare can be likened to a vase of artificial flowers: they may look like real flowers, be woven with the highest skill, and from a distance be mistaken for real flowers, but the living texture, the perfume—the life itself—is missing. They cannot grow. Or think of the works as a mansion donated to the state because the owner, whose family has inhabited it for centuries, can no longer afford to live there. The house is still beautiful and stuffed with treasures, and walking through it is a real pleasure, but its life, its true genius, has departed with the owner. It has become a museum rather than a home: that vital human element is missing. This is true of the current Shakespearean dispensation. The historian Stephanie Hughes has written that "in losing the true author's identity the world lost Shakespeare's biography, and with it, much of importance about what it means to be human."[20] It also lost one of the most absorbing stories of English history.

~ 2 ~

Blighted Rose

Who has a book of all that monarchs do,
He's more secure to keep it shut than shown.
(Pericles, I.i.95–96)

WHILE ELIZABETH WAS YET in the womb, her parents' relationship
was already deteriorating. King Henry VIII was weary of Anne
Boleyn's displays of temper, her sudden sarcastic wit, her overbearing manner at court. For her part, Anne was repelled by Henry's increasing bulk and choleric disposition; nor was it in her nature to
submit meekly to his affairs with other women. Even their joint
commitment to the English Reformation was sundered by Anne's
more radical ideas, which to her ill-wishers bore the stamp of Lutheran
heresy. Her unpopularity in the country grated on her; people whispered that she was a whore, an enchantress even. During her coronation procession at the end of May 1533, when she was heavily
pregnant, the crowds only broke their silence to cry out words of
support for the abandoned queen, Catherine of Aragon, or titter "Ha
Ha" in mockery of the banners bearing the intertwined initials of
Henry and Anne. The couple were spending more and more time
apart; and under the strain of it all Anne became anxious about the
child she was carrying.

In many ways, Anne and Henry were similar in temperament.
Both were high-strung, abrasive, short-tempered. The electricity
between them was often uncomfortable and resulted in violent rows.
Anne was heard to hector the king and lord it over his ministers.
The court found her dark, magnetic beauty disturbing; here was no
demure English rose, but an outspoken, freethinking woman who

sang and danced and knew all the arts of seduction from her years at the French court. Her bronze-black hair reached down to her waist, and her lithe frame exuded sexual energy. Rumors of witchcraft clung to her, and it was reported that she had a sixth finger on her left hand. She was an accomplished musician, which appealed to Henry, and aside from the fact that her bewitchment of the king (as his early infatuation was later parsed) caused England's break from Rome, she and her brother George were leading lights of the religious reform movement. So long as she could secure the Tudor succession for Henry, which meant producing a son, Anne looked set to become one of the most dominant and influential queens of English history.

It was not to be. Not only was Anne unable to secure the succession on Henry's terms, but her own regal status was frustratingly ambivalent. She was married and not married, queen and not queen, chaste mother and incestuous whore. She and Henry married secretly in January 1533; that June she was crowned queen, an honor conferred on only one other of Henry's wives, the royal-born Catherine of Aragon; then in September she gave birth to Elizabeth, her only child. Abetted by his astrologers and fortified in the belief that his divorce from Catherine was divinely sanctioned, Henry had convinced himself that the baby would be the prince he so desperately desired. Elizabeth, in other words, was meant to be a boy, and when she wasn't, Henry's anger and self-pity were colossal. Yet the birth had been easy, and the baby was healthy. Henry kenneled his violent feelings; Anne could still produce a male heir.

Since his divorce from Catherine, Henry had demoted both her and their daughter, Mary. Catherine, once the wife of Henry's elder brother Arthur, who had died suddenly at age fifteen, was now dowager Princess of Wales and Mary simply "the Lady Mary." Neither mother nor daughter recognized her diminished status, and in this both were supported by a large percentage of the court and country. In his First Succession Act (1534), Henry officially declared Mary a bastard and disinherited her from the throne, while Anne was affirmed as his legitimate queen and their daughter, Elizabeth, in the absence of male progeny, next in line to the throne. But for all his boyish faith in his will as king and his ability to bully Parliament, Henry could not legitimize Anne and Elizabeth in the eyes of the people, statute or no statute; nor was their own anxiety over their identity more than sleeked over by the good offices of ink and parchment. Mary's supporters at court, especially among the imperial envoys of Charles V, spread rumors that the queen's baby daughter had been born deformed: a demon-child of a witchlike mother. Disqualified by her dubious status, the infant Elizabeth was not considered a viable candidate for a princely continental match.

Anne's insecure identity had its roots as much in her origins as in Henry's bigamous marriage to her. Rumors abounded that the king had had an affair with her mother, Elizabeth Howard (and with her sister, Mary Boleyn), and that Anne was his daughter. When Sir George Throckmorton, who bitterly opposed his remarriage, accused Henry of sleeping with both the sister and the mother, the stunned king managed to stammer, "Never with the mother." According to the doctrine of carnal contagion (by which siblings-in-law fell under the incest prohibition), even Henry's affair with Mary Boleyn rendered his marriage to Anne incestuous, just as his marriage to his sister-in-law, Catherine of Aragon, was similarly prejudiced.

Anne, it seems, suspected she was Henry's daughter. In a book of hours handed to the king at Mass one day, she had inscribed the following couplet beneath an illumination of the Annunciation: "Be daly prove [i.e., by daily proof] you shalle me fynde / to be to you bothe loving and kynde." "Loving" connoted the love of a wife, and "kynde" that of a daughter or blood relative.[21] On becoming queen, Anne had chosen as her motto "The most happy," the word "happy" designating the special grace and felicity that attended the possession of royal blood. (The phrase "all happiness" in the dedication to *Shakespeares Sonnets,* 1609, uses the word in the same sense.) If Anne was the daughter of Henry VIII *and* his wife, she would be doubly royal, and thus "most happy." She would also be a bastard.

When Anne failed to produce a male heir after suffering several miscarriages, Henry, instead of divorcing her as he had Catherine, determined to put her to death. Even Anne's enemies were surprised by the king's sudden, unrelenting will to destroy his second queen. That he charged her with incest is revealing (she was accused of sleeping with her brother George), as it says much about Henry's projection of his own guilt, if he suspected that Anne was his daughter. Henry even claimed that George Boleyn was the father of Elizabeth, thus making Anne not only the child's mother but her aunt—like Gertrude, described by Hamlet as "aunt-mother."[22] For the king, killing Anne was perhaps a way of killing his own feelings of self-loathing. She was also accused of adultery with five men, a treasonable offense in a queen, and of having mesmerized her royal husband. The trial was a formality; no one dared defy the king. Only one man, the court musician Mark Smeaton, confessed to adulterous relations with Anne, an admission obtained by torture. It was the first public execution of an English queen. With faultless wit, Anne sent Henry a last note thanking him for elevating her from queen to saint. Ten days later the king had a new wife.

In many ways Elizabeth's was a transgressive birth, her origins partaking of much that was chaotic and taboo. The demons of incest and bastardy leered into her cradle, and before long she had come to be known as the "little whore," her mother being the "great whore." After Anne's execution Henry concocted a Second Succession Act (1536), which declared his marriage to Anne unlawful, thus making a bastard of Elizabeth and barring her claim to the throne "by lineal descent." Clause XII of the act made it high treason for anyone to "accept or take, judge or believe" that either of the king's former marriages was lawful, or to call Mary or Elizabeth legitimate.[23] It should be noted that the king's bastard son by Elizabeth Blount, Henry Fitzroy, Duke of Richmond and Somerset, was still alive at the time of the act, though he was to die later that year, aged seventeen. There was much talk at court about the king's plans to legitimize him.

Elizabeth was living at Hunsdon in Hertfordshire when her mother died, and soon felt Anne's absence. For one thing the flow of rich dresses dried up, leaving her governess to complain to Thomas Cromwell that Elizabeth had nothing to wear. The three-year-old, by all accounts gravely precocious, was fully aware of her relegation in the ranks of the royal family, and put the governor of her household, Sir Thomas Bryan, on the spot by asking, "How haps it, Governor: yesterday my Lady Princess, and today but my Lady Elizabeth?" Lifting her banishment from court, Henry eventually renewed his public shows of affection toward his second daughter, but "her fate," writes Lytton Strachey, "varied incessantly with the complex changes of her father's politics and marriages; alternately caressed and neglected, she was the heir to England at one moment and a bastard outcast the next."[24]

By any standards Elizabeth was a brilliant student, whose fluency in Latin, French, and Italian is attested to by her youthful translations, praised by the Reformation scholar and playwright John Bale, among others. She also read Greek, and could discuss ancient history and philosophy with many pointed comparisons. Her tutor Roger Ascham described her as his "brightest star," even taking into account Sir Thomas More's brainy daughters. In 1597, at the age of sixty-four, she responded extempore to an impertinent speech in Latin from the Polish ambassador. Enjoying to the full the bewildered admiration of her assembled courtiers, she congratulated herself with the words, "I have been forced this day to scour up my old Latin that hath long been a-rusting." She made translations throughout her life and, like her father, was a fine musician and a composer of verses. In a letter of 1549 to her brother, King Edward, in pleading her recent ill health, she apologized for neglecting "my old custom of bringing something or other out of my scanty literary store-house."

In 1544, at the age of eleven, Elizabeth translated from French a long devotional poem by Queen Marguerite of Navarre, *Miroir de L'Âme Pécheresse* (*Glass of the Sinful Soul*) and presented it to her stepmother, Queen Catherine Parr, as a New Year's gift. Marguerite had gotten to know Elizabeth's mother, Anne, when she was a girl at the French court, and had renewed the acquaintance when Anne became queen. It is likely that the copy of *Miroir* used by Elizabeth came from her mother's library. Marguerite was believed to have had an incestuous relationship with her adored brother Francis I, King of France, and *Miroir* is an outpouring of self-hatred, in which Marguerite depicts herself as a vile sinner beyond the pale of God's grace. This proves somewhat disingenuous, however, for casting herself in the roles of daughter, mother, sister, and wife to the Almighty, she goes on to draw four examples from the Bible in which a daughter, a mother, a sister, and a wife achieve redemption and union with the godhead. Describing herself as the sister of the Almighty, Marguerite appears to blur the distinction between God and her brother the king. By elevating the sin of incest to a spiritual plane, she justifies it to her guilty soul.

It is extraordinary that an eleven-year-old girl should have chosen this tortured penitential text as an object of study and translation.

However, considering the singular circumstances surrounding Elizabeth's birth and early childhood, the choice becomes a strong index of her inner torment as she approached puberty. Perhaps through *Miroir* she was attempting to come to terms with the legacy of incest and bastardy bequeathed by her parents; certainly, it is not hard to understand the appealing alchemy of Marguerite's approach. Because the fervent, fourfold relationship between the human soul and God is incestuous, physical incest between a royal couple can be seen as a spiritual union removed from the mundane prohibitions of moral law.

It is possible that what attracted Elizabeth above all to Marguerite's text was the dissolution of traditional kinship distinctions. As she writes in her translation, "Alas, my God, of the fraternity that Thou hast toward me through Thy humbleness in calling me sister, didst Thou ever say anything of it? Alas, yea, for Thou hast broken the kindred of my old father, calling me daughter of adoption."[25] *Thou hast broken the kindred of my old father.* Despite her rhetoric about being her father's daughter, Elizabeth's life wove a transverse thread, even down to her refusal to countenance an heir, either by blood or election. Indeed, she was to snuff out the royal line whose continuance had been her father's dearest wish. Gone was his patriarchal concept of monarchy, which relied heavily on the mystery of blood, and which she replaced with a more feminine, consultative model. *Calling me daughter of adoption.* In her attempt to exorcise the demons of her Tudor inheritance, Elizabeth re-created herself as a changeling, imagining a monarchy based on qualities of mind and soul.

In the context of Marguerite's thought, the divine incest of the Virgin Mary as bride, sister, daughter, and mother of God the Father and God the Son would not have been lost on Elizabeth. Even at eleven, she seems to have made a vital unconscious connection between the fallen soul as bride, sister, mother, and daughter of Christ, and herself, the future queen, in this same fourfold relationship to England. From being the *sponsa Christi* (bride of Christ) she would become the *sponsa Angliae* (bride of England). As she aligned herself with the spiritual libertine ideas that Anne Boleyn had imbibed at the French court, Elizabeth's throne became the throne of her mother, in both its religious and its intellectual underpinnings, and in the realization that Anne's sacrifice was the foundation stone of the new monarchy. She even adopted one of her mother's mottoes, *Semper eadem* ("Always the same"), for it spoke of an immutable selfhood above and beyond the chaos of her father's life and reign. Her resolution not to marry and not to share her throne was part of this unyielding determination to create an image for herself that transcended her origins.

Miroir is a kinship riddle (like that confronting Pericles at the opening of Shakespeare's play), an attempt by the young Elizabeth to conceal and reveal her origins. But kinship in her case extends beyond the immediate family to the national family, altering the foundations of government. Yet in 1547, at the time of her father's death, there seemed little chance that Elizabeth would ever succeed to the throne. Although restored to the line of succession, she still bore the stigma of bastardy.

When Henry VIII died, he was succeeded by his sickly nine-year-old son by Jane Seymour, Edward VI. Elizabeth, then thirteen, was transferred to the household of her stepmother, Queen Dowager Catherine Parr, at Chelsea. This would have been a welcome move, as Catherine and Elizabeth shared numerous affinities of mind and spirit, and Elizabeth had enjoyed the discussions on religious reform and literature at Catherine's court salon. Catherine too had shepherded the princess's return to her father's favor. But peaceful and scholastic her days at Chelsea were not, for just two months after the old king's death—the funeral baked meats coldly furnishing forth the marriage tables—Catherine, Henry's chaste queen, married the new king's uncle, Lord Admiral Thomas Seymour, a virile, piratical, impetuous knight of vaulting ambition, whose favorite oath was "God's precious soul!" He was also a cultured if rather flamboyant man, who wrote verses, including one, composed days before his death, which begins, "Forgetting God to love a king / Hath been my rod." Seymour had his eye as much on the girl whom intuition pronounced the future queen as on his new bride, and Elizabeth, starved of affection, was easily drawn into his love games. She was seen to blush when his name was mentioned, and in defiance of her usual modesty, appeared more pleased than affronted by his bold wooing.

Seymour took the teenage princess down the Thames on his barge at night, and made it his habit to creep into her chamber in the mornings "in his undress" in the hope of surprising her. He would tickle her, slap her jovially on the buttocks, and make as if to leap into her bed. Her maids, besotted themselves, laughed at his antics, but these were more than high-spirited pranks. Sometimes Catherine would join in the romping, helping hold Elizabeth down while the admiral tickled her. On one notorious occasion in the garden at Chelsea, Catherine gripped the girl tight while Seymour slashed her black dress to ribbons with his knife. What could have induced the normally modest queen dowager to have become an actor in these strange games? After all, she and Seymour were Elizabeth's surrogate parents. (Elizabeth signed her letters to Catherine, "Your highness' humble daughter.")

What is certain is that Elizabeth, despite the demure and chaste front she presented to the world—to her brother Edward she was "Sweet Sister Temperance"—exuded the same magnetic sexuality that had been her mother's bane. Though she tried her best to hold it in, veiling herself with devotion's visage, her presence had a disturbing, electric effect in the Seymour-Parr household that worked on both husband and wife, manifesting itself in episodes of aggressive and hysterical behaviour.

The trauma of Elizabeth's origins and any oedipal tensions that might have been triggered by her mother's execution were revived with unhappy intensity in her relationship with her stepparents, but now she was a fully sexual adult. Elizabeth's crush on Seymour, who was not only her stepfather but her uncle—thus making any sexual relationship between them incestuous—may have aroused feelings of animosity toward her aunt-mother, Catherine, to whom nevertheless she looked for protection from the increasingly overt advances of the swashbuckling admiral. The symmetry with her own parentage was uncannily exact, for Catherine and Seymour were themselves in an incestuous match, Catherine being Henry VIII's widow while Seymour was his brother-in-law (the king had married Seymour's sister Jane). Through her union with Seymour, Catherine was in effect marrying her brother. (To put it another way, Seymour was marrying his sister's husband's wife![26]) Thus, both Elizabeth's parents *and* her stepparents were incestuous, making her a child of incest twice over.

It was not long before Seymour managed to get a key to Elizabeth's apartments and was letting himself in at all hours, even interrupting her studies. Then, one day in 1548, Catherine, who had gone in search of her fourteen-year-old stepdaughter, found her in the arms of the lord admiral. Whether they were making love or just kissing, the sight was sufficiently shocking for Catherine to raise the house with her cries. Her anguish was the more poignant because she was carrying Seymour's child. That May, no doubt at Catherine's insistence, Elizabeth and her servants left the Seymour household and went to live at Cheshunt in Hertfordshire, under the care of Sir Anthony Denny, who had tended her father on his deathbed and whose wife, Joan, a former lady-in-waiting to Anne Boleyn, was the sister of Elizabeth's beloved governess Kat Ashley. Sir Anthony's sister, Joyce Denny, was the mother of Francis Walsingham, the future head of Elizabeth's secret service; and Joyce's second husband, Sir John Carey, had been Anne Boleyn's brother-in-law. Cheshunt, then, was a safe haven for Elizabeth, surrounded by Boleyn cousins and confidants, and there she and her household remained for nearly five months.

Catherine Parr gave birth to a daughter, Mary Seymour, on August 30. A few days later she contracted puerperal fever, and in the ensuing delirium made wild charges against her husband, accusing him of attempting to hasten her death so that he could marry Elizabeth. With uncanny synchronicity Catherine died on September 7, 1548, Elizabeth's fifteenth birthday. Elizabeth herself had been sick from around midsummer (June 24) through October, when she wrote to thank the lord protector for sending his physician Dr. Bill to tend her. Much of the time she was confined to her bed, and as late as November she was still complaining of poor health.

Following his wife's death, Seymour put into action an outrageous plan to usurp his brother's place as lord protector and seize control of the throne. To the lord admiral's giddy mind, this meant kidnapping the eleven-year-old King Edward and marrying the younger of his sisters, Princess Elizabeth. Seymour had been showering the king with gifts of money for some time, and intriguing to make a match between the boy and his own eleven-year-old ward, Lady Jane Grey, another claimant to the throne under the will of Henry VIII. (Failing this, Seymour reserved the right to marry the girl himself.[27]) His prime focus, however, was Elizabeth, and he worked hard to win support for his marriage plans from her closest advisers, Kat Ashley and Thomas Parry. Indeed, that Christmas there were widespread rumors in London that Elizabeth was to marry the admiral. Knowing he couldn't win the assent of the Council (required under the late king's will), Seymour was already assembling troops and minting his own money in preparation for a coup, risking not only his own life but the princess's. In a final indiscretion, he was caught trying to enter the king's bedchamber at night with a loaded pistol. In the succeeding mêlée, Edward's pet dog was shot dead. Seymour was arrested on January 17, 1549, and executed without trial two months later, having been condemned under act of attainder (i.e., "taintedness"), whereby all his titles and properties were forfeited to the crown. "This day died a man with much wit and little judgment," Elizabeth is said to have remarked.[28] In a sermon at court Bishop Latimer condemned the dead man in no uncertain terms: "He was, I heard say, a covetous man: I would there were no more in England. He was, I heard say, a seditious man, a contemner of common prayer. I would there were no more in England. Well, he is gone. I would he had left none behind."

Soon after Seymour's imprisonment in the Tower, Elizabeth's trusted servants Ashley and Parry had been arrested. The government wished to ascertain the degree to which Elizabeth had known about or aided Seymour's plans, whether she intended to marry him, and whether, as rumor declared, she had had a child by him. So began months of nerve-racking interrogations for the fifteen-year-old, in which she used her wits to brilliant effect to save her life and protect her servants. The government interrogator Sir Robert Tyrwhit realized that Elizabeth and her servants had already composed their story and were singing from the same sheet. He wrote to the lord protector, "I do see it in her [Elizabeth's] face that she is guilty, and do perceive as yet she will abide more storms ere she accuse Mistress Ashley." Even when presented with confessions from Ashley and Parry, Elizabeth kept cool, insisting that nothing improper had happened between her and the admiral, though she'd been told of his desire to marry her.

The rumor that Elizabeth had a child by Seymour was so widespread that in January 1549 she wrote to the lord protector to defend her "honour and honesty [i.e., chastity]" which she said she esteemed above all things. "My Lord," she complained, "these are shameful slanders, for the which, besides the great desire I have to see the King's Majesty, I shall most heartily desire your Lordship that I may come to the Court after your first determination, that I may show myself there as I am." By this time, the strain on Elizabeth was immense, and following Seymour's execution she suffered a total nervous collapse and was debilitated for most of that year and much of 1550.

If Elizabeth did give birth, it most likely was in September of the previous year, just before she left her seclusion at Cheshunt to go to Hatfield, and could easily have been hushed up among her inner circle. Jane Dormer, Duchess of Feria, wrote in her memoirs:

> In King Edward's time what passed between the Lord Admiral Sir Thomas Seymour and her [i.e., Elizabeth] Doctor Latimer preached in a sermon, and was a chief cause that the Parliament condemned the Admiral. There was a bruit of a child born and miserably destroyed, but could not be discovered whose it was; only the report of the mid-wife, who was brought from her house blindfold thither, and so returned, saw nothing in the house while she was there, but candle light; only, she said, it was the child of a very fair young lady. There was a muttering of the Admiral and this lady, who was then between fifteen and sixteen years of age.[29]

If the child had been a boy, it is highly unlikely that he would have been "destroyed," miserably or otherwise, given the lack of male heirs in the Tudor line. Bastard or no bastard, he was a Protestant, who would have been seen as a possible successor to the sickly King Edward. (Somerset, in particular, would have been keen to control the destiny of this other Edward, who was, after all, his nephew. The birth of a royal son would also have aided Thomas Seymour's dynastic ambitions, providing his attempted coup with real teeth.) William Cecil, who was secretary to the protector and already a part of Elizabeth's life, could have placed the child as a changeling, ensuring that a close eye was kept on him and that the best education was provided.

Elizabeth's subsequent refusal ever to name an heir becomes more understandable if she had a hidden child of her own, and was in a perpetual quandary over whether or not to shatter her carefully crafted image as the Virgin Queen by revealing him to the world. When the possible restoration of Mary, Queen of Scots to the throne of Scotland was being discussed, as a precondition of English assistance Elizabeth insisted on the ratification of the Treaty of Edinburgh, a document that Mary had always refused to sign. One of its terms stated that Mary was to renounce her claim to the English throne during the life of Elizabeth and "any issue" Elizabeth might have. Mary rather saucily replied that the words "any issue" should be replaced by "lawful issue," signaling her awareness that Elizabeth was already the mother of bastard offspring.

Clause V of the Treasons Act of 1571 made it illegal for anyone during the lifetime of the queen to name her successor in print (in the absence of an Act of Parliament affirming the same), "except the same be the naturall issue of her Majesty's body." In other words, it was lawful to nominate only a child of the queen's own flesh and blood as heir to the throne, for such a child would have an undeniable claim by virtue of blood. (The word "natural," of course, tended to connote bastardy.) By means of this extraordinary clause, Elizabeth was opening the door to the possibility that even if she refrained from naming an illegitimate child as her successor, others might in time take the opportunity to do so.

It was a highly significant clause, and much discussed, both at the time and subsequently. In a letter to Philip II of Spain, dated July 22, 1587, concerning Arthur Dudley, the purported son of Elizabeth and the Earl of Leicester, Sir Francis Englefield wrote:

> It is true that his claim [to the throne] at present amounts to nothing, but, with the example of Don Antonio [bastard claimant to the throne of Portugal] before us, it cannot be doubted that France and the English heretics, or some other party, might turn it to their own advantage . . . especially as during the Queen's time they have passed an Act in England excluding from the succession all but the heirs of the Queen's body.

It is interesting to note that there were no succession acts under Elizabeth, only treason acts, for merely to be in the line of succession constituted treason in the queen's eyes. When Mary Queen of Scots was deposed by the Scottish Parliament and her thirteen-month-old son crowned in her stead, Elizabeth remarked that a sovereign could not even trust the children who were to succeed her. Given her own troubled background and suspicious nature, to have no heirs seemed to be a psychological necessity for Elizabeth, which would explain why she did her best to destroy or disable all possible successors. Her cousins Katherine and Mary Grey, for instance, lived miserable, curtailed lives under the rod of her perpetual displeasure. Prince Arthur in Shakespeare's *King John* poignantly illustrates the pitiful fate of those unlucky enough to find themselves "in line" during Elizabeth's reign. As he says to his jailer, Hubert, who has been given the task of murdering him: "Is it my fault that I was Geoffrey's son?"—Geoffrey Plantagenet being the elder brother of the usurping John.

For all her public nonchalance on the matter, Elizabeth inherited from her father the Tudor obsession with succession. To keep the Tudor dynasty going had been Henry's dearest wish, and Elizabeth's own mother had been sacrificed to that imperative. With her sensual appetite and frank appreciation of virile beauty, not to mention her early induction into the world of sex, it seems likely that Elizabeth had children. On the other hand, it makes sense that she would have seen a male child as a threat to her throne. Had not the birth of her father's male heir, Edward, in 1537 thrust her from her place at the center and made a bastard of her? Elizabeth's reluctance to acknowledge her offspring is as understandable as her aversion to the married state.

Most historians object that Elizabeth led too public a life to give birth in secret, but her many mysterious illnesses and long periods of confinement provided a perfect cover.[30] A more durable cultural argument concerns the queen's personal mythology and her considerable charisma in impressing it upon society. Having already broken so many taboos as a strong female leader who used her sex to devastating political effect, Elizabeth was in a strong position to create a myth of ethereal purity and self-sacrifice around herself for all the mystified courtiers dying to believe it. They may have been living in a world turned upside down, but their fears were allayed by the illusion of magical virginity spun from the depths of her belly. She was the bride of her country (and, therefore, of every Englishman, be he ne'er so humble), an idea impossible to resist after the dismal persecutions of Mary's unglamorous reign. Elizabeth did not so much brainwash her courtiers in the matter of her sexuality as they brainwashed themselves. This is not to say they did not realize the truth; rather, they saw with parted eye, for their livelihoods depended on maintaining the official truth. Elizabeth, as ever, had her eye on the history books, and it is her mythology that has emerged triumphant.

Whether she bore a child by Seymour or not, the scandal almost cost Elizabeth her life, and was probably the motive force behind her eventual transformation into the Virgin Queen. The earliest known portrait of her, commissioned shortly after the Seymour scandal, seems to mark this rite of passage. The composition of the picture resembles the trump of the high priestess in the major arcanum of the tarot. Elizabeth, looking very demure, penitential almost, stands holding a book, her right hand on the cover, her left partially inside to denote hidden knowledge. Another, much larger volume, probably the Bible, sits on the table to her right. She is wearing a red dress, which signified virginity in the Renaissance. Unusual in the portraits of the time, here it clashes somewhat with the red of the subject's hair. She is covered in pearls—on head, neck, chest, and waist—symbols of purity and spiritual transformation. In this she follows the known portraits of her mother. Behind her, the heavy dark draperies of her bed (the veil of the temple, shrouding the mysteries of her private life) are parted in the middle to form the letter A, for her mother Anne, a queen beheaded for her secret sexual life. The overwhelming aura is one of sanctuary and devotion: a woman fit for the cloister. Yet the red of virginity is also the red of passion, and the edging of the curtain covering the table is curled like a serpent on the floor. This is very much a fallen Eve.

Determined to maintain the good opinion of the people, Elizabeth needed a screen of chastity behind which to indulge her licentious will. When her old governess Kat Ashley begged her to show restraint in her relations with Robert Dudley in order to curb the scandalous rumors dogging her early reign, she replied that if she were inclined to compromise her honor in the manner that wagging tongues suggested she had compromised it, then "she did not know of anyone who could forbid her."[31] Thus spake the daughter of Henry VIII.

The monarch possessed two distinct bodies, and with them two distinct wills: the body natural was the physical body, incorporating the personal will, with its capacity for error; the body politic, on the other hand, was the kingdom he or she embodied, and with it came an impersonal, political will, which was incorruptible. It was fortunate for Elizabeth's sanity that she had these two bodies and two wills, so that while her private will and body natural yielded to Dudley, her public will and body politic remained chaste. Or, as David Starkey put it, "Dudley had sex with her but she did not have it with him." This dualistic theory of the monarch's two bodies was to serve Elizabeth as a "get-out-of-jail-free card" throughout her reign, allowing her to rationalize some of her more scandalous and high-handed behavior. Since Elizabeth's private life was penetrated at every point, some would say wholly subsumed, by her public life as queen, it was little wonder that she came to believe that her fallible will and corrupted body were purified by participation in the transpersonal body that symbolised the sovereign state of England. As the spiritual libertines believed, *ubi spiritus ibi libertas:* where the spirit of the Lord is, complete liberty prevails—the subject is above the law. Obedience to the moral law was not a prerequisite of salvation for the spiritual daughter of Marguerite of Navarre.

Once the Seymour affair had died down, Elizabeth returned to court, where she usurped the place of her absent sister, Mary, who was out of favor for her Catholic recalcitrance. Celebrated for her plain dress and demure bearing, Elizabeth was treated with genuine respect and affection by her grave twelve-year-old brother, Edward VI, who paraded her as a kind of consort on ceremonial occasions. Her instinct for survival, which was naturally alert, had been further sharpened by the dangers she had passed. In addition, she was revealing a shrewd, acquisitive streak in her various land investments. With the help of William Cecil, Elizabeth was beginning to amass quite a territory, especially in the strategic county of Hertfordshire to the north and northwest of London, and at just sixteen, she became the proud owner of Hatfield House, her principal seat.

After the fall of Somerset, it was noted that Elizabeth was friendly with his successor, John Dudley, Earl of Warwick (father of Robert Dudley), and there were rumours that their relationship was not altogether innocent. The imperial ambassador Jean Scheyfve even reported that Warwick intended to divorce his wife and marry the princess. Where sex was concerned, Elizabeth it seems could never banish rumors of wantonness and misconduct; they would follow her to her grave.

Despite his love for his favorite sister, Edward had a nasty surprise for Elizabeth in his "Device for the Succession," a deathbed document composed in June 1553, in which she was once again declared a bastard and excluded from the throne. This exclusion was then ratified by law in the first Parliament of Mary's reign. Life under her Catholic sister soon became intolerable for Elizabeth, who was the unerring object of Mary's resentment and mistrust, even her scorn. (The queen, for instance, let it be known that she suspected Elizabeth was the child of Anne Boleyn's alleged lover Mark Smeaton, and not the daughter of Henry VIII at all.) Following the Wyatt uprising of 1554, Elizabeth was summoned to court under suspicion of treason. According to Simon Renard, Charles V's ambassador, Elizabeth's pallor and "swollen body" when she arrived in London were sure signs that she was pregnant, the result, he surmised, of "some vile intrigue."

Elizabeth spent two months as a prisoner in the Tower, never knowing when she might be called to the block. The experience would haunt her for the rest of her life. Even twenty years later she was heard to praise God for "pulling [her] from the prison to the palace." After the Tower there followed a year of house arrest under the guardianship of Sir Henry Bedingfield at Woodstock, near Oxford. In a letter to the Marquis of Winchester in October 1555, Elizabeth wrote, "none of my state hath been and yet is, more misused with them of mine own family than myself." Ironically, Elizabeth's greatest ally with her sister proved to be Mary's husband, Philip II of Spain, who urged his wife to recognize her younger sister as her rightful successor.

For ten years from 1549 to her accession in 1558 Elizabeth had played a dangerous game of cat and mouse with the authorities, often swallowing pride and principles for the sake of survival. She became an unrivaled equivocator—or worse—as when her sister, Mary, on finally nominating her as her heir, sent a messenger to Hatfield to seek assurance from the princess that she would maintain the Catholic religion, to which Elizabeth "prayed God that the earth might open and swallow her up alive, if she were not a true Roman Catholic."[32] When news finally reached her of Mary's death in November 1558, Elizabeth already had her government in place. Her transition to power, thanks to Cecil, was smooth and efficient, and the fairy-tale glamour that her sufferings under Mary had bestowed upon her ensured that the people were ready to take her to their hearts.

Elizabeth's relationships with men seemed to bring out the worst in her. Where there was sexual attraction, she used her power to cut them down to size, making it hard to resist the conclusion that she was motivated by an unconscious desire to avenge the murder of her mother. Her wooing of men for political ends was a painful charade: she teased them, lured them, cajoled them, lied to them, kept them waiting interminably, then dumped them. Toward the end of her grotesque and protracted courtship of the French king's brother, François Hercule d'Alençon, Elizabeth kissed her frog prince, as she called him, on the mouth and, slipping a ring onto his finger, declared before the French ambassador that she had decided to make him her husband. Alençon in turn drew a ring from his finger and, with a reciprocal vow, placed it on the queen's hand. This was the time-honored marriage by ring and pledge, which still had force in law. The very next day Elizabeth told one of her councillors that she would not marry Alençon, even to be empress of the world. Deeply sensitive herself, she had little consideration for the feelings of others. All that mattered was her own survival.

Describing the queen's cold-blooded dominance over men, the historian Carolly Erickson makes a penetrating analogy:

> In a larger sense what King Henry had done was to assert his personal sovereignty in the sexual realm as ruthlessly as he had asserted it in the political realm. The women he became entangled with, whether as wives or lovers, emerged much the worse from the encounter, while the king remained unshackled and dominant. By proclaiming her preference for the single life, by refusing the suitors who pursued her, by her seeming indifference to the urgent issue of the succession, and most of all, by her shameless liaison with Dudley, Elizabeth was achieving the same results her father had achieved: sovereign mastery of her sexual life, at the expense of others.[33]

Shortly before she conferred on Robert Dudley the quasi-royal title Earl of Leicester (once held by the usurper Henry Bolingbroke, later Henry IV), Elizabeth told the Scottish envoy Sir James Melville that had she ever been minded to take a husband, Leicester would have been her choice. The son and grandson of traitors, and a traitor himself, Leicester was hell-bent on winning the throne, and like Claudius in *Hamlet,* a character almost certainly modeled on him, he would not stop short of murder to achieve his goal. Like Seymour before him, he possessed a perfidious charm that Elizabeth found irresistible. A sort of unofficial husband, Leicester mitigated the anomaly of her position as unmarried queen, which to most people, including Elizabeth's councillors, was an almost monstrous phenomenon, certain to bring shame and misfortune upon the realm.

Her emotional cruelty toward Leicester was typical of her dealings with the men she loved, and is exemplified by her scheme to marry him off to the Scottish queen, whom she described as "the serpent that poisons me." Indeed, it was said that she had raised him to the earldom of Leicester only to make him a fit offering for Mary. Unwilling to marry him herself, she seemed to get a vicarious thrill from the idea of his wedding her great rival, and having them both under her thumb. For Elizabeth, this was a matter of control. Men might wield power over her as a woman—but as a queen, *never*. After one memorable bit of impudence on Leicester's part, she fulminated at him, crying, "I will have here but one mistress and no master!" In the end, the interminable courtship broke Leicester's will and pride. Denied the usual pleasures of married life and an heir to succeed to his titles, browbeaten and humiliated beyond the endurance of any self-respecting man, he was emasculated by the queen whose throne he longed to share.

Like Persephone (raped by her uncle Pluto, god of the underworld), Elizabeth spent only half the year aboveground, under the broad sky; for the other six months she reigned in Hades, a shadow queen prostrated by nervous ailments and tormented by self-doubt. For the first thirty years of her reign, from 1558 to 1588, the facade of chastity held up through the sheer force of her personality. After the Armada, it finally crumbled and she became increasingly undignified, living in semi-incestuous bondage to her dashing young "son" —Dudley's stepson—Robert Devereux, Earl of Essex. She fondled him in public with her robe open to the waist, and they spent all night "playing cards" until interrupted by the chirping of birds at dawn. For those who could see, the secret was out in the open.

This is not to say that the cult of the Virgin Queen fell into abeyance at the royal court; on the contrary, it was bolder and more exaggerated than ever, while the mock chivalry that grew up to vindicate it had an almost impossibly garish, even morbid quality to it. When Essex appeared in black armor at the Accession Day tilt of 1590, accompanied by a black-clad pageant, the object of his mourning was not just Philip Sidney, but chivalry itself. That same year Elizabeth's secretary of state, Francis Walsingham, had died, leaving the Cecils, who exemplified the new ruling class, to gather even more power into their hands. It was Essex who led the reaction to the *regnum Cecilianum,* as it was sometimes called. The 1590s were a time of poverty and famine, with the queen herself having to sell crown lands and auction off royal heirlooms from the jewel house at the Tower. Gloriana was aging visibly, and the Council sent out an order "to suppress all likenesses of the Queen that depicted her as being in any way old and hence subject to mortality."[34]

Elizabeth functioned in two worlds—the mundane and the mythic— and the two gradually melted into each other. To draw a metaphor from *Antony and Cleopatra,* she inhabited both Rome and Egypt, and like Cleopatra managed to keep rejuvenating herself in the fount of her royalty. As Enobarbus says of the Egyptian queen: "Vilest things become themselves in her." In December 1560, when Nicholas Throckmorton, Elizabeth's ambassador to France, complained about rumors in Paris that the queen had secretly married Robert Dudley, William Cecil wrote, counseling him "not to meddle with the matters of this Court, otherwise that ye may well be advised from hence. What her Majesty will determine to do only God, I think, knoweth; and in her His Will be fulfilled. . . . But in one word I say, contend not where victory cannot be had." Rumors of a secret marriage were accompanied by reports that the queen was expecting Dudley's child. "I am no angel," Elizabeth confided coyly to the Spanish ambassador Bishop Alvarez de Quadra.

On October 30, 1566, Roger Ascham, Elizabeth's old tutor, began his classic work *The Scholemaster* with a long dedication to the queen entitled "Divae Elizabethae." Informally commissioned by Elizabeth herself, *The Scholemaster* was not published until 1571, three years after Ascham's death. The dedication, moreover, was omitted, and didn't see the light of day until 1761, when it was published by James Bennett. The reasons for the suppression are not hard to determine. Ascham went out of his way to compare Elizabeth to David in the blessings that God had bestowed on her (e.g., in bringing her safely to the throne after many trials), including the Almighty's promise to Israel's greatest king that "Thine own seed shall sit in thy seat." "And so David," writes

Ascham, "made king by God's goodness, made also not only his present time happy, but his posterity also blessed." But David's life was far from blameless: he committed adultery with Bathsheba and engineered her husband's death. Ascham refuses to gloss over these sins, making them part of his analogy:

> But David was wrapt in a stranger case and kind of misery; for when God had showed him his greatest favour, and had given him the highest benefits that man in earth could receive, yet God suffered him to fall into the deepest pit of wickedness; to commit the cruellest murder, and shamefullest adultery, that ever did man upon earth. Whereinto he did not stumble by ignorance, nor slide by weakness, nor only fall by wilfulness, but went to it advisedly, purposing all practices, and finding out all fetches that mischief could imagine, to bring mischief to pass. . . .
>
> And therefore was I very willing to offer this book to your Majesty, wherein, as in a fair glass, your Majesty shall see and acknowledge, by God's dealings with David, even very many like good dealings of God with your Majesty.[35]

Ascham closes by wishing the queen what in the end David was granted, "most prosperity, and surest felicity, for you, yours, and your posterity." The analogy with David's wrongdoing would have reminded readers of Elizabeth's alleged connivance at the death of Dudley's first wife, Amy Robsart, in 1560, and her subsequent "punishment" in falling prey to smallpox. David had many children by different wives, and his forty-year reign was plagued by confusion and infighting over the succession, until he finally named Solomon, his surviving son by Bathsheba, as his heir.

Aware of Elizabeth's shortcomings and the ugly rumors surrounding her throne (which to many *was* the throne of David), Ascham uses the example of the King of Israel not only to hold up the mirror of history to his former pupil, but to elevate her in the national imagination. But because he had been too scrupulous in weighing her misdoings, his contemporaries were denied his wisdom.

In a dedication addressed directly to the queen, there was nowhere to hide. In a work of fiction, on the other hand, an author could camouflage his criticism. Shakespeare, whose works reflected his awkward position at court, had much to say about Elizabeth. He also had much to say *to* her. His portrayal of her as Gertrude in *Hamlet* is clearly not the sort of literal depiction a historian might present, but it is one of great emotional and psychological depth—and full of surprises. This "most-seeming virtuous queen," as the Ghost calls Gertrude, is hardly the Elizabeth that history has taught us to admire. For one thing, she has a son, a poet-prince living in the shadows, who uses the theater to hold the mirror up to her and speak out about abuses of state. In the closet scene, when Gertrude and her son are completely alone, it is as if we are trespassing upon a private, wholly forgotten moment of history, of incalculable import. Hidden away in some dim recess of the world soul, Shakespeare and Elizabeth, as even the most daringly imaginative of novelists could never have conceived them, are baring their hearts. If we were not so enthralled, we might be tempted to turn away in disbelief. "O Hamlet," cries the Queen, "Speak no more. Thou turn'st my eyes into my very soul."

The state, as reflected in *Hamlet,* was not only in crisis, but in danger of collapse. There were many comparisons in the rhetoric of the time between England's perilous condition and the fall of Troy. The speech Hamlet gives the First Player in Act II scene II describes the moment Troy's citadel falls to the ground, its king murdered by the avenging Pyrrhus. The fall of Troy led to the founding of a new civilization, Rome, by the Trojan hero Aeneas, whose great-grandson Brutus was said to have founded Britain.

After the lurid description of Priam's slaughter comes a passage about his queen, Hecuba, famous for her fertility (Shakespeare mentions her "all o'erteemed loins"). She is described as "mobled" (or "mob-led"); in other words, her face was muffled, or she was being led astray by the mischievous fairy, Queen Mab or Mob. She runs up and down barefoot, with a cloth on her head and a hastily snatched blanket to cover her naked body. The passage continues with an extraordinary couplet:

> Who this had seen, with tongue in venom steep'd,
> 'Gainst Fortune's state would treason have pronounc'd.
> (II.ii.506–507)

Why would witnesses to the queen's actions be tempted to cry treason? (Fortune was a common trope of the time for Elizabeth, so we're talking about something paradoxical, not to say heretical: the monarch accused of treason.) Could it be that not just the walls of Troy were breached during that fateful hour? The historian H. H. Holland remarks that in 1582–3 "scandalous stories were being circulated by the Countess of Shrewsbury, who had presumably received them from some lady or gentleman-in-waiting, to the effect that Queen Elizabeth had been seen going to meet Simier, the French envoy, in a lady's chamber, that she had met Alençon, his master, at the door of her bedchamber with only her shift and nightgown on, and that he had remained with her for three hours. . . . That after retiring to her private rooms . . . the Queen is disturbed by her impassioned suitor; that in fear she comes out, having thrown a blanket over herself, that far from being amenable to his passion, she flies into a blinding rage and threatens him."[36] We must remember, too, that Elizabeth's flirtation with Simier, whom she called her "monkey," was so brazen that Dudley retired from court in a fit of jealousy. Shakespeare, it is clear, was deliberately juxtaposing the fall of Troy (Britain) with the compromising love life of its queen.

He broached this same theme more overtly in *Troilus and Cressida,* written around the same time as *Hamlet.* Here the play's heroine, Cressida, is shadowed by the object of the war, that "mortal Venus," Helen of Troy; and at times the two become indistinguishable. That Elizabeth is meant is clear in the first scene, when Troilus applies the red-and-white Tudor rose signature to Helen, saying "[she] must needs be fair / When with your blood you daily paint her thus." The comments about her are overwhelmingly cynical and negative. Through her the sexual and political realms merge, her wantonness sowing discord and worse. Though she is more sinned against than sinning, her relationship with Paris has created the Trojan war and threatens the survival of Troy itself. Diomedes speaks for the majority when he says:

> She's bitter to her country: hear me, Paris—
> For every false drop in her bawdy veins
> A Grecian's life hath sunk; for every scruple
> Of her contaminated carrion weight
> A Trojan hath been slain.
>
> (IV.i.69–73)

Professor Marjorie Garber of Harvard observes that Cressida and Troilus struggle "blindly against their own mythic identities."[37] Like Elizabeth, Cressida is ever conscious of how history will judge her, and must wear a mask to defend her reputation for chastity ("honesty"). When her uncle Pandarus, another lampoon of William Cecil, Lord Burghley, says, "You are such a woman, a man knows not at what ward you lie," she replies:

> Upon my back, to defend my belly; upon my wit, to defend my wiles; upon my secrecy, to defend mine honesty; my mask, to defend my beauty; and you, to defend all these; and at all these wards I lie, at a thousand watches.
>
> (I.ii.265–269)

"Lie," of course contains its other meaning, "to speak falsely." On her back to defend her belly suggests she uses sex as a form of defense, just as she uses quick-wittedness as a cover for craftiness. As for chastity, she must be secretive to defend her reputation; keeping others in the dark is vital. As far as Cressida's beauty goes, the application to Elizabeth is clear, for the latter certainly used her mask of godlike virginity to create an aura of unfading youth. She employed Cecil-Pandarus to watch and lie for her, keeping the lid on her indiscretions ("and you, to defend all these," as Cressida says). When Pandarus says to her, "If my lord [i.e., Troilus] get a boy of you, you'll give him me," we hear Cecil, as master of the royal wards, offering to take Elizabeth's son under his wing.

Cressida's wounds go deep. Despite her eloquent protestations, she seems incapable of faith in her relations with men. Her language reflects the alien soulscape of *Miroir de L'Âme Pécheresse* when she says, "I have forgot my father. / I know no touch of consanguinity."[38] Like Elizabeth, she has no mother; and her father has abandoned her, leaving her under the charge of an uncle-father. Troilus strives to reconcile Cressida's seeming purity with the rank faithlessness with which she gives her love from him to Diomedes. In the end, all he can do is to split her in two:

> This is, and is not, Cressid . . .
> Instance, O instance! strong as Pluto's gates:
> Cressid is mine, tied with the bonds of heaven.

Instance, O instance! strong as heaven itself:
The bonds of heaven are slipp'd, dissolv'd, and loos'd;
And with another knot, five-finger-tied,
The fractions of her faith, orts of her love,
The fragments, scraps, the bits, and greasy relics
Of her o'er-eaten faith are given to Diomed.

(V.ii.145, 152–159)

Antony and Cleopatra, which contains the most glorious and damning portrait of Elizabeth in the canon, also juxtaposes a queen's sensuality and the fall of a civilization. Cleopatra, like Helen of Troy, is a mortal Venus, a woman who inhabits the myth she has created for herself. It was to the cult of the moon goddess Isis, divine mother and sacred bride, that she attuned herself, appearing in public, according to Plutarch, "in the habiliments of the goddess." Like Isis, known as "Myrionymus" for her myriad names, Shakespeare's Cleopatra is protean, changing form as it suits her. As part of her cult of the virgin goddess, Queen Elizabeth was addressed by poets under countless epithets. In the prologue to Thomas Dekker's *Pleasant Comedy of Old Fortunatus* (1600), one old man asks another if he is on his way to the temple of Eliza, and receives the reply: "Even to her temple are my feeble limbs travelling. Some call her Pandora: some Gloriana, some Cynthia: some Delphoebe, some Astraea: all by several names to express several loves: yet all those names make but one celestial body, as all those loves meet to create but one soul."

Nevertheless, to Caesar and the Romans, Cleopatra is little more than a high-class prostitute, and Antony for doting on her "a strumpet's fool" or "the bellows and the fan to cool a gipsy's lust." Even Antony calls her a "triple-turned whore," taunting her with her opportunistic love affairs with the great of the world:

I found you as a morsel, cold upon
Dead Caesar's trencher: nay, you were a fragment
Of Gnaeus Pompey's, besides what hotter hours
Unregister'd in vulgar fame, you have
Luxuriously pick'd out. For I am sure
Though you can guess what temperance should be,
You know not what it is.

(III.xiii.116–122)

How Elizabeth must have winced when she heard those lines, not least because the reference to Caesar was a gibe at her alleged affair with Philip of Spain in the mid-1550s. Cleopatra's relationship with Antony is erotic, and jealous, and proves politically suicidal. (Though she had incestuous relationships with two of her brothers and had many children by Antony and others, Cleopatra turned out to be the last of the Ptolemaic dynasty; after her death, Egypt became a Roman province.) Yet her charisma is such that the goddess in her is not contradicted by the whore, but strangely enhanced, as if she made a cult of her sins. So great is her diversity that all opposites are reconciled in the magic of her personality ("she did make defect perfection"). Antony's general, Enobarbus, praises her in spite of his better judgement:

> Age cannot wither her, nor custom stale
> Her infinite variety: other women cloy
> The appetites they feed, but she makes hungry,
> Where most she satisfies. For vilest things
> Become themselves in her, that the holy priests
> Bless her, when she is riggish [i.e., wanton].
>
> (II.ii.235–240)

Shakespeare's Cleopatra enjoys cross-dressing, and going through the streets at night as a commoner. She is a mistress of disguise; she loves revels, acting, feasting, flattery, and all the arts of seduction. She is endlessly vain, as was Elizabeth, who if the "Scandal Letter" is to be believed, thought "as highly of [her] beauty as if [she] were a goddess of heaven . . . and took such great pleasure in flatteries beyond all reason that [she was] told for example that at times one dared not look full at [her] because [her] face shone like the sun."[39] Cleopatra is sensual, too, and adores Antony's body; yet she is false and faithless, an equivocator who delights in sending false messages (her final one, imparting her death, proves fatal), and who repeatedly betrays the man she loves. She is majestic and noble-hearted, yet coarse, spiteful, vicious, and vainglorious. Vital rather than beautiful, it is her charm and quick-wittedness that captivate, her erotic and cultured mind and gift for languages. Her temper is intimidating and sometimes violent and she would prefer to hear good news or flattering words, even if false, to uncomfortable truths. She strikes and berates

the messenger who brings her news of Antony's marriage to Octavia,
dragging him up and down by the hair and threatening to have him
"whipp'd with wire, and stew'd in brine." (Elizabeth was infamous
for her violence toward her servants, on one occasion breaking the
finger of one of her maids of honor, on another sticking her knife
into the hand of a serving lady.) Later, when she has calmed down,
Cleopatra quizzes the messenger about Octavia's appearance, much
in the manner that Elizabeth interrogated the Scottish envoy James
Melville about Mary Queen of Scots, turning his neutral answers to
deprecation. (When told that Octavia is "low-voic'd" and not as tall
as her, Cleopatra pronounces her "dull of tongue, and dwarfish!")
Like Elizabeth on the eve of the Armada, rousing her troops at Tilbury
"with the heart and stomach of a king," Cleopatra insists on taking
the field at Actium: "A charge we bear i' the war, / And as the president of my kingdom will / Appear there for a man."

These three heroines (Gertrude, Cressida-Helen, and Cleopatra)
reveal Elizabeth to have been a liability to the state, her licentiousness
—like theirs—having grave political consequences for the monarchy. All, however, are the center of the hero's universe—of Hamlet's,
Troilus's, and Antony's—he being something of a political outcast,
alienated from power by his idealism and poetic spirit. Each woman
proves or has proved faithless, betraying her son or lover, whose
anguish is voiced poignantly through the lips of Antony:

> Betray'd I am.
> O this false soul of Egypt! This grave charm
> Whose eyes beck'd forth my wars, and call'd them home,
> Whose bosom was my crownet, my chief end,
> Like a right gipsy, hath, at fast and loose,
> Beguil'd me, to the very heart of loss.
>
> (IV.xii.24–29)

~ *3* ~

Budding Genius

Albeit by the learned view and insight of your Lordship,
whose infancy from the beginning was ever sacred to the
Muses.
　　　　　　　—Angel Day to the Earl of Oxford, 1586

GIVEN THE VAGUENESS AND uncertainty that shroud contemporary
accounts of Shakespeare, it would be incredible if the man behind
the name, when correctly identified, did not present a mysterious
and baffling figure to his contemporaries, whether or not they suspected the extent of his activities and his stature as an artist. Even
today, more than 400 years after his death, controversy rages about
who Oxford really was, for there is much in his life, as it has been
handed down to us by the records of the time, that does not add up.
There is a missing dimension, which is not wholly explained by his
secret life as William Shakespeare.

The history books tell us that Edward de Vere was born on April
12, 1550, at Hedingham Castle in Essex, the only son of John de Vere,
16th Earl of Oxford, and his second wife, Margery Golding. According to the Victorian historian Lord Macaulay, the de Veres were "the
longest and most illustrious line of nobles that England has seen."
Originally Norsemen, the Veres were said to have moved from
Denmark to Normandy, where they settled in and around the village of Ver. Others claim they were originally from Veere in Holland (*veer* in Dutch rather charmingly meaning a feather or quill).
Alberic de Ver arrived in England with William the Conqueror,

and for his part in the invasion was granted land in the counties of Middlesex, Cambridge, Huntingdon, Suffolk, and Essex. His son, Alberic II, created lord great chamberlain by King Henry I, built the family's principal seat of Hedingham Castle, whose towering Norman keep still pierces the Essex sky. His grandson, Aubrey, was made Earl of Oxford in 1142 by Empress Matilda, mother of Henry II. The earldom, which was the most senior in the land during Elizabeth's reign, lasted for 561 years, expiring with the death of Aubrey, the twentieth earl, in 1703.

There is no record of Edward's birth in the registers of the time. Instead, we owe the date of his appearance in the world to his future father-in-law, William Cecil, Lord Burghley, who made a note of it more than a quarter century later, as if he needed to remind himself of the official truth. On April 17, 1550, however, the Privy Council, under the leadership of Lord Protector Edward Seymour, Duke of Somerset, authorized the gift of a baptismal cup for the christening of "our very good Lord the Earl of Oxford's son." This is not proof of a birthdate in April 1550, for if Oxford was a changeling, as some have claimed, born up to eighteen months earlier, an official baptism could have been arranged at any time.

What we do know is that John de Vere and Margery Golding were married quite suddenly on August 1, 1548, and some people would later challenge their children's legitimacy, arguing that the parents were unlawfully wed. John de Vere had a daughter, Katherine, by his first wife, Lady Dorothy Neville (d. 1547); while still wedded to Dorothy, he contracted a bigamous marriage with Joan Jockey of nearby Earl's Colne. Various other amours followed. At the time of his wedding to Margery Golding he was engaged to be married the very next day to another woman, Dorothy Fosser, who was a servant of the earl's nine-year-old daughter Katherine. The banns for their marriage had already been called twice when he abandoned her—seemingly under duress—in favor of a hasty union with Margery.

Lord Protector Somerset, intent on forcing a match between Oxford's daughter Katherine and his own son Henry Seymour, had been blackmailing the earl for some time. Though it is not known what he had on him, Somerset managed to extort de Vere's ancestral lands under two separate fines dated February and April 1548. According to eighteenth-century historian, the Reverend Philip Morant:

Edward Seymour, Duke of Somerset, Protector of the Realm, out of his extreme avarice and greedy appetite did, under color of justice, convent before himself for certain criminal causes John Earl of Oxford and so terrify him that, to save his life, [he] was obliged to alienate to the said Duke by deed all his estates, lordships, manors etc.[40]

What might these undivulged crimes have been, and did they involve the earl's extramarital affairs? Whatever the answer, from that moment until his death John de Vere fell into line, becoming little more than a puppet of Somerset's private secretary, Sir William Cecil. Under the "recognizance" signed between the men, Somerset even removed Oxford's control over his own household, denying him the basic power to dismiss servants. Moreover, he used Thomas Golding, the brother of Oxford's future bride Margery, and Thomas Darcy, the earl's brother-in-law, to spy on the hapless nobleman and report back to Somerset's office. This pinioning of John de Vere may have been in preparation for the arrival of a royal changeling. If so, the timing fits with the rumored birth of a child to the king's sister, Princess Elizabeth—later Queen Elizabeth—in the autumn of 1548; and if this child was Edward de Vere, then a birth date of September or October 1548 would make sense of many subsequent anomalies in the biographical record.

William Cecil, already indispensable to Elizabeth in the wake of the scandal involving Thomas Seymour, most likely masterminded the placing of the child. Cecil's influence at court had been steadily rising as Somerset had come to rely more and more on the younger man's unrivaled head for detail and his ability to broker deals. Cecil had a way of tacking and turning with the tide, while appearing to those around him as a model of unexampled loyalty. After Somerset's fall he quickly became the eyes and ears of his successor, John Dudley, Duke of Northumberland. Although a Puritan at heart, he began attending Mass on the accession of Mary in 1553, worming his way into the counsels of the Catholic queen with little strain on his conscience. At the same time, he remained indispensable to Mary's sister, Princess Elizabeth, helping manage her lands and keeping her abreast of political developments.

he Cecils, originally "Sitsylts," were from the Welsh borders, and
iam's father and grandfather had both been minor court officials
er Henry VII and Henry VIII. They were the new bureaucratic
ed. When William died in 1598, he had been in Elizabeth's service
half a century. Though extremely ambitious for himself and his
nily, he also harbored larger goals and had the patience and cunning
advance them. Having seen all the upheavals of the Tudor succes-
ion at close quarters, through four reigns, he had grown somewhat
cynical about the divinity that hedges a king. His lawyerly mind
began to work toward a form of constitutional monarchy, whereby
the Council shared power with the queen, acting as a sort of collective consort, both protecting and restraining her rule, and assuming
the power to decide the succession by choosing the next monarch.
This way, the Protestant state could be preserved; and that, more than
the preservation of the monarchy, was Burghley's ultimate goal. It was
unfortunate for him that the security of the state should depend on
the health and virtue of the monarch (especially a female monarch);
by strengthening the Council and weakening the powers of the queen,
he attempted to bring greater political stability to the realm. The much
vaunted *regnum Cecilianum* was a kind of monarchical republic, perhaps with Venice as its model; hence Shakespeare's portrait of Burghley
as Shylock in *The Merchant of Venice.*

The other quasi-royal child born in the second half of 1548, but
orphaned by the death of both parents, was Mary Seymour, daughter of Queen Catherine Parr and Lord Admiral Thomas Seymour.
Mary disappears from history about a year after her birth (c. August
1549), having spent her infancy in the household of Catherine
Willoughby, Duchess of Suffolk. The duchess kept what appears to
have been an unofficial royal orphanage at her Lincolnshire estate,
Grimsthorpe Castle, and it may be that Edward de Vere was originally placed there, too, before being transferred to Hedingham. There
is no record of Mary's death, so it could be that she turned up in the
Oxford household as Edward's sister, Mary Vere, who would later
marry Catherine Willoughby's son, Peregrine Bertie. Mary Vere is
said to have been born in 1554, but there is no recorded birth or
baptism (if she was Mary Seymour, she would have been Edward's
half-sister). No children were born to John de Vere and Margery
Golding.

One chronological anomaly that should be dealt with immediately concerns the suit brought in 1563 by Edward's half-sister in the de Vere line, Katherine, and her husband, Lord Windsor, to have the marriage of Edward and Mary's putative parents—the Earl and Countess of Oxford—declared void, and the children illegitimate. In responding to the suit on behalf of his nephew and niece, Arthur Golding, the countess's half-brother, who was also Edward's tutor, refers to both children as minors of fourteen years, which of course would be their correct age if they were the children of Thomas Seymour, born in August and September 1548 respectively. If, however, they were de Vere siblings, as history claims, then Edward would have been thirteen at the time, and Mary just nine. It is difficult to mistake a nine-year-old girl for fourteen.[41]

In *Thomas of Woodstock*, or *Richard II, Part I* as it is often called, which many scholars now attribute to Shakespeare, Richard's birth date becomes a matter of contention. His uncles have led him to believe that he is younger than he actually is. When Richard learns the truth through Sir John Bushy, who has been combing through the English Chronicles, he exclaims:

> O treacherous men that have deluded us!
> We might have claimed our right a twelve month since.
> (II.i.114–115)

As far as I have been able to discover, this discrepancy over Richard's age is Shakespeare's innovation rather than a matter of historical record.

Whether Oxford was born in September or October 1548 to Princess Elizabeth by Thomas Seymour, or in April 1550 to Margery Golding by John de Vere, Earl of Oxford, the shadow of bastardy hung over him. As B. M. Ward, Oxford's first biographer, wrote in 1928: "It is curious to see how scandal accompanied Edward de Vere into the world; and we shall find as [his] story develops that the voice of scandal steadily pursued him throughout his life, and has continued to pursue his memory during the . . . years that have elapsed since his death."[42] My own view, which determines the perspective from which I write, is that Oxford was the bastard son of Elizabeth and Seymour, the infant whom rumor declared "miserably destroyed" at birth. Throughout his life, no one knew quite how to treat Oxford. He was alternately deified and demonized, as one would expect of a hidden prince, whose presence promised a bright new future—and blew a hole in his mother's carefully crafted myth.

Whether Seymour-Tudor or de Vere, Edward was clearly named for the boy king, Edward VI, Elizabeth's brother, who was on the throne at the time of his birth and who reigned at first under the regency of Seymour's brother, Edward, Duke of Somerset. A frail, scholarly child, he died of consumption at the age of fifteen, in July 1553, when Oxford was not quite five. The name Edward sticks out like a sore thumb in the list of Aubreys, Johns, and Roberts that constitute the long line of Oxford earls, marking him as an outsider from the start. The young Oxford was a deeply sensitive and impressionable child, who read widely in history and romance literature, so the death of the boy king who shared his name must have made an impression on him, stirring associations, perhaps, with the princes in the Tower. One of those princes, Edward V, was another minor prevented from fulfilling his royal destiny. This archetype of the boy king lay buried in Oxford's unconscious, rising later in the tragic figure of Prince Arthur in *King John,* or the apparition of the crowned child that so astonishes Macbeth.

Oxford was born at a quintessentially Shakespearean moment, when there was only the ghost of a king on the throne—a pale, consumptive boy—and no settled succession, the land being governed by the lord protector and his council. To many daring minds, including that of Oxford's possible father, Thomas Seymour, the crown seemed there for the taking. Seymour, as was his nature, made a lunge for it, his subsequent execution undermining the popularity of his brother Somerset. John Dudley, Earl of Warwick (father of Elizabeth's lover, Robert Dudley), saw his opening and began to intrigue for the privilege of protecting the boy king. Warwick won out, becoming president of the council and Duke of Northumberland. When he knew he was dying, Edward VI drew up what he termed the Device for the Succession, a desperate and unrealistic attempt to secure a successor who was both male and Protestant. Under Salic law, the document barred both Mary and Elizabeth, and indeed all females, from the line of succession, thus contradicting Henry VIII's

third and final Succession Act of 1543, and his will. In the absence of (legitimate) male heirs, however, Dudley persuaded Edward to alter the Device, so that his cousin, the sixteen-year-old Lady Jane Grey, Dudley's own daughter-in-law, could inherit the throne. This she did, but for a mere nine days. The puppet queen and her master had no support, and in July 1553 Henry's eldest daughter, Mary, swept into London on a sudden swell of popular affection. The Protestant king of Edward's imagination had turned into a Catholic queen.

Oxford's birth was also a time when the Continental Renaissance was taking hold in England, bringing with it a new aesthetic of learning. The rediscovery of the artistic life of ancient Greece and Rome through their vast treasury of literary and philosophical texts was stimulating a revolution in language, literature, and court culture in general. Nothing of value was left unaffected: music, painting, poetry, politics, architecture, horticulture, fashion, and of course drama. Castiglione's cult book *Il Cortegiano* inspired a new generation of courtiers to reconcile their old profession of arms with a new passion for the mind. Above all, perhaps, it inculcated a faith in their own individuality. A wave of young noblemen poured into Oxford and Cambridge to avail themselves of the new learning, not just for itself, but aware that they were now competing for political office with highly talented "new men" of the ilk of Wolsey and Cromwell. "In this first, heroic, phase of the educational revolution," writes Lawrence Stone, "peers and gentry possessed an enthusiasm for pure scholarship that far outran the practical needs of an administrative *élite*."[43]

At the same time, the Reformation brought with it a revolution in education and social attitudes, a new critical and humanistic spirit that fostered changes in economy and statecraft. For the reformers, learning was a tool of moral and spiritual development. The ruler must learn the lessons of history, his own and his country's, in order to become a fit embodiment of Plato's philosopher-king. The reformers' emphasis was on history, philosophy, and political theory (i.e., the collective); the fine arts they regarded with suspicion, in particular poetry and drama, as having the potential to corrupt a young man's allegiance to God and country. National interest was the driving force behind the political and educational reforms; and a new awareness of self was both cause and effect of the artistic and scientific flowering. These two great agents of European change—the Renaissance, taking its life from the Catholic south; and the Reformation, from the Protestant north—produced tensions in England which, when mediated in a creative fashion, as happened in the psyche of Shakespeare, produced the highest art.

Of Oxford's earliest years we know nothing, though his biographers have assumed that he spent them chiefly at the de Veres' ancestral estate at Castle Hedingham in Essex, with occasional visits to the capital, where the family would have stayed at Vere House by London Stone. Though details are sparse, Oxford first emerges into the light of day in December 1554, when he was sent to Ankerwick, the Buckinghamshire seat of Sir Thomas Smith, to become the scholar of that formidable Reformation intellectual. Smith would later describe Oxford as "brought up in my house." If Oxford was the bona fide child of John de Vere, he would have been only four when this crucial move took place—too young, even for those precocious times. If, however, he was the child of Elizabeth and Seymour, then he would be leaving home at six, an age better conforming to the standard of the time. (His namesake, Edward VI, had begun his formal education at age six.)

Sir Thomas Smith was noted for his direct manner, his rigorous, rather puritanical mind, and his general lack of affectation, which made his a rather uncomfortable presence at court. Oxford would later immortalize him as "plain Thomas" Woodstock, King Richard II's "plain protector" in his chronicle play *Thomas of Woodstock*.[44] Smith was the finest classical scholar of his day, and one of the brightest stars of the new learning at Cambridge, where in 1530 he became a fellow of Queens' College at sixteen. He was appointed the first Public Reader in Greek three years later, and his oratory drew crowds of students from the university, among them the future prime minister William Cecil; fellow classicist, John Cheke; the future Archbishop of Canterbury, Matthew Parker; Nicholas Bacon, the father of Francis; and Roger Ascham, who would one day tutor Princess Elizabeth. Smith did much to encourage the study of Greek at Cambridge, and reformed its pronunciation. He also lectured on natural philosophy (he was a Platonist) and was appointed the first Regius Professor of Civil Law by Henry VIII. In this last capacity he spent eighteen months lecturing at the renowned University of Padua in northern Italy.

Smith's ability as a teacher was widely praised, and his gifts of expression, both literary and rhetorical, were of the highest order. He was a literary stylist with a strong feel for the emerging genius of English, for which he invented a new alphabet of twenty-nine letters. According to his biographer Mary Dewar, Smith "tried to revolutionize the writing and spelling of the English language." He was also a politician and diplomat, at one time serving as Elizabeth's ambassador to France. His most celebrated work, *De Republica Anglorum; the Manner of Government or Policy of the Realm of England* (1562–1565), gives proof of his deep constitutional knowledge and his abiding interest in the political institutions of his native land. In it, he grapples with the perennial problem of the succession by providing a monarchical model that is broadly constitutional in our modern sense. Smith's other passions included Roman history, astronomy and astrology, architecture, gardening, hawking, beekeeping, medicine, and mathematics. Dewar writes, "His colleagues and students were always dazzled by his wide range of interests and impressed by his capacity to discuss any topic and pronounce learnedly in almost any field of study."[45] Linguist, orator, historian, lawyer, translator, physician, astronomer, horticulturalist, and statesman, Smith was a true Renaissance polymath. Moreover, his principal fields of expertise—namely Latin and Greek, classical civilization, law, history, horticulture, medicine, rhetoric, and the development of the English language—are all profoundly reflected in the works of Shakespeare.

Shakespeare's knowledge of Greek tragedy and philosophy in the original Greek is so ingrained, and so intrinsic to his imaginative self-expression, that hardly a phrase goes by in his plays without some reminiscence of an image or trope from Sophocles, Euripides, Aeschylus, or indeed Plato. His learning, however, is worn with the lightness of the truly erudite mind; therefore many of his classical references are missed by all but the most vigilant scholars. A good example occurs in *Henry VI, Part 1,* when Charles, the Dauphin, congratulates Joan of Arc after their success at the siege of Orléans:

> Thy promises are like Adonis' gardens,
> Which one day bloom'd, and fruitful were the next.
>
> (I.vi.6–7)

The surface meaning is obvious. The Dauphin, exulting in Joan's promises of success, marvels at the speed with which her predictions are coming true. Yet a knowledge of Plato's *Phaedrus,* in which Socrates warns Phaedrus of the folly of planting one's seeds in a garden of Adonis, where they will spring up in eight days and as suddenly fade, undercuts the superficial reading with a deep irony. Joan's promises will prove ephemeral and, like the blooms of Socrates's magic seeds, wither before their time. This is Shakespeare's full meaning, and yet the *Phaedrus* had not been translated into English in his day. Oxford's thorough early drilling in the classics was an essential part of the literary apprenticeship of the genius we know as Shake-speare.

Sir Thomas Smith, a former servant of Edward Seymour, Duke of Somerset, was a member of a coterie of Protestant scholars assembled by William Cecil to bring home the English Reformation, not only by translating ancient texts and composing treatises on statecraft and philosophy, but by instructing the sons of noblemen in the new learning. As such, Smith knew and came into contact with many of the most eminent thinkers, educators, explorers, and writers of his day, and it is reasonable to suppose that his young charge, Edward de Vere, was permitted to meet and question these luminaries, which included the theologian and collector of early English manuscripts Matthew Parker; the scholar and educationalist Roger Ascham, who did much to promote English as a literary language; the classical scholar and former tutor to King Edward VI, Sir Anthony Cooke; the Regius Professor of Greek at Cambridge Sir John Cheke; the historian, playwright, and Protestant polemicist John Bale; the Anglo-Saxon scholar Laurence Nowell; the Latin scholar and rhetorician Bartholomew Clerke; the mathematician, astronomer, and occultist John Dee; Dee's pupil Thomas Digges; the alchemist and translator of geographic works Richard Eden; and the explorer, writer, and Member of Parliament, Sir Humphrey Gilbert. Nearly all these men were involved in politics at one time or another, as advisers to the monarch. It was a stimulating environment in which to grow up, and Edward also had access to Smith's impressive library. A list of his books compiled by Smith himself in 1566 gives 411 titles, many consisting of multiple volumes. A good number of these titles provide source material for Shakespeare's plays.[46] Oxford seems to have been drawn most powerfully to Greek and Roman literature, in particular poetry and drama, which is one reason the poet and translator Angel Day described him as someone "whose infancy from the beginning was ever sacred to the Muses."

We don't know who made the decision to place Oxford with Smith, but it was likely to have been William Cecil. John de Vere was reported to be an unstable character, of unsettled beliefs—what today we might describe as a loose cannon—and Essex during the reign of Mary, because of its cells of radical Protestantism, became one of the hot spots of government reprisals. If Cecil was in charge of Oxford's overall upbringing, then he would be at pains to ensure that the boy was in safe hands, and with a family who would keep his royal origins in complete confidence. Smith and his wife Philippa, who were themselves childless, fit the bill to a T. In October 1558, a month before Queen Mary died, the ten-year-old Edward was enrolled at Smith's alma mater, Queens' College, Cambridge, and then at St. John's the following January. How long he remained at the university is uncertain, but Smith, it seems, continued to be responsible for his all-around education.

When Smith took up residence at his new home, Hill Hall in Essex, Edward probably spent more time up at Hedingham visiting his foster father, whose extorted lands had been restored by Parliament in January 1552. He would have enjoyed fooling around with his father's actors, the Earl of Oxford's Men (the de Veres had kept players since 1492), who, when they weren't traveling, put on plays before their lord and lady. Edward was being brought up as an only child under the care of a rigorous mentor, who was in touch with some of the most exciting minds of the time, and literature and the theater quickly became his refuge and delight. Through them he was able to orient himself to the world, and imagine a role for himself that was in keeping with the power and daring of his imagination. Masked from the moment of his birth, and brought up under a false identity, he was a born actor. Seeing the players re-create the world through the power of the spoken word (a humble actor being transformed into a king), Edward—if he was aware of the rumors that hovered about him—must have felt the shame of his bastardy washing away in the stirring speeches of these fellow outsiders. At Hedingham, he may have witnessed a performance of John Bale's *King John,* the first historical verse drama in English. Bale wrote

Protestant propaganda plays for the 16th Earl of Oxford, and his *Chronicle of the Blessed Martyr Sir John Oldcastle* would influence Shakespeare's portrayal of Sir John Falstaff (originally named Oldcastle).

Edward would have accompanied both Smith and John de Vere on their frequent hunting and hawking expeditions through the Essex countryside, and possibly kept a bird of his own. Certainly the hawking imagery he uses in his early poems, such as "Woman's Changeableness," appears utterly instinctive. In the autumn of 1559 he may well have accompanied John de Vere, Sir Thomas Smith, and Lord Robert Dudley when they traveled to Colchester to meet John, Duke of Friesland, and accompany him to London. The duke had arrived with an embassy from Sweden to negotiate on behalf of his brother, Prince Eric, for the hand of the queen.

It was Edward's intellectual pursuits, however, that held center stage. In 1557 there had appeared a volume of poetry known as *Tottel's Miscellany* that would have a profound influence on Shakespeare's development as a writer. The book was also known as *Songs and Sonnets, written by the right honourable Lord Henry Howard late Earl of Surrey*, Surrey being the principal contributor. As a poet Surrey was a considerable innovator, helping introduce Italian meter and versification to England. He was, in addition, the first poet to write blank verse (in his translations from *The Aeneid*) and the first to employ the Shakespearean sonnet form. According to George Puttenham, he and Thomas Wyatt "greatly polished our rude and homely manner of vulgar Poesie, from that it had been before, and for that cause may justly be said the first reformers of our English meter and style."[47] Surrey was also Edward de Vere's uncle. A copy of the precious volume no doubt found its way into the nine-year-old's hands via his aunt Frances Vere, Surrey's widow.

The roots of the English Renaissance can be traced back to the middle years of Henry VIII's reign, after the dissolution of the monasteries had led to the suppression of Mary. A dammed-up chivalry burst forth in defiance of the new mercantile and bureaucratic ethos, perhaps as a belated act of valor toward Henry's brutalized and abandoned wives. The new poetry championed the feminine, with Venus-Mary reborn in the figure of the poet's unattainable mistress. Disaffection with the treacheries and timeserving of court life, its overbright cult of the Sun King, and the prying officialdom that burrowed into the hearts of men, seeps up into the leaves of the new verse. Surrey's upbringing as the boon companion of Henry's adored bastard son, Henry Fitzroy, had been quasi-royal, and he himself had played the prodigal to Henry's stern father, only in this case there was no homecoming. When Fitzroy died suddenly, everything changed.

During his sojourn at the French court with Fitzroy, Surrey had fallen under the spell of Marguerite of Navarre, who, with her brother King Francis I, created a highly cultured circle of artists known as the New Parnassus. It may be that Marguerite became Surrey's muse or nursed his genius in some way, rather as Elizabeth would do for Shakespeare. Henry, on the other hand, was no patron of literature, and back in England Surrey found the Machiavellian court stifling and demeaning to his sense of nobility. He disparaged the "new men," in particular the Seymour family and, proud of his royal descent, was in the habit of referring to himself in the third person. The Dutch humanist Junius described him as "a truly royal young man." In a final act of hubris Surrey quartered the royal arms with his own, surmounting his coat with what looked like a crown rather than an earl's coronet, or so it was alleged, and it was this allegation that led to his execution for treason a week before the end of Henry's reign.

A soldier-poet, using his pen as a sword to cut through the craft and seeming of court life, Surrey was a knight-errant in a distinctly unchivalrous age. As Alexander Pope would later write of him, "Matchless his pen, victorious was his lance, / Bold in the lists, and graceful in the dance."[48] Like Shakespeare after him, he embodied the alienated son at court, whose principal channel of expression was literature. Nor was he afraid to hold up "a mirror clear" where his erring monarch could see "the bitter fruit of false concupiscence," hinting that the purpose of such poetry was to awaken tyrants "out of their sinful sleep." The note of realism and subjectivity that he sounded in his verse, flowing as it did from his sense of isolation at the mercantile court of Henry Tudor, identified the Renaissance poet as an exile in his own land. For the first time in English verse, words became a true instrument of feeling. And if we accept T. S. Eliot's dictum that "every development of language is a development of feeling as well," Surrey's verse marks the start of a new self-awareness, cultivated in defiance of the state, that would find its fullest expression in Shakespeare's soliloquies. Had he survived Henry's reign, Surrey might well have turned to the theater to sublimate his rebellious instincts, as his more famous nephew would one day do.

As well as spending time at Hedingham during his absences from Cambridge, Edward probably had his first taste of the court at Whitehall or one of the other palaces along the Thames, such as Greenwich, Richmond, or Hampton Court, for John de Vere officiated as lord great chamberlain at Elizabeth's coronation in January 1559 and was afterward ordered to stay at court with his wife, a newly appointed maid of honor. In this case Edward would have set eyes on his real mother, possibly for the first time. We can only guess at the overwhelming emotions he must have felt at being in the presence of this earthly goddess, whether or not he was conscious of their consanguinity. Having grown up not quite knowing whose he was and where his roots lay, he must have been a deeply receptive child, and I imagine that where love and allegiance joined hands, as later testimony avers they did in this case, the feeling of being in love must have been especially intense for this ten-year-old. He had been given the name of "Truth" ("Vere"), and discovering and bearing witness to the truth would be his self-appointed task in life. Looking at the queen might have been, for the young nobleman, like looking in a mirror in which he saw reflected not only his own brilliance and royalty but the demons of his house. Certainly, one can imagine how he came alive to himself and to a fledgling sense of power and identity through his first encounter with the woman who would dominate his life with the binding force of fate.

Edward may have come to suspect the true story of his birth around this time. A work that appeared in 1560, the first translation of Ovid to be published in English, seems to provide a clue. The anonymous work, consisting of 192 lines of verse, preceded by an "argument" in prose, renders the story of Narcissus and Echo from Book III of the *Metamorphoses*. The title of the work, "The Fable of Ovid Treating of Narcissus," was arranged so that the top line read simply, "The Fable of O" in bold type. Though he hadn't inherited the Oxford earldom yet, might this have been Edward's way of announcing not only that he was telling his own story through the myth of Narcissus, but that he knew his Oxford lineage was a fable, and he himself a nobody? A premonition perhaps of the Fool's words to Lear after the loss of his kingdom, "Now thou art an 'O' without a figure."

Narcissus was a product of rape, his mother (the river nymph Liriope) having been violated by the river god Cephisus—just as Elizabeth, who was living on the Thames at Chelsea at the time, was most likely forced by Lord Admiral Thomas Seymour (certainly she was what we would call today "under the age of consent"). From the moment he was born, Narcissus's exceptional beauty was apparent; both men and women fell in love with him. The seer Tiresias predicted that he would live to a ripe old age *so long as he did not come to know himself.* (For Oedipus too, knowing his true identity proved fatal.) Narcissus was so filled with pride that he scorned the love of all those who fell in love with him, in particular the nymph Echo. His passion—like Adonis's—was for hunting. One of those he had rejected prayed to the gods that Narcissus himself might fall in love, so that he could feel the pain of those who had loved him. Wearied with hunting one day, the beautiful young man knelt down beside a stream to drink, and there fell in love with his own reflection, believing it to be the visage of a divine being. Even when it dawned on him that the reflection was his own image, he could not tear himself from the riverbank, and there pined away from self-longing. The wood nymphs mourned his death and, going to retrieve his body, found that it had disappeared. In its place was a flower—the narcissus.

It is easy to imagine how this tale of desire and transformation might have appealed to the boy who would one day be Shakespeare, the poet for whom Adonis, another narcissistic youth, acted as a mythic self-reflection. Like Hamlet, Narcissus cannot indulge in ordinary love relations or casual affairs; he is as one removed. Desiring nothing more than to be reunited with his true self, he turns his focus inward; hence the intense self-reflection that results in death. Ultimately, this falling in love with his reflection is a wonderful image for the artist who can see himself only by creating characters who reflect his reality, and whose attempt to embrace the self pulls him down into the unconscious.

Also evident in the tale of Narcissus is Edward's fear of isolation, and his sense of despair at being exiled from himself, for the image of the youth yearning for his reflection in the brook marks a divided personality, someone alienated from himself. His cry of recognition (which in Ovid reads *iste ego sum,* "I am he!") signals the birth of self-awareness engendered by suffering, and reminds us of Hamlet's cry, "It is I, Hamlet the Dane!" It also points to that shattering moment when young Edward saw himself reflected in the queen's face, and so died to his old self. The narcissus or death flower, being sacred to the god Hades, opened the gates of the underworld, where the hero had to go in quest of his identity. In sum, "The Fable of O(vid) Treating of Narcissus," though a youthful experiment, reaches deep into the psychology of the boy who would be Shakespeare, giving us a snapshot of the mythic life out of which his themes and imagery grew.

In August 1561 the queen, on a progress to East Anglia, spent five days at Hedingham Castle as the guest of the Earl and Countess of Oxford. As usual on such occasions, there would have been a succession of entertainments: masques, plays, banquets, dancing, jousting, hawking, hunting, and trips to notable sites or monuments, with a great many of the lords and ladies of the court in attendance. Perhaps Elizabeth had chosen Hedingham so that she could spend some private time with her son, who was almost thirteen. Certainly there would have been opportunities for the two to ride or walk together, away from the busy eyes of the court. The queen was not yet twenty-eight and, according to B. M. Ward, "one of the most striking personalities in Europe." An enchanting and charismatic woman, she had the natural authority that comes to one who has learned her political lessons early, and from bitter experience. Elizabeth was a survivor, who had suffered the same emotional privations as Edward de Vere growing up, and was tougher as a result. "I thank God," she would tell a delegation of parliamentarians in 1567, "that I am indeed endowed with such qualities that if I were turned out of the realm in my petticoat, I were able to live in any place of Christendom." Few could get the better of her, yet she wore her ample learning lightly and unaffectedly and loved nothing better than the cut and thrust of witty conversation, whether in her own orbit or onstage. Edward must have been utterly fascinated by this mysterious and commanding woman, so masterly and yet so fragile. This was a unique chance not only to talk to her, but to gain her confidence. He could also observe her at close quarters, seeing what delighted her and what excited her wrath, how quickly she changed from one mood to the other, and who among her closest followers had her interests at heart, and who were timeservers.

The queen's visit to Hedingham followed on the heels of one of the major crises of her reign, the death, possibly by murder, of Robert Dudley's wife, Amy Robsart. Amy was found dead at the bottom of the stairs at her house in the country. Foul play was immediately suspected. It was no secret at court that Elizabeth and Dudley had been talking of marriage, and it seems that in the late summer of 1560 Elizabeth had become pregnant with their first child (Arthur Dudley, born in May 1561).[49] Thus it was widely assumed that Dudley had had his wife murdered, and that Elizabeth herself was complicit. In retrospect, it seems more probable, judging from some rather unguarded remarks he made to the Spanish ambassador Alvarez de Quadra, that William Cecil had engineered the "accident" to ensure that his own preeminence in the counsels of the queen was not challenged by a Dudley monarchy. Cecil may have had his eye on Edward de Vere as a future sovereign, and his appointment as master of the court of wards in early 1561 paved the way for "Pondus," as Elizabeth sometimes nicknamed him, to take the boy into his care. Only one thing stood in his way, however, and that was John de Vere, the boy's putative father.

In July 1562 a marriage contract was drawn up whereby Edward de Vere (then almost fourteen) would marry either Mary or Elizabeth Hastings, the younger sisters of Henry Hastings, Earl of Huntingdon, on reaching his eighteenth birthday. Though nothing came of it, the contract is significant for two reasons. First, Henry Hastings was a Plantagenet, descended twice over from King Edward III, and a popular choice to succeed Elizabeth. In March of the previous year Alvarez de Quadra had told Philip of Spain that he was convinced Elizabeth would name Hastings her successor. Cecil was also said to favor his claim, though, true to form, he was playing both sides of the field. Second, it is important to note that the legal age of consent for such contracts was fourteen, so that if Edward was born in 1550 he would be considerably too young. The only real exception to such a rule was in the case of royal marriages: here the parties were often younger.

It looks as though John de Vere had taken it into his head to arrange a royal marriage for his teenage charge, an action that would have called forth the wrath of Cecil, who had marked out Edward for his own daughter, Anne. John de Vere was only in his mid-forties and there were no signs of failing health; but a month after the wedding contract he was dead, and Edward, now the seventeenth Earl of Oxford and lord great chamberlain of England, was on his way to London to take up residence with Sir William Cecil and family as one of the queen's wards of court. Ever since Lord Protec-tor Somerset had bullied John de Vere into promising his daughter Katherine to Somerset's son Henry Seymour in 1548, the earl and his patrimony had been shamelessly exploited by the ruling powers for their own designs, whether by blackmail or raw political thuggery. More than that, two quasi-royal children had been placed cuckoo-like in his ancestral nest for the purpose of concealing their true parentage. Now that he had served his purpose as surrogate father, it was clearly thought prudent to dispose of him. As for his estates, they fell under the control of Cecil, who as master of the court of wards was responsible for administering them, and Robert Dudley, the queen's favorite, who managed to acquire for himself the revenues from the de Vere lands in Essex, Suffolk, and Cambridgeshire. It was Dudley who benefited most in the short term, and it is his presence as a supervisor of the will that causes suspicion, because he and Oxford were not closely associated. Dudley was rumored to be a dab hand with a bottle of poison, having learned the most sophisticated techniques from Italians in his employ; if so, this plum grant of lands may have been his reward for performing an unpleasant but necessary task.

One immediately thinks of the plot of *Hamlet,* in which Claudius, who is based on Dudley, poisons the King his brother and seizes the kingdom. Young Hamlet, meanwhile, looks on in dismay as his mother, so recently widowed, marries her former husband's murderer. This also occurred in the case of Edward de Vere, for his putative mother, Margery Golding, remarried within a year of her husband's death, possibly much sooner. Her second husband was Charles Tyrrell, a former equerry for the Dudley household; and although he didn't literally murder a king, he did bear the name of one of the most famous regicides of history, Richard Tyrrell, who murdered Edward V and Edward's brother Richard in the Tower.

Margery herself had very little to do with Edward after the earl's death, and her letters to Cecil betray a deeper concern for the estate of her late husband than for the fate of her supposed son. If she did feel maternal affection toward him, it is not expressed. In one letter she seems to hint that she did not know of Edward's royal origins until after her husband's death. "I confess," she writes, "that a great trust hath been committed to me, of those things which in my Lord's lifetime was kept most secret from me."

The contention between Claudius and old King Hamlet is also reflected in the political rivalry between the Seymour and Dudley families during the early 1550s, with Elizabeth's affections passing from one to the other. It is fascinating to learn, for instance, that Thomas Seymour was lord of the manor of Stratford-upon-Avon, and John Dudley (Robert's father), who owned the monastic lands around Stratford, attempted to acquire Seymour's lordship and landholdings in return for more valuable property elsewhere. Seymour, however, would not part with them.

Oxford never mentions his father in his letters or other writings, though we learn from Charles Arundel that the ghost of his stepfather Charles Tyrrell appeared to him carrying a whip. The father remains a ghostly presence, haunting the mythopoeic margins of his son's soul, hence Shakespeare's idealized portrayal of Hamlet's father. The death of Oxford's surrogate father, John de Vere, just as the son was crossing the threshold of adolescence, plunged him into that lifelong struggle with the "great mother," which shaped his literary work. Oxford found himself under the queen's thumb for the rest of his life, alternately cherished and deserted, as fortune dictated.

His desire to assert himself as his mother's eldest son, and the rightful heir to the kingdom, would find itself in perpetual conflict with an equally forceful drive to cut himself free from her all-powerful influence. The would-be king fought in the depths of his nature with the would-be artist, like the white and red dragons of Saxon legend wrestling in the bowels of earth.

According to diarist Henry Machyn, Oxford rode into London after his father's funeral "with seven score horse all in black"; in other words, he entered the capital like a Prince of Wales, with no fewer than 140 retainers (the Elizabethan historian John Stow puts the number at 180). He was accompanied by the soldier-poet and future laureate George Gascoigne. His new home was Sir William Cecil's palatial residence on the north side of the Strand, with high brick turrets raised upon its four corners. Cecil House, which had been completely renovated by Sir William, was light and spacious and had one of the finest libraries in England. Its extensive gardens were under the care of John Gerard, the Dutch horticulturalist, whose *Herbal: Or General History of Plants* influenced Shakespeare. Here Oxford's continuing education was overseen by the master of the queen's wards, Cecil himself, who would have been glad finally to have the queen's son under his vigilant eye. Cecil's watchword had always been "control"; he was like a great spider at the center of the web of state, and no vibration of the threads, however slight, escaped his notice. While admiring his political and administrative acumen, Oxford soon found his guardian's outlook too narrow-minded and puritanical for his own tastes, not to say suffocating in his constant need to supervise and interfere. In Oxford's private mythology it seems that Cecil, the monstrous serpent guarding the throne, was incorporated into the "great mother" archetype from which he was struggling to free himself. Elizabeth called Cecil her "Spirit," in the sense of her guardian angel; together they were the grit in the oyster that shaped the pearl of Oxford-Shakespeare's genius.

If Cecil thought of Oxford as a potential king, then marrying him one day to his daughter Anne, who in 1562 was only six years old, was an enticing prospect. That way, Cecil blood would flow in the veins of a future monarch, and William himself would be the founder of a royal dynasty. The crux, as ever, was how to reveal Oxford to the world in his true colors without bringing the whole Seymour affair to light and disgracing the queen. In October 1562, at the age of twenty-nine, Elizabeth almost died of smallpox. In her delirium, with her councillors crowded round her bed, she named Robert Dudley as lord protector, an office that would have made sense only if the heir to the throne was a minor—in which case Dudley might conceivably have been appointed to govern until the lad reached his majority—or if Elizabeth intended to create a republic. If Elizabeth had died, the meaning of her extraordinary appointment would doubtless have been called into question; but as she survived, no one, even today, seems to have thought to ask for whom Dudley was supposed to be protector. After all, her heir under the will of her father, Katherine Grey, was alive and well, and with a healthy son of her own, Edward Seymour.

It is uncertain whether Oxford's residence at Cecil House was permanent during his teenage years, or whether he returned to Cambridge to complete his studies. In a letter that he wrote to Cecil in fluent and courtly French in August 1563, he begs to be excused from explaining the order of his studies, as it would take too long. Cecil himself had drawn up a detailed timetable of study and exercises for his charge, which included French, Latin, cosmography, writing, drawing, dancing, and prayers. Among Oxford's tutors at this time was the Anglo-Saxon scholar Laurence Nowell, who in 1563 appears to have discovered the only known copy of *Beowulf* in a volume of manuscripts now known as the Nowell Codex. This Scandinavian epic of a warrior-prince's heroic deeds, in particular his ridding the kingdom of Denmark of the monster Grendel and Grendel's fiendish mother, would be an important source for *Hamlet,* yet it is hard to see how Shakspere of Stratford could ever have gotten his hands on this unique, privately owned manuscript copy.

Also in 1563, Oxford's legitimacy was challenged by his half sister Katherine, and his name was made a common recreation at court. Even the queen was said to have called him "her little bastard," which goes to prove that many a true word is spoken in jest. Oxford's misery at this public humiliation must have reached deep, reviving perhaps the haunting uncertainty of his origins. One can imagine his shame; the smug, pitying looks of those he passed at court must have been an unendurable taunt to his pride. As his only salve he turned to the written word, his consolation since studying the Greek tragedies under Sir Thomas Smith, with their rhythmic expression of strong feeling. The result was a wonderfully spirited poem, alive with raw indignation. The device of calling upon creation to bewail the loss of his good name gives the impression through a sort of echo effect that the poet can hear his disgrace reverberating through the universe, and speaks poignantly of the depth of alienation that Oxford felt at this time in his life:

Fram'd in the front of forlorn hope, past all recovery
I stayless stand, to abide the shock of shame and infamy.
My life, though ling'ring long, is lodg'd in lair of loathsome ways,
My death delay'd to keep from life the harm of hapless days:
My sprites, my heart, my wit and force in deep distress are drown'd,
The only loss of my good name is of these griefs the ground.

And since my mind, my wit, my head, my voice, and tongue are weak
To utter, move, devise, conceive, sound forth, declare and speak:

Such piercing plaints, as answer might, or would my woeful case,
Help, crave I must, and crave I will, with tears upon my face:
Of all that may in heaven or hell, in earth or air be found,
To wail with me this loss of mine, as of these griefs the ground.

Help gods, help saints, help sprites and powers that in the heaven do dwell,
Help ye that are to wail aye wont, ye howling hounds of hell:
Help man, help beasts, help birds, and worms, that on the earth do toil,
Help fish, help fowl, that flocks and feeds upon the salt sea soil:
Help echo that in air doth flee, shrill voices to resound,
To wail the loss of my good name, as of these griefs the ground.

In charge of Oxford's defense during the bastardy affair was his uncle Arthur Golding, a Cambridge-educated scholar and author employed by Cecil to act as receiver for the young earl. Golding accompanied Oxford to Cecil House in 1562, and the two were in close contact there for many years. It has been suggested that Golding tutored Oxford in history and the classics; at the very least the two shared their literary and intellectual enthusiasms, though Golding's Puritanism (he was a follower of Calvin) was not to Oxford's taste. Golding dedicated at least two works to Oxford, the first being his translation of Justin's abridgement of the *Histories of Trogus Pompeius* in 1564, in which his admiration of his nephew's precocious talent shines through. Describing Oxford as a "jewel" in the eyes of his queen and country, he refers to his "great forwardness" and the hope and expectation that his contemporaries have of him:

> For . . . it is not unknown to others, and I have had experience thereof myself, how earnest a desire Your Honour hath naturally graffed in you to read, peruse, and communicate with others, as well as the histories of ancient times and things done long ago, as also of the present estate of things in our days, and that not without a certain pregnancy of wit and ripeness of understanding. The which do not only now rejoice the hearts of all such as bear faithful affection to th'honourable house of your ancestors, but also stir up a great hope and expectation of such wisdom and experience in you in time to come.

The following year the first five books of Ovid's *Metamorphoses* were published with Golding's name on the title page. The full fif-

teen books appeared in 1567, constituting a work that scholars have
described as Shakespeare's favorite book. To say that this bubbling,
effusive translation of Ovid's masterpiece with its exuberant and juvenile turns of phrase consorts oddly with the rest of Golding's published canon (which in its earnestness and gravity includes *The Psalms
of David* with Calvin's commentary, Calvin's *Sermons,* Caesar's *Gallic Wars,* and other improving works of ancient history and philosophy) would be a considerable understatement. Rather, it sticks out
like a sore thumb. There is nothing in Golding's life or philosophy
to suggest even remotely that he would or could bridge the gulf in
style and outlook between Calvin and Ovid. Even the Renaissance
mind could not imagine two such strange bedfellows. In its tales of
the transforming power of love in the lives of gods and mortals, under-
pinned throughout by the Pythagorean philosophy of reincarnation,
Metamorphoses is a tremendous exploration of that quintessentially
Shakespearean theme, trespass. Venus's son Cupid is the presiding
deity, his love arrows passing all pales. Here is an extract from his
rendering of the myth of Actaeon from Book III. The goddess has
just been interrupted bathing:

> And casting back an angrie looke, like as she would have sent
> An arrow at him had she had hir bow there readie bent,
> So raught she water in hir hande and for to wreake the spight
> Besprinckled all the heade and face of this unluckie knight,
> And thus forespake the heavie lot that should upon him light:
> Now make thy vaunt among thy Mates, thou sawste Diana bare.
> Tell if thou can: I give thee leave: tell hardily: doe not spare.
> This done she makes no further threates, but by and by doth spread
> A payre of lively olde Harts hornes upon his sprinkled head.
>
> (III.223–231)

There is an exhilarating, headlong energy to the fourteeners, which
could so easily have become cumbersome, and what John Frederick
Nims describes as a "rugged English gusto," almost as if a new language is being hammered out before our eyes. Ezra Pound famously
called it "the most beautiful book in the language." It is hard to imagine such rough and callow riches flowing from the pen of the mature
Golding, but if we substitute a youthful Shakespeare, then all contradictions vanish and the master of our modern language takes his place

among those who enriched English through translation of the classics. Indeed, in his preface to the reader, the translator describes Ovid's work in terms that later critics would apply to Shakespeare, as if he is witnessing his own creative powers coming alive under the influence of the Roman poet:

For this doo lerned persons deeme, of Ovids present woorke:
That in no one of all his bookes the which he wrate, doo lurke
Mo darke and secret misteries, mo counselles wyse and sage,
Mo good ensamples, mo reprooves of vyce in youth and age,
Mo fine inventions to delight, mo matters clerkly knit,
No, nor more straunge varietie to shew a lerned wit.
The high, the lowe: the riche, the poore: the mayster, and the slave:
The mayd, the wife: the man, the chyld: the simple and the brave:
The yoong, the old: the good, the bad: the warriour strong and stout:
The wyse, the foole: the countrie clowne: the lerned and the lout:
And every other living wight shall in this mirrour see
   His whole estate, thoughtes, woordes and deedes expresly shewd to bee.
                                                              (lines 185–196)

There is a jocular allusion to the authorship of Golding's *Metamorphoses* in the early Shakespearean play *Thomas of Woodstock*. When plain Thomas of Woodstock, the king's uncle, who is a portrait partly of Oxford's uncle Arthur Golding and partly of his early guardian Sir Thomas Smith, arrives at a court function gorgeously attired instead of in his usual modest dress, King Richard cries (emphasis mine):

How comes this *golden metamorphosis*
From home-spun huswifery? Speak, good uncle,
I never saw you hatched and *gilded* thus.
                              (I.iii.75–77)

The pun on Golding's *Metamorphoses* is obvious, as is the implication that Golding's homespun style and puritanical concerns are inconsonant with the quicksilver of Ovid's sophisticated poetry. Oxford's court audience would have picked up the hint.

Volume XIX of the archival series of Fairleigh Dickinson University in New Jersey is a little-known untitled manuscript by a former professor there, Dr. Walter Freeman, who composed it around 1950, although it did not become available to students until 1991. Freeman is the first to propose the theory that Edward de Vere was the son of Queen Elizabeth by Lord Admiral Seymour. Freeman furthermore suggests that Oxford had no permanent residence or identity as a boy, but as he was transferred from the protection of one nobleman to another, so his names and titles changed. He has Edward under the protection of the Earl of Pembroke in Wales up to the age of three, then with the Earl of Derby in Lancashire, who adopted him and gave him the name William Stanley (or W.S.) before he was spirited off to Lord Clifford's castle in the wilds of Westmoreland to live out Bloody Mary's reign. Finally, with Elizabeth's accession in 1558, Freeman places him with John de Vere, 16th Earl of Oxford. Although Freeman produces no evidence for his claims, which seem far-fetched on the surface, there is an emotional truth to the story he tells, which is harder to dismiss. Even in Oxford's conventional biography, metamorphosis is a key theme.

Ovid's *Metamorphoses* chart the transgressions and transformations of human and divine figures from the beginning of the world to contemporary times (i.e., the reign of Caesar Augustus). It is easy to understand their profound appeal to a teenage boy, whose very birth was transgressive and who was punished by being transformed from what he was to what the authorities deemed he could safely be; a boy, moreover, who would soon learn to transform himself, not only by adopting different pseudonyms, but by creating a raft of literary characters behind which he could take cover. These dramatic personae, begotten from the depths of his soul, afforded an emotional and political protection that he could not expect from others. Oxford was fast realizing that he could recoup his lost power through words, and that literature was the best means of criticizing the "gods," though even here—as Ovid himself had discovered—there lay tremendous risks. This belief in the predominance of the word is boldly proclaimed by the Roman poet in the final paragraph of the *Metamorphoses,* where he suddenly sneaks precedence over starry Caesar, asserting in effect the superiority of poetry over politics:

> My work is complete: a work which neither Jove's anger, nor fire nor sword shall destroy, nor yet the gnawing tooth of time. That day which has power over nothing but my body may, when it pleases, put an end to my uncertain span of years. Yet with my better part I

shall soar, undying, far above the stars, and my name will be imper-
ishable. Wherever Roman power extends over the lands Rome has
subdued, people will read my verse. If there be any truth in poets'
prophecies, I shall live to all eternity, immortalized by fame.[50]

Both Ovid and Shakespeare became scapegoats of the political regimes under which they lived, and were deeply transformed as a result. The record of these transformations is to be found in their works,
to such an extent in Shakespeare's case that his plays could plausibly
be entitled *The Metamorphoses of Edward de Vere, Earl of Oxford*.

It is difficult to ascertain the exact moment when Oxford turned
to the theater as a means of expressing his disaffection. When the
queen attended his graduation from Cambridge in August 1564, a
play was performed containing certain anti-Catholic gibes, which gave
offence to her Majesty. As would happen in *Hamlet* twenty years
later, the queen's attendants called for lights, the play was halted,
and Elizabeth swept out of the hall with a train of trembling university officials in her wake. The title of the play and its author were
not recorded, but might not this have been the debut of a naively
ardent Oxford, who at Cecil House was directly under the influence of Cecil himself, the chancellor of Cambridge; his wife, Mildred
Cooke; and Arthur Golding—all radical Protestants?

That year, during the Christmas season at court, the first tragicomedy in English, *Damon and Pithias,* was performed by the Children of Her Majesty's Chapel. Attributed to Richard Edwards, it is
a raw, fledgling piece, more likely to have been written by a sixteen-year-old prince as a pledge of devotion to his vulnerable queen.
Punning repeatedly on "true" and "truly" (i.e., "Vere"), the poet
addresses Elizabeth directly in the epilogue:

> The strongest guard that Kings can have
> Are constant friends their state to save.
> True friends are constant both in word and deed;
> True friends are present, and help at each need;
> True friends talk truly, they glose for no gain;
> When treasure consumeth, true friends will remain;
> True friends for their true Prince refuseth not their death.
> The Lord grant her such friends, most noble Queen Elizabeth!
>
> (lines 1–8)

Another probable early effort by Oxford was *The Famous Victo-ries of Henry V,* a prose drama which he would later revamp and magnify into the two parts of *Henry IV* and *Henry V.* His portrayal of Prince Henry (later Prince Hal), the renegade son of Henry IV, a wild prince living beyond the pale, royal and base, haughty and demo-cratic, is derived from his fascination with the strange dichotomies of his own character. A prince who is chronically short of money and lacks the dignified trappings of royalty, whose idealistic, self-dramatizing spirit is drawn to bohemian rather than courtly or po-litical types, yet who suffers shame for giving rein to his humors in such a giddy fashion—the youthful Earl of Oxford was becoming just such a character. One certainly gets the sense of someone strug-gling to know himself and make sense of his chimerical gifts. Little wonder that he cries, "Curst be the day wherein I was born, and accursed be the hour wherein I was begotten!" It is a high-spirited and energetic piece of writing by a dramatist who is still finding his wings, and who almost betrays his authorship by giving such unwar-ranted emphasis to the nobility and heroism of the then Earl of Oxford. He would quickly learn greater discretion.

Oxford was also busy writing verses, not just under the initials E.O., but using names such as "Ignoto" (the unknown one) and "Ever or Never" (a play on Elizabeth's motto, "Ever the same"). In addi-tion to his literary and academic studies, Cecil House provided the teenager with a unique education in domestic and international af-fairs, for Cecil ran his own private state department and held meet-ings there with the prime movers in European politics. Truly, Oxford could be said to have spent the key years of his youth in the engine room of English political life, and the insights he gained would be profitably used in his mature plays, which demonstrate an extraordi-nary knowledge of what if feels like to be in the heat of the political kitchen.

From accounts that have survived of Oxford's time at Cecil House we know that in addition to books (which include a Geneva Bible, a Chaucer, Plutarch's works in French, Cicero, and Plato) he spent lavishly on many of the appurtenances of high living. "Long before his seventeenth birthday," writes Professor Alan Nelson, "Oxford evinced deeply rooted habits of self-importance and fiscal extrava-gance, spending heavily on clothes, personal weapons, horses, and retainers."[51] It seems that, whatever his means as the holder of the premier earldom in the land, Oxford always thought of himself as royal, and spent accordingly. In a lawsuit brought by the widow of one of Oxford's tailors concerning his expenditures in the late 1570s, one of the deponents, a hosier by the name of Bennett Salter, referred to the earl at that time as "in the chiefest of his Royalty."

If, as seems likely, Oxford was involved in putting on plays before the queen, who never paid for her own entertainment, then he would have borne at least part of the cost of the productions. If the court was on summer progress, there would be the extra expense of transporting cartloads of costumes and props, not to mention the actors themselves. The lord chamberlain of the household and the master of the revels were responsible for the overall organization and licensing of the queen's entertainments, but neither man was in any sense an artistic director. This raises the question of who Elizabeth's court impresario was during the 1570s and 1580s when the golden age of Elizabethan theater was born, i.e., the person who chose and directed the plays and masques. Oxford, who had inherited his father's company of players in 1562, would seem to be an ideal choice.

When Oxford received his degree from Oxford University in 1566, the queen was again present; this was the second such graduation, out of a total of three, that she would attend during her reign. The play put on for her amusement and instruction was *Palamon and Arcyte,* an early version of Shakespeare's *The Two Noble Kinsmen.* Both plays are dramatizations of Chaucer's "Knight's Tale" and tell the story of the cousins Palamon and Arcite, devoted friends who, because they love the same woman, become deadly foes. Oxford-Shakespeare was fascinated by the themes of twinship and the rival brothers, and seems to have split himself instinctively into opposing characters (such as Edgar and Edmund in *King Lear*) as a way of exploring the pronounced contradictions of his own nature. Some Oxfordians have speculated that Oxford was himself a twin, and that his brother was Edward Manners, later Earl of Rutland, who joined him as a royal ward at Cecil House in 1564.

The character of Edricus in *Edmund Ironside,* another early play by Oxford-Shakespeare, gives an idea of the self-tormenting voices his shady origins may have engendered in him. Edricus is a lowborn, sharp-witted man who has been made a duke for his "villainy," as

he expresses it, and would now rather forget his origins. When his wretched mother turns up with his stepfather and half brother (a cobbler by the name of Stitch), Edricus reacts angrily to the suggestion that his dolt of a stepfather is in fact his father. He proceeds to deny his mother as well:

WIFE:
Oh he is a wise man, for in faith my husband is none of his father, for indeed a soldier begot him of me as I went once to a fair. But son, know ye me?
EDRICUS:
Thee, old hag, witch, quean, slut, drab, whore and thief, how should I know thee, black Egyptian?
WIFE:
This is his old tricks, husband. Come, come, son, I am sure ye know me.
EDRICUS:
Ay, if not too well.

(II.ii.498–504)

It was through rough characters such as Edricus that Oxford came to terms with the darker elements of his history, and vented his rage at the queen who had locked up his identity and thrown away the key. Oxford's sense of being nobody created a void from which his characters teemed forth, so that No-man begat Any-man begat Every-man. Equally, his identification with mother—mother as patriarch, mother as taboo—generated the rage or *furor poeticus* that periodically swallowed him up. A horrifying thought, "I am she; I am the spider spinning its web from the depths, then drawing it in again," drove him on to seek a freer space in the farther reaches of his being. According to the novelist and philosopher John Cowper Powys, great writers are "genuinely dangerous writers . . . writers who exploit their vices, lay bare their weaknesses, brew intoxicating philters of sweet poison out of their obsessions and lead humanity to the edge of the precipice!" Such a description is deeply alien to our traditional understanding of Shakespeare's artistry, yet for those who know him as the Earl of Oxford, it makes perfect sense. In another youthful poem, one is left in no doubt as to the cathartic function of Oxford's art, and his intention to use it for his own requital:

Fain would I sing, but fury makes me fret,
And rage hath sworn to seek revenge of wrong;
My mazed mind in malice so is set,
As death shall daunt my deadly dolours long;
Patience perforce is such a pinching pain,
As die I will, or suffer wrong again.

I am no sot, to suffer such abuse
As doth bereave my heart of his delight;
Nor will I frame myself to such as use,
With calm consent to suffer such despite;
No quiet sleep shall once possess mine eye
Till Wit have wrought his will on Injury.

My heart shall fail, and hand shall lose his force,
But some device shall pay Despite his due;
And Fury shall consume my careful course,
Or raze the ground whereon my sorrow grew.
Lo, thus in rage of ruthful mind refus'd,
I rest reveng'd on whom I am abus'd.

The word "device" in the final stanza means a theatrical device
or masque. Like Hamlet with his *Mousetrap,* Oxford, even as a teenager, understands the power of drama to effect revenge. It is fascinating, too, to see a Shakespearean soliloquy taking shape before our
eyes in the unsophisticated magic of Oxford's lines, which appear to
have been written in a white-hot fury. As the final line attests, it is
the poem itself that in the end satisfies the poet's thirst for revenge.

In February 1567 Oxford enrolled at Gray's Inn, where he received a thorough grounding in the common law, an essential training for those faced with the task of managing their estates or holding
political office. In the sixteenth century, the Inns of Court were more
like finishing schools than formal law academies, at least for those
sons of the nobility and gentry who were not intent upon a career in
the law. Sir George Buck described them in 1612 as "the third university of England." The revels played a significant role in the rou-
tine of the Inns of Court, and plays and masques were a regular feature
of life there. It was a good training for Oxford's Blackfriars days, when
he would produce plays for private performance before the brightest

young men in the capital. Oxford's old friend George Gascoigne was
already at Gray's Inn, and Philip Sidney entered at the same time.
Two plays performed that year, later attributed to Gascoigne, were
a comedy of mistaken identity, *The Supposes,* translated from the Italian of Ariosto and thought to be the first prose drama in English;
and *Jocasta,* an adaptation of Euripides's *Phoenissae,* a tale of royal incest,
and the first such "translation" of its kind. To what extent Oxford
was involved in the writing or production of these plays is unknown,
but this was clearly a stimulating environment for a budding dramatist, especially now that other literary men, such as Thomas Churchyard and Gabriel Harvey, were beginning to gather round him. So
fervent were Oxford's literary pursuits at this time that two years later,
in the dedication of his translation of Heliodorus's *Aethiopian History,* Thomas Underdown suggested the earl was becoming "too
much addicted that way."

An entry in William Cecil's diary that summer reveals that Oxford had killed one of the servants at Cecil House, and the matter
had been hushed up. "Thomas Brincknell, an under-cook," Cecil
wrote, "was hurt by the Earl of Oxford at Cecil House in the Strand,
whereof he died; and by a verdict found *felo-de-se* [i.e., suicide] with
running upon a point of a fence sword of the said Earl's." It may be
that Oxford had discovered Brincknell spying on him for his master,
and had run the man through in a sudden rage. Suborning servants
seems to have been one of Cecil's favorite tricks.

In May 1568, the presence in England of Elizabeth's dynastic rival,
Mary Queen of Scots, brought the question of succession to the fore
again, and Elizabeth thought long and hard about naming a successor. According to the author Hank Whittemore, she spent time alone
that summer with Edward de Vere at Havering-atte-Bower, an ancient estate in the Forest of Essex, with the intention of coming clean
about his parentage. Instead, she ended up making overtures to the
bewildered young man, for this was Elizabeth's habitual way of controlling men she felt threatened by. Oxford may have been her son,
but he was unruly and ambitious, and might one day make a bid for
the throne; therefore, Elizabeth would not think twice about using
her sexual charms to subdue him. (Many years later, the Catholic
malcontent John Poole would say that "the Queen did woo the Earl
of Oxford but he would not fall in."[52]) This episode would be

dramatized in Oxford's first published work under the name William Shake-speare, *Venus and Adonis*.

Oxford's foster mother, Margery Golding, died the same year, but it is not known whether he attended her funeral. The following year, Oxford spent more time with the queen at Windsor Castle, and on this occasion she may have finally gathered the courage to tell him that he was her son. As Whittemore writes, the "shock" of this news caused Oxford to "fall into a severe melancholy or depression." This, it seems, was followed by a nervous collapse, which resulted in a period of prolonged sickness, lasting on and off until the spring of 1570. For part of his illness he lay in rented rooms in the town of Windsor, and it was here, no doubt, that he discovered the legend of Herne the Hunter, a former keeper of Windsor Forest who prowled about an ancient oak at night, wearing a pair of "great ragged horns." Herne, whom Falstaff impersonates in *The Merry Wives of Windsor,* is a sort of resurrected Actaeon, and the appearance of this myth in Oxford's life would have been a fitting symbol of the life-changing truth he had stumbled upon. He had seen the queen "naked," and from now until the end of his life he would be the hunted stag, whose only refuge was the theater. Whatever comforts he could press to his bosom, Edward de Vere knew for certain that there were those about him who saw through his "Oxford" mask; nor could he draw solace from the fact that the blood of the Tudors flowed in his veins, for his royal birth was far from being a political reality. Neither earl nor prince, he was a kind of nobody, who would have been arrested and charged with treason had he made a move to proclaim himself Elizabeth's heir. As it was, only his genius and the fickle protection of his mother stood between him and annihilation.

In November 1569, still not fully recovered, Oxford wrote to his guardian William Cecil requesting that he be given employment in her majesty's forces, then engaged in putting down the northern rebellion. In the letter he remarks upon a certain strangeness which has recently colored their relationship, and which he now wishes to dispel. ("But at this present, desiring you if I have done anything amiss that I have merited your offence, impute [it] to my young years and lack of experience to know my friends.") At the bottom of the letter he used a new and wholly remarkable signature, which sported a coronet or crown above the name "Edward Oxenford" and a line with seven dashes beneath it. Moreover, the whole signature, which is unique in the annals of the Elizabethan age, was shaped like a crown. To those who did not suspect the secret of de Vere's birth, it did no more than signify his status as the 17th Earl of Oxford; but to those who were in the know, like William Cecil, it proclaimed a royal title, that of "King Edward VII." Furthermore, the line with the seven strokes beneath the name resembles the individual scoring marks, known as "cheques," used to count the number of staves broken at the tilt—a premonition perhaps of his subsequent pen name Shakespeare. It is worth remembering that Oxford's uncle the Earl of Surrey had been executed for treason in 1547 for surmounting his coat of arms with a crown rather than the earl's coronet. Unless Oxford was secure in the knowledge of his royal birth, he was treading on very dangerous ground indeed.

Oxford would use this signature on all his letters to the Cecils, William and Robert, for as long as the queen was alive. Only on her death in 1603 and the accession of James of Scotland did he finally drop it and, with it, any claim to the throne. When Cecil saw the signature for the first time, he must have realized that Oxford finally knew who he was—and did not intend to keep quiet about it. He must have known, too, that this brilliant young man, with a company of actors at his beck, would prove a subtle and formidable adversary. As one of Oxford's early poems expressed it:

> I am not as I seem to be,
> Nor when I smile, I am not glad:
> A thrall although you count me free,
> I, most in mirth, most pensive sad.
> I smile to shade my bitter spite.
>
> . . . .
> Thus contraries be used I find,
> Of wise to cloak the covert mind.

The duel between Oxford and Cecil, the poet and the politician, would prove one of the most dramatic and far-reaching of English history.

Part Two

Prodigal Son

Consort of the Goddess

A phoenix, captain, and an enemy,
A guide, a goddess, and a sovereign,
A counselor, a traitress, and a dear.
(*All's Well That Ends Well*, I.i.164–166)

THE RED KNIGHT

Thomas Radclyffe, Earl of Sussex, who was to become Oxford's most outspoken ally at court, was an inveterate adversary and critic of Robert Dudley, Earl of Leicester, whose ruthless pursuit of power he rightly feared. "Beware of the gypsy," he warned on his deathbed, "for he will be too hard for you all." As lord chamberlain of the queen's household, Sussex took a keen interest in theatrical performances and from 1569 kept his own company of players, sometimes known as the Lord Chamberlain's Men. The famous comedian and jester Richard Tarlton, who later joined the queen's company, was a member of Sussex's troupe. His influence on Shakespeare's conception of the fool was profound. Sussex helped facilitate Oxford's own dramatic experiments, which in turn spurred the young man's ambition to produce drama of real quality and depth at the court of Elizabeth. With the Earl of Leicester's company the chief rival to Oxford's, Sussex no doubt saw the virtue of espousing his charge's literary-political agenda. After all, theater was the most effective way of undermining their rival's attempt to control the throne. As Richard Simpson writes:

In Elizabeth's days, and later, the drama and stage occupied not only a literary position, but a political one also. The play was the review of the period. It was only by the stage that the lay politician could be sure to find his audience. Dramas were part of the machinery of political propagandism, and malcontents whose ideas were not realized in the actual government were fond of indulging themselves with the triumph of their principles exhibited in a private play.[53]

Sussex, who was twenty-three years his senior and had no offspring, quickly became a father figure to Oxford. His mother, Elizabeth Howard, was the sister of the queen's great-uncle Lord Howard of Effingham, making Sussex a first cousin of Anne Boleyn and a sort of uncle to Elizabeth. Thus, if Oxford was Elizabeth's son, Sussex was a blood relative and may have known or surmised the truth of his parentage. He was also closely connected to the Southampton family, being a cousin of Mary Browne, the 2nd Earl's wife, and having married Elizabeth Wriothesley, the daughter of the 1st Earl. The list of high political offices that Sussex occupied is impressive, including lord lieutenant of Ireland and lord president of the Council of the North. Soldier, scholar, statesman, he was, according to the Spanish ambassador Bernardino de Mendoza, "a man of much valour and understanding." Oxford may have accompanied Sussex on his embassy to Vienna in 1567, and certainly served under him in Scotland, putting down the northern rebellion of 1569–1570.

On one occasion Oxford openly defied his queen as a gesture of solidarity with Sussex. The queen had humiliated her lord chamberlain in front of the Duc d'Alençon's special envoy for providing insufficient plate at dinner. Sussex's arch-enemy, Leicester, could not hide his delight at the older man's discomfort. The following day, according to Mendoza, "the Queen sent twice to tell the Earl of Oxford, who is a very gallant lad, to dance before the Ambassadors; whereupon he replied that he hoped her Majesty would not order him to do so, as he did not wish to entertain Frenchmen. When the Lord Steward took him the message the second time he replied that he would not give pleasure to Frenchmen, nor listen to such a message, and with that he left the room."[54]

In 1571, having officially turned twenty-one, Oxford took his seat in the House of Lords. He had little appetite for administrative work and was never a conscientious attendee but would occasionally appear in the chamber or on a committee. In May 1571 the queen ordered at Westminster "a solemn joust at the tilt, tournay, and barriers," possibly in honor of her son's majority. Oxford was one of the four defendants, competing as the Red Knight. He performed "far above the expectation of the world," receiving from the queen a "tablet of diamonds" for a prize. This was a diamond-embossed notebook or set of "tables," as Hamlet calls it, a significant gift to one who had given early notice of his devotion to letters. In Sonnet 122, Shakespeare writes of a precious set of tables that he has given away, and justifies his deed by claiming that the gift is impressed upon his heart "with lasting memory." George Delves, one of Oxford's fellow defendants, wrote, "There is no man of life and agility in every respect in the Court but the Earl of Oxford." In another tribute later that year, Giles Fletcher wrote of Oxford as a spear-shaking hero in the making:

> But if at any time with fiery energy he should call up a mimicry of war, he controls his foaming steed with a light rein, and armed with a long spear rides to the encounter. Fearlessly he settles himself in the saddle, gracefully bending his body this way and that. Now he circles round: now with spurred heel he rouses his charger.
>
> Bravo, valiant youth! 'Tis thus that martial spirits pass through their apprenticeship in war. Thus do yearling bulls try the feel of each other's horns. Thus too do goats not yet expert in fighting begin to butt one against the other, and soon venture to draw blood with their horns.
>
> The country sees in thee both a leader preeminent in war, and a skilful man-at-arms. Thy valor puts forth leaves, and begins to bear early fruit, and glory already ripens in thy earliest deed.[55]

Here Oxford's genius is perceived in terms of fire and air, and the effortless delicacy with which he manages his steed could serve as a metaphor for his mastery of language. It certainly prefigures the famous passage in *Henry IV, Part 1* in which Sir Richard Vernon describes the bewitching horsemanship of Prince Hal, with Hal himself compared to "feather'd Mercury" and his comrades in arms figured forth as "young bulls" and "youthful goats." As for Oxford's valor "putting forth leaves" and "bear[ing] early fruit," only a literary context would seem to make sense.

The fact that Oxford rode out as the Red Knight must have sent a powerful message to the queen. In the Grail legends the Red Knight is the mortal foe of King Arthur. He it is who rides into the king's banqueting hall and steals the golden cup from under the monarch's nose. In grabbing it, he spills its contents over the queen, who withdraws to her apartments in anger. As he is leaving the gates of the castle, goblet in hand, the Red Knight is met by Perceval in Welsh homespun, who rides past him into the presence of the king. When he learns of the affront Arthur has suffered at the hands of the Red Knight, Perceval asks to be knighted on the spot, and rides out to challenge the king's foe. Overtaking the knight, he kills him by hurling a spear through his eye. Having donned the red armor of the slain man and appropriated his horse, he retrieves the golden goblet and sends it back to the king. From this time forth he too goes by the title of the Red Knight.

In his early twenties the Earl of Oxford was viewed by contemporaries as someone brimming over with animal spirits: highly gifted, but not a little wild. Like a firework, he could either light up the sky or go off in your face. Oxford's contemporaries were challenged by his contradictory character and iconoclastic mind, few seeing through the spear-shaking exterior to the healing beams beyond. The Red Knight was a perfect symbol for this potent combination of high-voltage potential and waywardness, and Oxford may have worn the red armor as a means of advertising the martial persona that would one day inspire his enduring literary identity. (It is interesting to note that *The Red Knight* was one of the plays in the repertory of the Earl of Sussex's Men.)

As Elizabeth's Red Knight (or "Turk," as she often called him), Oxford was appearing before the crowds at Westminster as the flowering forth of that blood which the queen, for the sake of political expediency, had chosen to suppress; indeed, he was the living embodiment of it. Now that the sacred goblet had been spilled, it was up to the queen to respond. Would she acknowledge the stain, or retire to her apartments in a fit of pique?

An Unwilling Husband

Oxford's religious leanings, no less than his literary bent, were a matter of concern to the establishment, for he was popular with the people.

That he harbored Roman Catholic sympathies in his twenties was well known, as was his interest in the Rosicrucianism of John Dee and others. In his 1571 dedication to Oxford of his translation of *The Psalms of David* (with Calvin's commentaries), Arthur Golding writes rather disingenuously, "I assure your Lordship I write not these things as though I suspected you to be digressed from that soundness and sincerity wherein you were continually trained and traded under that vigilant *Ulysses* of our commonwealth [i.e., the Protestant Burghley] . . . or as though I mistrusted your Lordship to be degenerated from the excellent towardness, which by forward proof [you] have given glad foretokens." He also calls upon Oxford to be mindful of his tremendous influence: "I beseech your Lordship consider how God hath placed you upon a high stage in the eyes of all men, as a guide, pattern, example, and leader unto others." This is the language used to address monarchs. When Elizabeth was being pressured by Parliament into executing Mary Queen of Scots, she indignantly reminded members that princes cannot act lightly, for they stand upon a stage in sight of all the world.

Having achieved his majority, Oxford was free to leave the confines of Burghley's sphere and follow his chosen path. But what that path might be seemed to wring more fear than hope from the hearts of the older generation of statesmen and royal observers. If Oxford was indeed the Prince Hal of his day, a wild and untried youth, alienated from his royal inheritance, the dazzling vessel of all Elizabeth's own untamed, promiscuous impulses, and with the sort of glamour and fascination at his disposal to command the loyalty of large swaths of the population, it is little wonder that the queen's chief councillors might consider how such "hydra-headed wilfulness" was to be kept in harness. Though deeply wary of such a course, Sir William Cecil (as Burghley still was) seems to have used his power as the custodian of Elizabeth's darkest secrets to strike a deal whereby he would work behind the scenes to pave the way for Oxford's eventual succession, on condition that the Cecils would join the royal family through marriage. This could happen only through the union of the 17th Earl of Oxford and Cecil's daughter Anne, who in 1571 was—like Juliet on the eve of her wedding—still only fourteen.

How the free-spirited Oxford felt about this arranged marriage can easily be imagined, yet he had little choice in the matter, as the queen was largely at the mercy of Cecil, whose monumental discretion and aranean skill in holding together the threads of government policy (threads often as gossamer as the whims of the queen herself) bolstered her sense of security. Cecil was duly ennobled to make Anne a worthier match for a prince. On February 25, 1571, Elizabeth placed the titular cloak about the shoulders of her fifty-year-old secretary of state, pronouncing him Baron Burghley in the County of Northampton. Then in December, ten days after her fifteenth birthday, Anne and Oxford were married at Westminster Abbey, with the queen in attendance. A few months earlier Burghley had written rather disingenuously to Oxford's boyhood companion, the Earl of Rutland, feigning surprise at Oxford's "motion," as he put it, to marry his daughter. He continued:

> Now that the matter is determined betwixt my Lord of Oxford and me, I confess to your Lordship I do honor him so dearly from my heart as I do my own son, and in any case that may touch him for his honor and weal I shall think him mine own interest therein. And surely, my Lord, by dealing with him I find that which I often heard of your Lordship, that there is much more in him of understanding than any stranger to him would think. And for mine own part I find that whereof I take comfort in his wit and knowledge grown by good conversation.[56]

It is a strange letter with Burghley sounding defensive about the match, as if he wanted to assure Rutland that it was not of his own making; yet, as always, Burghley protests too much. The underage Anne was given no voice at all, being little more than a pawn in her father's political games. One is reminded of Polonius protesting Hamlet's ardent love for his daughter before the King and Queen, even citing it as the cause of his madness, and all by way of drawing the prince into his matrimonial net.

The previous month, on hearing of the engagement, Lord St. John had also written to Rutland, but in very different terms:

> The Earl of Oxford hath gotten him a wife, or at the least a wife has caught him; this is Mistress Ann Cecil, whereunto the queen hath given her consent and the which hath caused great weeping

and sorrowful cheer of those that had hoped to have that golden day.[57]

Months after the wedding, there were rumors that Oxford had rejected Anne and was refusing to consummate the marriage, and, further, that he had instructed his servant Rowland Yorke to deny her access to his chambers—to which, by contrast, his riotous friends had easy resort. The marriage of Richard II and Anne of Bohemia in Shakespeare's early play *Thomas of Woodstock* provides vivid insights into Oxford's wedded life with Anne before he left for the Continent in 1575. In the play Queen Anne suffers her husband's neglect in silence, returning love for dereliction, grateful for what fleeting affection he does show. Richard evinces no malice toward his wife; he is too busy living it up with his cronies (or "flatterers," as his uncles call them), putting on masques, and designing new Continental fashions to be worn at court. He even calls her "Nan," the nickname Anne Cecil's family bestowed on her. Richard's sartorial innovations are by no means frivolous, if read as a metaphor for the new language in which Oxford and his literary cohorts were dressing English culture. As Richard says to his Queen:

> Thou seest already we begin to alter
> The vulgar fashions of our homespun kingdom.
> I tell thee, Nan, the states of Christendom
> Shall wonder at our English royalty.
> We held a council to devise these suits.
>
> (III.i.47–51)

Shakespeare is referring not only to the literary revolution that he intends to create, but also to the new monarchy of the poet-king.

Aside from his resentment of Burghley's pervasive meddling in his affairs, Oxford may have felt that marrying Anne was tantamount to marrying his sister, for they had been brought up as virtual half-siblings at Cecil House; also, although her sweetness of nature was universally praised, her submissiveness to her father nettled him. Oxford was, it seems, saving himself for an altogether more complex and sophisticated woman, one with the gifts of mind and independence of spirit to inspire his budding genius. It was in the queen alone that he found these heady qualities, and she alone became his muse. There were, however, deeper, mythic-dynastic reasons that fired his love, casting him in the role of son-consort of the goddess. Elizabeth, in the dance of veils that she performed in masking and unmasking herself before her fascinated subjects, made of herself "a thousand loves," appearing to him, in the words of Helena, as "A mother, and a mistress, and a friend, / A phoenix, captain, and an enemy, / A guide, a goddess, and a sovereign, / A counsellor, a traitress, and a dear." The harsh fact was that Oxford had already pledged himself to his queen, as his youthful Shakespearean sonnet, "Love Thy Choice," attests (emphasis mine):

> Who taught thee first to sigh, alas, my heart?
> Who taught thy tongue the woeful words of plaint?
> Who filled your eyes with tears of bitter smart?
> Who gave thee grief and made thy joys to faint?
> Who first did paint with colors pale thy face?
> Who first did break thy sleeps of quiet rest?
> *Above the rest in court who gave thee grace?*
> Who made thee strive in honor to be best?
> In constant truth to bide so firm and sure,
> To scorn the world regarding but thy friends?
> With patient mind each passion to endure,
> In one desire to settle to the end?
> Love then thy choice wherein such choice thou bind,
> As naught but death may ever change thy mind.

Grace was the queen's alone to bestow.

In May 1573 Gilbert Talbot wrote to his father, the Earl of Shrewsbury, with the latest gossip from London:

My Lord of Oxford is lately grown into great credit; for the Queen's Majesty delighteth more in his personage, and his dancing, and valiantness, than any other. I think Sussex doth back him all that he can; if it were not for his fickle head he would pass any of them shortly. My Lady Burghley unwisely hath declared herself, as it were, jealous, which is come to the Queen's ear, whereat she hath been not a little offended with her, but now she is reconciled again. At all these love matters my Lord Treasurer [i.e., Burghley] winketh, and will not meddle in any way.[58]

Not only was Oxford supreme in the queen's regard but, according to the French ambassador, he had "more followers and [was] the object of greater expectations than any other in the realm." The Spanish ambassador Mendoza concurred; in his dispatches to Madrid he described Oxford as "a lad who has a great following in the country." In *Hamlet,* Claudius refuses to make a direct move against the prince because "he's lov'd of the distracted multitude." But why should Oxford have been so popular, unless it was at least suspected that he was the queen's son? After all, there were many charismatic noblemen at the court of Elizabeth. Or maybe Oxford was already famous for mounting public spectacles, such as the mock battle he helped stage at Warwick Castle in 1572. We know from a description of the queen's progress to Plymouth in 1580 that a public appearance by Oxford was an occasion for general mirth, so his reputation as a court jester may have traveled far. "Then came the Lord Chamberlain with his white staff, / And all the people began to laugh," wrote the anonymous poet, referring of course to the histrionic lord *great* chamberlain. (The lord chamberlain of the time was the proud and elderly Earl of Sussex.)

Oxford was also an inveterate prankster, with a taste for the picaresque, and it sometimes seemed that he undertook adventures simply for the purpose of writing them up, and collecting a stock of humorous stories with which to amuse his friends. His men, for instance, were involved in an incident at Gadshill on the road between Gravesend and Rochester on May 20, 1573. According to William Faunt, he and John Wotton, servants of the lord treasurer, Lord Burghley, while "riding peaceably by the highway from Gravesend to Rochester had three calivers [light muskets] charged with bullets discharged at us by three of my Lord of Oxenford's men . . . who lay privily in a ditch awaiting our coming with full intent to murder us."[59] Though Faunt fell from his horse, the two men escaped; and it was from Gravesend that Faunt wrote his account to Burghley, in which he regretfully states that he believes Oxford to have been "the procurer of that which is done," i.e., the mastermind of the operation. One is reminded of a similar plan hatched by Poins and Hal in *Henry IV, Part 1* and executed at the same locale.

Two other elements of Oxford's character that captured the attention of contemporaries, in this case inducing a certain wariness, were his violent temper and sensitivity to slights. He could be willful, too, and under provocation possessed a sharp tongue. William Faunt referred to Oxford's "raging demeanor," while Sir Christopher Hatton, whom Elizabeth had nicknamed her "Sheep," wrote to the queen beseeching her to reserve her favor to him, for the Sheep "hath no tooth to bite, where the Boar's tusk may both raze and tear"—a pointed reference to Oxford's family crest, a blue boar. His uncommon sensitivity, along with his violently passionate nature, made him a bewildering figure to less complex souls, and here one thinks of Friar Laurence's astonishment at Romeo's ardent emotionalism:

> Art thou a man? Thy form cries out thou art.
> Thy tears are womanish, thy wild acts denote
> The unreasonable fury of a beast.
> Unseemly woman in a seeming man,
> And ill-beseeming beast in seeming both!
>
> (III.ii.108–112)

In 1581, Charles Arundel would call Oxford "a beast stained with all impudicitie."

Those rare few who understood him, such as his fellow poet Edmund Spenser, could see that the violence masked a profoundly vulnerable and feminine nature. In portraying Oxford as Clarion in his long poem *The Fate of the Butterfly,* Spenser conjures up an almost monstrous image of a dazzling butterfly with delicately painted wings, armed to the hilt, like a fearsome warrior. Despite its disconcerting juxtaposition of beauty and violence, the exquisite butterfly in full battle dress works as a metaphor for the poet who goes in fear of his life, obliged at every point to protect himself against charges of sedition. Before the reader dismisses the armor-clad butterfly as a vain conceit on Spenser's part, void of allegorical application, he should remind himself of Hamlet, a highly sensitive and imaginative prince—and a writer to boot—who, on his own admission, is capable of drinking hot blood and doing "such bitter business as the day would quake to look on." In his extended description Spenser compares Clarion with Achilles, Heracles, Phoebus, and Cupid, once again pointing up the apparent contrast between artist and warrior. Cupid was the son of Venus, while Heracles—raised in ignorance of his divine parentage—was doomed to serve Hera, the goddess who sought his death and from whom he took his name. Clarion, the poet tells us, was the eldest son and heir of Muscaroll, whose dearest wish was that his son would one day prove worthy of his throne. To pin down the identification with Oxford, Spenser addresses the butterfly in terms of disappointed royalty (emphasis mine):

> O Clarion, thou fairest thou
> Of all thy kinde, *unhappie happie* Flie.
>   (lines 233–234)

Oxford is "happy" because he is royal, and "unhappy" because his royalty is tainted.

Gilbert Talbot's letter suggests that Oxford and Elizabeth were lovers in 1573, and this finds corroboration seven years later in a letter from Henry Howard to the queen declaring that Oxford had "vaunted [i.e., boasted] of some favors from your Majesty which I dare take mine oath upon the sacred testament were never yet imparted unto any man that lived on this earth"—meaning, presumably, sexual favors. Oxford had been married less than eighteen months when Talbot wrote this letter, so perhaps the rumors that he was not sleeping with Anne were true. It is certainly to be expected that Elizabeth, who was the keeper of his identity, the wellspring of his blood, and the most powerful woman in England, should dominate his thoughts and affections, especially now that he was the object of her amorous pursuit.

There was only one person in Elizabethan England for whom Hamlet could possibly stand, and that is Edward de Vere, Earl of Oxford. Not only was Oxford married to the daughter of the queen's chief minister, Lord Burghley (long recognized as the inspiration for Polonius), but like Hamlet he was, it seems, the son of the queen. Ophelia, like Anne Cecil, is sweet and pretty, and a tool of her father, and the fact that she and Hamlet have not had sexual relations contributes to her nervous breakdown. Anne, who was of a fine nature and extremely well educated, probably fell in love with Oxford's poetic genius. As Laertes warns his sister, Ophelia:

Then weigh what loss your honour may sustain
If with too credent ear you list his songs.

(I.iii.29–30)

Burghley's interference in Oxford's relationship with Anne, using his daughter to feed him information about his maverick son-in-law, conforms with the dynamics of *Hamlet,* as does Oxford's furious reaction to these antics. In the end, Oxford rejected Anne completely, writing with icy dignity to Burghley:

> Wherefore, as your Lordship very well writeth unto me that you mean (if it standeth with my liking) to receive her into your house, these are likewise to let your Lordship understand that it doth very well content me; for there, as your daughter or her mother's more than my wife, you may take comfort of her, and I, rid of the cumber thereby, shall remain well eased of many griefs.[60]

Hamlet is mapped out along the mythic coordinates of this tense family drama, and the fact that Oxford's life illuminates some of the darkest corners of that play and vice versa is a strong argument for his authorship. Anne Cecil was always devoted to Oxford—that much is clear from her distraught letters during the years of their separation—and he may eventually have come to love her. At first, however, he was highly resentful of the union that had been foisted upon him, considering it beneath his dignity to have been matched with someone of relatively humble birth. (Ophelia is told that "Hamlet is a prince out of thy star," and Helena uses identical imagery to express her inferiority to Bertram—that "bright particular star"—lamenting, "The hind that would be mated by the lion / Must die for love.") As Oxford's guardian, Burghley was entitled to choose a bride for him and levy a punitive fine should he refuse. Being significantly in debt, both to Burghley and to the crown, Oxford would have had little option but to adhere to his guardian's choice of a mate. Yet his heart was not in it. What, then, was really going on?

It is possible that Oxford and the queen were playing a complex, esoteric game, and had devised a secret scheme to secure the Tudor monarchy through a child of their own. If so, Oxford was most likely refusing to sleep with Anne so that in time he could sue for divorce on the grounds of non-consummation. Even so, Elizabeth, who hated to be tied down to a determined course of action, could have been playing her customary double game, using the promise of a child to keep Oxford quiet about his own royal claim. Recognizing Oxford as her son and heir would ruin the queen's reputation and act as a trumpet call to the skeletons in the royal cupboard; marrying him as her premier nobleman was quite another matter, however, and might conceivably have worked—though Burghley would always be a stumbling block. Oxford would have become king consort, and the child of their marriage the future sovereign. Royal incest was nothing new; it had been practiced openly by the ancient Egyptian monarchy. The pharaohs, following the example of the gods, regularly contracted incestuous marriages to keep the royal blood pure, the practice being said to have begun with Isis and Osiris, whose myth inspires the relationship between Antony and Cleopatra in Shakespeare's last great tragedy.

Whatever the truth, we are left to tie together the threads as best we can from the literature of the time, which was "of purpose . . . written darkly."

Passing Deformity

Some historians have suggested that Queen Elizabeth and the Earl of Oxford, at the height of their amorous involvement, pledged themselves to each other before the most senior priest in the land, Elizabeth's old friend and mentor Archbishop Matthew Parker. (Parker was, of course, the only man in the land who could marry the sovereign.) Indeed, the queen made three visits to Parker at Lambeth Palace and Croydon between January 1573 and March 1574, and she was accompanied by Oxford on each occasion. Parker had been chaplain to Elizabeth's mother, Anne Boleyn, who had entrusted her infant daughter to his spiritual care before being arrested in 1536. If anyone knew the origins and secret life of Elizabeth, it was the queen's confessor.

If Oxford's marriage to Anne Cecil was unconsummated after three years, then an exchange of rings and vows with Elizabeth before a holy witness would have constituted a legal union, whether it was revealed to the world or not. Secret marriages and betrothals are common—one might almost say de rigueur—in Shakespeare. Olivia in *Twelfth Night* is forced to make known her secret marriage to her young lover, Sebastian, though she had "intended to keep in darkness what occasion now reveals before 'tis ripe." The priest confirms the legitimacy of the union:

> A contract of eternal bond of love,
> Confirm'd by mutual joinder of your hands,
> Attested by the holy close of lips,
> Strengthen'd by interchangement of your rings,
> And all the ceremony of this compact
> Seal'd in my function, by my testimony.
>
> (V.i.154–159)

This "contract of eternal bond" may have been sealed when the queen first realized she was pregnant with Oxford's child, and would certainly have been kept secret from Burghley, who would hardly have condoned such a recklessly naive plan. In *Two Gentlemen* much is made of Silvia's "passing [i.e., temporary] deformity"—that is to say, her pregnancy—and Valentine's "folly" in causing such a condition, Valentine-Oxford being "the secret, nameless friend" with whom she is in love. "The auburn-haired Silvia, rash and reckless, steps somewhat beyond the sphere of a woman's nature," writes G. G. Gervinus. So did Elizabeth.

Surprisingly little is known of the queen's movements from autumn 1573 to the end of her summer progress in 1574, but it sounds as though she was in something of a funk from May 1574, when she deferred yet another visit to Archbishop Parker, going instead to stay with Oxford at Havering-atte-Bower, a royal demesne since the time of Edward the Confessor, for whom it had served as a favorite retreat. A beautiful wooded sanctuary high above the Thames, Havering and its royal palace appear to have been leased or granted to Edward de Vere during the 1570s, possibly as a private getaway for the royal lovers. Even today it remains a deer-haunted oasis of green high above the suburban turmoil of Greater London. On this occasion we are told that the queen was "melancholy," perhaps on account of "some weighty causes of state" (which are not named), and that she intended to remain at Havering until her summer progress to Bristol began. Accounts of Elizabeth's engagements and whereabouts for June 1574 are sketchy, but we do know that she was at Greenwich on June 8 and that Oxford was in attendance. Her depression had not lifted, and it was reported that she and Oxford had been involved in a spat over a suit he brought before her. Gilbert Talbot wrote of it to his mother, Lady Shrewsbury:

> The young Earl of Oxford, of that ancient and Very family of the Veres, had a cause or suit, that now came before the Queen, which she did not answer so favorably as was expected, checking him it seems for his unthriftiness. And hereupon his behaviors before her gave her some offense.[61]

At the end of June she moved to Richmond in preparation for her progress to the West Country, which began on July 7. Just as she was departing, the court was rocked by the news that Oxford had fled to the Continent. His companion on this occasion was Edward Seymour, Earl of Hertford, whose sons were next in line to the throne. Elizabeth immediately dispatched Thomas Bedingfield to bring the erring noblemen back. The 2nd Earl of Southampton also fled the country, taking refuge in Spain.

It could be that the queen had given birth to Oxford's child at Havering in late May or early June, and that in a sudden panic about the possible repercussions for her political security had gone back on her promise to acknowledge the child, deciding instead to place it with foster parents, whereupon Oxford had flown into a rage (hence the reported spat). Shakespeare's Sonnet 33 refers to the birth of the child, and Elizabeth's change of mind:

> Even so my Sun one early morn did shine
> With all-triumphant splendour on my brow;
> But, out alack, he was but one hour mine,
> The region cloud hath masked him from me now.
>
> (lines 9–12)

The same story is told in the Ditchley portrait of Elizabeth, which depicts the queen standing on a map of England, with the county of Oxford immediately beneath her feet. With the little finger of her left hand she points downward, and if one follows the line of the finger it passes first through Oxford and then Southampton, with no cities between. Behind the queen is a large cloud, which hides the sun, though streaks of what looks like dawning light are visible in the top right-hand corner of the picture. Beneath the zigzags of emerging sunlight is a sonnet which, owing to damage and reframing, is partly obscured. The first line, however, reads: "The prince of light. The Sonn by whom . . ."

If news of the birth had leaked out into the court, Oxford would have been in danger of arrest on charges of treason. As Dorothy Ogburn and Charlton Ogburn Sr. point out, "[The Earl of] Leicester ran away in 1561, the year his son [Arthur Dudley] was said to have been born to the Queen."[62]

Oxford was duly brought back, and after certain bitter speeches he and the queen were reconciled, at least for the moment. Elizabeth, true to her genius for equivocation, probably kept Oxford believing through half promises and finely judged asseverations that she would one day acknowledge their child as her heir. Meanwhile the bone of contention seems to have been the boy's custody and future education, and here the wrangle between Titania and Oberon over the changeling child might provide clues as to what was going on. Oxford, it seems, wanted his royal son to be brought up in his household rather than being placed with the Earl of Southampton, where he would be under the control of Burghley's henchman Thomas Dymocke, who dominated the Wriothesley household with the same easy-borrowed pride that Thomas Golding had evinced in lording it over the de Veres.

As it happened, Oxford lost out—at least to begin with—and the child was placed with the Southamptons. Mary Browne, the Countess of Southampton, had given birth to a son on October 6, 1573, but there is no record of a baptism for the baby, who may have died in infancy or been placed with another family in preparation for the adoption of the queen's son. Either way, her child was probably illegitimate and not a Wriothesley at all, for the earl, her husband, was in the Tower when the child was conceived and she was rumored to be having an affair with "a common person" by the name of Donesame, pretext enough in those days for the removal of the baby. Moreover, although this child was the 2nd Earl's first son, the boy who stepped into his shoes, Henry Tudor-Wriothesley, later 3rd Earl of Southampton, is frequently referred to as "the second son," again suggesting that the child born in October 1573 either died or was farmed out. Southampton's indefatigable biographer Charlotte Stopes confessed that she had been able to find "only two manuscript references to the Wriothesley baby (i.e., the 3rd Earl) during his whole childhood."

Just as the 16th Earl of Oxford had conveniently died in his early forties in 1562, so that Burghley could take control of the royal changeling, the 2nd Earl of Southampton suffered the same fate in 1581, aged thirty-six. The death of fathers was indeed a "common theme," as Claudius reminds Hamlet with perfect sangfroid. Edward de Vere himself had been rendered invisible by the "Oxford" mask that he was forced to wear; now, as his thoughts turned to his royal son, he was determined that Southampton should be spared this fate.

In October 1574, not long before Oxford's grand tour of the Continent, he and Anne shared rooms at Hampton Court, a rare interlude of intimacy in what had been a remote and one-sided marriage, and it is possible that the daughter born the following year, Elizabeth Vere, was conceived at this time, though Oxford would later deny that the child was his. As Hamlet says to Polonius, "Conception is a blessing, but not as your daughter may conceive." There are two separate, almost identical traditions according to which Oxford was tricked into sleeping with his wife, believing that she was his mistress; from this "virtuous deceit," one of his daughters was said to have proceeded. Thomas Wright, in his *History of Essex,* tells how Oxford "forsook his lady's bed, [but] the father of Lady Anne by a stratagem contrived that her husband should unknowingly sleep with her, believing her to be another woman, and she bore a son [*sic*] to him in consequence."[63]

Such a trick is played in both *All's Well* and *Measure for Measure;* hence their reputation as dark comedies. The confusion of mistress and wife was certainly one that loomed large in Oxford's life at this time, and the real "bed trick," in psychological terms, was the substitution of Anne for Elizabeth as Oxford's wife, the "substituter" being Anne's father, Burghley. The result of the substitution in both plays is that Bertram and Angelo appear to make love to a virgin without defiling her. In other words, their enjoyment of her does not compromise her purity. If we understand the bed trick in terms of Oxford's relationship with the Virgin Queen, then its inclusion in the plays—which grates so harshly on modern sensibilities— becomes meaningful. Subconsciously at least, Oxford-Shakespeare is creating a scenario, a little dreamscape, in which he can be the queen's lover or husband without destroying the "virginity" or purity on which her crown and reputation rest. In effect, he is imagining a situation in which her virginity—official, relentless, ironclad —does not usurp their relationship or his identity. On the other hand, because she is his mother, her virginity becomes an essential component of their union, a sort of amulet to protect them against the taboo they are transgressing.

Helena, the heroine of *All's Well,* embodies the contradictions at the heart of Elizabeth's sexual life: she is, in the words of Janet Adelman, both "a miraculous virgin" and "a deeply sexual woman seeking her will." She quickly finds an ally in Bertram's mother, the Countess of Rossillion, who connives at the maiden's pursuit of her son. In fact the two become one, a process predicted by the very first words of the play when the countess, in mourning for her late husband, says, "In delivering my son from me, I bury a second husband." The buried theme of incest is thus announced *ab initio,* and it can be seen that the sleight of hand with the virgin (the bed trick) is introduced as a way of purifying the mother before she gets into bed with her son. Bertram, let us not forget, will only marry Helena if she gives birth to his child immaculately, without sex having taken place. There is a deep guilt at work here, as if his own desires are somehow transgressive. What this means in terms of the author's soul-life is that the concept of virgin birth—in particular *his* virgin birth and that of his son—becomes essential to the mythology of his relationship with the queen: indeed, it is made the foundation for a kind of spiritual marriage that ennobles incest and keeps the queen's virginity intact. If he is born of the virgin, he is somehow immune to ordinary sexual sin, and can enter into a union with his virginal mother without defiling her.

Shakespeare's extraordinary sexual psychopathology, as revealed in the plays, is nothing less than his attempt to legitimize his carnal love for his mother, the Virgin Queen, Elizabeth of England. His unconscious works overtime to devise all manner of ingenious justifications, so that he can avoid falling into the abyss marked *taboo.* His anxiety is often deflected from the hero, in this case Bertram, onto another character, providing the author with the necessary license and safety to explore his dilemma. This dialogue between Helena and the countess is a good example:

HELENA:
What is your pleasure, madam?
COUNTESS:
You know, Helen, I am a mother to you.
HELENA:
Mine honourable mistress.
COUNTESS:
Why not a mother? When I said "a mother,"
Methought you saw a serpent. What's in "mother"
That you start at it? I say I am your mother,
And put you in the catalogue of those
That were enwombed mine. . . .
God's mercy, maiden! Does it curd thy blood
To say I am thy mother?

(I.iii.132–139; 144–145)

If the countess is Helena's mother, then it would be incest for Helena to make love to Bertram. Behind the surface dialogue we hear Shakespeare's own anxiety over the confusion of mistress and mother.

All's Well ends up being Shakespeare's most thorough exploration of virginity and gives us an insight into the potent myths at work behind Elizabeth's public image. Though the queen's virginity helped absolve Oxford's own stain, at least psychologically, it nevertheless barred him from the throne. Parolles's Falstaffian diatribe against the maiden state releases some of Shakespeare's bitterness:

To speak on the part of virginity is to accuse your mothers, which is most infallible disobedience. He that hangs himself is a virgin; virginity murthers itself, and should be buried in highways out of all sanctified limit, as a desperate offendress against nature. Virginity breeds mites, much like a cheese; consumes itself to the very paring, and so dies with feeding his own stomach. Besides, virginity is peevish, proud, idle, made of self-love which is the most inhibited sin in the canon. . . . Your date is better in your pie and your porridge than in your cheek; and your virginity, your old virginity, is like one of our French wither'd pears: it looks ill, it eats drily; marry, 'tis a wither'd pear; it was formerly better; marry, yet 'tis a wither'd pear. (I.i.134–143; 154–159)

Realizing the absurdity of the idea that this passage could have been written by William of Stratford during the reign of Elizabeth, the writer and broadcaster Barry Took, like so many of his fellow commentators, is forced to alter the chronology of the plays to accommodate Shakespeare's Stratfordian identity:

> This denigration of virginity, together with the gloom of the opening scene, where everyone is in mourning, gives us a very good clue as to when the play was written. Shakespeare clearly could not have written *All's Well* while Queen Elizabeth, a celebrated virgin, was alive and well and living just up the road. I doubt if his feet would have touched the ground before his neck hit the block if he had written [such] lines . . . while Gloriana was still on the throne.[64]

Helena, like Ophelia, is based on Anne Cecil. All three girls are brought up as stepsisters of a kind to the hero, who cannot help looking upon them with a certain incestuous horror. And just as Helena becomes an involuntary channel for the countess's feelings of desire toward her son, and Ophelia the unwitting agent of Gertrude's primitive lust, so Anne Cecil, it seems, was the lightning rod for the queen's incestuous passion for Oxford. In the same vein Hamlet projects his feelings of rage toward his incestuous mother upon his innocent lover; hence his tirade against Ophelia: "Get thee to a nunnery!"

ORPHAN OF THE STORM

On his way back from Italy toward the end of March 1576, Oxford stopped in the French capital, where the adventurer Rowland Yorke, who had been one of his men for several years, appears to have made certain suggestions regarding the paternity of Oxford's eldest daughter, born to Anne Cecil the previous year, that threw his master into a state of profound agitation. Although the missive hasn't survived, Burghley would later write in his diary that in a letter of April 4 from Paris, Oxford had signified some misliking concerning his wife but had then dismissed it, saying he had been abused by "a man of his which was his receiver." (The "doubleness" or treachery of servants is a leitmotif of Oxford's letters from abroad, and was a problem he was to encounter all his life. Springing partly from his overgenerous nature, it had its roots in his own "baseness" or bastardy which, shut it out as he might, returned to haunt him in the form of double-dealers who undermined his status and ensnared his higher self.)

Like Othello, stung by the promptings of his servant Iago, Oxford, as his subsequent behavior would reveal, remained in a state of torment. "By the world!" exclaims Othello,

> I think my wife be honest, and think she is not,
> I think that thou [Iago] art just, and think thou art not;
> I'll have some proof: my name, that was as fresh
> As Dian's visage, is now begrim'd, and black
> As mine own face: if there be cords, or knives,
> Poison, or fire, or suffocating streams,
> I'll not endure it: would I were satisfied!
>
> (III.iii.390–396)

Oxford left Paris for England in a rage. While he was crossing the Channel in mid-April, his ship was captured by pirates and his goods plundered. He was stripped to his shirt and "left naked" on the shore, and might well have been killed had he not been recognized by one of his attackers, a Scotsman. Hamlet, too, is overtaken by pirates on his way to England, and in his letter to Claudius refers to himself as having been "set naked on your kingdom." Hell-bent on a course that would separate him from his wife and baby daughter, and would leave him dangerously exposed at court, Oxford, in crossing the Channel, changed the course and tenor of his life, or at least experienced the nightmare that marked his entrance into a new, more intense phase of the inner struggle. Claudius repeats the words "naked" and "alone" from Hamlet's letter, and it was essentially naked and alone that Oxford was returning to the English court, where he had so lately jetted it with the finest. (The gorgeous Italian dresses he had brought back for the queen were lying at the bottom of the ocean.) Betrayed by Elizabeth, intrigued against by Burghley and his ilk, divorced in effect from his young wife, mistrusted by his contemporaries, heavily in debt, and with no political office or sinecure to sustain him, Oxford had only literature between himself and despair.

What had happened in his absence may never be fully known, but there were people close to the queen who would have been glad to put an end to Oxford's royal favor and, with it, his dreams of kingship. Burghley, as ever, was playing a double game, unsure whether he could control Oxford or would be better off disposing of him. Burghley's immediate aim was to force Oxford to honor his marriage to Anne, and the best way to do that was through the birth of a child. Herein lay the rub, however, for Oxford had told Elizabeth's physician Richard Masters in her majesty's presence, before he left for the Continent, that if Anne was pregnant the child could not be his. Nevertheless, while abroad, he had greeted the news of her pregnancy with genuine warmth, and had sent her gifts as a mark of his pleasure. News of her delivery, however, coming as it did so long after the fact, was acknowledged but coolly by him, toward the end of his letter to Burghley dated September 24, 1575. The child, Elizabeth, who was baptized at the end of September and named for the queen, had most likely been born earlier that month; if so, Oxford could *not* be the father—hence Burghley's fabricated birth date of July 2.

The picture is made more confusing by the ramblings committed to paper by Burghley, who was clearly unsettled by Oxford's newly engendered misgivings about Anne's conduct and his own. In a long, barely coherent letter to the queen of April 23, 1576, whose guilt-driven involuted discursions invite comparison to Polonius's worst mumbo-jumbo,[65] he pleads for her majesty's defense of him "in anything that may hereof follow [i.e., in the matter concerning Oxford and his daughter], whereof I may have wrong with dishonesty offered to me," and protests his daughter's honesty, chastity, and entire love toward—and indeed infatuation with—her husband. He even prefaces his protestations by "renounce[ing] nature," which appears to be a Freudian slip for renouncing art or artifice, something he is clearly incapable of doing. For once, Burghley was lost in his own labyrinth.

When Oxford arrived at Dover, he was met by Burghley's elder son, Thomas Cecil, but declined either to accompany Thomas or to divulge his own discontent. Instead, he took another boat, sailing around and up the Thames to London, missing a second, even less desirable welcoming party, comprising his sister Mary and wife, Anne, who had thought to intercept him at Gravesend. With him was Rowland Yorke, and it was to the house of Yorke's brother Edward in the City of London that Oxford headed. From there he visited the queen at Greenwich, though what happened is not recorded. From Greenwich he wrote Burghley a letter of barely suppressed rage:

I must let your Lordship understand thus much: that is, until I can better satisfy or advertise myself of certain mislikes, I am not determined, as touching my wife, to accompany her. What they are, because some are not to be spoken of or written upon as imperfections, I will not deal withal. Some that otherways discontent me, I will not blaze or publish until it please me. And last of all, I mean not to weary my life anymore with such troubles and molestations as I have endured; nor will I, to please your Lordship only, discontent myself. . . .

This might have been done through private conference before, and had not needed to have been the fable of the world if you would have had the patience to have understood me.

In a memorandum to himself two days later, Burghley made a list of Oxford's grievances, from which it is clear that Oxford refused at this stage to reveal his true suspicions to his father-in-law (he may never have revealed them). The document also indicates Oxford's slightly paranoid feelings toward Lady Burghley, Anne's mother, whom he accuses of slander, of trying to alienate Anne's affection toward him, and of causing divisions in his household. He also charges Burghley with suborning his servants and usurping his authority as a husband. But what were Oxford's real doubts? Given the barrage of references to incest and unnatural conception leading up to Ophelia's suicide at the end of Act IV, and the confusion of father and lover in her "mad" songs, it is not outrageous to suggest that she kills herself because she is pregnant with her father's child. It is rarely noted that when Hamlet taunts Polonius with being a Jephthah, the judge of Israel who sacrificed his daughter, he throws in a second reference to another Old Testament grandee, Abraham's nephew Lot, who committed incest with his daughters:

POLONIUS:
If you call me Jephthah, my lord, I have a daughter that I love passing well.
HAMLET:
Nay, that follows not.
POLONIUS:
What follows then, my lord?
HAMLET:
Why

"As by lot [i.e., *Lot*] God wot,"
And then you know
"It came to pass,
As most like it was."
The first row of the pious chanson will show you more.

(II.ii.407–416)

Earlier in this scene, in telling the King and Queen of his advice to his daughter, Polonius says:

And then I prescripts gave her,
That she should lock herself from his resort,
Admit no messengers, receive no tokens;
Which done, she took the fruits of my advise,
And he, repelled—a short tale to make—
Fell into a sadness, then into a fast.

(II.ii.142–147)

Intruding upon the surface meaning of Polonius's words is a darker message that the speaker is no doubt at pains to hide, for it betrays his own incest. Ophelia, we learn, shuts Hamlet out, taking instead the fruits (read "seed") of her father's "advise" (i.e., "visit"—from Latin *ad* = "to, toward" and *viso* = "visit"). As a result Hamlet feels rejected and, not to put too fine a point on it, loses his erection ("a short tale-tail to make"). There is a clear sense here of sexual competitiveness in Polonius's language, as if he is the prince's rival in his daughter's affections. Following the death of her father, Ophelia's madness makes a truth teller of her, and the politicians are predictably alarmed. As a gentleman of the court advises the Queen:

'Twere good she were spoken with, for she may strew
Dangerous conjectures in ill-breeding minds.

(IV.v.14–15)

This is not to suggest that Burghley literally impregnated his daughter Anne in Oxford's absence, but the sensitive young poet may have harbored such a suspicion, his own incestuous origins no doubt predisposing him to this kind of thinking. There is a possibility that Oxford suffered from bipolar disorder (manic depression), and may have been more susceptible to paranoid thoughts during phases of heightened stimulation. Certainly, he swung from moods of high comedy, in which he drove others to hysterical laughter with uproarious, improvised accounts of his fantastic adventures, to melancholy brooding, wherein he imagined himself the sole target of fortune's blows. The axis that joined these two poles of feeling was his compulsive self-dramatization, which was forever prompting him to try on different hats and act out different roles. His were the "female humors" and "Protean rages" attributed to Amorphus in Ben Jonson's play *Cynthia's Revels.*

Whatever the whispering campaign initiated by Oxford's servant Rowland Yorke and his friend Lord Henry Howard, both of whom were deeply hostile to Burghley, this episode, combined with his harrowing Channel crossing, seems to have pulled Oxford back into the waste spaces of his taboo and nameless origins.

When Hamlet returns to Elsinore after the pirates' attack, he comes upon the funeral of Ophelia, who has taken her life in his absence. The full significance of his jumping into her grave, it seems to me, has been missed, and can best be understood through this brief dialogue between Hamlet and Polonius in Act II:

POLONIOUS:
Will you walk out of the air, my lord?
HAMLET:
Into my grave?
POLONIOUS:
Indeed, that's out of the air. How pregnant sometimes his replies are—a happiness that often madness hits on, which reason and sanity could not so prosperously be delivered of.

(II.ii.206–211)

The pun on "air" and "heir" was common in Elizabethan literature. Walking "out of the heir" (i.e., surrendering his position as royal heir) is clearly a kind of death for Hamlet; hence the reference to his grave. Conversely, leaping into Ophelia's grave marks his acknowledgement, deep down, that he can no longer succeed to the throne of Denmark. The odds are against him. He is, as it were, no longer in the air-heir, but a king of the underworld like his ghostly father. Oxford knew on his return from the Continent that whatever deal he and Elizabeth had made was off. He too was out of the heir. Why? Read

Polonius's next words. The imagery is that of childbirth. Getting the queen pregnant may have been felicitous, but it was also madness. When Claudius asks Hamlet, "How is it that the clouds still hang on you?" the prince replies with a bawdy pun that would have set Elizabeth's temples throbbing, "Not so, my lord, I am too much *in the sun*," "sun" being a common trope for the monarch.

In the end, Anne lived with her parents, while Oxford took up with his literary cronies. His return from the Continent, marking as it did a cutting of ties with his family, initiated a period of intense literary and dramatic activity, which coincided with the construction of the first public theater in England in 1576. Situated in Shoreditch, outside the City walls, and called simply the Theatre, it was run by James Burbage (the father of Richard), whose patron the Earl of Leicester used it as a venue for his company of players. Oxford, too, may well have been one of the original patrons; certainly his newfound familiarity with Italian innovations in theater design and performance would have been put to good use.

While the world of the poet in Elizabethan England, as in the France and Italy of the time, was—with very few exceptions— courtly and aristocratic, the world of the public theater was classless and bohemian, attracting talent from some of the rougher elements of London life as well as the emerging middle class. Unlicensed actors were branded as vagrants, and left to wander the countryside. Shakespeare, the consummate poet-playwright, must have had a foot in both worlds. This was no easy thing, for despite Hamlet's complaint that class distinctions were crumbling, social privilege was jealously guarded in Elizabethan times, and Elizabeth herself, the fantasies of Victorian artists notwithstanding, never attended a performance at the public theaters (Charles II was the first English monarch to do that). Shakespeare, the bohemian aristocrat, must have appeared déclassé to his peers at court. Certainly the Sonnets register his sense of shame at trespassing in a public and commercial world forbidden to men of his station. Sonnets 110 and 111 make this lament famous:

> 110:
> Alas, 'tis true I have gone here and there
> And made myself a motley to the view.
>
> (lines 1–2)

III:

O for my sake do you with Fortune chide,
The guilty goddess of my harmful deeds,
That did not better for my life provide
Than public means which public manners breeds.
Thence comes it that my name receives a brand.

(lines 1–5)

For the poet who had affixed the haughty tag from Ovid to the front of *Venus and Adonis,* translated by Jonson as "Kneel hinds to trash: me let bright Phoebus swell / With cups full flowing from the Muses' well,"[66] his association with the public theaters was a bitter pill indeed. "A poet-playwright," writes the Shakespeare scholar Harold Clark Goddard, "is a contradiction in terms. But a poet-playwright is exactly what Shakespeare is."[67]

Two of his earliest plays after his return, *Pericles* and *The Historie of the Solitarie Knight* (*Timon of Athens*), speak eloquently to the isolation he felt, and his apparent helplessness in the face of fortune's buffets. His separation from Anne and the ensuing scandal, together with the exclamations of his creditors, contributed to a growing sense of alienation, further exacerbated by the demands of his genius. As an escape from these pressures Oxford focused his attention on his child with the queen, the young Henry Wriothesley, who once again fueled his fantasies—if only vicarious—of royal recognition. It was as if Oxford were waking from one dream only to find himself acting in another.

Pericles, in particular, is eerily reflective of Oxford's world at the time. The hero, Pericles, Prince of Tyre, pays suit to the daughter of Antiochus, King of Antioch, who—unknown to him—is being sexually abused by her father. Like the long line of suitors before him, Pericles must either solve the riddle of Antiochus's incest, and so win his daughter, or else perish. Having solved the riddle, yet fearful of provoking the King's wrath by divulging the truth, Pericles flees for his life. "Who has a book of all that monarchs do," he tells the King, "[is] more secure to keep it shut than shown." Thus begins a life of wandering on the high seas, pursued by Antiochus's henchmen and the elemental fury of nature. The princess, kept in thrall by her abusive father, is Anne Cecil and Queen Elizabeth telescoped into one, while Antiochus himself is Burghley. Pericles, whose acute perception puts his life in danger, stands for Oxford, and although this is Pericles of Tyre, not Athens, no one hearing the name could fail to recall the Athenian aristocrat turned democrat, who did so much to develop the cultural splendor of the Greek capital.

"Yet cease your ire, you angry stars of heaven!" cries Pericles, finally washed up after a mighty tempest on the shore of Pentapolis, where he is found by fishermen. He has lost everything in the storm except his father's old suit of armor, which, rusty with the salt surge, is hauled onto the beach in the fishermen's nets. As it happens, the King of Pentapolis, Simonides, is holding a tournament to celebrate his daughter Thaisa's birthday, and princes and knights from all corners of the world have come "to joust and tourney for her love." Pericles decides to take part, destitute as he is, and asks the fishermen to direct him to the court. The rival knights parade before the king and his daughter with their devices and mottoes. Pericles, the last to appear, shieldless and in rusty armor, holds a withered branch that's green at the top, bearing the motto *In hac spe vivo* ("In this hope I live"). This branch probably represented Oxford's only true lineal hope, his royal son.

Although Pericles wins the tournament and, with it, the love of Thaisa, his troubles are by no means over. While he is returning home to Tyre with his pregnant wife, his ship is once more battered by a storm. His wife dies (or appears to die) giving birth to a girl, Marina, and the sailors insist that she must be thrown overboard to calm the tempest. Pericles decides to stop at Tarsus, where he places his baby daughter for protection with the governor, Cleon, and his wife Dionyza. Having lost both wife and child, Pericles returns home. He is eventually reunited with his family through the divine offices of Diana, goddess of chastity and childbirth, who appears to him in a dream. Incest casts Pericles upon the waves and divorces him from the name of king, but his own child, legitimately born, redeems him; hence his description of Marina as "Thou that begett'st him that did thee beget." Marina, born from the wrath of the goddess (like the flower born from the blood of Adonis), represents Oxford's true child, the poetry that gives him new life.

Oxford would live apart from his wife and daughter for five years before their reconciliation, during which time Anne bore his ill-treatment with an almost saintly patience, never swerving in her love for him, and trusting to time to clear her name. In the end, Oxford came to realize that he had behaved toward her with great cruelty, and Anne's early death at the age of thirty-three would cause him untold remorse, which he attempted to purge in play after play. *Much Ado About Nothing, All's Well That Ends Well, Hamlet, Othello, The Winter's Tale, Cymbeline,* and *Pericles* all tell of an entirely loving wife rejected by a suborned husband, who allows his jealous imaginings to run away with him (though in *All's Well* the "wife" is rejected for her inferior birth, and the hero, as in *Hamlet,* is not suborned). There is also the case of *Measure for Measure,* in which the loving Mariana is spurned by her husband, Angelo, both because her promised dowry did not materialize and "for that her reputation was disvalu'd in levity" (i.e., there were rumors of improper behavior). Since her rejection at the hands of her husband, Mariana has lived in a sort of limbo, "neither maid, widow, nor wife." Her separation from Angelo, like Oxford and Anne's, lasts five years. When the Duke learns of her nebulous status, he exclaims, "Why, you are nothing then," at which Lucio interjects, "My Lord, she may be a punk; for many of them are neither maid, widow nor wife." This seems to be a hit at Elizabeth, whose feminine status was a mystery to her contemporaries, and raises once again the ghost of the queen behind the author's furious rejection of his wife.

Oxford had bypassed his wife and her family on landing to make straight for the queen: it was to her and their son that he now looked for a sense of identity and purpose. For a time, Elizabeth managed to flatter Oxford's hopes and keep all doors open, but this happy interlude could not last. Further rude awakenings were in the offing.

~ 5 ~

England's Literary Champion

Triumph, my *Britaine,* thou hast one to showe,
To whom all scenes of *Europe* homage owe.
—Ben Jonson, 1623

THE ENGLISH MAECENAS

The notion that the golden age of Elizabethan literature began with
Marlowe in the late 1580s (fully thirty years into the queen's reign)
is hard to dislodge, despite the fact that it leaves twenty-five years of
literary activity—much of it of the highest quality—stranded on the
sands of time. It also leaves us with little option but to believe that
neither Marlowe nor Shakespeare had any form of literary apprenticeship, but rather that both emerged in all their finery from a vacuum.
Much of the work produced from 1560 to 1585 has not been properly assigned to an author, or its attribution has been taken at face
value, without any understanding of its political context. The plays
of John Lyly are a good example. To accept a Shakespeare who began
writing dramatic masterpieces in 1590 without earlier efforts in poetry and prose is as unrealistic as proposing a Chekhov who wrote
the great plays of the late 1890s without the formative sketches, short
stories, and juvenile dramatic efforts of the previous two decades. We
would be nearer the mark if we thought of the First Folio of 1623 as
the tip of the Shakespearean iceberg.

The writing of the time was highly diverse and experimental, with censorship spurring authors to keep one step ahead of the authorities in their development of literary forms and tropes. Shakespeare in particular, as "the glass of fashion and the mould of form," had to be like a snake, shedding the skin of one identity to make room for another as his genius developed and, with it, his power to awaken the conscience of his peers. As political realities changed, so he metamorphosed, outgrowing old modes of expression.

It was on the back of Shakespeare's example and innovations that the first professional writers emerged at the end of the 1570s. Yet great literature required great patrons, and literary historians have yet to come up with an Elizabethan literary patron of any stature, leaving us to wonder who or what inspired the most dramatic and sustained outpouring of literature in the history of the English-speaking peoples.

Not only was Oxford not prepared to settle down to a life of domestic responsibilities with the woman who was his wife in name only; he was eager to seek the glory that would make him a worthy knight to his sovereign lady. Restless for adventures, he petitioned the queen for a license to travel and see action abroad, but she was determined to keep him at her side, for he was fast becoming the brightest ornament of her court. Oxford sublimated his military energies through literature, a common enough displacement of the time for the feudal nobility, whose "dragon rancors" of old required new outlets. He had the passion for letters to make this happen, his rejection of Anne providing him the absolute freedom to pursue his maverick course.

By means of two seminal publications, which he sponsored and for which he wrote eloquent introductions, one only weeks after his marriage and the other a year later, Oxford quickly nailed his literary colors to the mast. The first work was a translation from the Italian into Latin of Castiglione's *The Courtier* made by his old tutor Bartholomew Clerke. Castiglione's work became something of a best seller at the courts of Europe, and Hamlet has clearly studied it with great care, not least Ottaviano Fregoso's concept of the courtier's proper function "of not allowing his prince to be deceived, of ensuring that he always has the truth about everything, and of standing

in the path of flatterers and slanderers and all those who might scheme
to corrupt the soul of the prince through shameful pleasures." In his
prefatory letter to the reader, also in Latin, which the literary critic
Gabriel Harvey described in 1578 as "more polished even than the
writings of Castiglione himself," the elements of Castiglione's style
and philosophy that Oxford picks out for special praise tell us much
about his own literary aspirations. Indeed, his letter reads, in part,
like Shakespeare's artistic manifesto. Oxford is delighted by the natu-
ralness and variety of Castiglione's dialogue, and his praise seems to
foreshadow future panegyrics of his own character creation in the
plays:

> I will say nothing of the fitness and the excellence with which he
> has depicted the beauty of chivalry in the noblest persons. Nor
> will I refer to his delineations in the case of those persons who
> cannot be courtiers, when he alludes to some notable defect, or
> to some ridiculous character, or to some deformity of appearance.
> Whatever is heard in the mouths of men in casual talk and in so-
> ciety, whether apt and candid, or villainous and shameful, that he
> has set down in so natural a manner that it seems to be acted be-
> fore our very eyes.

Not only has Castiglione "resuscitated that dormant quality of
fluent discourse," writes Oxford, but he has succeeded in perfectly
attuning his language to his subject matter—both accomplishments
of which Shakespeare was to prove himself a master:

> For who is clearer in his use of words? Or richer in the dignity of
> his sentences? Or who can conform to the variety of circumstances
> with greater art? If weighty matters are under consideration, he
> unfolds his theme in a solemn and majestic rhythm; if the subject
> is familiar and facetious, he makes use of words that are witty and
> amusing. When therefore he writes with precise and well-chosen
> words, with skillfully constructed and crystal-clear sentences, and
> with every art of dignified rhetoric, it cannot be but that some
> noble quality should be felt to proceed from his work.

Having stated that Castiglione "has been able to lay down principles for the guidance of the very monarch himself"—a liberty that

may not have been altogether pleasing to Elizabeth, yet one that Shakespeare was to make his own—Oxford ends with a rousing encomium to the queen, "to whom alone is due all the praise of all the Muses and all the glory of literature." *Gloria literarum,* "the glory of literature": the phrase leaves one in no doubt of the reverence in which Oxford held the practice of fine writing. "For the first time in our annals," writes B. M. Ward, "we find a nobleman taking immense trouble to recommend a book in which he was interested. We shall find Oxford in the following year not only doing the same thing again, but actually paying for the publication of the book himself. Here was a literary patron indeed."[68]

The second work, which according to the title page was "published by commandment of the right honourable the Earl of Oxenford," was a translation by Thomas Bedingfield of the Italian mathematician and philosoher Jerome Cardan's *De Consolatione* (or *Cardanus Comforte,* as it was more commonly known). In his dedication to Oxford, Bedingfield, another soldier-scholar in the Hamlet mould, makes play of the metaphorical link between arms and letters beloved of aristocratic authors of the time. Indeed, "arms" almost becomes a code word for literature. "Sure I am it would have better beseemed me," he writes, "to have taken this travail in some discourse of arms (being your Lordship's chief profession and mine also) than in philosopher's skill to have thus busied myself: yet sith your pleasure was such, and your knowledge in either great, I do (as I ever will) most willingly obey you."

Oxford's prefatory letter on this occasion is even more remarkable, and rings the changes throughout on another convention of aristocratic writing: the notion that the author's work is but a trifle, something tossed off in his spare time for his own amusement and that of his friends, not for wider dissemination and the instruction of the public. In his dedicatory epistle to Oxford, Bedingfield notes that the earl desired and encouraged him to make the translation, which he has duly and dutifully undertaken. Yet now, for all that, he begs Oxford to show it only to those who, because of their love for Bedingfield or their reverence for the earl, will look upon the work with an indulgent eye. In his letter, Oxford explains with considerable panache his reasons for overriding Bedingfield's request:

But when I had thoroughly considered in my mind of sundry and diverse arguments whether it were best to obey mine affections or the merits of your studies, at the length I determined it better to deny your unlawful request than to grant or condescend to the concealment of so worthy a work. Whereby as you have been profited in the translating, so many may reap knowledge by the reading of the same, that shall comfort the afflicted, confirm the doubtful, encourage the coward and lift up the base-minded man to achieve to any true sum or grade of virtue whereto ought only the noble thoughts of men to be inclined.

And because next to the sacred letters of divinity nothing doth persuade the same more than philosophy (of which your book is plentifully stored), I thought myself to commit an unpardonable error to have murdered the same in the waste-bottoms of my chests, and better I thought it were to displease one than to displease many, further considering so little a trifle cannot procure so great a breach of our amity, as may not with a little persuasion of reason be repaired again.

Oxford is not merely toying with the retort courteous for convention's sake, or playing an elaborate literary game; he is making a declaration of artistic intent for his own and future generations of writers. Important works of literature deserve a wide readership, and if that means sweeping aside conventions of anonymity and private distribution, so be it. At the same time, as the following passage reveals, Oxford senses that, for all his resolution, not to say bravura, this may prove to be easier said than done. Images of fever, graves, and death alert us to the fragility underlying the boldness of his claims; and his talk of an author's works as his monument, in its premonition of his own fate (which he was to describe in identical language in the Sonnets) sends an elegiac thrill down modern-day spines.

Wherefore considering the small harm I do to you, the great good I do to others, I prefer mine own intention to discover your volume before your request to secret the same. Wherein I may seem to you to play the part of the cunning and expert mediciner or physician, who although his patient in the extremity of his burning fever is desirous of cold liquor or drink to qualify his sore thirst, or rather kill his languishing body, yet for the danger he doth evidently know by his science to ensue, denieth him the same.

So you being sick of too much doubt in your own proceedings, through which infirmity you are desirous to bury and insevill your works in the grave of oblivion, yet I, knowing the discommodities that shall redound to yourself thereby (and which is more unto your countrymen), as one that is willing to salve so great an inconvenience, am nothing dainty to deny your request.

Again we see if our friends be dead, we cannot show or declare our affection more than by erecting them of tombs: whereby when they be dead indeed, yet make we them live as it were again through their monument. But with me behold it happeneth far better, for in your lifetime I shall erect you such a monument that, as I say, [in] your lifetime you shall see how noble a shadow of your virtuous life shall hereafter remain when you are dead and gone. And in your lifetime, again I say, I shall give you that monument and remembrance of your life whereby I may declare my goodwill.

Oxford's repeated protestation belies his anxiety about the renown and immortality of authors in a land that had not, as yet, learned to value literature. Determined as he was that writers should not remain hidden, he nevertheless seemed to sense that he himself would be subject to this fate, as witness these lines from the commendatory poem he appended to his letter:

> So he that takes the pain to pen the book
> Reaps not the gifts of goodly golden Muse,
> But those gain that, who on the work shall look.

We must remember that by 1573 Oxford had already published a great many works either anonymously or under others' names, or in some cases had circulated them among his friends, so we should not be taken aback by the matter-of-fact resignation of these words. For all his passionate idealism, he was a veteran of submitting to his fate. Maybe this was one reason why *Cardanus Comforte* appealed to him, for it was written as a consolation to those, like Cardan himself, who had in some way been crushed by fate. (Cardan, whose mother had tried to abort him, had been born illegitimate, and frequently met with discrimination for that reason.) Cardan's philosophy of adversity and consolation, which in essence holds that men suffer through their perception of things rather than through the things themselves, owes much to the stoicism of Cicero and Marcus Aurelius. Men, he believed, suffer most in the mind and can use this knowledge to banish sorrow. "I perceive that in this life," writes Cardan, "there is nothing found that may justly be called good or evil, and do allow of those philosophers as wise, who thought that all things consisted in opinion." It was important, therefore, to realize that every pleasure is accompanied by its contrary. There are many passages in the book in which Cardan philosophizes about death and suicide; at one point he compares death first to a sleep and then to a long journey, as well as describing it as the end of all griefs.

Shakespeare's play *Hamlet* is steeped in the philosophy of *Cardanus Comforte,* and shot through with quotations and reminiscences from the work. Hardin Craig has gone so far as to call *Cardanus Comforte* "Hamlet's book"; likewise, Lily B. Campbell confessed herself inclined to believe that "Hamlet was actually reading or pretending to read it as he carried on his baiting of Polonius" in the scene that opens with the stage direction "Enter Hamlet, reading." Hamlet himself is a perfect example of someone who is led to the brink of self-destruction by his own dark-tormenting thoughts. His famous soliloquy beginning "To be or not to be" bristles with Cardan's tart observations on man's apprehensions of death; and his praise of Horatio's ability to accept triumph and adversity with equal indifference ("Give me that man that is not passion's slave . . .") is a masterful summation of Cardan's recipe for a contented life. Hamlet gives the speech just before he puts on *The Mousetrap* in front of the king and queen, highlighting the fact that through theater he achieves dispassion, which is, in Cardan's view, essential to the clear and contented mind. In other words, by choosing the appropriate role and playing it with understanding, we make peace with our lot. Thus *Cardanus Comforte* gives us an insight into the way Shakespeare used theater as a means of coming to terms with his fate.

Oxford signed his letter to Bedingfield "from my new country muses at Wivenhoe" (one of the de Vere properties at the mouth of the river Colne), where he was taking a break from the court to concentrate on his writing in the Essex countryside. He may have been joined by some of the writers who were beginning to gather about his standard, such as George Gascoigne, Thomas Churchyard,

Gabriel Harvey, Thomas Twyne, Angel Day, Edmund Elviden, John Hester, Arthur Golding, and Bedingfield himself. All these men were engaged in translation, as the first step in creating an effective contemporary English that would possess the range and suppleness to produce the great literature of the 1580s and 1590s, as well as the late 1570s. It was a question, too, of expanding the available vocabulary, and this proliferation happened with such suddenness that it was as if men were breathing in new words with the air. "Words from the classical languages, in particular," writes Ted Hughes, "poured into learned use, and from there into popular literature. . . . With some authors this liking for new words became a mania, a collector's craze. And Shakespeare, according to the evidence, was more susceptible to this craze than any other." In his prefatory letter alone Oxford used four new English words: "base-minded," "ornify," "secret" (as a verb), and "insevill" ("bury"). In 1580, Gabriel Harvey, referring to Oxford's exceptional ability to coin words, described him as "a diamond for nonce."

There was considerable pride in this burgeoning language, and when the first anthology of Elizabethan verse, *A Hundred Sundrie Flowres,* was published in 1573, sponsored and largely written by Oxford, the title page declared that the flowers had been gathered "partly (by translation) in the fine outlandish gardens of Euripides, Ovid, Petrarch, Ariosto and others: and partly by invention out of our own fruitful orchards in England." Oxford chose *Meritum petere grave* ("To seek serious merit") as his principal literary signature and proudly placed it on the title page. Looking back from the vantage point of 1592, Thomas Nashe wrote in *Pierce Penniless:*

> To them that demand what fruits the poets of our time bring forth or wherein they are able to prove themselves necessary to the state, thus I answer. First and foremost, they have cleansed our language from barbarism and made the vulgar sort here in London, which is the fountain whose rivers flow round about England, to aspire to a richer purity of speech than is communicated with the commonalty of any nation under heaven.

The literary salvos that Oxford fired in the early 1570s—or rather, the spears that he and his associates shook—must have raised more than a few eyebrows at court. By elevating literature's profile, Oxford was in effect declaring his realization that art would have to play an important role if the monarch was to be transformed from tyrant to philosopher, and if his subjects were to be enlightened under his benevolent rule. Literature must not be suppressed!

Around this time, Oxford took rooms in the Savoy, a former royal palace. It had been refounded as a hospital at the beginning of the century, but in Elizabeth's time it had become, among other things, a writers' haunt. Here he rented rooms for his literary cronies, and found for himself a congenial place to write and rehearse when he was in the capital. In addition to his burgeoning efforts as a poet and playwright, he was fast becoming the most generous and committed patron of arts in the country. The dedications to him speak eloquently of his dazzling breadth of interests, from literature and music to science and medicine, from history and warfare to philosophy and religion. In 1573 Thomas Twyne, known for his translations of Virgil and Petrarch, dedicated his English version of Humfrey Lluyd's *Breviary of Britain* to Oxford, beseeching him to bestow on it "such regard as you are accustomed to do on books of geography, histories, and other good learning, wherein I am privy Your Honor taketh singular delight." Oxford, Twyne makes clear, was "hoped and accounted of to become the chiefest stay of this your commonwealth and country," which gives us more than an inkling of why his devotion to literature was causing such alarm among the mandarins of Whitehall. But Oxford was a patron with a difference. He did not simply dispense funds to indigent and aspiring writers, but read their work with a critical eye, and as one who understood the creative process gave well-directed encouragement to their efforts. Indeed, as some of the dedications aver, he often provided the idea or inspiration for a work, and launched fledgling writers on their literary careers. When Anthony Munday dedicated *The Mirror of Mutability* to Oxford in 1579, he referred to Oxford's "riper invention" and declared, "I rest, Right Honorable, on your clemency, to amend my errors committed so unskillfully." Robert Greene, in his dedication of *The Card of Fancie,* wrote: "Your Honor being a worthy favorer and fosterer of learning hath forced many through your excellent virtue to offer the first fruits of their study at the shrine of your Lordship's courtesy." More than a patron of literature, Oxford was its leading practitioner. Even after he had fallen from grace and lost his influence in society, writers still laid their works at the altar of his genius.

At Vere House, near London Stone—against which the rebel leader Jack Cade struck his sword as a mark of self-appointed sovereignty—one can picture the Earl of Oxford, the architect of the English literary Renaissance, part Hal, part Timon, presiding over a bohemian school, as rowdy as it was cultured. Apollo was honored with music and dancing, gifts of jewels, and the performance of masques, many of them, no doubt, Oxford's own (he was, after all, praised as "the best for comedy"); and Dionysus was, with no less reverence, lifted up among the revelers. According to Charles Arundel and Henry Howard, when Oxford was in his cups extravagant tales cascaded from his lips, embellished with each new recital, one of his favorites being a story that the Duke of Alva had placed him in command of the King of Spain's forces in the Low Countries, whence his fame had spread to Italy. No wonder Gabriel Harvey wrote of Oxford, "Not the like discourser for Tongue and head to be found out." Flavius, Timon's steward, recalls his master's wild parties, at which the vaults "have wept with drunken spilth of wine" and "every room blaz'd with lights and bray'd with minstrelsy." And yet this same steward speaks of the sense of duty and zeal that Timon's "unmatched mind" inspires in him, an attitude shared by the artists who bring their works to him for approval and patronage.

In July 1582, John Lyly, who was in effect the Earl of Oxford's steward, wrote in a letter to Lord Burghley, "All my thoughts concerning my Lord [Oxford] have been ever reverent, and almost religious," a feeling we see repeated in numerous literary dedications. Another of Oxford's followers, Henry Lok, reminisced, again to Burghley: "I have bent my self wholly to follow the service of the honorable Earl of Oxford, whose favor shone sometimes so graciously upon me that my young years were easily drawn thereby to account it as impossible that the beauty thereof should be eclipsed." Yet Oxford, like many artists, could be overtrusting, and later in the same letter Lok refers to "the overmany greedy horse leeches which had sucked too ravenously on his [Oxford's] sweet liberality." Oxford ruinously overstretched himself both in fostering the artistic talent of his contemporaries and in his management and subsidy of court theater, including his patronage of his own acting companies (Oxford's Men and Oxford's Boys). Consequently, in 1586, he had to be rescued by the queen with a sizable stipend, though this was no more than a long overdue acknowledgment of his unexampled service to the arts.

Can we really imagine the English Renaissance without an inspired and obsessive figure like Oxford to drive it along, like Hermes driving the cattle of Apollo across the hills and plains of Greece? If not he, who was its prime mover and chief instigator through all the years of experimentation? Who else had the genius and influence to promote literature to an exalted station of its own?

THE ITALIANATE ENGLISHMAN

Oxford left England in February 1575 with an entourage of about ten men, and made straight for Paris and the Louvre, where he was presented to the new king, Henri III, and Henri's formidable mother, Catherine de' Medici. Henri had been seriously mooted as a potential husband for Elizabeth in the early 1570s, before his derogatory remarks about her age, physique, and character had reached London. Henri had called the Queen of England "putain publique" ("public whore") and "an old creature with a sore leg."

Oxford was just in time for Henri's wedding and coronation at Reims Cathedral on St. Valentine's day, after which the court repaired to Paris. Oxford made a favorable impression on the king, using himself—according to the English ambassador—"with great commendation," and presenting a "device" (i.e., a masque or short play) before the court that was "very proper, witty and significant." At the French court Oxford no doubt met the "prince of poets" Pierre de Ronsard and other members of the Pléiade, a group of seven poets and playwrights committed to creating from the French tongue a modern literary language to rival those of ancient Greece and Rome. If Richard Malim is correct, Oxford had already met Ronsard in the early 1560s while his tutor Sir Thomas Smith was ambassador in Paris, and this meeting had prompted Ronsard to make an extraordinary prediction in verse regarding English literature in 1565, by which time Oxford was already several books into his landmark translation of Ovid's *Metamorphoses,* published in its entirety two years later under his maternal uncle's name. Here is the verse from the 1584 edition of the *Bocage Royale:*

> Soon the proud Thames shall see
> A flock of white swans nesting on his grass,
> His holy guests, they mount to the heavens
> In circles over those delightful banks
> Uttering song which is the certain sign
> That many a Poet, and the heavenly troop
> Of sister Muses quitting Parnassus
> Shall take it for their gracious dwelling place,
> And tell the famous praise of England's Kings
> Unto the crowded nations of the world.[69]

It seems that Ronsard had met the young Shakespeare—then in the first flush of his genius—and could well have been the one to inspire the future Bard with his ideal of a classically based literary language with the scope and suppleness to lift English culture above the collective consciousness of the Middle Ages. Oxford was already well along this path with his translations of Ovid, and his perceptive and wide-ranging interest in history had been noted by Golding in dedicating his *Histories of Trogus Pompeius* (1564) to him.

While in Paris, Oxford had his portrait painted (probably the Welbeck portrait), sending it back to England as a gift for his wife, together with a pair of coach horses, for he had just learned of Anne's pregnancy. "My Lord," he wrote to Burghley on March 17, "your letters have made me a glad man, for these last have put me in assurance of that good fortune which your former mentioned doubtfully." Declining to come home on account of his wife's condition, Oxford speculates about his travel plans. He intends to visit Germany, and has letters to the duke in Venice from the Venetian ambassador in Paris, as well as to the Turkish Court, for he is considering "bestow[ing] two or three months to see Constantinople and some parts of Greece." As it turned out, his next stop was indeed Germany, where he visited the great Protestant scholar Sturmius at Strasbourg. The two conversed in Latin. In addition to being a towering figure of European letters—the "German Cicero," no less—Sturmius was a gatherer of political intelligence, a vital node in the English government's Continental spy network, and sent regular reports to Burghley. At Elizabeth's behest, Oxford himself may have been entrusted with political and diplomatic missions involving espionage, in the same way that Philip the Bastard acts as King John's eyes and ears on the Continent in Shakespeare's history play. After all, spying and literature were allied disciplines in those days, requiring the same canniness and flair for concealment. Gabriel Harvey wrote of Oxford on his return from the Continent, "Not the like Lynx to spy out secrets and privities of States." At the very least, he had audience with a number of European leaders.

After Germany he crossed the Alps via the Saint Gotthard Pass, and thence went on to Venice via Milan. Venice in 1575 laid claim to be the cultural capital of Europe. Apart from its incomparable artistic salons, where musicians, painters, poets, and courtesans gathered, there were two public theaters in the city and several annual festivals with processions, music, and plays in the tradition of the commedia dell'arte. The Earl of Oxford made it his base for traveling around Italy and, according to Sir Henry Wotton, so took to it that he had a house built for himself there and spent more time in Venice than in any other Italian city. We know that he worshipped at the church of San Giorgio dei Greci (the "church of the Greeks"), a favorite haunt of Greek exiles, and at Santa Maria Formosa, where he met the chorister Orazio Cuoco, who was to return to England with him and join his household. Cuoco remarked on Oxford's fluency in Latin and Italian; he also noted that his master never tried to convert him from his Catholic faith, but "let each person live in his own way." Oxford had been deeply impressed by the youth's singing, and once back in England had him perform before the queen, whose consort of Italian musicians was justly renowned.

Free at last from the close attentions of his father-in-law, Oxford could give his passion for the arts free rein. He was no stranger to the courtesan culture of Venice (a pillar of its artistic life), for one of its most notorious sisters, Virginia Padoana, later declared that she honored "all [the English] nation for my Lord of Oxford's sake." Another lady of the night, the poet Veronica Franco, whose *Terze Rime* was published in 1575, would have rubbed shoulders with Oxford at Santa Maria Formosa, as would her patron Domenico

Venier, a retired senator who presided over one of the most celebrated literary coteries in Italy. Franco, who was painted by Tintoretto at the time of her literary debut, had been the lover of Henri III of France, so Oxford may have heard of her first from the lips of the French king during his five-week sojourn in Paris. The three great painters of late-Renaissance Venice, Titian, Veronese, and Tintoretto, all had their studios in the city. Titian in particular enjoyed entertaining foreign dignitaries and artists at his villa-studio on the Birri Grande.

A highly spiced and semifictionalized account of Oxford's adventures in Italy occurs in Thomas Nashe's picaresque novel *The Unfortunate Traveller* (1594), dedicated to the twenty-one-year-old Earl of Southampton. The work purports to be a narrative of the adventures of one Jack Wilton, page to Oxford's uncle, the poet-soldier Henry Howard, Earl of Surrey, during his continental travels.[70] In Nashe's account Surrey, who stands for Oxford, is consumed by his love for the fair Geraldine, a redheaded beauty on whom he sets his cap at Hampton Court, before traveling abroad to do her honor. "The fame of Italy," Surrey tells Jack, "and an especial affection I had unto poetry, my second mistress, for which Italy was so famous, had wholly ravished me unto it." In Rotterdam Surrey pays his respects to Erasmus, "aged learning's chief ornament," before continuing on through Germany. When they finally arrive in Venice they stay at the house of a famous courtesan, Tabitha the Temptress, "a wench that could set as civil a face on it [her whoring] as chastity's first martyr, Lucretia." They are cozened by her into taking counterfeit gold and end up in prison, from which they are released through the good offices of the poet and playwright Pietro Aretino, known for his satire as "the scourge of princes." Jack's eulogy of Aretino, which includes these lines, reads like a comprehensive list of Shakespeare's peculiar virtues as a writer: "His tongue and his invention were forborne; what they thought, they would confidently utter. Princes he spared not, that in the least point transgressed. His life he contemned in comparison of the liberty of speech." The Puritans, we are told, spewed forth their venom at him.

From Venice, Oxford visited Padua, Mantua, Verona, Florence, Siena, Genoa, Milan, Naples, Palermo (and Messina?), and possibly Rome. We don't know whether he made it to Greece and Constantinople; however, reports of an injury he sustained in a Venetian galley suggest that he set off down the Adriatic coast that summer. If so, his route would have taken in towns such as Ragusa on the Illyrian coast, a sovereign city-state that had once been a Venetian colony; and Trogir—also in Illyria—with its famous Orsini chapel. He may even have disembarked on the coast of Bohemia, which did indeed exist between 1575 and 1609, and from there sailed to Sicily. In his *Travels* (1590), Edward Webbe wrote that when he was in Palermo, Oxford challenged all and sundry to single combat for the honor of his queen and country, "for which he was very highly commended, and yet no man durst be so hardy to encounter with him, so that all Italy over he is acknowledged the only chevalier and nobleman of England." Likewise in *The Unfortunate Traveller,* Surrey issues a proud challenge against all comers in Florence, "in defence of his Geraldine's beauty" (Florence was Geraldine's birthplace, just as it is that of Bertram's mistress, Diana, in *All's Well*). His armor was "intermixed with lilies and roses," and his helmet was "round-proportioned like a gardener's water-pot" (Don Quixote–style), from which "seemed to issue forth small threads of water." In *Much Ado* Beatrice mocks a similarly romantic gesture on Benedick's part: "He set up his bills here in Messina, and challenged Cupid at the flight." Given that the Spanish dramatist Miguel Cervantes was in Palermo in the late summer of 1575, the author Mark Anderson speculates that he may have witnessed Oxford's quixotic challenge and so caught a glimpse of his most famous hero in the making.[71]

This aristocratic artist—who enjoyed the rough-and-tumble of commedia dell'arte, put on his own "devices," spun hilarious yarns of his adventures, consorted with all estates of men and women, and lavished alms upon beggars—must indeed have presented a quixotic spectacle to those who observed him on his travels, though judging from the report of Francis Peyto in Milan it is possible that he undertook some parts of his journey incognito. (In *The Unfortunate Traveller* the Earl of Surrey changes names with his page for a while in order to enjoy "more liberty of behavior.") In Venice, Oxford seems to have gone native, throwing himself into the life of the city-state, and becoming something of a cultural icon. In a work by Andrea Perrucci, *Dell'Arte Rappresentativa Premeditata ed all'Improviso,*[72] published in 1699, the section on commedia dell'arte includes a tirade of the tournament (*tirata della giostra*) read out by the stock character Graziano, the talkative Bolognese doctor. "I found myself ambassador of my illustrious

country of Bologna at the court of the Emperor Polidor of Trebizond,"
begins the doctor, before reeling off a list of the dignitaries attending
the tournament to celebrate the emperor's marriage to Irene, Empress
of Constantinople. Among the names appears that of "Elmond, milord
of Oxford." Having described Oxford's horse, weapon, device, and
motto, Graziano relates a comic episode in the joust in which Oxford
and his opponent, Alvida, Countess of Edenberg, are thrown simultaneously, both landing facedown in the dust. The emperor distributes
prizes to all the participants, Oxford being presented with "the horn
of Astolf, paladin of Charlemagne, the magic horn to rout armies—a
spear of sorts to shake, with enchanted consequences." Julia Cooley
Altrocchi writes that Oxford's inclusion in the tirade signifies:

> that he was well and very companionably known at the perfor-
> mances of the *Commedia dell'Arte* and that he was recognized as
> being not only so good a sportsman but so good a sport and pos-
> sessed of so resilient a sense of humor that he could be introduced
> into a skit and, with impunity, described as meeting a woman in
> tilt and being unhorsed and rolled to the ground with her in the
> encounter. One can see him sitting in the performance-room at
> the Doge's Palace, or at the theatre, and hear him roaring during
> this recital of the *Tirade of the Tournament,* delivered hilariously in
> the stage-doctor's Bolognese dialect![73]

Perrucci may have been describing a mock tournament or piece
of theater in which Oxford actually participated. If so, the fabulous
prize that he receives from the emperor may be a witty reference to
the sobriquet that the earl had already adopted for himself ("the spear-
shaker"), or, less likely, may have actually suggested what was to become the most famous pseudonym in literature. That Astolf or Astolfo
was the son of the English king Otto would certainly not have been
lost on those who selected the prize. Oxford would once again be
associated with a celebrated paladin when one of his literary secretaries, Anthony Munday, published *The Famous, Pleasant, and Vari-
able Historie of Palladine of England* on April 23, 1588, Palladine being
the son of King Milanor of England. The ending of the romance is
particularly significant, for it relates Orbiconte's prophecy of the glory
of Palladine's son, Florano, whose deeds "shall be correspondent to
his name, flourishing above all the knights of his time, he being the

only flower that ever grew in England." Significant because it mirrors the mythology of Shake-speare's royal son, whose name, Wriothesley (pronounced "Rose-ly"), was indeed the only flower, i.e., the Tudor Rose of the Sonnets.

Munday also translated the other great works of knight-errantry from the Continent, *Amadis of Gaul, Palmerin d'Oliva, Palmerin of England* (much admired by Cervantes), and *Primaleon of Greece*. A number of these were dedicated to Oxford, citing his "matchless virtues" and deep knowledge of the languages from which the romances were translated—French, Italian, and Spanish. More important, the adventures of the heroes of these romances read like parables of Oxford's own life, and it is clear from Perrucci's anecdote that Oxford saw himself as the hero of a chivalric romance enacted in Tudor England, in which he played the nameless knight who after many trials recovers his inheritance. Amadis de Gaul, for instance, is born of the illicit love of King Perion of Gaul for Elisena of England. Born in secret, he is placed at birth in an ark, which carries him downriver. With him is entrusted his father's sword together with the ring of betrothal Perion had given his beloved, Elisena; and about his neck is placed a parchment with the words, "This is Amadis, son of a king." The baby, who is discovered and adopted by a Caledonian knight, Gandales, comes to be known as "the Child of the Sea." The Earl of Oxford was powerfully drawn to such tales, identifying strongly with their forsaken heroes.

During Oxford's visit, much of Italy, including Milan, Naples, and Sicily, was under Spanish control. Don John of Austria, the bastard brother of Philip II of Spain, was ferrying back and forth between naval bases in Naples and Messina, preparing to take a force north to intervene in the civil war between the old nobility and the new men in Genoa, a city-state vital to Spanish financial interests. Since his victory over the Turks at Lepanto, Don John was a figure of unexampled glamour in Europe, as both a soldier and a womanizer. Unacknowledged by his father, Emperor Charles V, Jeromin, as Don John was known in childhood, had been moved from one foster home to another, until finally taken into the household of the emperor's majordomo as a page (this was a familiar story in the annals of royal bastards). Later, he would become close to his half brother, Philip, who, perhaps envious of his military prowess and

wary of his obvious political ambition, never quite trusted him. Don
John's dream was to liberate Mary Queen of Scots from captivity,
marry her, and occupy the throne of England (to which he had a
strong claim by virtue of his descent from John of Gaunt). He had
also, at one time, put himself forward as a possible husband of Elizabeth. It seems the Earl of Oxford did at times fantasize about being
the English Don John, a modern knight-errant whose deeds would be
celebrated throughout Christendom, and whose bastardy would be
redeemed in a blaze of matchless virtues. (In 1578 Oxford would apply
to the queen to serve under Don John, but was refused.) Lord Henry
Howard, in a letter to the queen of December 1580, claimed that
Oxford had boasted that "Don John sent him fifteen thousand men
to surprise the state of Genoa during the civil war." Charles Arundel,
another erstwhile friend of Oxford's, was to expound upon the theme:

> I have heard him [Oxford] often tell . . . that at his being in Italy
> there fell discord and dissension in the city of Genoa between two
> families whereupon it grew to wars, and great aid and assistance
> given to either party; and that, for the fame that ran through Italy
> of his service done in the Low Countries under the Duke of Alva
> [another tall tale], he was chosen and made general of thirty thou-
> sand that the Pope [supported by the Spanish under Don John]
> sent to the aid of one party, and that in this action he showed so
> great discretion and government, as by his wisdom the matters
> were compounded, and an accord made, being more for his glory
> than if he had fought the battle. This lie is very rife with him and
> in it he glories greatly, diversely hath he told it, and when he enters
> into it he can hardly out, which hath made such sport as often
> have I been driven to rise from his table laughing.

Although Arundel is writing in condemnation of Oxford—and
to save his own skin—he cannot help speaking in flattering terms
of the earl's powers of oratory. As we learn in the very next paragraph, Oxford's apparent accomplishments in Italy, in keeping with
his ideal of the soldier-scholar, were as much intellectual as military and diplomatic:

> His third lie, which hath some affinity with the other two, is of
> certain excellent orations he made, as namely to the state of Venice

at Padua and Bologna, and divers other places in Italy, and one which pleased himself above the rest to his army, when he marched toward Genoa, which when he had pronounced it he left nothing to reply, but everyone to wonder at his judgement, being reputed for his eloquence another Cicero, and for his conduct a Caesar.

Oxford's imagination, it seems, was always at work refashioning his experiences on a mythic plane. After all, self-mythologization is bound to be an essential element of the creativity of a man who feels a constant and powerful need to repair his shattered identity. Oxford's frail sense of self, like a storm-battered tree, once touched by the solar rays of the Italian Renaissance, felt a new surge of energy and warmth. To him Italy was a rebirth. For the first time in his life he felt that the king and the rebel could coexist inside him, and that their friction could act as a spur to his political-artistic ambitions. Not only did he indulge his bohemian propensities there; but, free from the puritanical sanctimony of Burghley and his circle, he and some fellow travelers are said to have converted to Catholicism while on a trip to Rome, a conversion he would later retract. (Oxford, like Don John, had considerable sympathy with Mary Queen of Scots, who embodied the plight of the exiled monarch.) But for now his purpose was to penetrate to the very heart of this miraculous culture so that he could return to England with its essential flame, like Prometheus returning to earth with the fire of the gods in a fennel stalk. No palace, church, or tomb he visited, no play or masque attended, no concert heard, no conversation had with the great creative intellects of the day, but he packed the life-enriching pollen in his thighs, ready to utilize and distribute to his hive of fellow writers.

Writing to Burghley from Venice in September 1575, Oxford, who had just recovered from a fever, feared that his time was no longer sufficient for his desire, "for although I have seen so much as sufficeth me, yet would I have time to profit thereby." He was concerned, too, about his finances: he needed enough money to keep traveling and to pay off his creditors at home. To that end, he instructed Burghley to proceed with the sale of his lands. A letter from Padua dated November 27, 1575, requests his father-in-law to "make no stay of the sales of my land." On January 3, 1576, his tone takes on a greater urgency and he notes that he has authorized Burghley to sell "any portion" of his land, just so long as the capital starts flowing again. Mark Anderson describes Oxford's life since crossing the Alps as one of unabated prodigality, and claims that over the course of fourteen months he spent a total of £4,561, about $1.2 million in today's money. "A traveller!" exclaims Rosalind to the melancholy Jaques in *As You Like It*. "By my faith, you have great reason to be sad. I fear you have sold your own lands to see other men's. Then to have seen much and to have nothing is to have rich eyes and poor hands." To which Jacques replies, "Yes, I have gained my experience." The richness of that experience would furnish Oxford's creative works for decades to come.

Oxford became notorious on his return from the Continent for his Franco-Italian affectations of dress and language, and his interminable traveler's tales. Indeed, the word "traveler" (as in Nashe's *Unfortunate Traveller*) soon came to be one of the principal epithets applied to Oxford by his fellow authors. Ben Jonson, for instance, in *Cynthia's Revels or The Fountain of Self-Love* (1600), a play about his literary rivalry with Oxford-Shakespeare, lampoons him as Amorphus, "the traveler that hath drunk of the fountain, and there tells the wonder of the water"; he did the same in *Every Man Out of His Humour* (1599) in the character of Putarvolo, "a vain-glorious knight" who "over-English[es] his travels." Like Oxford, Amorphus tells tales of meeting all the great leaders of Europe, and having magnificent ladies pay court to him; and he too issues an eccentric challenge to which no one responds. In his *Speculum Tuscanismi* (1580), Gabriel Harvey mocks Oxford as the Italianate Englishman, and having complimented his delicacy of speech, quaintness of array, and conceitedness in all points (i.e., his wit or ingenuity), apostrophizes him thus:

> O thrice ten hundred thousand times blessed and happy,
> Blessed and happy Travail, Travailer most blessed and happy!

"Travail" in Elizabethan times not only meant to toil or be in labor but was a variant of "travel." By harping on "most blessed and happy," Harvey is dropping a heavy hint that he knows of Oxford's royal origins. (Nashe may have applied the title "unfortunate traveller" to the earl as a retort to Harvey.) He also highlights Oxford's eccentricity, calling him "a passing singular odd man." Another likely skit on Oxford, Amoretto, the poet and admirer of Ovid in the *Parnassus* plays (1598-1602), is described as a traveler as well as a "great linguist" who reads in Italian, French, Spanish, and Hebrew. "Farewell, Monsieur Traveller," Rosalind takes her leave of Jaques. "Look you lisp and wear strange suits; disable all the benefits of your own country; be out of love with your nativity, and almost chide God for making you what countenance you are; or I will scarce think you have swam in a gondola."

In his letter of January 3, 1576, Oxford again reminds Burghely that he has decided to continue traveling, "the which thing in nowise I desire your Lordship to hinder, unless you would have it thus *ut nulla sit inter nos amicitia* [that there be no friendship between us]." Yet shortly after his letter from Siena, Oxford headed back over the Alps into France and Germany. It is possible to trace his likely route, knowing as we do that he traveled via Milan and Lyon. As Anderson points out, it is almost certain that he stayed at Tournon-sur-Rhône, where the count of Roussillion (as in Shakespeare's Bertram) held court—one more indication that Oxford revealed his complete Continental itinerary in the plays. In Chapman's *The Revenge of Bussy d'Ambois* (c. 1606), the character of Clermont d'Ambois, who is Chapman's Hamlet, recalls having encountered Oxford in Germany on his way back to England (emphasis mine):

> I overtook, coming from Italy,
> In Germany, a great and famous Earl
> Of England; the most goodly fashion'd man
> I ever saw: from head to foot in form
> Rare and most absolute; he had a face
> Like one of the most ancient honour'd Romans
> From whence his noblest family was deriv'd;
> He was beside of spirit passing great,
> Valiant and learn'd, *and liberal as the sun,*
> Spoke and writ sweetly, or of learned subjects,
> Or of the discipline of public weals;
> And 'twas the Earl of Oxford.
>
> (II.i.259–270)

Chapman is not praising Oxford as Oxford here; he is praising him as Hamlet, royal son and man of the Renaissance.

A HUNDRED SUNDRIE FLOWRES

In trying to trace Shakespeare's lost juvenilia, we would do well to read some of the seminal works of early Elizabethan literature, for many of them bear the stamp of his peculiar psychology. *A Hundred Sundrie Flowres,* for instance, an anthology of verse and prose published in 1573, is covered with Oxford-Shakespeare's fingerprints. It opens with *The Adventures of Master F.I.,* a prose narrative interspersed with poems that has been described as the first novel in English. It is, in effect, a fusion of the stories told in Shakespeare's two long narrative poems, *Venus and Adonis* and *The Rape of Lucrece,* which, taken together, tell the tale of the rape of an exalted figure and the resultant birth of a royal heir. The letters F.I. stand for "Fortunatus Infelix," meaning "the fortunate unhappy," and refer to Oxford's status as Fortune's (Elizabeth's) bastard son, who is unhappy ("infelix") because he cannot be acknowledged as royal ("happy"). The main difference is that the hero F.I., unlike Adonis, does not reject the Venus figure (Elynor); rather, he vows to use his spear to defend her honor:

> Let mighty Mars himself, come armed to the field:
> And vaunt dame Venus to defend, with helmet spear and shield.
> This hand that had good hap, my Helen to embrace,
> Shall have like luck to foil her foes, and daunt them with disgrace.

On more than one occasion the narrator, called G.T., refers rather ominously to "the secret causes why they [F.I.'s poems] were devised," and confirms our suspicions that *Adventures* is a roman à clef by declaring his unwillingness to reveal the true names of its characters. He also discusses problems of interpretation, saying that F.I.'s references in verse to Helen of Troy might be taken to refer to a real Helen at court, rather than Elynor. He explains that F.I. has written the poems in order to express what social convention has dictated he keep to himself:

> and therewith enjoined both by duty and discretion to keep the same covert, [he] can by no means devise a greater consolation, than to commit it into some ciphered words and figured speeches in verse, whereby he feeleth his heart half (or more than half) eased of swelling.

One is reminded of Hamlet's words, "But break my heart, for I must hold my tongue."

The author splits himself between G.T. and F.I., narrator and poet, the one rational and objective, the other emotional and inspired, while Elizabeth's character divides into the faithless Elynor, on the one hand, and Frances, who is chaste and loyal, on the other. We find the same dynamics in Shakespeare's plays. *The Two Gentlemen of Verona,* an early work from the mid-1570s, sees Shakespeare-Oxford splitting himself into Valentine and Proteus, the loyal and treacherous sides of his nature. Qua Valentine he is the loyal lover banished for the sake of his love; qua Proteus he is the double-crossing friend who attempts to rape the object of his passion. Understanding as we do, however, that Shakespeare-Oxford is trying to take back his very identity through this "rape," we can share Julia's tender sympathy for the tortured Proteus and see in it the poet's fantasy of redemption:

> Poor wounded name: my bosom, as a bed,
> Shall lodge thee till thy wound be throughly heal'd;
> And thus I search it with a sovereign kiss.
>
> (I.ii.115–117)

It is interesting to note that Shakespeare's principal source for *Two Gentlemen* was Jorge de Montemayor's *Diana Enamorada* (1542), meaning "Diana in Love," which was not translated from Spanish into English until 1598.

The remaining sections of the anthology, all in verse, ring the changes on *Adventures,* plumbing the emotional depths of the relationship between F.I. and Elynor under different names. While F.I. metamorphoses into "Meritum petere, grave," "Fato non fortuna," "Ever or Never," Dan Phoebus or Dan Bartholomew of Bath, Elynor becomes Dame Nature, Bathsheba, "Ferenda Natura," "sovereign," Helen of Troy, Cleopatra, "mighty goddess"—and even Lucrece. But the name that occurs most often in conjunction with this commanding lover is Cressida, who stands for treachery, with Troilus embodying truth. The tale that emerges is one of broken troth and perfidy on the part of the "goddess," and despite the poet's frequent attempts to assert her ultimate virtue in the teeth of manifold deceptions, his bitterness is unmistakable: "and in deed I must confess that the opinion which I have conceived of my Mistress hath stirred my pen to write very hardly against all the feminine gender."

More striking for our purposes, however, is the poet's sense of duty toward the moral health of his sovereign lady, and his deep desire to redeem her. We are reminded of Hamlet's concern for Gertrude:

> So labor'd I to save thy wandering ship,
> Which reckless then, was running on the rocks,
> And though I saw thee seem to hang the lip
> And set my great good will, as light as flocks:
> Yet haul'd I in, the main sheet of my mind,
> And stayed thy course by anchors of advice,
> I won thy will into a better wind,
> To save thy ware, which was of precious price.[74]

There is even a premonition of Hamlet's "The play's the thing / Wherein I'll catch the conscience of the King," especially when one remembers that Hamlet's priority throughout is to save his mother, rather than convict his father's murderer:

> And so to beate my simple shiftlesse brayne,
> For some device, that might redeeme thy state.[75]

A "device" was commonly an interlude or masque put on at court. Like Hamlet, this poet stands for truth, which in turn seems to partake of the idea of royalty or a rightful claim to share in the power that his lady possesses. Hence the following lament, made by Dan Bartholomew of Bath:

> Is this the right reward for suche desart?
> Is this the fruite of seede so timely sowne?
> Is this the price, appoynted for his part?
> Shall truth be thus by treason overthrowne?[76]

The "fruit of seed so timely sown" most likely refers to a royal child conceived by the poet's sovereign mistress. The poet burns and freezes according to her moods, not only submitting himself to the transforming power of the alchemical bath, but vowing "to serve this Saint for term of all his life" even though he knows her to be "both root and rind of all his strife." The saint in question is of course Diana, the goddess of chastity—a pointed reference to the English queen's cult of virginity or, less grandly, her plastering art. In his "Dolorous Discourses" Dan Bartholomew is explicit about his lady's self-canonization:

> Not so content, thou furthermore didst swear
> That of thy self thou never meant to swerve,
> For proof whereof thou didst the colors wear,
> Which might bewray what saint you meant to serve.
> And that thy blood was sacrificed eke,
> To manifest thy steadfast martyred mind.[77]

Thus the lady's intention is placed above her acts, and the fact that she "never meant to swerve" becomes the basis of her official chastity. The colors that she wore to mark her allegiance to Diana were Elizabeth's favorite combination: black and white (the colors of the moon), which offset her red hair to such effect. Hence she is called Dame Cynthia in other verses in the collection, while he—her sun—is Dan Phoebus ("the shining one"). The blood that was sacrificed to maintain the queen's martyred status was that of her off-spring, i.e., Fortunatus Infelix (F.I.) himself. His truth was denied in order to preserve her reputation as the dedicated bride of her people. Her treachery ("the wasted vows which fled every wind") will not diminish his devotion to her, but the truth that has been abnegated or made taboo—the truth of his identity—will become the heart of his poetry. For good or ill, she is his muse. More than that, she is his life. As Valentine says of Silvia in *Two Gentlemen:*

> She is my essence; and I leave to be,
> If I be not by her fair influence
> Foster'd, illumin'd, cherish'd, kept alive.
> (III.i.182–184)

Literature in those days was often a means of political one-upmanship or revenge, and Oxford may have used the publication of *Flowres* to strike a blow at Christopher Hatton, his principal rival for the queen's love at that time, knowing that the surface story could be construed by court readers as a parody of Hatton's extravagant and self-abasing courtship of Elizabeth. Hatton got his own back three years later, when Oxford was on the Continent, for he had a bowdlerized version issued under the title *The Posies of George Gascoigne,* with *The Adventures of Master F.I.* explained away as a translation of an Italian fable. Thus at one stroke the work was depoliticized and all traces of Oxford's authorship were removed. To add insult to injury, the queen awarded Gascoigne the post of poet laureate. Oxford expressed his feelings by writing a song called "The Forsaken Man," which begins:

> A crown of bays shall that man wear
> That triumphs over me.

She was punishing her "Turk" for writing too freely of royal affairs.

Shakespeare as Euphues

The critics of the nineteenth century and the early twentieth century were baffled by what they perceived as Oxford's sudden disappearance after a blazing start in the world of letters. They were no less bemused by his apparent exclusion from public life, which they deemed to be a result of his "fickle head" and emotional instability. In fact Oxford took advantage of his alienation from family and society by going underground and creating a literary school that rallied to his cause. Far from disappearing or going silent, he had simply dived down to that same riverbed where Ophelia met her end.

There is no doubt that great artists are self-absorbed, and they are often accused of egocentricity by their kith and kin. Oxford himself has been censured for appalling selfishness and hard-heartedness by historians and English professors, who have in many cases convinced themselves that such behavior disqualifies him from having been Shakespeare. As if moral rectitude has ever been a valid index of artistic greatness! A brief glance at the lives of Mozart, Beethoven, Liszt, Wagner, Marlowe, Coleridge, De Quincey, Byron, Dickens, Auden, Pound, Picasso, and a host of others might convince us that the reverse is true. In a letter of July 13, 1576, Oxford wrote to Burghley, "For always I have and will still prefer mine own content before others," and this was not an unusual sentiment coming from his pen. What Oxford never complained of, however, was the company of other artists; indeed, he seemed inspired by their presence, and was able to write fluently and with total concentration in the company of his literary fellows; this—together with the fact that he did not have to earn a living—may help explain his prolific output. Jonson wrote of Shakespeare that certain actors had said "he never blotted [i.e., crossed out] a line," suggesting that like Mozart he composed in his head, the writing itself being no more than dictation. Oxford-Shakespeare is mocked by his fellow writers (notably Ben Jonson) in the guise of characters like Amorphus for using every occasion to improvise some fancy speech or other. Dickens had the same talent. He would extemporize both aloud and in his head in the idiom of his characters, often acting them out in front of his children, envisaging a whole chapter in detail before putting pen to paper.

As we've seen, Oxford's return from Italy prompted a dam-burst of works (poetry, drama, romances), some put out anonymously, others published under the name of one or other of his literary confreres. In 1576 a poetical anthology, *The Paradyse of Daynty Devises,* appeared, presenting works by ten different authors. In the best poems of the collection we feel art taking its life from the soil of personal experience rather than the conventional themes of the collective. True imagination as opposed to mere fancy is at work, and a refreshing realism breaks through. One senses a culture on the brink of discovering new personal depths, a feeling encapsulated by this couplet from Thomas Lord Vaux's "He desyreth exchange of lyfe":

> *Narcissus* brought unto the water brink,
> So aye thirst I, the more that I do drink.[78]

This new self-awareness is most fully embodied in the poems that come from the pen of "E.O." (Edward Oxenford), in some of which one can hear the Shakespearean soliloquy taking form. One in particular, "Not attaining to his desire, he complaineth," could have been spoken by a youthful Hamlet and expresses the sense of self-division and inner paradox that are characteristic of Shakespeare's mature heroes. The poet E.O. has the same narcissistic streak as F.I., and in "His good name being blemished, he bewaileth" he calls upon the powers of nature to join him in lamenting the loss of his good name (see p. 75). In another poem he complains that he is not receiving credit for his (literary) achievements; and in the song "The Forsaken Man," it becomes apparent that the poet's literary and amorous ambitions are woven of the same cloth: in both he aims for the highest prize. All in all, E.O.'s work transmits an energy that cannot be confined within the compass of court convention. If we are looking for the early footprints of Shakespeare the lyric poet, *Paradyse* is a good place to continue the search.

Before the appearance of Marlowe on the literary scene, the 1580s were dominated by the figure of John Lyly, whose two *Euphues* romances (1578, 1580) ran to thirty editions in fifty years and sparked a linguistic fad—Euphuism—that held court culture in thrall for a decade. The technique and themes of the two novels, *Euphues: The Anatomy of Wit* and *Euphues and His England* (the second dedicated to the Earl of Oxford), are close to those of *The Adventures of Master F.I.* In many ways *Euphues* is a creation myth of the English renaissance, an allegory of the process by which England assimilated cultural influences from the Continent and developed its own literary language. But as important as the process is the man who was its principal vehicle, Euphues himself, who travels from Athens to Italy and England, and back again, sowing his wild oats and imitating the pattern of the prodigal son. Busy pollinating English language and culture from the treasury of European literature, Euphues is none other than our old friend Oxford-Shakespeare, "the Traveller." And being a traveller, he wanders beyond the confines of the two *Euphues* books and into the literary world of Elizabethan London, where he is feted by the leading writers of the time. Anthony Munday, for one, in dedicating his *Zelauto* (1580) to Oxford, drops a very broad hint as to Euphues's true identity:

> Zelauto. The Fountain of Fame. Erected in an Orchard of Amorous Adventures. Containing a Delicate Disputation, gallantly discoursed between two noble gentlemen of Italy. Given for a friendly entertainment to Euphues, at his late arrival in England. By A.M. Servant to the Right Honourable the Earle of Oxenforde.

Moreover, Euphues's love for Queen Elizabeth, to whom he delivers an encomium in the section entitled "Glass for Europe," is more than hinted at, and has a martyred, self-sacrificing quality that is also a pronounced element of *Flowres*. At the very end of the second volume, the narrator questions whether Euphues's constancy toward his love isn't a form of madness. In terms of poetic inspiration, this is of course exactly what it is.

Euphues ("witty") and his alter ego Philautus ("self-loving") are the rival brothers of Shakespearean drama, forming a composite hero from conflicting character traits within the author. Thus at the end of *Euphues* one can sense the competing pulls of solitary and married life, as expressed in the divergent fates of the two friends. "Gentlemen, Euphues is musing in the bottom of the Mountain of Silixsedra, Philautus married in the isle of England. Two friends parted: the one living in the delights of his new wife, the other in contemplation of his old griefs. What Philautus doth they can imagine that are newly married; how Euphues liveth they may guess that are cruelly martyred."[79] Despite a strong reclusive streak, Euphues revels in company and conversation, and his wit, we are told, is like wax, "apt to receive any impression," there being none more witty than he.

The doubleness and self-division in *Euphues,* the conflict between instinct and intellect, will and wit, is highly Shakespearean. The characters' actions continually contradict their arguments and discourses. As Steinberg observes, "The characters almost always mean something besides what they say; advice is never followed, either by the advisor or advisee; ambiguities abound."[80] The more they attempt to use their intellect to impose order on their lives, the more unconsciously they appear to act. And although they may not be quite ready to welcome indiscretion as an ally (like Hamlet in his sea gown), nevertheless one can see in Euphues himself the same protean genius that Shakespeare later fashioned into his most famous hero, as well as the same core psychological insight that "*Nature* workes her will from contraries."[81] Likewise, the root of their self-contradictoriness is the same: for political reasons Euphues and Hamlet cannot say what they really mean and cannot reveal the true nature of their love. Behind both heroes the paradoxical figure of Queen Elizabeth smiles her Gioconda smile. As Euphues writes in holding her up as a "glass for Europe":

> As this noble prince is endued with mercy, patience, and moderation, so is she adorned with singular beauty and chastity, excelling in the one Venus, in the other Vesta. Who knoweth not how rare a thing it is, ladies, to match virginity with beauty, a chaste mind with an amiable face, divine cogitations with a comely countenance? But such is the grace bestowed upon this earthly goddess that, having the beauty that might allure all princes, she hath the chastity also to refuse all, accounting it no less praise to be called a virgin than to be esteemed a Venus, thinking it as great honour to be found chaste as thought amiable.[82]

Come *Hamlet,* honesty and beauty would no longer hold discourse with each other.

From the late 1570s John Lyly was secretary to the Earl of Oxford, who in 1580, upon taking the lease on the Blackfriars theater, installed him as manager. (Gabriel Harvey described Lyly as "the fiddlestick of Oxford.") The name Lyly would be highly fitting as a front for Oxford to hide behind, as the flower of that name denoted both virginity and royalty (e.g., the fleur-de-lis of the Prince of Wales). Lyly's plays, which were privately produced during the 1580s by Oxford's company of boy players, both at Blackfriars and at court, were all (very oddly for a professional playwright) published anonymously. They possess a seamless interweaving of myth, history, politics, and dream that is so enchanting a quality of Shakespeare's best work.

Lyly is adept at diving down into the unconscious of Queen Elizabeth and her court and bringing up the myths that animate their psychology of love. Thus the plays become deeply personal and revealing, and must have been written by one who partook profoundly of the queen's psyche. In the court prologue to *Sappho and Phao,* the author addresses the queen thus: "and I on knee for all, entreat that your Highness imagine yourself to be in a deep dream that, staying the conclusion, in your rising your Majesty vouchsafe but to say, 'And so you awaked.'" The "deep dream" is the cathartic experience of art offered by the author.

Through the tale of the mortal man falling in love with the goddess, Lyly explores the relationship between the poet and his queen. In a sense, all Lyly's plays are hymns to the moon goddess—*not* panegyrics, for that would be too simplistic, but hymns, half celebrating, half lamenting the devotional pains of the mortal who pursues the love of the divine. For madness, whether in the form of inspiration or insanity, is the price of wearing the moon's livery. As Niobe says to her suitor Sylvestris, "Beleeve me . . . the onely way to be mad is to be constant."[83] This notion is taken to its extreme in *Endimion,* where the poet (or shepherd) becomes the man in the moon, the ultimate image for the alienation of the artist.

The moon goddess is, on one level, a representation of Elizabeth, and the daring with which Lyly treats his theme precludes a writer from outside the court as the true author of these remarkable plays. For instance, *The Woman in the Moone,* Lyly's only verse drama, seems to be a satire on the chaos that Elizabeth created in her love relations at court through her fickleness, deceit, and inconstancy. As the heroine Pandora she chooses the moon, of all the planets, to live on. The moon, Lyly seems to say, is Elizabeth's ruling planet, for it best reflects her arbitrary nature. As Nature instructs Pandora in her closing speech:

> Now rule, *Pandora,* in fair *Cynthia's* stead,
> And make the moon inconstant like thyself;
> Reign thou at women's nuptials, and their birth;
> Let them be mutable in all their loves,
> Fantastical, childish, and foolish, in their desires,
> Demanding toys: and stark mad
> When they cannot have their will.[84]

Tellus in *Endimion* repeats the sentiment with greater economy in the words, "There are no colors so contrary as white and black." In the same play, the oracle on the bed of the sacred fountain describes the moon goddess by inverting Elizabeth's motto "Ever the same" (*Semper eadem*) to "Always one, *yet never the same:* still inconstant, yet never wavering." The queen, remember, was in the audience: the play was addressed to her. Lyly, like Shakespeare, positions himself as Cupid, the rebellious son of Venus, who sets the drama in motion by shooting one of his love arrows. In *Love's Metamorphosis,* Cupid even triumphs over the chaste goddess Ceres and her icy nymphs, for whether divine, semidivine, or mortal, everyone, including Queen Elizabeth, must acknowledge the power of love. Hiding in the moon is no solution. If the monarch denies love, Lyly seems to say, she will become an emotional tyrant.

It is curious that Lyly's first editor, Edward Blount, describes him as "a rare and excellent poet," since only one of his plays is written in verse (the blank verse of *The Woman in the Moone*), and he has left us no other poetry. If Lyly had written poetry, however, it would surely read like the verses that appeared under the name Thomas Watson, especially the *Hekatompathia or Passionate Century of Love*, which he dedicated to the Earl of Oxford in 1582. Again, the names of Oxford's associates are suggestive. Thomas means "twin," and doubting Thomas was the one who doubted Christ (as Shakespeare doubts the divinity of the Virgin Queen), while Wat-son in effect means "son and heir," with the usual pun on "hare," for which "wat" was a common dialect word. (One thinks of poor Wat the hare in *Venus and Adonis*.) The title page of *Hekatompathia* announces that the work is "Divided into two parts: whereof, the first expresseth the author's sufferance in love: the latter, his long farewell to love and all its tyranny. Composed by Thomas Watson Gentleman; and published at the request of certain Gentlemen his *very* friends" (*very* being a pun on Oxford's family name, Vere). The scholarly commentaries accompanying the poems have long been thought to be Oxford's work, and according to C. S. Lewis "are the most interesting part of the book." He also remarks, "Watson is perhaps closer to Shakespeare than to any other sonneteer in his conception of the sonnet."

Here, in 100 eighteen-line sonnets, we witness the same devotional philosophy of love that sustains Lyly's plays, as well as the life-and-death struggle with the goddess that was so marked a feature of another poetic century, *A Hundred Sundrie Flowres* (1573). Here too are all the mythic and historical characters, from Alexander to Gallathea, that we find in Lyly, and the manifold exchanges between gods and men. We feel in the author the gentle, hypersensitive spirit that in King Lear is driven beyond the bounds of sanity. Unsurprisingly, the poet of *Passionate Century* identifies with Actaeon, but cannot reveal the name of his goddess:

Diana was afraid he would report
What secrets he had seen in passing by:
   To tell but truth, the selfsame hurt have I
   By viewing her, for whom I daily die . . .
         life availeth nought
Where service cannot have a due reward:
   I dare not name the Nymph that works my smart.[85]

In the commentary preceding the sonnet, the anonymous anno-
tator remarks that Ovid compared himself to Actaeon after his banishment at the hands of Augustus Caesar, and quotes the relevant Latin
passage from Book II of the *Tristia*. The implication is that Watson,
too, whoever he may be, is suffering some form of exile. In Sonnet
X the poet is blinded for gazing on Minerva's "naked side," and in
Sonnet 49 of *The Tears of Fancie or Love Disdained,* published anonymously in 1593, the author—long thought to be Watson—again treats
of Actaeon, punning throughout on hart and heart, and lamenting
the fact that he "would speak but could not, so did sigh and die."

If one examines the mythic forces that drove and shaped the
English literary Renaissance, from *The Songs and Sonnets of Henry
Howard* in 1557 to the anonymous *Tears of Fancy* in 1593, one is forced
to conclude that rather than springing out of nowhere in 1593 with
the publication of *Venus and Adonis,* Shakespeare was busy developing his distinctive voice and style throughout the 1560s, 1570s, and
1580s, and may have used other names during this period of experimentation and transformation or created a school of literature that
bore the stamp of his guiding mythology. (Robert Greene—the
French for Green being *vert,* which is how Vere was pronounced in
Elizabethan times—is another highly significant name in the Oxford-
Shakespeare circle.) No one writes a 1,200-line poem of the quality
of *Venus and Adonis* without an extended literary apprenticeship.

In 1592 Thomas Nashe dedicated his *Strange Newes* to a mysterious gentleman, "his *verie* friend Maister *Apis Lapis*"—again the pun
on Vere—whom he describes as "the most copious carminist of our
time" (*carmen* in Latin being a song, poem, or verse). In other words,
Nashe is hailing his dedicatee as the most prolific poet of the age. Since
he goes on to address this poet as "Gentle M[aster] William," it has
been widely assumed that he is referring to Shakespeare. Ovid himself

describes his *Metamorphoses* as "*perpetuum carmen,*" which also implies a sense of copiousness, and is echoed in Polonius's pompous phrase "poem unlimited." Jonathan Bate, in *Shakespeare and Ovid,* describes the Roman poet as "the most copious of authors." In 1598 the critic Francis Meres wrote of Shakespeare, "As the soule of Euphorbus was thought to live in Pythagoras: so the sweete wittie soule of Ovid lives in mellifluous and hony-tongued Shakespeare." (The reference to Pythagoras alerts us to the idea that Shakespeare kept reincarnating himself by assuming different literary identities.)

One can trace Shakespeare's flight from the hounds of the goddess, from Master F.I. through to the appearance of Jaques in *As You Like It.* Euphues, the court dramas of Lyly, the sonnets of Thomas Watson, and the romances of Greene and Munday all form a bridge between *Flowres* in 1573, when the young Shakespearean poet first records his divine trespass in verse, and *Venus and Adonis,* Shakespeare's mature poetic testament twenty years later. It is difficult at this remove to sort out exactly who wrote what, for Oxford's literary studio, first at the Savoy and then in Bishopsgate, was a busy place, and like any genius he had many imitators. What is certain is that the work known as the First Folio of Shakespeare's comedies, histories, and tragedies is the crown of this poet's work, not its entirety. And though others may have followed his standard, dipping their quills in his cause, he alone lived the life of allegory on which his plays comment with such lasting power.

In the summer of 1578, during the queen's progress to East Anglia, when Elizabeth and her court were at Lord Henry Howard's estate Audley End, the Cambridge scholar and rhetorician Gabriel Harvey presented her majesty with several printed speeches in Latin in honor of herself and her leading courtiers—Leicester, Burghley, Hatton, Sidney, and Oxford—entitled *Gratulationes Valdinenses.* In his address to Oxford, Harvey cunningly used the pretext of encouraging him to take up arms in defense of his country (which was then happily at peace) as a means of outing him as a professional writer. This was not a speech written out of concern for the security of England, nor indeed for the court career of the Earl of Oxford, but a spiteful attempt to shame a literary genius of whom Harvey was bitterly envious. Using the sort of exaggerated rhetoric that was the hallmark of Oxford's traveler's tales, he paints a picture of this literary earl as a fearsome champion of his native land. Harvey's snide agenda notwithstanding, the oration speaks volumes about Oxford's prolific talent and broad cultural interests, not to mention the spear-shaking persona that he had already created for himself. Here is an extract from B. M. Ward's prose translation of Harvey's hexameters (emphasis mine):

> O great-hearted one, strong in thy mind and thy fiery will, thou wilt conquer thyself, thou wilt conquer others; thy glory will spread out in all directions beyond the Arctic Ocean; and England will put thee to the test and prove thee to be a native-born Achilles. Do thou but go forward and without hesitation. Mars will obey thee, Hermes will be thy messenger, *Pallas striking her shield with her spear shaft will attend thee,* thine own breast and courageous heart will instruct thee. For a long time past Pheobus Apollo has cultivated thy mind in the arts. English poetical measures have been sung by thee long enough. Let that Courtly Epistle[86]—more polished even than the writings of Castiglione himself—witness how greatly thou dost excel in letters. I have seen many Latin verses of thine, yea, even more English verses are extant; thou hast drunk deep draughts not only of the Muses of France and Italy, but hast learned the manners of many men, and the arts of foreign countries. . . . Neither in France, Italy, nor Germany are any such cultivated and polished men. O thou hero worthy of renown, throw away the insignificant pen, throw away bloodless books, and writings that serve no useful purpose; now must the sword be brought into play, now is the time for thee to sharpen the spear and to handle great engines of war.
>
> In thy breast is noble blood, Courage animates thy brow, Mars lives in thy tongue, Minerva strengthens thy right hand, Bellona reigns in thy body, within thee burns the fire of Mars. Thine eyes flash fire, *thy countenance shakes spears;* who would not swear that Achilles had come to life again?[87]

~ *6* ~

The one word that explains the Shakespeare miracle is unconsciousness.
                                                    —Henry David Thoreau

SHAKESPEARE'S THREEFOLD IMAGINATION

In *Shakespeare Identified,* Thomas Looney gave us a single believable author, a human Shakespeare. In his hands the works made sense as the poet's attempt to understand his experiences by turning them over on the anvil of his imagination. Looney could be said to have re-united Shakespeare with his corpus—and thus with the history of his times—or at least to have begun this heroic task. A vital part of the process is to see the works as a single story, for despite their apparent diversity, the tales Shakespeare dramatized have a strong thematic unity, bound together as they are by the author's inner story. Even the genre divisions of comedy, tragedy, history, and romance seem false.

Shakespeare's choice of plots for his plays was not arbitrary; he chose them because they reflected themes that were crucial to his life. All were taken from classical or medieval sources, which on the political level provided him with a vital tool, deniability. As Clare Asquith writes in her discussion of Shakespeare's sources for *Richard III,* "Like Hamlet who defends his political court play by claiming it is a harmless translation from the Italian, [Shakespeare] can point to an innocent precedent."[88] In other words, offensive material could be laid at the door of the source. Shakespeare did not wake up one morning and decide to write a play about honor because his last one had been about ambition; like all true writers, he wrote to heal the wounds to his soul, to remake the shattered world in which he found himself. Indeed, once one has noted the extraordinarily personal nature of his works, the author's soul journey emerges very clearly, from exuberant Renaissance prince (Berowne) to disillusioned courtier and political dissident (Hamlet) to social outcast (Timon) to visionary philosopher (Prospero). As for Shakespeare's motifs (which are the motive power of his works), they speak volumes about his own predicament: usurpation of royal right; the fall from grace; loss of power; loss of name; exile; disinheritance; banishment; the alienated courtier; the royal bastard; the concealed heir; the court fool who tells his truth in jest; the hidden man revealed; the lost man found; the poet-prince; the philosopher-king.

It is through an author's imagery and themes that one learns how ideas associate themselves in his mind, and gains an insight into the nature of his obsessions. As Caroline Spurgeon writes:

> Like the man who under stress of emotion will show no sign of it in eye or face, but reveal it in some muscular tension, the poet unwittingly lays bare his own innermost likes and dislikes, observations and interests, associations of thought, attitudes of mind and beliefs, in and through the images, the verbal pictures he draws to illuminate something quite different in the speech and thought of his characters.[89]

The key phrase here is "unwittingly lays bare," as the process of making images is largely unconscious, fashioned from the invisible components of the individual imagination, rather like an alphabet arising out of the unconscious of a new race. Some of the elements that go to make up an author's images are conscious, but many are unknown to him—are hidden or repressed—and constitute the material from which the formative myths of his life are woven. In this hinterland of the soul, where images hatch, we are very close to the heartbeat of motivation, of sensing *why* an author writes as he does.

Spurgeon points out that in drama, as opposed to more formal types of poetry, especially the Elizabethan drama, which was written "red-hot," the images poured forth in a surge of heightened feeling unimpeded by the conscious mind. This seems to have been particularly true in Shakespeare's case. Ben Jonson, for instance, wrote that Shakespeare "had an excellent phantasie, brave notions, and gentle expressions, wherein *he flow'd with that facility, that sometime it was necessary he should be stopp'd*." It is true, too, of all those fabulous talkers he created, including Hamlet, Romeo, Berowne, Benedick, Beatrice, Bottom, Falstaff, Philip the Bastard, Petruchio, Parolles, and Prince Hal.

The imagery and themes in Shakespeare's plays often operate as an undercurrent that goes against the tide of the primary or overt plot (the surface story), forming what might be described as an ulterior plot of their own, which gives depth and complexity to the characters' motives. This ulterior or subconscious plot is highly personal to the author and functions as a parallel drama within the play—a kind of soul drama in which the characters represent warring elements in the poet's being, of which he will be largely unaware. Nor are these characters in the least discreet; instead they resemble the players of whom Hamlet says, "[They] cannot keep counsel: they'll tell all."

In *Hamlet,* for example, the incest theme, of which very little overt mention is made during the play, branches out willy-nilly in Shakespeare's imagination (and far beyond his conscious intention) to penetrate the lives of Hamlet, Gertrude, Ophelia, Laertes, and even Polonius. In *A Midsummer Night's Dream* the royal marriage of Theseus and Hippolyta, together with the happy reconciliation of the four parted lovers, is undermined by a darker story, fraught with menace: the story of Bottom's lost kingdom, Bottom being an impolitic weaver of words, who enchants the fairy queen with his singing (poetry), but whose tongue must be tied in case he blabs. His "most rare" vision, which is beyond the wit of man to relate, is nothing as banal as the dream-like memory of an ass's head; it is the specter of the crown which the fairy queen's love for him seemed to portend. "Methought I was—and methought I had, but man is but a patch'd fool if he will offer to say what methought I had." As Caroline Spurgeon writes:

> It is noticeable how continually [Shakespeare] associates dreaming with kingship and flattery, so much so that one might almost deduce that he had often dreamed he was himself a king of men, surrounded by homage and sweet flattering words, and had awakened to find this but empty and vain imagining.[90]

The power of Shakespeare's ulterior plots bespeaks an intensely subjective art, a sort of literary narcissism, if that's not too strong a word. This subjectivity was noted by T. S. Eliot, who pronounced *Hamlet* an artistic failure on that score. He found that Hamlet's powerful emotions toward his mother, which dominate his actions, are "in excess of the facts [of the play] as they appear." In other words they have no objective foundation in the plot, or, in Eliot's special phrase, no "objective correlative." This is true. What Eliot didn't see, however, is that such excess of emotion is everywhere in Shakespeare and flows out beyond the confines of the plays; this is why his heroes are so disarmingly real and give the impression that they are speaking directly to us, over the heads of the other characters. King Lear's colossal unprovoked fury at Cordelia's honest profession of love has its origin outside the play, as does Timon's loathing of female sexuality: these emotions overwhelm the action, flooding the margins of Shakespeare's text and pulling us into his psychic flow.

Because there is no objective correlative for these overpowering emotions in the characters and plot of a given play, we must look instead to the life of the author himself (to what might be termed the *subjective* correlative). In *Hamlet,* the hero's suicidal despair, yoked as it is to his violent sense of disgust at the Queen, is likely to proceed from Shakespeare's own incestuous or quasi-incestuous relationship with his mother. And if his mother was the Virgin Queen, one can understand why he could not be more explicit (and why there is no objective correlative for Hamlet's horror of female sexuality); it would also explain his displaced rage toward Ophelia. Incest, it seems, is the cause of Hamlet's dissolving sense of identity and his inability to take his father's place on the throne.

The guardedness that Shakespeare necessarily exercised in his dealings with the state activated the unconscious to an extraordinary degree in his literary work, forcing hidden content into the light through the revelations of his characters. This happens most patently when characters are attempting to control their thoughts and hide their true feelings. For it is a truism that the more one tries to curb one's thoughts and speech, the more active the unconscious becomes in introjecting slips of the mind and tongue, which reflect the true feelings of the subject. Good examples in *Hamlet* are the speeches of Claudius in his lengthy conversation with the rebellious Laertes, in

which the two plot to kill the prince. In his final speech before
Gertrude enters, Claudius unwittingly describes the dynamics of the
repressed thought: "If this should fail, / *And that our drift look through
our bad performance,* / 'Twere better not essay'd." (Claudius cannot
reconcile that he is both king and murderer.)

This same tide of feeling informs Shakespeare's humor, flowing
through his works with wonderful indiscretion and filling the characters of his invention, as if the entire canon were one colossal Freudian slip. "Masters," cries Bottom to his fellow players, "I am to
discourse wonders: but ask me not what; for if I tell you, I am not
true Athenian. I will tell you everything, right as it fell out." Hamlet
perhaps comes closest to describing the involuntary creativity of the
unconscious mind when he says to Horatio:

> And prais'd be rashness for it: let us know
> Our indiscretion sometime serves us well
> When our deep plots do pall.
>
> (V.ii.7–9)

No character illustrates the power of Shakespeare's indiscretion
better than Falstaff, who as king of misrule represents an essential
function of Shakespeare's art. His priceless reply to Colevile of the
Dale, one of the rebels at York, when Colevile kneels before him
with the words "I think you are Sir John Falstaff," gives a perspective rather different from Hamlet's. "I have a whole school of tongues
in this belly of mine," exclaims the fat knight, "and not a tongue of
them but speaks any other word but my name. And I had but a belly
of any indifferency, I were simply the most active fellow in Europe:
my womb, my womb, my womb undoes me." This great teeming
womb of Falstaff's is, of course, Shakespeare's almost monstrous creativity, which is his undoing both because of its wide-ranging indiscretion and because of its obsession with the author's identity (i.e.,
speaking his name). No wonder Jonson, in *Cynthia's Revels* (1601),
satirized Shakespeare as Amorphus, a man "so made out of the mixture of shreds and forms, that himself is truly deformed."

All of this is to say that the unconscious supports and nurtures
Shakespeare's text in a unique manner, which has much to do with
the author's anonymity and frail sense of identity. The power of

Shakespeare's art lies in its boundlessness; the fact that his characters transcend the roles they play in their allotted dramas, and engage us in the larger drama of the author's identity crisis. In this way, we partake of Shakespeare's mythic field of experience—his unconscious life. Indeed, the unconscious is an excellent metaphor for the concealed poet, because although it lies hidden, it uses its untold ingenuity to "break cover" and make itself known through arresting images and involuntary revelations, constantly balancing a character's assertions with their hidden antitheses. The unconscious *is* in fact a concealed author or, in the words of D. H. Lawrence, a "secret agent," a carrier of ideas disowned by the individual or his society, or both. That Shakespeare himself was a concealed poet goes some way toward explaining why the unconscious mind was so active in his art.

Because the coordinates of Shakespeare's art lie in the unconscious, not in consistency of plot and character, he engages us more profoundly than any other writer. For this reason, too, his work is a gift to actors: their interpretive space is greatly expanded by all that is going on between the lines. The objective correlative in Shakespeare, the consciously contrived plot, takes second place to this vast unconscious intention, which is ultimately the remaking and assertion of the author's identity. It is the ulterior plot that fashions the hidden, poetic crown. As Richard II says, "Now is this golden crown like a deep well / That owes two buckets, filling one another, / The emptier ever dancing in the air, / The other down, unseen, and full of water."

There is another type of plot in Shakespeare's plays, between the primary and ulterior plots, which is an expression of the author's conscious attempt to tell the untold history of his time, and is very much the creation of Shakespeare the satirist, who, in disguising his portraits of court and government figures, carefully calculated how thin a coat of camouflage would protect him from the wrath of his victims. It was like playing a game of verbal cat and mouse. Through it, Shakespeare's verbal ingenuity was refined, making double meanings and hidden messages second nature. Even the names of characters contain clues as to their nonfictional identity. In the first quarto of *Hamlet,* for instance, the Polonius figure is called Corambis, meaning "double-hearted," a clear swipe at Lord Burghley's motto *Cor unum, via una* ("One heart, one way").

What might seem obscure or unmotivated to us may well have made more sense to Shakespeare's court audience and in particular to the queen, for they shared with the author a common field of experience that has been largely lost over time. Certain things did not need to be spelled out, such as private court feuds or who was sleeping with whom. Audiences would have picked up on the innuendo immediately, as when Hamlet holds up the portraits of his father and Claudius and asks Gertrude, "Have you eyes? / Could you on this fair mountain leave to feed / And batten on this moor?" One of Leicester's nicknames at court was "Gypsy," which, like "Moor," connoted dark looks. Equally, Hamlet's curious declaration to Claudius, "I eat the air, promise-crammed. You cannot feed capons so" is a gibe at Sir Christopher Hatton (cap-on = hat-on), one of Elizabeth's most richly rewarded favorites, for whom assurances of favor were never mere "promises."

The semi-royal prominence given to Laertes can seem puzzling to us, but Shakespeare's court audience would have understood the web of contemporary relationships that determined or reshaped those at Elsinore. With Elizabeth as Gertrude and her lover Robert Dudley, Earl of Leicester, as Claudius, it is not hard to see that Laertes, who is treated as a surrogate son by Claudius, stands for Leicester's stepson Robert Devereux, Earl of Essex. This identification makes sense of the mob's otherwise baffling cry of "Laertes shall be king, Laertes king!"—for such was the reaction of the London mob to the dashing Essex, who was rumored to be the bastard son of Elizabeth and Leicester. Claudius's earlier description of the disaffected Laertes, that he "keeps himself in clouds, / And wants not buzzers to infect his ear," is a brilliant evocation of the volatile and suggestible young earl. Finally, when Ophelia gives wildflowers to Laertes with the words, "You must wear your rue with a difference," she is punning on the name Devereux (rue with a difference = divers rue = dever-reux). Of course Laertes can have no possible claim to the throne, being the son of the king's chief minister, but if in Shakespeare's mind he is the Earl of Essex, such an anomaly becomes both natural and topical. Moreover, Shakespeare's own status and aspirations can be understood when one remembers Hamlet's expression of regret that "to Laertes I forgot myself; / For by the image of my cause I see / The portraiture of his."

One soon becomes adept at seeing both the primary and the secondary plots at once, or, in the words of Hermia in *A Midsummer Night's Dream,* seeing "with parted eye."

There are, then, three interlocking plots in any given Shakespeare play. The first or primary plot is the fictional foundation of the play and is determined largely by Shakespeare's sources. They provide him with a basic tale, which then acts as a stalking horse for the real story he wants to tell: the secondary plot. This plot is essentially topical satire based on the author's experiences of court life and could not have been told in an uncamouflaged form without endangering his life. It is in essence the story of his lost identity, with all its political ramifications. The interplay of the primary and secondary plots can lead to anomalies between what a character should plausibly be saying and what the author himself wants to say through that character. Thus, for instance, Hamlet's persistent complaints about his poverty and lack of status (he even goes so far as to refer to himself as a beggar) are contradicted by the facts of the plot; that is, they have no objective correlative. Hamlet is, according to Claudius, "the most immediate to our throne" and "has the voice of the King himself" for his succession in Denmark. There is no suggestion that he is being denied the perks and privileges pertaining to his elevated status. Yet for Shakespeare himself the feeling of dispossession is very strong. In comprehending these "rival" plots, we should bear in mind Puttenham's definition of allegory, from *The Art of English Poesie* (1589), as those instances when "we speak one thing and think another, and that our words and meanings meet not."

The manner in which Shakespeare alters and modifies his sources is nearly always highly significant and is motivated by the demands of the secondary plot. In *Hamlet,* for instance, the Ghost, Polonius and his family, the play within the play, the prominence of Gertrude, and the death of Hamlet are all examples of material introduced by Shakespeare, and all serve his autobiographical designs.

The third or ulterior plot is the "soul story," a narrative created by the unconscious itself to give voice to the author's hidden interior life or mythic existence. This comprises the material that, according to Eliot, Shakespeare "could not drag to light." A good example is Shakespeare's treatment of Gertrude, or rather her treatment of him, for he evidently finds it difficult to keep her within the confines of the plot. Her general weakness as a character, for instance, is contradicted by the huge archetypal power—the king-killing, identity-annihilating power—with which Hamlet invests her. This is because Shakespeare's concept of Elizabeth has taken precedence over his portrayal of Gertrude, so that the demands of the plot are subjugated to his own psychic needs. The story of England, rather than Denmark, determines the inner logic of the play.

At the base of Shakespeare's portrayal of Gertrude, especially her extraordinary power over Hamlet's imagination, is the displaced theme of incest. When Hamlet confronts his mother in the closet scene, he pleads his dead father's virtues in the comparison of the two lockets (the one depicting old King Hamlet, the other the usurping brother, Claudius). His vehemence is such, however, that one gets the feeling he is pleading *his own* charms—that he is Claudius's competitor, not just for the throne, but for the hand of the queen, his mother. This hint of a sexual relationship between Hamlet and Gertrude is given by Polonius at the very opening of the scene with a series of unintentionally bawdy puns addressed to the Queen:

> A [i.e., Hamlet] will come straight. Look you lay home to him,
> Tell him his pranks have been too broad to bear with
> And that your Grace hath screen'd and stood between
> Much heat and him. I'll silence me even here.
> Pray you be round.
>
> (III.iv.1–5)

It is also made vivid by the explicit language Hamlet uses in describing his mother's licentiousness, both in soliloquy and to her face. The language is simply not consistent with a straightforward mother-son relationship, however strained. It is clear, too, that Hamlet has tormented himself a good deal with fantasies of his mother having sex with Claudius; he even associates the two of them making love with his mother's (imagined) betrayal of him. In this, he comes perilously close to casting himself in the role of jealous lover.

"What shall I do?" pleads Gertrude, to which Hamlet replies:

> Not this, by no means, that I bid you do:
> Let the bloat King tempt you again to bed,
> Pinch wanton on your cheek, call you his mouse,
> And let him, for a pair of reechy kisses,
> Or paddling in your neck with his damn'd fingers,
> Make you to ravel all this matter out
> That I essentially am not in madness,
> But mad in craft.
>
> (III.iv.183–190)

The theme of incest emerges in Hamlet's first soliloquy in Act I, scene ii, and though the prince does his best to project his own uncomfortable feelings onto Claudius and Gertrude (who are brother- and sister-in-law), he cannot help expressing a sense of self-disgust so violent that it leads to thoughts of suicide. It is as if he himself has partaken of the incestuous relationship, and his body has been polluted as a result:

> O that this too too sullied flesh would melt,
> Thaw and resolve itself into a dew,
> Or that the Everlasting had not fix'd
> His canon 'gainst self-slaughter. O God! O God!
>
> (I.ii.129–132)

He cannot assuage his feelings by killing Claudius; such a course of action would only make things worse because he would in effect be replacing his stepfather as his mother's consort. *A little more than kin, and less than kind.*

The fact that commentators endlessly discuss Hamlet's motives, and those of Shakespeare's other protagonists, is surely evidence that we are dealing with the author's unconscious mind. This, as Thoreau pointed out, is the "miracle" of Shakespeare. We respond to him on a preconscious level—*between the lines*—almost as if we were cocreators, for the dynamic field in which his unconscious mind intersects with ours is intensely alive, making his work strongly akin to music.

Another wonderful example of the ulterior plot at work is Ophelia's death (half accident, half suicide), reported by Gertrude at the end of

Act IV. This is a symbol-picture in little of Shakespeare's own fate. Ophelia is hanging her garlands of wildflowers on a willow when an envious sliver breaks, and she falls into the brook with her "weedy trophies." Taken together, the willow tree, sacred to the moon goddess and her priestesses (the nine Muses); the crown of flowers; the broken bough; the figure poised between land and water, all bespeak a striving toward some otherworldly kingship. It is an energy that Elizabeth and Shakespeare shared: she as a mythical virgin queen, he as a poet-king, both attempting to transcend the horror of their common background. Ultimately, Ophelia weaving her crown of flowers is Shakespeare composing his works in service to the moon goddess, who abandons him to the waters of the unconscious, which bear him up while he sings his songs (writes his poetry) before pulling him down to his death (anonymity). Ophelia's flowers floating on the water are a beautiful image for Shakespeare's poetry welling up from the unconscious, and the phrase "weedy trophies" suggests a laureate's wreath. If we are in any doubt about this fleeting identification of Ophelia with Shakespeare, Claudius's strange comment at the end of the graveyard scene should dispel it: "This grave [i.e., Ophelia's] shall have a living monument." This is the very image that Shakespeare uses in his Sonnets to assure the Fair Youth that he will live forever through the poet's works.

As Thomas Carlyle wrote in "The Hero as Poet" (1841), "There is more in Shakespeare's intellect than we have yet seen. It is what I call an unconscious intellect: there is more virtue in it than he himself is aware of. . . . Shakespeare's art is not artifice; the noblest worth of it is not there by plan or pre-contrivance. It grows up from the deeps of Nature."

More than anything else, perhaps, it is the intense suffering in the plays that goes to the heart of Shakespeare's reality. The deep psychic wounds that his characters bear are like shafts down into the soul of the poet. As no one consciously suffers, the expression of intense suffering in an author—whether Dickens, Dostoyevsky, Byron, or Shakespeare—is peculiarly revealing of the unconscious archetypes that shape the individual's life and thought. The suffering of Edgar in *King Lear* is a vivid case in point. There is no objective basis in the plot for Edgar's terrible suffering, least of all the agony he inflicts upon himself. This is a case of the author's emotional pain overwhelming the outer logic of the text with its own inner rationale. Without conscious intention on Shakespeare's part, it seems, Edgar is transformed from the curled darling of the court to the lacerated figure of Oedipus, the self-pierced pariah, half mad from grief. Yet in this no-man's-land of psychic disintegration a new language and, with it, a new mythology emerge into consciousness.

Tracing the roots of Shakespeare's pain brings us to an understanding of his identity, and his work. And when one realizes that Shakespeare's pain is real, the realization that Shakespeare himself is real cannot be far behind. It is a question of retrieving that vital connection between an author's characters and his soul life.

Just as it is an axiom of psychoanalysis that what we deny in ourselves drives our lives, so with Shakespeare what remains unsaid becomes the motive power of his corpus. Is it surprising that the works of an author who must remain hidden should be dominated by the theme of identity? And this excessive emotion, this field of potential: what is it but the mourning garment of a man who was forced to give up his identity and become nothing? And because Shakespeare's works have a hidden purpose, i.e., to reveal the author's identity and his claim to the throne, all his characters must in a sense *collude* in this undercover operation, helping to bear the burden of his secret. Each character, like its author, possesses a double identity.

Mistaken identity, concealed identity, loss of identity, enforced anonymity—all are crucial Shakespearean themes. Though Shakespeare explores them to great effect for dramatic purposes, his very real disquiet about his own identity breaks through, often in the figure of the fool, who is beyond name and status, or by means of another outsider, the bastard. Even with a historical figure like Richard II, Shakespeare chooses—without any basis in fact—to present this troubled king as racked by an identity crisis: "I no, no I; for I must nothing be," laments Richard. *I know no I:* even his basic sense of self has dissolved. The emotion, however, is real. "Who is it that can tell me who I am?" cries Lear, whose preceding words—"Ha! waking? 'tis not so"—recall the final line of Sonnet 87, "In sleep a king, but waking no such matter."

Shakespeare's anxiety over his identity is dramatized by means of the fool, the bastard, and the king without a crown. They are the principal vehicles for his exploration of identity, and often merge. For instance, Philip, the royal bastard in *King John,* plays the fool, as do Hamlet, Lear, Edgar, and Richard II, all kings without crowns. Prince Hal, the heir to the throne, covers discretion with a coat of folly. Feste, the fool in *Twelfth Night,* assumes a quasi-royal status by describing himself as the "eldest son" of his mistress, Olivia, and calling her "madonna" to underscore the satire of the Virgin Queen. Another aspect of this same complex theme of the alienated man is the maverick prince or royal scapegrace, who rebels against the restraints of his birth, preferring the downright truths of his social inferiors to the finespun hypocrisy of the court.

The kingly fool finds its highest expression in Hamlet, yet it takes him by surprise, as it were, almost inhabiting him on the sly. When he is in his mother's closet, taking her to task for her promiscuity, he unleashes a volley of insulting remarks about Claudius, calling him "A king of shreds and patches." At that very moment the ghost of his father enters the room. The appearance of the ghost reminds us that Hamlet's princely identity is by now almost illusory, swallowed up as it is by his mother's incest. Thus Hamlet's insult rebounds on himself. He, not Claudius, is the royal fool or "king of shreds and patches," the truth teller believed by none. It is fascinating to note that, according to Charles Arundel, Oxford told "how God was fallen into a strange vein of crowning none but coxcombs [i.e., fools]."

Thersites, the Greek fool in *Troilus and Cressida,* is a bastard and not just any bastard, but the bastard son of "the mortal Venus," Helen of Troy—or so it is hinted. In a remarkable passage toward the end of the play, Thersites is encountered on the battlefield by Margarelon, the bastard son of Priam, who orders him to "turn and fight." When Thersites learns that his adversary is illegitimate, he responds with a mad insistence that recalls Edmund's obsessive repetition of the words "base" and "bastardy" in *King Lear.* "I am a bastard, too" he cries. "I love bastards. I am bastard begot, bastard instructed, bastard in mind, bastard in valour, in everything illegitimate. One bear will not bite another, and wherefore should one bastard? Take heed: the quarrel's most ominous to us—*if the son of a whore fight for a whore, he tempts judgement.* Farewell, bastard." This, I can't help feeling,

was Shakespeare's predicament exactly: the son of a whore fighting
for a whore. How was he to uphold Elizabeth's honor, and with it
England's, if she was no better than a whore? As for bastardy, Shakespeare evinces an uncanny insight into the psychology of the bastard. Harold Bloom, referring to Edmund's dying words "The wheel
is come full circle; I am here," writes: "'I am here' reverberates with
the dark undertone that . . . to have have been born a bastard was to
start with a death wound."[91]

Identity in Shakespeare is closely linked to the idea of authority or
power. The fool, the bastard, and the king without a crown are dis-
empowered figures who have no place in society. On the surface their
lack of identity engenders a lack of power, but what they lose in status
they gain in self-awareness. Through exclusion and suffering they find
a voice, and with it a deeper, more permanent identity. "And I am I,
howe'er I was begot," cries Faulconbridge. They are figures who make
it their business to speak out against the ills and injustices of society:
Thersites, Faulconbridge, and Lear on the heath, all in their different
ways, become the conscience of their nation.

They also serve as mouthpieces for the author, suggesting the sort
of authority that Shakespeare recovered for himself. That is, the authority he renounced or was denied in the world of government
and military affairs he recovered through authorship, and the theater.
This became his chosen form of authority. Through it, using the alienated characters of his drama, he challenged the power of the politicians. Let them write the history of the age as they might, he would
undermine their chronicles with the deeper truths of his art.

If there is a single leitmotif which directs the Shakespearean music,
it is alienation. When Hamlet cries, "The time is out of joint," he is
saying that he is out of sync with his age: he feels alienated from the
social and political culture. Hamlet, Othello, Macbeth, King Lear,
Edgar, Richard II, Richard III, Bertram, Jaques, Feste—all are mis-
fits. Prospero on his island is perhaps the supreme metaphor in Shakespeare for this sense of alienation, which washes through the canon
like a great tide of emotion. As Ted Hughes writes:

> Even more ominously than Goethe's Mephistopheles, or the venge-
> ful, pitiless, lonely hatred behind Dante's *Inferno,* Shakespeare's
> misfit, in its elemental otherness and ferocity, suggests an almost

pathological psychic alienation from the culture within which his plays triumphed, a radical estrangement that sits oddly with the traditional idea of the "gentle Shakespeare," the benign senior citizen of an English country town.[92]

SHAKESPEARE'S CORE MYTH

Every writer has a core myth or series of interlinking myths that sustain and nourish his work, even if he is considered a realist or naturalist: such a myth is the heart and destination of his work, the soil from which his images arise. Whatever he writes under the influence of this mythology—whether he knows it or not—becomes, in the words of Ted Hughes, "a subjective event of visionary intensity." The myth is like the author's own peculiar light, and whatever it touches it turns into itself or at least into its own frequency. According to Hughes, Sylvia Plath's work was shaped by a pair of interrelated myths—Phaeton and Icarus—both of which fed into and blossomed out of the early loss of her adored and inaccessible father. In his analysis of two closely allied poems, "Ariel" and "Sheep in Fog," Hughes shows how the Phaeton-Icarus myth, without being specifically mentioned, is at the very heart of Plath's later poetry, determining its catastrophic imagery. "Sheep in Fog," for instance, ends with Plath gazing at the "far fields" which "threaten / To let [her] through to a heaven / Starless and fatherless, a dark water"—like Icarus plunging away from his father toward the sea. As Hughes points out in the case of Plath, artists are hardly ever aware of the "working presence" of the myth while they are writing, even though the "mythic personality" is in control of selecting the imagery and directing the action of the poem or drama. In the end, it is the "blood-jet, autobiographical truth" that allows one to distinguish between a myth used consciously by a realist as literary ornament and "the mythic image as it appears in a truly mythic work."

Shakespeare's core myth, which represents his essential autobiography, is so distinctive that it becomes an invaluable tool in determining his identity, especially as he used it for the first work published under his name. Hughes writes:

Since Shakespeare only ever chose one mythic subject—Venus and Adonis—and since he chose it for his first and (considering

Lucrece as an automatic sequel) only long poem, one can believe that [it constituted] an obsessive nexus of images to which he was drawn by irresistible fascination.[93]

Venus and Adonis, as Shakespeare tells it, is the tragic story of a beautiful youth who rejects the advances of the goddess and, pursuing his passion for hunting instead, is killed by a boar. In dying, he is transformed by the goddess into a flower.

Shakespeare's most fundamental change to the myth of Venus and Adonis is Adonis's rejection of Venus. In Ovid's *Metamorphoses* (Book X), and in all other variants of the myth, Adonis reciprocates the love of the goddess. Another striking Shakespearean divergence from the classical myth is the difference in age between Venus and the "tender boy" Adonis; in the earlier myths there is nothing to suggest that they are not contemporaries, but in Shakespeare's version Venus is presented as an experienced lover well past her youth.[94] Indeed, although she boldly informs Adonis that she can still conceive, she is old enough to be his mother, and a good deal of maternal imagery is applied to her, as when she is likened to "a milch doe, whose swelling dugs do ache, / Hasting to feed her fawn, hid in some brake." Her fawn is Adonis, who bears the charge of the poem's son-sun images. Indeed, the very first lines of the poem clothe him in the mantle of the sun, which—like the flower that he becomes at the end of the narrative—is purple (i.e., royal):

> Even as the sun with purple-colour'd face
> Had ta'en his last leave of the weeping morn,
> Rose-cheek'd Adonis hied him to the chase.
>
> (lines 1–3)

If Adonis is the son of Venus in Shakespeare's personal mythology, then the youth's rejection of the goddess's love, which at times amounts to revulsion, is explained. There is a taboo here, which Adonis does not wish to transgress. After all, under normal circumstances, what young man would not give his right hand to make love to the goddess of love? For her part, although she pursues him as her sexual prey, Venus evinces a mother's concern and indulgence toward the pouting boy, and sees herself in him, his eyes being de-

scribed as "two glasses where herself herself beheld." Another clue
to the blood link between Venus and Adonis lies in the red and white
imagery that Shakespeare applies to both characters, red and white
being the colors of the Tudor rose. The boar, we are told, did not
see—when he pierced Adonis with his tusk—"the beauteous livery
that he wore." In other words, Adonis wore beauty's (i.e., Venus's)
badge; he was of her house.

Several times during the course of the poem Venus is referred
to as "queen," and there is no doubt that readers at court when the
poem first came out would have identified the goddess, in her bla-
zon of red and white, with the Tudor queen, Elizabeth. Nor would
they have been insensible to certain well-aimed gibes at the queen's
character—for instance, her notorious indecision:

> A thousand spleens bear her a thousand ways,
> She treads the path that she untreads again;
> Her more than haste is mated with delays
> Like the proceedings of a drunken brain,
> Full of respects, yet naught at all respecting,
> In hand with all things, naught at all effecting.
>
> (lines 907–912)

This is a very human Venus. Ovid in his account compares her
to Diana, the virgin goddess of wild places, for she accompanies
Adonis on the hunt, and this echo of Diana remains in Shakespeare's
portrait of Venus. Indeed, it could be argued that much of Adonis's
shocked revulsion at the goddess's behavior stems from the fact that,
being a hunter, he had expected the love and protection of Diana,
the patron deity of huntsmen, only to discover that Venus had usurped
her place. This "double vision" is brought home to us at the end of
the poem when Venus presides over the virgin birth of the purple
flower from Adonis's blood, and, with the flower-child between her
breasts, flies off to the island of Paphos, where she "means to immure herself and not be seen"—in other words, intends to hide the
fact that she has given birth. The idea of the virgin queen giving birth
incognito would not have been lost on Shakespeare's court readers,
who would have interpreted the poem as the revelation of a dynastic secret. Certainly, when Venus addresses the purple flower, it is in

terms of royal legitimacy: "Thou art the next of blood, and 'tis thy right." The curious language of Shakespeare's dedication of the poem to the Earl of Southampton bears out such an interpretation: "But if the first heir of my invention prove deformed, I shall be sorry it had so noble a godfather, and never after ear so barren a land, for fear it yield me still so bad a harvest."

Significantly, the boar also partakes of the red and white imagery, his "frothy mouth bepainted all with red, / Like milk and blood being mingled both together." As a heraldic animal, the boar is doubtless the badge of the author himself, as well as representing the transgressive passion that engenders the tragedy not only of this poem, but of all Shakespeare's subsequent works. He is both totem and taboo. The boar is also a powerful symbol of the mother at her most rapacious (we still use the term "boar mother"): what in psychological terms we might call the "devouring mother." In the context of the poem, it becomes the incestuous mother, intent on ravishing her own child. The poem then becomes a shamanic dream or nightmare initiation, in which the dreamer or hero is transformed by the confrontation with the mother. One could almost rename the poem "The Rape of Adonis." Such a title certainly emphasizes how perfectly it mirrors its companion piece, *The Rape of Lucrece*.

But even before the boar-goddess moves to destroy the youth, her behavior as the lovestruck Venus is puzzling and strongly suggests a contemporary political context for the poem. The statement of her love is so extravagant as to put us on our guard. The lady, it seems, doth protest too much. Could it be a ruse of some sort, a means of accomplishing an ulterior end? From the start, it is clear that the goddess is kissing Adonis to prevent him from talking, fearful no doubt of what he might say:[95]

> but soon she stops his lips,
> And kissing speaks, with lustful language broken,
> "If thou wilt chide, thy lips shall never open."

And:

> He saith she is immodest, blames her miss;
> What follows more, she murders with a kiss.
>
> (lines 46–48, 53–54)

Just as Queen Titania orders her fairies to "tie up my love's tongue" and "bring him silently," so Venus, for some unstated reason, tries to gag her lover. Adonis's "mermaid's voice," which is the voice of the poet, expresses "melodious discord," i.e., harsh truths in sweet poetry. Nor is there any denial of the youth's mortal aim; he clearly has the ability to hit his target. We are reminded of Philip the Bastard in *King John* delivering "sweet, sweet, sweet poison for the age's tooth":

> Once more the ruby-colour'd portal open'd
> Which to his speech did honey passage yield,
> Like a red morn that ever yet betoken'd
> Wrack to the seaman, tempest to the field,
>   Sorrow to shepherds, woe unto the birds,
>   Gusts and foul flaws to herdmen and to herds.
>
> This ill presage advisedly she marketh:
> Even as the wind is hush'd before it raineth,
> Or as the wolf doth grin before he barketh,
> Or as the berry breaks before it staineth,
>   Or like the deadly bullet of a gun,
>   His meaning struck her ere his words begun.
>   (lines 451–462)

The relationship between Hamlet and his mother, Gertrude, who complains that his words "like daggers enter in [her] ears," springs to mind. This "most seeming-virtuous queen," as the Ghost calls her, refuses to face the truth of what she has done. Both Hamlet and Adonis stand for Shakespeare, the truth teller, whose words are his chief weapon. Both relationships share the undercurrent of incest.

The goddess's love, then, is revealed as a means of silencing the outspoken young man. And when he does manage to speak out, it is easy to understand Venus's discomfort, for Adonis accuses the goddess of love of not knowing what love is:

> Call it not love, for love to heaven is fled,
> Since sweating lust on earth usurp'd his name;
> Under whose simple semblance he hath fed

Upon fresh beauty, blotting it with blame;
Which the hot tyrant stains and soon bereaves,
As caterpillars do the tender leaves.

(lines 793–798)

Thus Venus is using her sexual charms as a political tool, as Queen Elizabeth was notorious for doing. As for her motive for behaving in this manner, she is clearly anxious lest Adonis should reveal some indiscretion that might compromise her authority. If this is Elizabeth we're talking about and Adonis (Shakespeare) is her son, then it may be that she wishes to disguise her true relationship to him by courting him as a lover. After all, it was not politically expedient to have a disaffected royal bastard hovering in the wings. It may be that she held out the possibility of his becoming her consort instead of her son, thus conferring a quasi-royal status upon him through marriage. Either way, she is determined that he will not speak out. In the end, when she realizes that the headstrong youth will not be governed, she murders him in the form of the boar. In a reversal of normal male–female relations, it is Venus who penetrates Adonis (with her boar's tusk), suggesting an original model for Venus, who, although feminine by gender, possesses traditionally masculine attributes of power—for instance, the scepter of the monarch. The result of this piercing is "a purple flower" (or royal child), though in the imagery of the time "flower" also connotes a work of literature, especially poetry; thus this royal child becomes synonymous with the works of Shakespeare himself. In dying as the queen's son, Shakespeare becomes an artist.

The Rape of Lucrece tells the story of the rape and suicide of Lucrece, whose husband, le Collatine, boasts of her chastity to his fellow officers while they are encamped near Ardea. Sextus Tarquinius, the king's son, inflamed with lust, leaves the camp and makes his way privately to the house of Lucrece, where, having enjoyed the lavish hospitality of his hostess, he rapes her, and flees into the night. Having summoned her husband and father, Lucrece stabs herself in their presence. The outcry following her death is such that "the Tarquins [are] all exiled, and the state government changed from kings to consuls."

It is, in other words, a poem about the desecration of an idol or divinity, resulting in the death of a virgin and the end of the monarchy. The predatory, sexual aspects of the goddess that were so evi-

dent in *Venus* appear at first sight to have been purified and purged
in *Lucrece,* but they remain in muted form in the luscious sensual
descriptions of the sleeping maid. There are also enough vestigial
touches of an older myth for us to realize that Lucrece is the moon
goddess, Diana. Her essential royalty or divinity appears in countless
expressions and images. Collatine, for instance, boasts of her sovereignty; she is compared to the moon; and Tarquin's intended act is
described as "treason."

Nor can it be without significance that Tarquin's lust is yoked
with ambition for the throne; the many echoes of *Macbeth* in the poem
serve to confirm this reading. As Tarquin gazes at Lucrece's breasts,
Shakespeare writes:

> These worlds in Tarquin new ambition bred;
> Who like a foul usurper went about,
> From this fair throne to heave the owner out.
> (lines 411–413)

If we see the shadow of Queen Elizabeth behind the figure of
Lucrece, then lust and ambition become inseparable. After all, with
the Virgin Queen on the throne, how else could a man become
king but through sexual conquest? Rape in this context was tantamount to staging a coup. Moreover, the piercing of the virgin's
veil or exposure of the queen as a whore—symbolized by the rape
of Lucrece—could lead to the end of Elizabeth's reign, even the
end of monarchy itself.

But there is a metaphorical rape at work here too, perpetrated
by Shakespeare the iconoclast, who violates the queen's semidivine
image through his works, puncturing the screen of illusion with
the tusk of truth. Nor can Lucrece-Diana be entirely absolved from
the sexual act of which she is the apparent victim. The expression
of her shame, in contrast to the fugitive description of Tarquin's, rolls
out for page after page, often carrying a tone of self-accusation, as
if the breach of holy vow has been hers. She also betrays a curious concern—more suited perhaps to the psychology of Queen
Elizabeth—with how future generations will regard her:

> Make me not object to the tell-tale day:
> The light will show character'd in my brow

The story of sweet chastity's decay,
The impious breach of holy wedlock vow;
Yea, the illiterate that know not how
To cipher what is writ in learned books,
Will quote my loathsome trespass in my looks.

(lines 806–812)

That Lucrece, like Venus, is intended on the level of political myth to stand for Elizabeth is confirmed by these lines in Henry Chettle's poem "England's Mourning Garment," written on the death of the queen in 1603:

Shepherd, remember our *Elizabeth,*
And sing her Rape, done by that *Tarquin,* Death.

After the rape, Tarquin is described as "a heavy convertite," for, like Actaeon, he has been transformed. He "faintly flies, sweating with guilty fear," like Ovid's Actaeon fleeing the goddess.[96] Nor is he able to utter his shame, skulking off without words. Thus we can understand Tarquin, like Actaeon, as the sacrificed king. It is through him that the kingdom is renewed, like the stag shedding and renewing its antlers.

If, as Ted Hughes suggested, one takes *The Rape of Lucrece* as an "automatic sequel" to *Venus and Adonis,* an interesting transformation occurs. Venus, who at the end of the previous poem flew off to Paphos, where she meant to "immure herself and not be seen," is transformed into the chaste and cloistered Lucrece; and the boar-pierced Adonis becomes "lust-breathed" Tarquin, who in destroying the chastity of "the silver moon," as Shakespeare describes Lucrece—i.e., in *deflowering* the goddess—brings down the monarchy. Thus Adonis becomes both the flower and the serpent under it.[97] The flower that the goddess presses to her bosom is beautiful but deadly, rather like the asp that Cleopatra nurses at her breast. Thus the Shakespearean hero-archetype embodies within himself both the redeemer (Adonis) and the destroyer (Tarquin), though in many plays these are split into two rival characters, such as Hamlet and Claudius or Edgar and Edmund. The heroine, on the other hand, embodies both Lucrece and Venus, the chaste and lustful projections of the great goddess.

The love dance or life-and-death struggle between the goddess and her son-consort, or the poet and his muse, is in essence a struggle for higher consciousness. The poet or divine son, while serving the goddess, attempts to free himself from her relentless and interminable cycle of life and death through transcendence. In poetic terms, this is often seen as an attempt on the goddess's life, a desire to destroy her.

The two poems, taken as one, can be seen as an allegory of Shakespeare's story as an artist. Adonis, symbolized by the sun god Apollo, is Shakespeare the lyric poet, transformed by his rape-death at the hands of the goddess into Tarquin, who, as a god of frenzy, is under the sway of Dionysus, patron deity of the theater, and so represents Shakespeare the dramatist. Shakespeare, it seems, is telling us what it was that transformed him from lyric poet to dramatist, namely the "death" he suffered at the hands of the mortal Venus. As with Hamlet, the theater becomes a means of asserting his royal right in defiance of the goddess. Politics and the removal of his own political status drive Shakespeare into the theater, or rather inspire him to create modern drama.

Through the poems Shakespeare reveals his secret story. "I am the son of the Goddess," he is saying, "and her amorous pursuit of me is at base a political ploy to disguise the fact that she is my mother. Despite her posturing she is not the Virgin Queen. Since our royal son—the purple flower—was born, I have been officially annihilated while she has 'immure[d] herself,' hiding behind the virgin veil of her mythology. This death at her hands has provoked me to challenge her power by means of the theater, the realm of Tarquin-Dionysus, and this in turn has served to confirm my status as royal outcast." The poignancy of his fate as a dissident writer is told in the beautiful thirty-line parable of poor Wat the hare (read "heir") in the middle of *Venus and Adonis*. This is Shakespeare, the royal heir, trying to stay one step ahead of the hunter (censor) by means of his literary skill:

> And when thou hast on foot the purblind hare,
> Mark the poor wretch, to overshoot his troubles,
> How he outruns the wind, and with what care
> He cranks and crosses with a thousand doubles;
> The many musits through the which he goes
> Are like a labyrinth to amaze his foes.

Sometime he runs among a flock of sheep,
To make the cunning hounds mistake their smell;
And sometime where earth-delving conies keep,
To stop the loud pursuers in their yell;
   And sometime sorteth with a herd of deer:
   Danger deviseth shifts, wit waits on fear.

(lines 679–690)

There is also a sense in which the two long poems can be read as myths of Catholicism and Puritanism, the two forces that pulled upon the conscience of the nation during the Elizabethan age and threatened the stability of the throne. (Eventually, during the Civil War, they would tear the country apart.) Elizabeth herself embodied this religious split in the psyche of Reformation England, the Virgin Queen being her Puritan projection—her Lucrece persona—and Venus, the mother of her people, her Catholic projection. It was this split in both mother and nation that Shakespeare attempted to heal through his art.

The example of William Reynolds, the very first reader on record of *Venus and Adonis,* who bought a copy hot off the presses in 1593, demonstrates that this dual perception of Elizabeth registered strongly in the national psyche. Reynolds not only equated Elizabeth with the Venus of Shakespeare's poem ("You are Venus herself," he wrote directly to the queen), but also was conscious of her projection as an otherworldly, Titania-like creature. As he wrote to the Privy Council in September of that year:

> Also within these few days there is another book made of Venus and Adonis wherein the queen represents the person of Venus, which queen is in great love (forsooth) with Adonis, and greatly desires to kiss him, and she woos him most entirely, telling him although she be old, yet she is lusty, fresh and moist, full of love and life . . . and she can trip it as lightly as a fairy nymph upon the sands and her footsteps not seen, and much ado with red and white.

Reynolds lived with his widowed mother in or near the Strand, and other letters he wrote reveal a man suffering from an acute Oedi-

pus complex. Duncan-Jones describes "his intense devotion to her"
as "Hamlet-like."[98] All Reynolds's negative thoughts toward his mother
are repressed in his ecstatic panegyrics, being reserved instead for the
queen, whom he accuses of neglect and wantonness. In other words,
Elizabeth seems to fulfill the function of uncaring mother in Reynolds's
mental-emotional world. Because he sees himself as Adonis in Shakespeare's poem, it is clear that Reynolds has made an intuitive connection between Venus and Adonis as mother and son. In one of his letters
to Elizabeth, Reynolds accuses the queen of leading him on by means
of her sexual charms, only to humiliate him, but he will not be cozened, "for I know what I do, and I understand what I write, neither
will I be fed any longer with echoes nor appareled with shadows." Far
from seeing her as the caring mother of her people, Reynolds paints
her as wanton Venus, "trembling in her passion," a sex-crazed queen
who will not scruple to hit upon her own son.

It is easy to dismiss Reynolds's rambling letters as the ravings
of a madman, but the Privy Council took them sufficiently seriously
to call him in for questioning; nor is his characterization of Lord
Burghley as the robber of the realm wide of the mark. The importance of Reynolds lies in the fact that his Oedipus complex and frail
sense of self—qualities shared by Shakespeare—allowed him to tune
in to some of the deeper themes of the poem. Certainly Reynolds's
technique, if it can be called that, of splitting his mother into two
characters— the chaste, devoted mother living in the Strand, and the
devouring, promiscuous mother living in the palace of Whitehall—
is a signature of Shakespearean characterization.

The queen's suppression or "murder" of her son stimulated the
poetic life of the times, as if she had fertilized the garden of England's
imagination by sacrificing the king. This king-sacrifice was a constant theme or leitmotif in Elizabeth's life and in the Elizabethan
subconscious, and this is why we meet it so often in the literature.

The energy of the alienated son that Shakespeare's Adonis-Tarquin
embodies is a powerful, if suppressed force, in the politics of the Elizabethan age, and one that has been overshadowed by the traditional
historical archetypes of Elizabeth as mistress, Leicester as consort, and
Burghley as father of the realm. Like the three Fates passing their one
eye between them, these three dominant figures guarded the mysteries of government. There was, however, a powerful rogue energy

crouching beneath the table of state like the proverbial tiger (long before the Earl of Essex burst onto the scene in the early 1590s), which manifested itself principally through the arts, in particular the court revels. This "fourth dimension" or son energy had an iconoclastic edge that challenged the political orthodoxy of the age. A kind of fourth estate, bearing heavily on the genesis of the public theater, it became the principal medium for challenging the government. Thus the struggle at the heart of Elizabethan government is realized as one of art versus politics, or truth versus propaganda, the truth being embodied in the figure of the hidden prince, whose task it was to fight the dragon of false rule. The dynamics become visible once we treat the works of Shakespeare as historical chronicles, not just as works of art. The English theater, as we know it today, grew out of the profound sense of alienation felt by the true heir and those who gathered about his standard.

This son energy, repressed on the political level, created severe tensions at the helm of state, for great efforts were required to keep it belowdecks. It drove the succession crisis, for instance, and intensified the culture of paranoia that had insinuated itself into every nook and cranny of the polity. It was positive, too, suddenly flaming upon the mast of state as a brightly pennoned patriotism. Ultimately, Elizabeth seemed to benefit from it, as she made sure she benefited from everything. Indeed, it is no exaggeration to say that the queen renewed and rejuvenated herself by swallowing this son energy, like some great Babylonian fish goddess swallowing the sun. It fed her cult of ever-youthful virginity, and kept all eyes focused firmly on her as the living goddess. This is beautifully and eerily depicted in the famous "Rainbow" portrait of the queen, painted around 1600 by Isaac Oliver, which puns on sun and son. Though Elizabeth was in her late sixties at the time, the portrait depicts an ageless, highly erotic figure, her gown covered in eyes and ears, and slits that look like mouths. Her left thumb and forefinger are inserted into the folds of the gown; this gesture, together with the large serpent on her left arm, suggests an androgynous and self-sufficing sexuality that can produce offspring without the agency of a male. There is no sun to be seen in the portrait, even symbolically, yet the queen grasps a phallic-looking rainbow in her right hand, above which appears the legend NON SINE SOLE IRIS, "No rainbow without the sun"— in other words, *No reign without the son.*

Part Three

Fall from Grace

~ 7 ~

Love's Labours Lost

That instant was I turn'd into a hart,
And my desires, like fell and cruel hounds,
E'er since pursue me.
                    (*Twelfth Night*, I.i.21–23)

THE MYTH THAT PIERCES to the heart of Shakespeare's relationship
with Elizabeth is the tale of Actaeon, the hunter who stumbled upon
the virgin goddess Diana bathing nude in a woodland pool. Surprised
by the intruder, she stood blushing furiously while her nymphs gathered around to shield her nakedness. To punish Actaeon, and to prevent him from disclosing what he had seen, Diana turned him into a
stag. Thus transformed, he was hunted down and torn to pieces by his
own hounds. Ovid's life, no less than Shakespeare's, reflects this myth,
for the Roman poet was banished by the emperor Augustus for having witnessed some royal indiscretion, or so he tells us in the poems
he wrote from exile. In Shakespeare's case, the myth of Actaeon says
much about his ambivalent yet compulsive relationship with the goddess in his life, Queen Elizabeth.

Shakespeare's *Venus and Adonis* is almost a mirror image of the
Actaeon myth. Adonis sees a side of the goddess not permitted to
mortals (her sexual avarice), and for his transgression is pursued by a
boar that represents his own passions as much as those of the enraged
goddess. Like Actaeon, Adonis is a hunter hunted to death, the huntsman being a metaphor for the artist who pursues the truth of his
inspiration, come what may. The ferocity of the boar in this context
is the *furor poeticus* or creative rapture of the artist. Inevitably, one

comes to see Shakespeare's inspiration as an expression of the fury of the goddess. This makes sense both in terms of the emotional life of the poet and in the wider context of his rapidly changing society, for the ancient goddess culture was being extinguished in Elizabethan England by the growth of Puritanism and capitalism, and it fell to the son-consort to express her dying defiance.

It is significant, too, that the attraction between Actaeon and Diana is mutual. The goddess's arousal spells the mortal man's doom, for there was always a heavy price to pay for arousing her lust. To make love to the goddess was to court death. (Bottom is another Actaeon figure transformed into a beast for loving the goddess.)

The myth of Actaeon had its origins in the sacrifice of the stag-king, who was hunted to death wearing a deerskin. This was an ancient fertility ritual in the Aurignacian culture of southwest France, and the dying king, whose death renewed the land, was often depicted ejaculating, his seed forming a heap of corn. He was the god of the year and renewal, much like Adonis or Osiris. Such a king was both a redeemer figure and a scapegoat, a sort of shadow king, whose power could be incorporated into the national psyche only through death. He was a figure of fear, too, who was driven out into the wild places.

In *As You Like It,* the stag becomes a symbol of the exiled lords, in particular Jaques, who moralizes upon the weeping deer. The weeping stag is the theme of one of the most extraordinary and controversial portraits of Queen Elizabeth, known as the Persian Portrait, which depicts a pregnant Elizabeth crowning a weeping stag with a garland of pansies. She wears a loose silver gown decorated with Tudor roses, honeysuckle, exotic birds, and clusters of grapes, and a tall Oriental hat with a full-length veil. A string of pearls dangles from her right arm, coming to rest on the stag's head; and around her neck hang two rings (wedding bands?) suspended from a thread. Directly behind the stag's head, so that one of its horns appears to metamorphose into one of the branches, is a walnut tree in fruit. A cartouche at the bottom right of the picture displays a Shakespearean sonnet that bears quoting in full:

> The restless swallow fits my restless mind,
> In still reviving still renewing wronges;

Her just complaints of cruel[t]y unkind,
Are all the music that my life prolongs.

With pensive thoughts my weeping stagg I crown,
Whose melancholy tears my cares express;
His tears in silence and my sighs unknown
Are all the physic that my harms redress.

My only hope was in this goodly tree,
Which I did plant in love, bring up in care;
But all in vain, for now too late I see
The shales be mine, the kernels others are.

My music may be plaints, my physique tears
If this be all the fruit my love tree bears.

Little wonder such strenuous attempts have been made over the centuries to alter, rename, camouflage, and generally disguise the portrait, as in this single image the whole official version of Elizabethan history comes crashing to the ground. Here is the tale that Shakespeare tells repeatedly in veiled terms of royal union and broken troth. It is the tale of the life-and-death struggle of the poet and the goddess, the one made mute—and finally destroyed—by the fury of the other. But the portrait does more: it transcends the ancient Greek myth, for here before us is an image of Actaeon and Diana *reconciled*. This surely is the moment that all Shakespeare's works strive toward: the poet (son) and the goddess united in a new myth for the renewal of the kingdom—the union of truth and beauty forming a new and chastened royalty.

The walnut tree that appears to spring from the stag's head like a giant set of antlers ("this goodly tree, / Which I did plant in love") is not only the royal family tree that the queen and her stag-king are extending through the child ripening in her womb, but the tree of knowledge that has sprung from the head of Shakespeare-Actaeon (poet, trespasser, royal lover). In the third stanza of the sonnet, the queen seems to be saying that the birth of her child has been in vain, as she has not been able to acknowledge him; nor has she benefited from the fruits of the walnut tree (Shakespeare's works) in the sense of allowing them to change her life, having enjoyed them as entertainment alone. As a result, her love is barren. She has abused and rejected the one who loved her above the rest. It is worth noting, too, that the walnut tree is associated with the moon, the swallow is sacred to Isis and Venus, and the pansy, a favorite flower of Queen Elizabeth, is symbolic of chastity. The pearls touching the stag's head in the shape of an O (for Oxford) symbolize genius in obscurity.

What hits us squarely between the eyes is the quality of revealed truth. As Shakespeare wrote of King Leontes's reunion with Camillo in *The Winter's Tale,* "There was speech in their dumbness, language in their very gesture; they looked as they had heard of a world ransomed, or one destroyed."[99]

A KIND OF HISTORY

At the end of the induction to *The Taming of the Shrew,* the drunken Warwickshire tinker Christopher Sly, who has been tricked up as a lord for the amusement of the aristocrats and to whom a comedy is about to be presented, asks, "Is not a comonty [comedy] a Christmas gambol or a tumbling-trick?"—to which the page replies, "It is a kind of history." Comedy as a kind of history: this is an authorial comment we would do well to heed. Earlier, a brief dialogue between the Lord and First Huntsman on the quality of hounds stresses the ability of the best to follow a dull scent or one that has grown cold—another clue, perhaps, that we must develop a keen nose for the hidden history in each play. All Shakespeare's plays are "histories," for they tell *his story* and comment on his times. Records of court performances in the 1570s contain many titles suggestive of early versions of the plays. Most are comedies, yet they are entitled histories, as, for instance *The Historie of Error* for *The Comedy of Errors, An History of the Crueltie of a Stepmother* for *Cymbeline,* and *The Historie of the Rape of the Second Helene* for *All's Well That Ends Well.*

It is impossible to assign Shakespeare's works with any certainty to a particular genre; they defy classification. His comedies are tragicomedies, with a deep vein of melancholy, richly interwoven with elements of romance and pastoral. The author and lecturer Marguerite

Alexander refers to them, quite typically, as "romantic comedies," in contrast to Ben Jonson's "satirical comedies,"[100] for she has failed to heed the words of the page to read them as histories. Had she read them so, she would have been compelled to redefine Shakespeare's comedies as court satires. What they are not is whimsical: we are drawn into their world by a profound psychological realism. Ultimately, any attempt at a comprehensive definition is doomed to the sort of failure Polonius experiences when he attempts to describe the repertoire of the actors visiting Elsinore.

The very term "comedy" provides an opening into the secret behind Shakespeare's method. It comes from the Greek κωμος, "revel," a word which takes us back to ancient seasonal rituals and—deriving as it does from the Latin *rebellare*—connotations of riot and rebellion. These revels involved disguising and mumming, role reversal, and practical joking, and gave people an opportunity to release pent-up animal spirits and siphon off their frustrations at the restrictions imposed by law—in other words, to poke fun at authority. A form of communal catharsis, they provided an outlet for the pressures of everyday life.

Working like a vaccination, the revels allowed a controlled form of rebellion, thereby preventing the sort of full-scale revolt that brings down governments. During the Saturnalia of ancient Rome, masters threw off the toga and served their slaves, who wore freedmen's hats, feasted, gambled, and lechered to their hearts' content. The social order was reversed, not subverted. In the original rites, a man was selected to play the part of the god Saturn, enjoying the authority and privileges of his divine station before being sacrificed to ensure the fertility of the land. Thus, at the root of the revels, even in Shakespeare's day, was the idea of honoring the god of vegetation and the cycle of life and death he embodied. The ritual assassination of the god ensured the purification of the community—the primary function of the revels. The Greeks called him Dionysus, and drama as we know it today developed from the rites used to worship him. The mock god at the center of such "revels" survived in Shakespeare's time as the lord of misrule. At the revels of the Inner Temple in 1561, for instance, Robert Dudley, later Earl of Leicester, was chosen as the mock king. This was more than playacting: his appointment was understood as a broad hint to Elizabeth that she should make him her consort.

As practiced in the English countryside in medieval times, the revels celebrated the essential democracy of the universal life-energy. The mummers who processed through their village, targeting certain houses, were disguised as gods or animals and allowed this primal energy to be expressed through them. They could not be identified by their fellow villagers, so they acted with impunity. Much of their revelry was light-hearted and a source of merriment for everyone, but it also had a darker side, which involved scapegoating: revenge was taken against those perceived to have sinned against the community during the year. Naming and shaming by pinning notices to trees or public buildings was one form of retribution; other, more dramatic forms might involve turning farm animals loose or setting fire to someone's barn.

The Elizabethan court versions of such mummery were called masques because the actors, as in older rituals, were masked or disguised. Masques included music, singing, and dancing, as well as acting; and there was no clear demarcation between masquers and spectators, the latter often wearing masks themselves. The settings tended to be pastoral and mythological, with courtiers disguised as shepherds and shepherdesses, foresters, sea gods, and mermaids. A fairy court was another popular conceit. The masque arrived in England from Italy at the beginning of Henry VIII's reign, in 1512, and many of the performances were watched from behind a barrier by crowds of ordinary people, to whom the spectacles must have seemed like magical apparitions. On one occasion King Henry and his lords, decked in gold and silver tinsel, entered the banqueting hall at Richmond palace in a fantastic car. This was too much for the people in the crowd, who surged forward, pulled the chariot to pieces, and snatched as much finery as they could. Nor did Henry object when he and his lords were stripped to their hose and doublet, as the crowds tore the gold lettering from their costumes—perhaps a folk memory from the ancient carnivals at which people performed the same rite upon the mock king as prologue to his assassination.

Shakespeare makes use of masques in several plays, including *Love's Labour's Lost,* in which the king and lords of Navarre, disguised as Russians, visit the French princess and her ladies, who are masked to deceive their suitors. A glance at the records of the court revels reveals that, on Sunday, January 11, 1579, a "Double Maske" shown before the queen and the French ambassador was "an entertainment in imitation of a tournament between six ladies and a like number of gentlemen who surrendered to them."[101] This is likely to have been an early version of *Love's Labour's Lost*.

In many ways Shakespeare's whole dramatic oeuvre takes its life from the court masque. His works follow that genre in their use of allegory and in being addressed to the monarch, a key participant, whether mingling in disguise or seated *in propria persona*. Just as important, they serve the extra-dramatic function of advising or warning the sovereign on matters of state. Many early versions of Shakespeare's plays were court masques put on throughout the 1570s for official or ceremonious occasions such as the arrival of a special envoy come to pay court to the nubile Elizabeth. Berowne, the courtier-poet-cum-jester, says in anticipation of the masque he devises:

> In the afternoon
> We will with some strange pastime solace them,
> Such as the shortness of the time can shape;
> For revels, dances, masks, and merry hours,
> Forerun fair Love, strewing her way with flowers.
> (*Love's Labour's Lost*, IV.iv.372–376)

Such entertainments, often thrown together at great speed, adapted an existing work or made considerable use of improvisation. Courtiers, under the aegis of the master of the revels, would be expected to direct their wit, imagination, and histrionic flair toward the accomplishment of such enterprises. The court, after all, with the semidivine Elizabeth at its heart, was the source of all that was magical and fantastic, a fairy-tale world where dreams could be made manifest at the wave of the royal wand. Without fantasy to sustain it, how could the monarchy maintain its mythical status? Or how could the court remain a viable social organism without the revitalizing energy of carnival? In her examination of the roots of Shakespeare's dramatic art, Stephanie Hughes writes:

That Shakespeare's comedies were written originally as Court entertainments seems obvious, since so many facets of the ancient revels cling to them, the wooded settings, the sticking up of poems on trees, the evocation of animal totems or folk gods and the spells used to constrain or evoke them (Herne the Hunter, Bottom the ass, Sycorax and Caliban, Oberon and Titania, Puck, and Ariel), dancing and music. The tricks played on Malvolio by the revellers in *Twelfth Night,* and by Oberon and Puck in *A Midsummer Night's Dream,* are simply glorified mummers' pranks; and with both these plays the titles themselves make it abundantly clear for which of the seasonal festivals they were originally created.[102]

The mummers' prank is very much in evidence in *The Merry Wives of Windsor,* with Falstaff tricked by the Merry Wives into dressing up as Herne the Hunter and meeting them after midnight at the oak in Windsor Park, which was said to be haunted by the dead keeper. Sir John, wearing a pair of ragged horns, compares himself to "a Windsor stag, and the fattest, I think, i' th' forest." But no sooner has he come forward to greet the two married ladies whom he is courting than a troop of masked children dressed as fairies rush out from a saw pit and, surrounding the prostrate knight, dance an antic around him, pinching him and burning him with tapers.

The purpose of this "device" is to expose and humiliate Falstaff for his transgression, not as a way of excluding him from society, but to reincorporate the rogue element he represents into the community. The final effect is purgation or catharsis. Notable too is the specter of the Actaeon myth behind this play within the play.[103] Through his attempted sexual transgression, which rouses desire and fury in the goddess (in this case the Merry Wives), Falstaff is driven out of the city into the forest, transformed into a stag, and attacked by hounds (the fairies who pinch and burn him). But he is not left there to nurse feelings of bitterness. As Mistress Page says, "The truth being known, / We'll all present ourselves, dis-horn the spirit, / And mock him home to Windsor."

Fearing that Falstaff has made a cuckold of him, Master Ford finds that the buck—male deer—looms large in his thinking (he repeats the word seven times in two lines). The word, from the Old English *bucca,* "he-goat," leads us down a fruitful path to the satyr or man-goat, from which we derive the word "satire," an art form frequently featuring the scapegoat. Satire in Shakespeare's comedies is the final flowering of the old mumming and disguising rituals. Its purpose is to expose the sins of the community, though Shakespeare subverts the basic masque form he inherited so that, instead of having the monarch and courtiers don masks to participate in the action, the dramatist disguises them as characters in his play. This meant that he could subject even the monarch to the sort of roasting Falstaff endures. For who better to bear the sins of the people than the sovereign?

Falstaff does not know that he is the principal actor in a masque of others' devising. Only when he recognizes Hugh Evans, the Welsh parson disguised as a satyr, does he begin to understand that he has been duped. This confusion of illusion and reality is central to Shakespeare's concept and use of theater, and is supported by his awareness of the court as a stage. Duplicity, disguise, illusion, double-dealing—these were the tools for survival at court, a theater in which the monarch and her entourage staged themselves to the world. Shakespeare's theater, on the other hand, presented a deeper reality, which threatened the illusion of court life. As such, it was indeed a kind of history.

Self-portraits of the youthful Shakespeare, frequently self-mocking, abound in the comedies. The composite archetype is that of a brilliant courtier poet, reveling in his own linguistic exuberance, who, because he is not wholly at ease in the illusory, false-speaking world of the court, develops a distinctly satiric edge. Rosaline's description of Berowne's fascinating eloquence provides a vivid glimpse of Shakespeare's youthful charisma:

> Berowne they call him; but a merrier man,
> Within the limit of becoming mirth,
> I never spent an hour's talk withal.
> His eye begets occasion for his wit;
> For every object that the one doth catch
> The other turns to a mirth-moving jest,
> Which his fair tongue (conceit's expositor)
> Delivers in such apt and gracious words
> That aged ears play truant at his tales,
> And younger hearings are quite ravished;
> So sweet and voluble is his discourse.
>
> (*Love's Labour's Lost*, II.i.66–76)

Of the above passage Frank Harris writes, "Every touch of this self-painted portrait deserves to be studied: it is the first photograph of our poet which we possess—a photograph, too, taken in early manhood."[104] Berowne is Hamlet before disillusionment and cynicism take hold. For Armado, Berowne, Benedick, or Valentine, and for Shakespeare, it is love that inspires the courtier to become a poet. "By heaven, I do love, and it hath taught me to rhyme, and to be melancholy," sighs Berowne. For him love's high honor is the only creed, and he envisions a court where love transforms politics and "plant[s] in tyrants mild humility."

Problems of love and language are inseparable in Shakespeare. He explores his feelings in a torrent of words. His mastery of rhetoric, one of the core accomplishments of an educated Elizabethan gentleman, is absolute; indeed, his rhetoric has a flowing, fluent, prodigious quality that is unrivaled. He can be high-flown and fantastical too, even a trifle affected. The King's description of Armado is pertinent:

> A man in all the world's new fashion planted,
> That hath a mint of phrases in his brain;
> One who the music of his own vain tongue
> Doth ravish like enchanting harmony . . .
> (*Love's Labour's Lost,* I.i.163–166)

Berowne concurs, calling him "a man of fire-new words." Like Armado, the "refined traveler of Spain," Shakespeare was clearly a well-traveled aristocrat, who soaked up the Renaissance on the Continent and brought back new ideas and phrases to court, gaining for himself the reputation of an exotic. More important, he was one of the chief importers into England of the cultural flowering in Europe, and claims this distinction rather self-depreciatingly through Armado, Berowne, and others. His playful identification with the fantastical Spaniard reveals a tendency to see himself as an outsider, set apart by his eccentric brilliance. It is also through Armado that he gently mocks the culture of euphuism that he himself created to enrich the English language.

This youthful Shakespeare, like Orsino, is a courtly aesthete, a lover of music, poetry, and flowers, a highly refined sensualist with more than a touch of narcissism. "If music be the food of love," he declares, "play on; / Give me excess of it, that surfeiting / The appetite may sicken, and so die." Just as we are bewitched by the music of Orsino's words, so he himself is in thrall to the harmonies of his musicians. Like Hamlet, Orsino despises wealth or "quantity of dirty lands" and, though perfectly at his ease socially, prefers solitude ("for I myself am best / When least in company"). Like many a Shakespearean hero, he is a kind of jovial recluse. Music and poetry are food for his melancholy nature and lyrical talents, and provide a release for his more troubled feelings. As he says to Viola-Cesario:

> Give me some music. Now good morrow, friends.
> Now good Cesario, but that piece of song,
> That old and antic song we heard last night;
> Methought it did relieve my passion much.
> <div align="right">(<i>Twelfth Night,</i> II.iv.1–4)</div>

Somehow one cannot think of Orsino without imagining him calling for more music, more poetry.

This young Shakespearean hero not only has an insatiable appetite for language, but is hungry for renown and can say with Navarre in *Love's Labour's Lost,* "Let fame, that all hunt after in their lives, / Live register'd upon our brazen tombs." So various are his talents that he is unsure of the form his ambition should take: military? political? literary? Benedick is a soldier, and Bertram, longing for military glory, steals off to the wars. Ultimately, he is a Renaissance man, and the path he values above all is honor. The rich promise of his talent is undeniable. The only thing that can derail him is love; love and honor rarely join hands—at least at court. As Proteus says of Valentine, "He after honour hunts, I after love." The hero, with his fluid sense of identity, is nothing if not protean.

A born entertainer, he lets his humor and high spirits at times run away with him. Maria, one of the Princess's ladies, calls Berowne "the merry mad-cap lord," adding, "Not a word with him but a jest." When Beatrice describes Benedick as "the Prince's jester," he is stung into self-reflection: "The Prince's fool! Ha, it may be I go under that title because I am merry." Both Berowne and Benedick play the fool, though they are not formally fools (there being no court jester until Touchstone). Jaques, the cynical courtier in *As You Like It,* is in his own words "ambitious for a motley coat."

Feste in *Twelfth Night,* although written down as Olivia's jester, is
more a bohemian aristocrat who plays the fool when it suits him
(like Mercutio or Hamlet).[105] This fooling, then, has a purpose: to
make the truth palatable. As Duke Senior says of Touchstone, "He
uses his folly like a stalking-horse, and under the presentation of
that he shoots his wit."

   The Shakespearean fool, that highly individual and arresting figure, is no quaint anachronism from the courts of medieval kings,
but a highly sophisticated truth teller. He is a fool *because he tells the
truth*. He is also a deeply personal figure in Shakespeare's private mythology, an ironic comment on his own excluded status. The fool is a
metaphor for the author's alienation from court culture, and a reminder
of his parentless origins. It was, one senses, from Yorick the jester that
Hamlet received his only real affection in childhood:

> I knew him, Horatio, a fellow of infinite jest, of most excellent
> fancy. He hath bore me on his back a thousand times, and now—
> how abhorred in my imagination it is. My gorge rises at it. Here
> hung those lips that I have kissed I know not how oft. Where be
> your gibes now, your gambols, your songs, your flashes of merri-
> ment, that were wont to set the table on a roar?
>
> (V.i.178–185)

   Courtier, soldier, scholar, poet, lover, jester: the young Shakespearean hero is the complete Renaissance man longing for the fame
and self-vindication that disaffection demands and his talents so richly
promise.

   Even in the comedies we consider Shakespeare's most light-hearted,
the intrusive melancholy of the hero is hard to ignore. Through him
the shadow of alienation and dispossession falls across these early works,
making our laughter uneasy. Whether we speak of Antonio, Valentine, Berowne, Benedick, Jaques, Bertram, Feste, or Orsino, the hero,
like the scapegoat of mythology, is isolated to work out some private
sorrow. His fate seems strangely sealed, his only release poetry. "I hold
the world but as the world Gratiano, / A stage, where every man must
play a part, / And mine a sad one," laments Antonio in *The Merchant
of Venice*. Even Antipholus of Syracuse in *The Comedy of Errors* complains that "He that commends me to mine own content / Commends
me to the thing I cannot get." The melancholy note is everywhere

sounded, and from Berowne to Jaques is but a short step: both are jour-
neying toward Hamlet.

The transformation of Berowne the lyric poet into Hamlet the
dramatist drives the comedies toward their remorseless conclusion:
the impossibility of marriage and the isolation of the hero. The
melancholy refrain from Feste's final song, "For the rain it raineth
every day," seems to be the refrain for the entire series of comedies. At the heart of this bleak outlook seems to lie some sort of
shattered troth. Or maybe Antipholus of Syracuse's search for family
and identity reveals a dark secret that turns the hero's world upside
down. One thinks of the Ghost's revelation in *Hamlet* and the hero's
desperate cry, "I say we will have no mo[re] marriage!" But the
souring of Berowne's vision does not have to wait until the later
comedies, or the tragedies; the satirist in him already rubs shoulders with the merry madcap lord. As Rosaline says,

> Oft have I heard of you, my Lord Berowne,
> Before I saw you, and the world's large tongue
> Proclaims you for a man replete with mocks;
> Full of comparisons and wounding flouts,
> Which you on all estates will execute
> That lie within the mercy of your wit . . .
> (*Love's Labour's Lost*, V.ii.833–838)

He himself, having overheard the King and his fellow lords forswear
themselves, cries, "Now step I forth to whip hypocrisy!"

The satirist in Shakespeare is also the scapegoat, driven into lonely
exile for his transgressions, real or imagined. Even Berowne is exiled from his love for a year and a day, and must submit to a penance
to curb his flouting tongue. Nor is this done in wholly holiday fashion, as he concedes:

> Our wooing doth not end like an old play;
> Jack hath not Jill: these ladies' courtesy
> Might well have made our sport a comedy.
> (V.ii.865–867)

By locating the real target of Shakespeare's satire, it is possible to
identify what transformed him from royal favorite to royal scapegoat.

The bridge between these two figures is Jaques, the exiled lord and "traveler" who on his own admission "can suck melancholy out of a song, as a weasel sucks eggs." He is a poet as well as a musician, and sings one of his own songs:

> If it do come to pass
>   That any man turn ass,
> Leaving his wealth and ease,
>   A stubborn will to please,
> Ducdame, ducdame, ducdame,
>   Here shall he see
>   Gross fools as he,
> And if he will come to me.
>   (*As You Like It,* II.v.47–54)

A fellow lord asks the meaning of "ducdame" and receives the reply that it is an invocation "to call fools into a circle," i.e., to call gentlemen to court where they must strive to please "a stubborn will," that of the tyrant. Ducdame ("Duke Dame") is another name for Elizabeth, the mannish queen with the heart and stomach of a king. Elizabeth, the song implies, has created a cult of love, which turns men to asses. Jaques-Shakespeare is just such a courtier, as Duke Senior says of him, "I think he be transform'd into a beast, / For I can nowhere find him like a man." Yet he differs from the common herd of dupes in that he has become a man apart who makes it his business to rail upon the folly of the court. Why? Most likely because his love for his stubborn monarch was more personal than political, and was reciprocated until some sudden disillusionment. One thinks of a fellow scapegoat, Bottom, who for a spell enjoyed the love of the Fairy Queen.

Jaques articulates Shakespeare's satirical creed, with the fool or jester as his model:

> I must have liberty
> Withal, as large a charter as the wind,
> To blow on whom I please, for so fools have;
> And they that are most galled with my folly,
> They most must laugh . . .
> Invest me in my motley. Give me leave

To speak my mind, and I will through and through
Cleanse the foul body of th'infected world,
If they will patiently receive my medicine.

(II.vii.47–51, 58–61)

In many ways, Feste in *Twelfth Night* is the alienated courtier par excellence. Using his wit and the art of fooling to keep his strong emotions at bay, Feste's technique of creative self-censorship has been English literature's recipe for success for more than four hundred years. Other characters follow suit until the play is awash with repressed emotion, inundated with images of rain, water, tears, and drowning. This dark-swelling tide surrounds the court, cutting it off like a bright little island in the midst of an implacable ocean. Nearly all the characters who inhabit this island—living on the verge of hysteria—partake of the constant self-guarding, second-guessing, and holding in that are their cultural standard. Much of their wit is displaced anger, with words thrusting, glancing, parrying. This is a shockingly tense and angry play, full of bitterness, regret, and thoughts of vengeance.

Each character lives under the burden of hidden grief, not knowing what truly ails him or her, though the sin Olivia imputes to Malvolio comes closest to the heart of the malaise: self-love. The narcissism of the characters is stongly allied to their feelings of dispossession, and here Shakespeare shows great insight, for a person cannot fall in love with himself unless he is in some fundamental manner self-divided. Of all the characters Feste best maintains his self-control, perhaps because he is most conscious of what is going on around him, and can release his feelings through song.

As the play begins, Feste has just returned from a long absence without leave. Maria fears for him, believing that his mistress, Olivia, will be angry, but Feste seems unconcerned. A law unto himself, he comes and goes as he pleases. His stock-in-trade is poetry, song, and snatches of bittersweet wit, yet he evinces a certain detachment from the profession fate has conferred on him. Feste cannot get away from the idea that words are instruments of deceit. As he says to Viola of his role in Olivia's household, "I am indeed not her fool, but her corrupter of words." In other words, he bends meanings, both to deflect and to accommodate the will of his mistress.

Feste is nonchalant about his absences because he is, as he admits to Viola, largely invisible. This invisibility is not a result of low birth or lack of education; it stems from a secret shame that is hinted at, but never openly expressed. Olivia, like Elizabeth, is much courted yet veils herself in pretended chastity, in her case weeping over her brother's death. However, when her passion is aroused by Viola, she pursues the object of her desires with single-minded determination. How she is and how she wishes to appear are two different things.

Feste hints that there may have been some sort of marriage troth or love contract between him and Olivia, which the lady reneged upon. When Viola asks him, "Art not thou the Lady Olivia's fool?" he replies: "No indeed sir, the Lady Olivia has no folly. She will keep no fool, sir, till she be married, and fools are as like husbands as pilchards are to herrings, the husband's the bigger." Pilchards being little herrings, the logical conclusion is not hard to draw: the fool is a little husband—or an unregarded one. Thus Feste's earlier quarrel with Malvolio in front of Olivia should be played as a scene bristling with sexual jealousy. But there is more. In the only brief scene in which Olivia and Feste are alone together, Olivia admonishes the jester for putting Malvolio's back up: "Now you see, sir, how your fooling grows old, and people dislike it." Feste replies, "Thou hast spoke for us, Madonna, as if thy eldest son should be a fool: whose skull Jove cram with brains." The conclusion is just as inescapable: the fool is Olivia's son. Son, husband, court jester, invisible man: little wonder this fellow seems bitter and confused about his identity.

The literary historian G. G. Gervinus writes, "No other of Shakespeare's fools is so conscious of his superiority as this one."[106] Feste's problem is that he knows too much about his secretive mistress, and cannot reveal what he knows without giving away his identity. All he can do is keep telling the truth in his own sideways manner. One thing is certain: his dilemma is Shakespeare's dilemma.

The game of love and the game of power were played together at the court of Elizabeth. To seek power was to court the queen, and vice versa: both were dangerous pursuits. To win the queen without the consent of the Privy Council was to commit treason, and adultery could be construed as a capital offense. (Henry VIII's 1536

Act of Succession made it a capital offense to "espouse, marry or deflower being unmarried any of the King's female relations.") Here was no ordinary love object, but the liege lord of every man and woman in the realm. No wonder Olivia calls Orsino's marriage proposal "heresy."

Elizabeth herself was addicted to the game of love, for it was her way of exercising power as a woman rather than as a monarch. She led men on, delighting in elaborate rituals of courtship in which she was worshipped as a goddess, while she kept them in their place with lowly pet names, such as "pygmy," "elf," "sheep," "monkey," "boar," "lids," and so forth. The confusion of love and politics meant it was impossible to tell whether love was real or feigned, heartfelt or expedient, the reams of love poems written to the queen being as much political petitions as confessions of the heart. Writing to her from Dover, where he was to embark for Europe, Sir Christopher Hatton began his letter, "Madam, I find the greatest lack that ever poor wretch sustained. No death, no, not hell, no fear of death shall ever win me of my consent so far to wrong myself again as to be absent from you one day." He ended it, "Your bondman everlastingly tied."[107]

The romantic element in Shakespeare's comedies draws its life from the special form of courtly love Elizabeth generated, with herself as the object of adoration. Courtiers, whether married or not, were expected to pay court to the queen as their sovereign mistress. This love could rarely, if ever, be fulfilled, and languished for the most part in the realms of fantasy. As with the courtly love of the troubadors, its reality was gauged by the intensity of suffering it caused the suitor.

In 1579, at age forty-five, Elizabeth embarked upon the last great foreign courtship of her reign, one that excited dread and fascination both at court and in the country at large. Although she was almost certainly beyond her childbearing years, the queen and her physicians kept up the fiction that she could still produce an heir; all discussion of the succession remained off-limits. Her suitor, the only one to make the journey to England in person, was Hercule François, duc d'Alençon, youngest son of Henri II of France and Catherine de' Medici. He courted her for five years, from 1579 to his premature death in 1584, though the game had begun in earnest in 1578 when he sent his personal emissary Jean de Simier, whom Elizabeth nicknamed her "Monkey," to make love to the queen on his behalf. (If the jealousy of the Earl of Leicester is any measure, he was remarkably successful in his endeavor.)

At twenty-four, Alençon was young enough to be Elizabeth's son. Moreover, the tiny Frenchman with the crooked spine, who suffered from an acute form of acne that laid special siege to his enormous nose, presented an outlandish spectacle beside the erect, red-haired queen who prided herself on her smooth complexion and delicate features. Yet Elizabeth seemed genuinely enchanted by her "Frog," as she dubbed the French prince, whose Gallic charm and excessive gallantry did much to ameliorate any deficiencies of form. Alençon knew all the tricks of courtly lovemaking, and relished the playacting as much as she did. So convincing was Elizabeth's *grande passion* that even the ministers who had assumed she was merely dallying for political purposes grew alarmed. The prospective match was so unpopular in England that Alençon's visit of August 1579 was kept secret, but this only whetted the queen's appetite. The court looked on in astonishment at the grotesque charade, horrified at rumors that Elizabeth and the prince had slept together. The country was no less hostile. As Josephine Ross writes:

> Mendoza [the Spanish ambassador] gave it as his opinion that revolution was in the air. Loyal Englishmen did not want a Catholic king and they did not want a French king; in Alençon they would have both.[108]

Shakespeare mocked the queen's passion for the French monster in the sudden strange love of Titania, the Fairy Queen, for ass-headed Bottom in *A Midsummer Night's Dream*. In Act I, scene ii, Bottom is unsure whether the part he is to play before the Duke is that of lover or tyrant, but he says, "My chief humour is for a tyrant. I could play Ercles [Hercules] rarely, or a part to tear a cat in." Alençon played both parts, lover to the queen of England and tyrant in the Netherlands, presiding over what came to be known as the "French fury," a failed attempt to sack Antwerp. One of his Christian names, though rarely used, was Hercule. In Act IV Bottom addresses Titania's fairies as "Mounsieur," the term by which Alençon himself was known at the English court, and this is echoed when Puck says to

Oberon, "My mistress with a *monster* is in love." Bottom asks Cobweb to get his weapons in his hand and bring him "the honey bag." Shakespeare's court audience, aware of the playwright' hits at the expense of the French courtship, would have heard "money bag," given Alençon's continual demands for money from England to fund his anti-Spanish campaign in the Netherlands. Finally, Oberon's reference to the "mermaid on a dolphin's back" conjures up a picture of Elizabeth riding the dauphin, i.e., the heir to the French throne, Alençon being heir presumptive of his brother, King Henri III.

Beneath the surface satire of the queen and her frog prince lay an altogether more sinister story of broken troth and unrequited love, of lost sovereignty and a royal child spirited away, of art made tongue-tied by authority. This ulterior story is, as ever, Shakespeare's own. Bottom is a complex self-portrait of the author, spanning both worlds of his existence, court and theater. An artisan or theater man, who wants to direct the play before the Duke *and* act all the parts, Bottom is the professional showman who relishes the world of public entertainment, and "hath simply the best wit of any handicraft man in Athens." On the other hand, he is the "gentle [i.e., noble] mortal," weaver of words and stories, whose singing enchants the Fairy Queen, yet whose tongue must be tied, for he is not always as discreet as he might be. He is something of a paradox, this Bottom. It seems his theatrical career, unbefitting to a nobleman, has left him *at the bottom* of court esteem. He is Shakespeare's bitter acknowledgment of his own shameful status as professional artist, one that quite overwhelms the gentleness of his birth in the eyes of his peers. The ass head is also a self-mocking swipe at the Stratfordian mask Shakespeare was compelled to wear to protect his identity.

A deeper, more emotional component of the image of Bottom, alienated from his fellows and wandering in the wilderness, is that of Shakespeare the royal outcast. Like Caliban, Timon, and Poor Tom, Bottom is one of many characters in the canon who symbolize Shakespeare's feelings of ugliness and disaffection as pariah, bastard, prodigy, and nameless man, one who with Hamlet could "accuse [himself] of such things that it were better his mother had not borne [him]." The term "monster," used of Bottom and Caliban, suggests not only the unnatural and deformed, but the prodigious or divinely gifted. There is a royal dimension, too: whereas Caliban is heir to his mother, Sycorax, queen of the Island before Prospero arrived, Bottom, for however brief a term, is consort to the Fairy Queen.

To be monstrous or deformed was also to be *transformed*. The actor transformed himself each time he took on a new role. The writer who adopted different pen names and identities was *deformed* through his many transformations. Like Proteus, the sea god, he could become anything he pleased. Even Hamlet uses the word "monstrous" to describe the actor who "but in a fiction, in a dream of passion, / Could force his soul so to his own conceit." For a nobleman or— God forbid!—the heir to the throne to make his home among the outlaws and vagabonds of the theater world, to become like Oberon a "king of shadows," was to engender such deep feelings of shame and ostracism that he could well imagine himself transformed into a monster. Shakespeare, Renaissance poet and prince, was also Bottom the artisan or theater man, the *transformed man* who, in the words of Sonnet 110, made himself "a motley to the view," "gored [his] own thoughts," and "sold cheap what is most dear."

Many mythological strands, not least that of Actaeon, weave themselves into the figure of Bottom. Like Jaques in *As You Like It,* Bottom has been transformed into a beast, not by accident but because he has witnessed something he should not have—an affair of state, perhaps, or the mysteries of Diana. This contact with the divine engenders a form of divinity in Bottom himself, who resembles the ancient Egyptian gods with their animal heads. One of the reasons for his transmutation is to prevent him from speaking of what he's seen or done, and yet he does manage to speak out (not without many a disclaimer, of course[109]) by means of the play he puts on to celebrate the royal wedding of Theseus and Hippolyta.

Another vivid strand of Bottom's mythic DNA is the Minotaur, the monstrous son—half man, half bull—of Minos, King of Crete. Kept hidden away in a specially built labyrinthine palace, the Minotaur was found and killed by Theseus, who used a clew of wool (also known as a *bottom*) to find his way out of the maze of corridors. There is also the story of the Golden Ass by Apuleius, made popular in Elizabethan times by William Adlington's translation. Its hero, Lucius, a nobleman from Thessaly, seeks to penetrate the mysteries of Isis. In his indiscriminate enthusiasm for the magic arts, however, he finds himself transformed into an ass. Remaining in this form from one rose season to the next, he is eventually reborn as a devotee of the goddess. As Robert Graves reminds us, asses in western European folklore "are connected . . . with the midwinter Saturnalia at the conclusion of which the ass-eared god, later the Christmas Fool with his ass-eared cap, was killed by his rival, the Spirit of the New Year." In such a guise Bottom becomes the mock king of the ancient English revels, venerated for a brief time before being sacrificed. But his dream of kingship is no mere fantasy; it is the guiding myth of Shakespeare's art.

Shakespeare's ambivalent position vis-à-vis the Fairy Queen can be appreciated when one places Oberon beside Bottom, for they represent two perspectives on his relationship with Elizabeth. Oberon, "king of shadows," appears to be at the mercy of Titania as far as family life is concerned, but is able to exercise power over her through art (i.e., by means of Puck and his theatrical tricks). As the theater chief of the time—the king of Fairyland—he is a powerful man in his own right. The bone of contention between Oberon and Titania is a beautiful changeling child stolen, according to Puck, from an Indian king. Oberon wants the boy to be his "henchman," but Titania keeps him for herself, crowning him with flowers and making him her joy. Her description of the child's birth tips off those in the know that the child is hers and Oberon's, and that Shakespeare is talking about a child of his own born to the Virgin Queen:

> His mother was a votress of my order;
> And in the spiced Indian air, by night,
> Full often hath she gossip'd by my side;
> And sat with me on Neptune's yellow sands,
> Marking th'embarked traders on the flood:
> When we have laugh'd to see the sails conceive
> And grow big-bellied with the wanton wind;
> Which she, with pretty and with swimming gait
> Following (her womb then rich with my young squire),
> Would imitate, and sail upon the land
> To fetch me trifles, and return again
> As from a voyage rich with merchandise.
> But she, being mortal, of that boy did die;
> And for her sake do I rear up her boy.

(II.i.123–136)

Titania is used by Ovid as an epithet for Diana, the virgin goddess, and here the mother of the "changeling" is identified as a votaress
of Diana, a tag confirmed in the next line in the phrase "In**dian a**ir,"
which yields both "Diana" and "Dian['s] air [-heir]." The last lines
tell of a familiar story among highborn or royal families, whereby a
love child is brought up as a foster child, the mother pretending that
the baby belongs to a dear friend who died in childbirth. So might
Elizabeth have farmed out her son by Shakespeare. Not being able
to acknowledge her child, she would indeed have died—as a mother.
One is reminded of Shakespeare's epithet for Elizabeth in Sonnet 107,
"the mortal moon," a phrase that nicely captures the private-public,
mortal-divine dichotomies of her life.

Any doubt on the matter of this mysterious virgin birth is dis-
pelled by Oberon's recollection of a certain remarkable incident,
which has long been understood by scholars as a tribute to the Virgin
Queen:

> That very time I saw (but thou couldst not),
> Flying between the cold moon and the earth,
> Cupid all arm'd: a certain aim he took
> At a fair vestal, throned by the west,
> And loos'd his love-shaft smartly from his bow
> As it should pierce a hundred thousand hearts.
> But I might see young Cupid's fiery shaft
> Quench'd in the chaste beams of the watery moon;
> And the imperial votress passed on,
> In maiden meditation, fancy-free.
> Yet mark'd I where the bolt of Cupid fell:
> It fell upon a little western flower,
> Before milk-white, now purple with love's wound.
>   (II.i.155–167)

Titania and her childbearing votaress combine in the phrases "imperial votress" and "fair vestal, throned by the west," code words for
the quasi-divine Elizabeth. Shakespeare could not be more explicit
about what happened. The queen, pierced by Cupid's fiery shaft,
conceived; and though she "passed on, in maiden meditation, fancy-
free" (i.e., kept her mask of virginity firmly in place), a royal child
was born ("the little western flower"). He told the same story in *Venus*

and Adonis, where the fruit of Venus's love for Adonis was "a purple flower checker'd with white." This flower, also known as "Beauty's rose," is the Fair Youth of the Sonnets, and in these, too, Shakespeare complains of being denied access to his royal child.

At the heart of *A Midsummer Night's Dream,* like the Minotaur at the center of the labyrinth, is the secret love child of the Fairy Queen (Elizabeth) and the Fairy King (Shakespeare). Viewing the story through the lens of Bottom's dream—the love match between an ethereal queen and a "gentle mortal" who puts on plays before royalty—one begins to understand the depth of disillusion behind the humor. The play that Bottom and his fellow mechanicals put on before Theseus and Hippolyta is entitled "A tedious brief scene of young Pyramus and his love Thisbe, very tragical mirth." *Very tragical mirth:* a dark layer of tragedy lurks beneath the surface brilliance of Shakespeare's comedies.

The game of courtly love Elizabeth played to bolster her self-regard and humiliate the men dependent on her generated enormous anger at court, which in part was manifested in the vicious rivalry surrounding the throne. No one dared condemn her openly; criticism was deflected onto others. The savagery, for instance, with which Mary Queen of Scots was demonized by the Privy Council far outweighed any political threat she posed. Shakespeare alone voices his rage, but because he roars so wittily and eloquently, and in the context of what appears to be a different story, the force and direction of his anger are often missed. It wasn't until I saw a performance of *Twelfth Night* by the Acting Ensemble in Bread Loaf, Vermont, in the summer of 2008 that I understood Malvolio as one of Shakespeare's bitterest self-portraits. The remarkable performance of Olivia's steward by Brian McEleney played up the repressed hysteria of this most unhappy suitor. For all his absurdity and self-righteousness, his strange masochism even, one sensed something truly tragic about Malvolio, his refusal to be reconciled at the end being more than wounded pride.

Though Olivia herself does not write the letter that tricks her steward into believing she is in love with him, we know enough of this fickle mistress to see that she has led him on sufficiently in the past to make his credulity plausible. The letter, to "the unknown belov'd," is part of the web Olivia has woven over the years. Through it Malvolio is gulled into believing he will be her consort, and they will lead a life of royal felicity (with gold garters and smiles); instead, he is made the butt of a hypocritical and hedonistic court. Branded insane and placed in darkness, Malvolio has no access to his mistress and no means of redress. He is mercilessly mocked for his royal ambitions, and his vow of vengeance at the end feels like an expression of Shakespeare's own determination to avenge himself on those who have betrayed him.

When Sir Toby congratulates Olivia's gentlewoman Maria on the success of her letter, he says, "Why, thou hast put him in such a dream, that when the image of it leaves him he must run mad"; and Olivia describes her steward's amorous behavior as "very midsummer madness." We are back in the realm of disappointed royal dreams, so vividly evoked in *A Midsummer Night's Dream*. "Thus have I had thee as a dream doth flatter," writes Shakespeare in Sonnet 87, "In sleep a king, but waking no such matter." Maria signs Olivia's letter "The Fortunate Unhappy," whose Latin form "*Fortunatus Infelix*" we met in the context of *A Hundred Sundrie Flowres*. (Shakespeare is Fortune's—i.e., Elizabeth's—but he is "unhappy" because he cannot attain to that felicity which the realization of his royal inheritance would bestow upon him.) This use of "happy" brings home the irony of the advice Malvolio receives in the letter: "If thou entertain'st my love, let it appear in thy smiling; thy smiles become thee well. Therefore in my presence still smile, dear my sweet, I prithee."

When Malvolio imagines himself "sitting in [his] state," surrounded by attendants, he is imagining a royal state. Fantasizing about making love to the goddess, Olivia, he sees himself in his "branch'd velvet gown," a passing reference, perhaps, to the transformed Actaeon with his branched head. Olivia, for all her faults, truly values Malvolio, but for a quality that is never openly expressed. "Let some of my people have a special care of him," she says. "I would not have him miscarry for the half of my dowry." Miscarriages and dowries: no one can accuse Shakespeare of lack of persistence. Nor can we fail to marvel at the depth of his humor. "This does make some obstruction in the blood, this cross-gartering, but what of that?" says Malvolio to Olivia. Aware that his blood can always be called into question, Shakespeare glances poignantly at the story behind the foundation of the Order of the Garter. King Edward III, retrieving the Countess of Salisbury's garter at a ball, attached it to his leg with the words "Honi soit qui mal y pense" ("Shame to him who thinks ill of my action"). She duly became his mistress. Those who wear their garters crossed, however, can expect no such success.

The most endearing element of Shakespeare's genius is his extraordinary sympathy for the insulted and injured, which goes hand in hand with an ability to laugh at himself. Just when we might be tempted to despise a character such as Malvolio, Shakespeare inhabits him body and soul. No matter that he has already used him to satirize his sworn enemy Sir Christopher Hatton, and possibly several others; Malvolio is still a fit temple for a poet who not only celebrated the shadow side but lived in it.

Love, then, is at the heart of Shakespeare's creative life, his inspiration and his path to despair; it is also his undoing, being a kind of treason. To protect himself and speak his truth with impunity, he assumes the guise of the fool. Ultimately, his love can be only a kind of madness, for it leads to disillusion—or the block. If he lives, he will end up with horns (the cuckold's or Actaeon's). *A Midsummer Night's Dream* reveals how dangerous and illusory Shakespeare's love for the queen is, "illusory" because the politicians have the power to overshadow his truth by manipulating the historical record. No wonder the poet goes out of his way to stress that what appears fantastical is in fact the truth. Though Theseus is inclined to dismiss the experiences of the lovers in the wood as mere imagining, Hippolyta begs to differ:

> But all the story of the night told over,
> And all their minds transfigur'd so together,
> More witnesseth than fancy's images,
> And grows to something of great constancy;
> But howsoever, strange and admirable.
>
> (V.i.23–27)

As Touchstone says to Audrey in *As You Like It,* "the truest poetry is the most feigning."

Where Olivia-Elizabeth is concerned, love takes second place to the image she has created for herself. Even doting Orsino is finally compelled to voice his disaffection at her cruelty, and in his words one hears Shakespeare's rebuke to Elizabeth:

ORSINO: Still so cruel?
OLIVIA: Still so constant, lord.
ORSINO: What, to perverseness? You uncivil lady,
    To whose ingrate and inauspicious altars
    My soul the faithfull'st off'rings hath breath'd out
    That e'er devotion tender'd—What shall I do?
OLIVIA: Even what it please my lord that shall become of him.
ORSINO: Why should I not, had I the heart to do it,
    Like to th'Egyptian thief at point of death,
    Kill what I love?—a savage jealousy
    That sometime savours nobly. But hear me this:
    Since you to non-regardance cast my faith,
    And that I partly know the instrument
    That screws me from my true place in your favour,
    Live you the marble-breasted tyrant still.
                  (*Twelfth Night*, V.i.109–122)

Even in the early comedies, the Dark Lady of the Sonnets casts her shadow, through characters such as Titania, Olivia, Rosaline, Phoebe, the Merry Wives, and Hero (or at least Claudio's misperception of Hero). *For I have sworn thee fair, and thought thee bright, / Who art as black as hell, as dark as night.* Sometimes we glimpse her as a Circean figure, transforming men into beasts; at other times she is perceived through the double vision of the hero, as both whore and virgin. When Claudio suspects Hero of infidelity, he raves at her before the altar:

    Out on thee, seeming! I will write against it.
    You seem to me as Dian in her orb,
    As chaste as is the bud ere it be blown;
    But you are more intemperate in your blood
    Than Venus, or those pamper'd animals
    That rage in savage sensuality.
        (*Much Ado About Nothing*, IV.i.56–61)

Olivia, too, doth protest too much, and we find ourselves unconvinced by her show of reclusive mourning.

Few would argue with the notion that there is something disturbingly forced and unsatisfactory about the marriages at the end of

Shakespeare's comedies, with the possible exception of *The Merchant of Venice* and *As You Like It*. Those at the end of *Two Gentlemen, The Taming of the Shrew, Much Ado, Twelfth Night, All's Well,* and *Measure for Measure* all fail the test of emotional truth, and that is rare for Shakespeare, the master psychologist. Even the unions at the end of *A Midsummer Night's Dream* lose their authenticity in the shadow cast by Bottom's disillusionment. Despite his adherence to the forms and conventions of comedy, Shakespeare could not heave his heart where it would not go. Marriage for him did not signify reconciliation and a life of happiness ever after. Writing of *All's Well* and *Measure for Measure,* Janet Adelman observes: "The marriages that end these comedies fail to satisfy the desires of either the characters or the audience; and their failure marks the extent to which Hamlet's prohibition [about no more marriages] remains in force and hence the extent to which comedy is no longer a viable genre for Shakespeare."[110]

As Shakespeare matures, his emotional complexes become more evident. Even the comedic heroes are in a process of metamorphosing into Hamlet, a man overwhelmed by emotions he cannot express. The pervasiveness of water imagery in *Twelfth Night* acts as a sort of harbinger to the tragedies, as if Shakespeare's buried sorrows were all issuing to the surface in an accumulated surge of despair. From now on, the rain will rain every day, as Feste has it, with the hero heading for the political wilderness, his thirst the unslakable thirst of the banished man. *Water water everywhere, nor any drop to drink.*

In sum, the comic hero in Shakespeare is a sensitive aristocratic poet alienated from the court by his artistic sensibilities and secret relationship with the queen-goddess. The fact that this relationship is taboo engenders in him the beginnings of an identity crisis. Son, consort, royal father—we catch glimpses of all three in this complex, fugitive man, as if witnessing a Greek tragedy in the making. Revealing his identity becomes the purpose of his art, stirring up a political hornet's nest because of the constitutional implications of who he is. A royal outcast, his dreams of kingship become his plays. When they are over, he steps forward with the words, "The king's a beggar, now the play is done."[111]

~ 8 ~

Compassing the Crown

There is only one history, and that is the soul's.
—W. B. Yeats

IN CHAPTER 7 WE saw the ghostly form of the young Hamlet stalking the comedies in the guise of Berowne, Benedick, Jaques, Feste, and Bertram. The paradox they embodied—that of the alienated man at the heart of state—found its surest expression in the fool or jester who speaks out, like a kind of privileged child, against the monarch. This Shakespearean fool, despite his indeterminate status, is to the manner born; hence the special depth of his estrangement.

If we view Shakespeare's chronicle plays or histories as we might his tragedies, comedies, or romances, then we find that the alienated prince remains at the center of the dramatist's work, quill poised over parchment. Relieved of their historical onus, the histories reveal themselves to be deeply political as well as deeply personal works. The key is to think in terms of Hamlet, for the plays unfold out of his psyche. Hamlet is "the most immediate" to the throne of Denmark, yet curiously alienated from it; he can find no role commensurate with his birth and destiny. His problem is his inability to succeed.

The history plays, too, dramatize one long war of succession, as if England ("this teeming womb of royal kings") were undergoing the most unnaturally protracted birth throes in its efforts to produce a legitimate king, one worthy to sit upon the throne of David—a true successor, no less. And yet what do we find? A group of kings more in sympathy with failure than success, at odds with their destiny, and in love with the poetry and pathos of resignation.[112] As in *Hamlet,* the only true king seems to be a ghost. Scratch the surface of these plays and one finds oneself staring at the crowned figure of vanity holding a skull in one hand and the fool's bauble in the other. Far from ruling the realm, the king has turned storyteller, as witness Richard II:

> For God's sake let us sit upon the ground
> And tell sad stories of the death of kings:
> How some have been depos'd, some slain in war,
> Some haunted by the ghosts they have deposed,
> Some poisoned by their wives, some sleeping kill'd,
> All murthered—for within the hollow crown
> That rounds the mortal temples of a king
> Keeps Death his court, and there the antic sits,
> Scoffing his state and grinning at his pomp,
> Allowing him a breath, a little scene,
> To monarchize, be fear'd, and kill with looks;
> Infusing him with self and vain conceit,
> As if this flesh which walls about our life
> Were brass impregnable; and, humour'd thus,
> Comes at the last, and with a little pin
> Bores thorough his castle wall, and farewell king!
>
> (III.ii.155–170)

The fact that these words are spoken by a king makes them extraordinarily powerful as an indictment of the vanity of kingship. Through Richard, Shakespeare expresses his realization that monarchy itself will not endure unless the king transforms his understanding and exercise of power to more spiritual ends by assuming the role of the philosopher-king. If the sovereign remains identified with the temporal glory of his position and seeks to rule by fear, he and the whole system on which his power is founded will crumble. This is not what the Tudor monarchy under Elizabeth wanted to hear, and one can only assume that Shakespeare's outspokenness was driven by some personal imperative. In looking at Shakespeare's earliest history plays, the literary scholar E. M. W. Tillyard wonders where the poet's keen interest in politics, or rather his commitment to them, comes from.

> It is plain enough that much of the substance of Shakespeare's more serious thoughts in his early years must have been political: otherwise, he would not have spent himself on his great historical

tetralogy, the three parts of *Henry VI* and *Richard III*. But the intrusion of politics in the *Comedy of Errors* and *Titus Andronicus,* where there was no need for them, shows how strongly they gripped his mind. Was this surprising at such a time, and what were the likely alternatives?[113]

It is generally thought that Shakespeare wrote his histories as Tudor propaganda, to inspire national unity at a time when England faced war with Spain. This is true as far as it goes, but Shakespeare's history plays do not have the feel of publicly commissioned art, written to government specifications. After all, where does Falstaff, the deconstructor of kings and kingship—more anarchist than monarchist—fit into such a scheme? What spur to valor and unity is he? What benchmark of national honor? For it is he, not Henry IV, who wins our allegiance.

To go beneath the surface of the public face, the propaganda, is dangerous. There is only one monarch that Henry IV, whom Hotspur accuses of breaking "oath on oath," can possibly stand for, and that is the notoriously fickle and perjurious Queen Elizabeth. Falstaff, meanwhile, the mock king or lord of misrule, whose name is a play on Shake-speare, is a portrait of the dramatist. Henry's oath breaking, which tarnishes the sovereignty he is pledged to uphold, is contrasted with Falstaff's venial word bending, which is more an index of imaginative exuberance than of bad faith. It is the former who threatens good government, not the latter.

The concept of honor, and by extension truth, is important in Shakespeare; it is the oath or word-bond of the knight to serve his king and master and so live in good faith, just as his vassals pledge their service and obedience to him; above all, it is the sovereign pledge of the monarch to his subjects to rule in accordance with the law of God. That way, to paraphrase Polonius, he cannot be false to any man. This is the feudal contract, whose dissolution Shakespeare's plays so vividly dramatize. The broken oath, the oath given in bad faith, not only undermines the integrity of the king but tarnishes his sovereignty. The kingdom divides, and the very identity of those who govern breaks up. The center cannot hold. Now truth must be enforced by the sword. Kings are not kings; they are displaced; their crowns are lost, their heirs disinherited; the distinction between base and legitimate is obscured; in sum, the throne is there for the taking. But where was Shakespeare's personal interest in all this? Why was the word of a king crucial to his art?

It is easy to forget what a genealogical tour de force the history plays are. Shakespeare's deep knowledge of the ruling families of late medieval England, many of whom were still in power in his own time, and their various interrelationships, to say nothing of the complex threads leading from them to the throne, is quite astonishing. Talbot, Neville, Mowbray, Blunt, Hastings, Mortimer, Percy, Plantagenet, Beaufort, Stanley, Vernon, Grey, Scroope, Clifford, Woodville, Willoughby, de la Pole: these great figures from English history are treated as household names by Shakespeare.

These are plays of succession and royal right, written by an insider who had made it his business to master the legal and dynastic intricacies of succession from the reign of Richard II to his own day. Like Churchill in his *History of the English-Speaking Peoples,* Shakespeare writes history with an easy knowledge of the ruling class, and a subjective flair that is shaped by his deep investment in the destiny of his country. As G. M. Trevelyan, another aristocratic historian, wrote of his trilogy on the Italian patriot Garibaldi, "Without bias, I should never have written them at all. For I was moved to write them by a poetical sympathy with the passions of the Italian patriots of the period, which I retrospectively shared."

Shakespeare's intense sympathy with those whose guiding ambition is the crown prompted Walt Whitman to declare that the history plays were likely written by "one of the wolfish earls so plenteous in the plays themselves." The extraordinary power and authenticity of the language Shakespeare puts in the mouths of these medieval kings and feudal lords (and the brutal code of honor underpinning their every utterance) makes it reasonable to assume it was a register native to the author, and that their blood ran in his veins. Whitman clearly sensed Shakespeare's emotional identification with the story that these plays tell. They are no more a simple retelling of history than *Hamlet* is a straightforward chronicle of ancient Denmark. Rather, they are Shakespeare's personal intervention in the most pressing political debate of his day.

Andrew Hadfield argues that the Elizabethan theater was a public space where "political debates, commentary and allusion could be made by those who were excluded from the ordinary processes of political life." The Earl of Oxford was such a one, debarred from power by his status as royal bastard, yet with a passion to come into his own—to *succeed*—that is often expressed in the murderous rivalry of the royal houses competing for the throne.

It is as well Oxford was able to express his violent resentment at his exclusion through literature, or he may have become a regicide. (His deep fascination with king-killers is everywhere evident in the plays.) Instead, he cast himself as the hero of the histories in the shape of the maverick heir to the throne, who devises skits on his royal parent, yet metamorphoses into the victor of Agincourt. The anonymous play *The Raigne of King Edward III,* attributed to Shakespeare by a growing number of scholars, contains the figure of the book-loving warrior Edward Plantagenet, the Black Prince, in whom we descry Shakespeare's youthful self-image, as well as the significance of his nom de plume. Before the Battle of Crécy the young Prince Edward receives his spear from the herald with these words:

> Edward Plantagenet, Prince of Wales,
> Receive this lance into thy manly hand;
> Use it in fashion of a brazen pen
> To draw forth bloody stratagems in France
> And print thy valiant deeds in honour's book.
>
> (III.iii.192–196)

With the succession came the problem of legitimacy. All the claimants to the throne in Elizabeth's time were compromised in one way or another, though they could all make a case for their right. Under the will of Henry VIII (and his final Act of Succession), Elizabeth's rightful heir after 1559—in the absence of the queen's own issue—was Lady Katherine Grey, granddaughter of Henry VIII's younger sister Mary. In 1561, when Elizabeth discovered that Katherine had secretly married Edward Seymour, Earl of Hertford, himself of royal blood through his mother, her fury knew no bounds. Katherine, who was eight months pregnant, was arrested and thrown into the Tower, and Hertford with her. Elizabeth declared the marriage null and void and their child, Edward Seymour, Jr., a bastard. However, to many at court, including William Cecil, this Edward Seymour, the son of Protestant parents, was the true heir to the throne. The fact that the child bore the same name as Elizabeth's bastard son by Thomas Seymour could well have contributed to the queen's rage.

That same year, 1561, Thomas Norton and Thomas Sackville, both writers under the patronage of Hertford and sympathetic to his wife's claim, wrote a tragedy, *Gorboduc,* which was presented before the queen by the Gentlemen of the Inner Temple. It was the first English drama in blank verse. Through the dismal story of Gorboduc, an ancient king of Great Britain, and his dissentious sons, the play pointed up the dangers of leaving the succession uncertain and divided. In this case, the outcome was civil war and a land laid waste. It was a blatant appeal to Elizabeth to settle the succession upon her Grey cousins (and the Seymour line). It was also a faint premonition of what would come when that other Edward Seymour (Edward de Vere) began to assert his royal right in works of transcendent genius.

According to Tillyard, "the most deeply felt of all Shakespeare's political motives" is "the working out of a crime, the punishment of a villain, and the establishment of the Tudors."[114] This motive, as much personal as political, penetrates to the core of why Shakespeare wrote at all. Through it, we can comprehend why he was at pains to understand what constituted rightful kingship. It is not enough to say that succession was a pressing contemporary issue, and therefore of primary importance to Shakespeare. Not only does this leave out the question of personal motive, but it ignores the mystical reverence in which Shakespeare holds the English crown. As Richard of Gloucester says to the Duke of York:

> And father do but think
> How sweet a thing it is to wear a crown,
> Within whose circuit is Elysium
> And all that poets feign of bliss and joy.
>
> (*Henry VI, 3,* I.ii.28–31)

Shakespeare's cycle of eight history plays covers the great war of succession known as the War of the Roses (1455–1485), from the murder of Richard II in 1399 to the accession of Elizabeth's grandfather Henry Tudor in 1485. It comprises two tetralogies, the first (*Henry VI, Parts 1, 2, and 3;* and *Richard III*) postdating the second (*Richard II; Henry IV, Parts 1 and 2;* and *Henry V*) in historical time. The crime that sets the whole series of plays in motion is the murder of a poet-king, Richard II, who at the end of the second tetralogy is resurrected in the figure of Henry V, who in his younger days was more at home in the tavern, where he and Falstaff put on their satirical performances, than at court. Might not this death and resurrection of the poet-king have a deeply personal resonance for the author? After all, we find the same dynamic in the first tetralogy. Henry VI, the scholar-king, is deposed and murdered, then resurrected in the figure of the Earl of Richmond (Henry VII), whose rise he prophesied.

In the first tetralogy we quickly arrive at the eve of war and with it the symbolism of the roses, specifically in the scene in *Henry VI, Part 1*[115]—a scene invented by Shakespeare—in which the white and red roses are plucked in the Temple Garden by supporters of the Duke of Somerset, a leading Lancastrian, and Richard Plantagenet, later Duke of York, who see their respective roses as symbols of truth in their dynastic quarrel. In the ensuing wars, the white rose will become the badge of the House of York, the red rose that of Lancaster. When more roses are plucked for Plantagenet than for his opponent, he turns to Somerset and asks where his argument is now, to which Somerset replies, "Here in my scabbard, meditating that / Shall dye your white rose in a bloody red."

Although there is continual hypocrisy and treachery on both sides of the conflict, and none can claim the moral high ground, Shakespeare never loses sight of the deeper symbolic axis on which the red and white roses oppose each other: blood and spirit, violence and love, reason and impulse, imperialism and sovereignty—the very forces that must be reconciled if the English crown is to bear its true and destined radiance. The struggle between the two roses is the conflict between blood and spirit in the protagonists themselves, and through them the English nation striving for wholeness. This sense of inner strife and transformation is captured through the containing image of the Temple Garden, where the opposing sides first pluck the symbols of their antagonism. The real struggle between red and white takes place in the soul of the nation.

In alchemy, red and white symbolized the conjunction of opposites, or the union of sun and moon, and the combined red and white rose the union of fire and water. This is the mystical foundation of Shakespeare's rose imagery, which first becomes fully visible in the Sonnets, where the Fair Youth represents the final distillation of the red and white, or Tudor rose. We see it as well at the close of *Venus and Adonis,* where the slain Adonis is transformed into a purple flower "check'red with white." In Edgar, too, at the end of *King Lear,* the perfected rose finds expression in the restoration of the hero's name, which had been lost, "by treason's tooth bare-gnawn and canker-bit." Thus Adonis, Edgar, and the Fair Youth, through either suffering or royalty of nature, reconcile the warring factions of the rose on the spiritual plane. On the political plane, this union is effected by the Earl of Richmond (the future Henry VII, and the first Tudor king), who, after the Battle of Bosworth, marries the heiress of the white rose, Elizabeth of York. The union of York and Lancaster represents the culmination of a historical process, the birth of a new hybrid rose, although psychologically it is no more than a prelude to Shakespeare's exploration of the inner conflict of red and white that shaped the Tudor monarchy for the 118 years of its existence.

His depiction of the Wars of the Roses reflected religious divisions in Elizabethan England between Protestant and Catholic, which engendered numerous plots against the queen's life. The central issue was the succession, the ultimate question being, "What constitutes a rightful claim to the throne?" If there was no clear-cut claimant, no one anointed by God from birth, then what were the best criteria for kingship, and who should decide, Parliament or the incumbent sovereign? Whatever the answer, Shakespeare had his eye at all times on the Tudor monarchy and the succession. The ferocious struggle of the Plantagenet kings was a warning to the queen and her ministers that leaving the succession unsettled could lead to a strife-torn England, vulnerable to foreign invasion.

Shakespeare's history plays were first written and produced in the early and mid-1580s, the years leading up to the Spanish Armada, a time of national peril and foreboding. The earthquake that shook southern England in 1580 was the first of many dire portents during the decade. Preachers and doomsayers pounded the streets of London, crying their apocalyptic wares; and pretenders to the throne, including one Emmanuel Plantagenet, who claimed to be the queen's son by God the Father, appeared out of nowhere. There were countless sightings of Elizabeth's brother, Edward VI, who, it was rumored, had not died in 1553 but had been spirited away to the Continent. Government rhetoric aside, Elizabeth's power as a symbol of national unity was waning.

It was also a time of worsening poverty. As B. M. Ward has shown, from 1582 to 1604, when the major Shakespeare plays were being written, the proportion of government revenue spent on defense each year averaged 73 percent, and in 1588 rose as high as 101 percent. Food prices soared, taxation quadrupled, and large swaths of the population were forced to beg to fend off starvation. Ward exclaims, "What a very different background to the writing and acting of the Shakespeare plays is here presented from the 'peace, prosperity, and Merrie England' picture that biographers of Shakespeare would have us believe!"[116]

The discovery of the Throckmorton plot in November 1583 put England on the slippery slope toward war with Spain. The racking of Francis Throckmorton had revealed the extent of the web woven by the Scottish queen, whose co-weavers included the pope, Philip II of Spain, the Jesuit network in England, and the Spanish ambassador Mendoza, who was summarily expelled from London. Assassination of Elizabeth was a real fear, and the queen's spymaster Francis Walsingham did not hesitate to play up the danger in order to exacerbate anti-Catholic feeling. He and Burghley were behind the Bond of Association (1584), drawn up by the Privy Council, whose signatories pledged themselves to hunt down any potential successor to Elizabeth on whose behalf an attempt on the queen's life was made or planned.

The year of the Bond of Association saw the death of Alençon and the assassination of William of Orange, effectively severing the Anglo-French alliance that had kept the balance of power in Europe for twelve years. Now England was duty bound to protect the Dutch Protestants against Spanish oppression, and Elizabeth was offered, but turned down, sovereignty over the United Provinces. She did, however, send money,

and in 1585 an army led by the Earl of Leicester. The following year a
further plot was discovered, spearheaded by the rich young Catholic
Anthony Babington, whose correspondence with the Scottish queen
was intercepted. Mendoza, now Spanish ambassador in Paris, was once
again heavily involved. Walsingham's waiting game had paid off: in an
indiscreet letter to Babington, Mary implicated herself in plans to murder
Elizabeth and replace her on the throne; and after endless vacillation
on the part of the English queen, Mary was executed at Fotheringhay
in February 1587. Catholic Europe was outraged, and Philip of Spain
stepped up his preparations for invasion.

It was in response to such pressures that Shakespeare composed
his cycle of history plays, to instill a sense of national identity in the
English, a vital task if the country was to avoid becoming a province
of the Spanish empire, whose ruler Philip II, buoyed up by the never-
ending stream of gold and silver flowing into his treasury from the
Americas, had set his heart on world domination. Crowning the series
of eight dramas was *Henry V,* and its impact on the eve of the Armada
is not hard to imagine, considering the powerful rallying cry Lawrence
Olivier's 1944 film version became 360 years later, when England was
once again threatened by a would-be global dictator. Churchill himself, Ezekiel-like, swallowed the play whole, fashioning his rhetoric
along its magical lines. In fact, Churchill did exactly what Shakespeare
himself had done: in the words of the American journalist Edward R.
Murrow, he "mobilized the English language and sent it into battle."

An example of Shakespeare's weaving together of history and the
present is the way he drew on the Northern Rebellion of Elizabeth's
reign for his depiction of Hotspur's revolt in the *Henry IV* plays.
Details from the conflict of 1569–1570 show up so vividly and precisely in these plays, down to the actual names of the protagonists,
that the nineteenth-century Catholic scholar Richard Simpson
claimed Shakespeare must have "worked up his account with the aid
of someone with personal knowledge [of the rebellion]."[117] It proved
a turning point in Elizabeth's reign, the fuse unwittingly lit by Mary
Queen of Scots when she fled to England after her scandalous life,
including complicity in the murder of her husband, Lord Darnley, had
lost her the Scottish throne. Her presence in England and her mooted
marriage to the Duke of Norfolk crystallized the rebellious impulses
of the Catholic north. Then in 1570 Pope Pius V raised the stakes by

excommunicating Elizabeth as a heretic and usurper, and absolving English Catholics of their oath of allegiance to her: Mary of Scotland was their true queen and sainthood awaited anyone who assassinated the impostor. It was a full-blown fatwa. In *King John,* John, like Elizabeth, is excommunicated and his title to the throne undermined by papal decree. John's stirring defense of his prerogative, hurling the pope's words back in his face, could as likely have been spoken by Elizabeth, and for that reason must have fired the hearts of Shakespeare's patriotic audiences:

> Thou canst not, cardinal, devise a name
> So slight, unworthy and ridiculous,
> To charge me to an answer, as the pope.
> Tell him this tale; and from the mouth of England
> Add thus much more, that no Italian priest
> Shall tithe or toll in our dominions;
> But as we, under God, are supreme head,
> So under Him that great supremacy
> Where we do reign, we will alone uphold
> Without th'assistance of a mortal hand:
> So tell the pope, all reverence set apart
> To him and his usurp'd authority.
>
> (III.i.75–86)

The historical and political dimensions of the histories are obvious. A third dimension, almost wholly neglected, is the personal, reflecting the author's life journey and making sense of figures such as Falstaff, Hal, Richard II, and Philip the Bastard, who stretch the historical boundaries of the plays toward fiction.

It is remarkable how often the eight monarchs depicted in the two tetralogies, spanning eighty-seven years, are paired as "rival brothers": the one legitimate, the other base; the one contemplative, the other a man of blood (the rational and irrational brothers of mythology, like Jacob and Esau)—Richard II and Bolingbroke (Henry IV), Prince Hal and Hotspur, Henry VI and the Duke of York, Henry VI and Edward IV, and Richard III and Henry Tudor. This royal rivalry is a reflection of an inner conflict in Shakespeare engendered by his dual perception of himself as both base and legitimate. One moment he sees himself as a bastard or outcast, debarred from the throne by his illegitimacy, the next as rightful king or chosen one.

Richard II is a poet-king who speaks passionately and eloquently of divine right, but is too self-indulgent and inward-looking to be effective. Too caught up in the drama of being king to rule competently, he reserves his finest moment for renouncing the crown, an act that brings out his theatrical flair, and into which he pours his deepest feelings:

> With mine own tears I wash away my balm,
> With mine own hands I give away my crown,
> With mine own tongue deny my sacred state . . .
>
> (IV.i.207–209)

In Richard's self-deposing one can sense Shakespeare using theater to stage his own abdication, and so inscribe the secret history of his nation. Both he and Richard convert their loss of political power into an access of dramatic power.

Richard is identified with the crown to such an extent that its loss undermines his sense of self. The son of a shadow king (the Black Prince), Richard is in the end himself more shadow than substance. That Shakespeare voices his own despair through this unhappiest of kings is clear from the fact that Richard seems haunted more by the loss of his name than the forfeiture of his crown:

> I have no name, no title;
> No, not that name was given me at the font,
> But 'tis usurp'd. Alack the heavy day,
> That I have worn so many winters out,
> And know not now what name to call myself!
>
> (IV.i.255–259)

Richard is replaced by the exiled knight Henry Bolingbroke, who returns to England to claim the lands of his deceased father, John of Gaunt, a vast inheritance seized by Richard to fund his Irish wars. Bolingbroke's claim to the throne is suspect, and his subsequent rule as Henry IV plagued by rebellion, the curse of the usurper. More fateful still, he has the imprisoned Richard murdered, thereby sanctifying his old rival's memory and ensuring that the crown will sit heavily upon his own brows. Yet Henry, too, was once an outsider, a banished man stripped of his status and identity. Hotspur refers to the time when he was "Sick in the world's regard, wretched and low, / A poor unminded outlaw sneaking home."[118]

In the *Henry IV* plays Bolingbroke, like Richard before him, has become careworn and inflexible; the crown is his sole source of identity, and his only face a public one. His son Prince Hal, on the other hand, is an outsider whose affections "hold a wing quite from the flight of all [his] ancestors." He is "the nimble-footed madcap Prince of Wales," who keeps his own renegade court of rogues and jesters —in other words, his father's shadow. He may not usurp his father's throne, but he does take the crown while his father is sleeping, and puts it on his own head.

Richard II, Henry Bolingbroke, and Prince Hal are all dispossessed figures, with a self-conscious, almost histrionic approach to kingship. One can't help feeling that Hal's transformation from theatrical and bohemian prince to worthy and glorious king is Shakespeare's assertion that he has put his own wild days behind him, and is now fit to rule. But even as king, Henry cannot resist disguising himself on the eve of Agincourt to eavesdrop on his troops. Borrowing a cloak, he tours the camp under the alias Harry le Roy.

Henry V is succeeded by his infant son Henry VI, whose early reign is shaken by dissentious uncles. Introspective, spiritually-minded, and suffering bouts of insanity, Henry would rather be a shepherd (or poet) than a king. As his wife Margaret of Anjou sneers, "His study is his tilt-yard,"[119] a glancing reference, perhaps, to the name Shake-speare. Like his grandfather Bolingbroke, he endures a period of exile; and like that other boy king, Richard II, he is driven from the throne and murdered. Henry is succeeded by his third cousin, Edward IV, whose father, Richard, Duke of York, is taunted as a mock king by the tigerish Margaret.

Another exile and usurper, Edward was known for his womanizing and love of books, and it was during his reign that William Caxton returned from abroad and set up his printing press at Westminster. Edward put the realm on a sound financial footing, and had he not died suddenly at the age of forty-one, when his sons were still minors, the Tudor experiment in monarchy may never have happened. As it was, he was succeeded by his twelve-year-old son Edward V, who, together with his nine-year-old brother, was allegedly murdered by their uncle Richard, Duke of Gloucester, who usurped the throne as Richard III. Of all Shakespeare's kings, none has a greater passion for the crown than Richard; nor are his Machiavellian cunning and skills as an actor surpassed, not even by the non-royal Iago. Richard is unseated by his third cousin once removed, Henry, Earl of Richmond, who ends the internecine strife by marrying Edward IV's daughter Elizabeth, thus founding the House of Tudor.

A personal dimension to these plays might feel foreign to many people, yet their heroes speak so poignantly of their lost inheritance that it seems impossible for their creator not to have been somehow invested in their troubles. When, for instance, Henry Bolingbroke is upbraided by his uncle York for defying the terms of his banishment and returning to England, he replies (emphasis mine):

> Will you permit that I shall stand condemn'd
> A wandering vagabond, my rights and royalties
> Pluck'd from my arms perforce, and given away
> To upstart unthrifts? *Wherefore was I born?*
> (*Richard II*, II.iii.118–121)

The cry "Wherefore was I born?" echoes through the histories. It is the cry of the dispossessed king, the man with no status, whose fate has been thwarted in some essential manner. In *Henry VI, Part 3*, when King Henry disinherits his son and heir Prince Edward in favor of his great rival Richard, Duke of York, one cannot help thinking of Elizabeth's own Edward, set aside in favor of the rival Stuart line. "Father, you cannot disinherit me," complains the boy, "If you be king, why should not I succeed?"

There is another deeply revealing passage in *Henry VI, Part 3*, which goes to the heart of Shakespeare's crisis in the histories. Richard, Duke of Gloucester (later Richard III), is talking more frankly than he knows about his hunger for the crown:

And yet I know not how to get the crown,
For many lives stand between me and home;
And I—like one lost in a thorny wood,
That rends the thorns and is rent with the thorns,
Seeking a way and straying from the way,
Not knowing how to find the open air,
But toiling desperately to find it out—
Torment myself to catch the English crown;
And from that torment I will free myself
Or hew my way out with a bloody axe.

(III.ii.172–181)

Behind Richard's violent ambition is the image of a baby struggling to leave the womb (a forest being an ancient symbol of mother), suggesting that what prevents his assumption of the crown is his maternal inheritance. He has already told us that he was *deformed* in his mother's womb, this physical deformity perhaps being a metaphor for the corruption of his royalty. As a result, he becomes as nothing, "like to a chaos, or an unlicked bear whelp / That carries no impression like the dam." The reference to the crown of thorns might seem incongruous when applied to Richard III, until we remember that Christ was the son of the Virgin. In this context, Richard's image of suffocation in the womb ("Not knowing how to find the open air, / But toiling desperately to find it out") suddenly illuminates his—or rather Shakespeare's—identity crisis. If Shakespeare was indeed the son of the Virgin Queen, we have an answer to the enigma of why he portrays himself as an unacknowledged king, foiled by his maternal inheritance, reduced to nothing, the womb of the virgin becoming the tomb in which the prince must lie forever sealed—or hew his way out with an ax!

Such a reading makes sense of Shakespeare's twofold obsession with being king and being nothing. It also explains the extraordinary silence that surrounds his life, as if his very existence were somehow taboo. Yet, on a higher level, Shakespeare did come into his own, and this is reflected in the personal story of loss and redemption that weaves itself through the histories.

Shakespeare's anxiety over his lost identity and his compensatory fantasy of the hidden redeemer appearing at the eleventh hour to claim the throne run hand in hand through the histories. All his kings suffer from a sense of disinheritance, and even minor characters, such as Owen Glendower in *Henry IV, Part 1* (the last Welshman to hold the title "Prince of Wales"), are drawn from this archetype of "king manqué." After the failure of his rebellion against Henry IV, Glendower, a cousin of the Tudors, became a sort of bandit king, a ghostly fugitive wandering the wilds of Wales in disguise. He had once been a towering presence in his oppressed land, a munificent patron of bards and scholars, who inspired his countrymen with dreams of independence. Shakespeare praises him through the Earl of Mortimer as a Renaissance man, with more than a hint of self-portraiture:

> In faith, he is a worthy gentleman,
> Exceedingly well read, and profited
> In strange concealments, valiant as a lion,
> And wondrous affable, and as bountiful
> As mines of India.
>
> (III.i.159–163)

The Shakespeare canon is a vast web, all words and images miraculously cross-referenced and resonating with each other, both within individual works and across different plays and genres. If one touches a single thread, all the others instantly vibrate, providing subtle insights into the poet's motives. Why, for instance, does Prince Hal spend all his time in the tavern with Falstaff, yet complain of his father's untrusting attitude? Why has he completely divorced himself from the court and all trappings of royalty, if at heart he wishes to wear his father's crown? He unwittingly provides the answer in his very first soliloquy, when he says of his wild companions:

> I know you all, and will awhile uphold
> The unyok'd humour of your idleness.
> Yet herein will I imitate the sun,
> Who doth permit the base contagious clouds
> To smother up his beauty from the world.
>
> (I.ii.190–194)

The web vibrates at these words, and immediately we hear in our minds Claudius's opening question to Hamlet, "How is it that the clouds still hang on you?" Perhaps Hal's succession to the crown, despite the fact that he is the Prince of Wales, is not a foregone conclusion; maybe, like Hamlet, he is an obscured prince, made invisible by his own compromised status and the machinations of the politicians. Another vibration, and we remember Sonnet 33 about the sun "permit[ting] the basest clouds to ride / With ugly rack on his celestial face" and "from the forlorn world his visage hide"—a poem about an unacknowledged royal heir, one hidden from public view. We now realize that the reason for Hal's deep alienation from his royal inheritance is not rebelliousness per se, but rather an obscured or thwarted title to the throne. In other words, he is that quintessentially Shakespearean figure, the unacknowledged heir. In response to his father's taunt that he is merely "the shadow of succession," Hal vows to redeem his youthful folly on Hotspur's head.

From this perspective, we see Shakespeare himself addressing Elizabeth through Hal, and understand that his collaboration with Falstaff in the fat knight's satiric skits on the royal family constitutes a warning of sorts. If Elizabeth keeps him in the political wilderness, he will continue to shake his bells at her and cause all manner of embarrassment through his dramatic art. By the same token, his rejection of Falstaff at the end of *Henry IV, Part 2* is a pledge of his commitment to fulfil his royal destiny. If only she will trust him, he will lay aside his Falstaff persona and step up to the plate.

Standing outside the cycle of Shakespeare's chronicle plays, *King John* is a useful key to unlock the other histories, providing special insights into Shakespeare's personal-historical perspective on the crown. Through Philip the Bastard, the illegitimate son of King Richard the Lionheart (and Shakespeare's own creation), the playwright reveals his stake in the sovereignty of his country and his belief in the superiority of character over title. He also provides an answer to Bolingbroke's cry "Wherefore was I born?" with his bold declaration, "I am I, howe'er I was begot!" Throughout the ages the royal bastard, baffled by his prejudiced status, has fed on fantasies of vindication and success, of one day being recognized as the legitimate heir, yet there remains a nagging feeling that no one takes him seriously.

A tragic example is Charles II's bastard son, James, Duke of Monmouth, who spread rumors of a mysterious black box containing his parents' marriage deed. When that did not convince the country, he took the chance of open revolt.

Shakespeare's Philip the Bastard is similarly opportunistic, but never to the point of treason. Stationing himself as the king's fool, he uses his sharp wit and eloquence, his brazen truth telling, to further his country's interests. Significantly, it is he, not Prince Henry, who is given the rousing final lines of the play (reserved for the most senior character left onstage):

> Come the three corners of the world in arms
> And we shall shock them! Nought shall make us rue
> If England to itself do rest but true!
> (*King John,* V.vii.116–118)

The king who does not wear a crown but teaches other kings how to wear theirs, exulting instead in the wild card status of court jester: this is a figure close to Shakespeare's heart. That he is prepared to rip the fabric of history by interpolating a fictional self-portrait into a chronicle play speaks volumes about his own compromised standing and the purpose of his art. Could there be any more certain sign that he himself was a royal outsider, a king without a crown?

A KINGDOM FOR A STAGE

A powerful component of the personal dimension in the history plays is the desire for vengeance on the part of the dispossessed—to use any means, however bloody, to come into their own, because their very identity is at stake. The *Henry VI* plays and *Richard III* are bedeviled with this bloodlust and the rage of dispossession underlying it. In *Richard II* and the *Henry IV* plays the tone changes. While the desire for vengeance remains—and with it the search for identity—it has found an outlet in art, imagination, and language. Richard II decides not to fight, but to renounce the throne, creating a poetic tragedy out of his self-sacrifice. Prince Hal wears the mask of the jester and joins in Falstaff's theatricals, happy even to let his corpulent friend take credit for the slaying of Hotspur. And then as Henry V, the philosopher-king, he makes it his task to raise the consciousness of the nation by honoring the sovereignty of the individual. His vision of kingship is shared, however fleetingly, by Richard II, who says, "Our holy lives must win a new world's crown."

The highly personal tale that Shakespeare tells through the histories continues with the tragedies, and in *Hamlet* we see the blood vengeance of the chronicle plays transmuted into the more creative redress that art brings through consciousness: holding up a mirror rather than a sword, speaking daggers rather than hurling them. Instead of rushing to stab his uncle, Hamlet puts on a play before him. This is where Shakespeare, then, finds his true compensation for the loss of the crown—in art. Theater becomes his surrogate kingdom: a stage for a kingdom and *a kingdom for a stage.*

These words from the prologue to *Henry V* are justly famous, yet few people are aware that they perfectly describe Shakespeare's sacrifice. The king renounces his crown and becomes a playwright, making the theater his kingdom and his characters his subjects. Many Shakespearean scholars, though hostile to any hint of a royal or aristocratic author, seem to sense this exchange. Harold Clark Goddard writes: "What Hamlet's succession might have meant may be seen by asking: What if, on the death of Elizabeth, not James of Scotland but William of Stratford had inherited the throne! That would have been England falling before William the Conqueror indeed. And it did so fall in the sense that, ever since, Shakespeare has been England's imaginative king."[120]

The exchange of a kingdom for a stage is in one form or another true of all Shakespeare's kings in the two tetralogies. Henry VI, more addicted to learning than power, is a case in point. On the run after the battle of Towton, in disguise and carrying nothing but a prayer book, he is overheard by a pair of gamekeepers lamenting the loss of his throne. They decide to confront him:

Second Keeper:
Say, what art thou that talk'st of kings and queens?
King Henry:
More than I seem, and less than I was born to:
A man at least, for less I should not be;
And men may talk of kings, and why not I?

SECOND KEEPER:
Ay, but thou talk'st as if thou wert a king.
KING HENRY:
Why, so I am, in mind; and that's enough.
SECOND KEEPER:
But if thou be a king, where is thy crown?
KING HENRY:
My crown is in my heart, not on my head;
Not deck'd with diamonds and Indian stones,
Nor to be seen: my crown is call'd content;
A crown it is that seldom kings enjoy.

(*3 Henry VI*, III.i.55–65)

The true king in Shakespeare is the king without a crown. This archetype, invested with the author's deepest and rawest feelings, carries an emotional charge like no other in the canon. That such an archetype can hijack a character whose personality is unsuited to bear it reinforces its integrity to Shakespeare's soul-life. Even in the case of a Machiavellian dissembler and man of blood such as Richard, Duke of York, champion of the white rose, Shakespeare's bias, fraught with the emotional stress of his own story, stamps its character on the text, yielding one of the most painfully moving passages in the plays.

York, who has sought tirelessly to make good his claim to the throne, is finally captured by the forces of Queen Margaret at the Battle of Wakefield. He is planted upon a molehill in open view and Margaret, mocking his dynastic ambitions, places a paper crown upon his head. In York's humiliation one feels the bitter shame of the author himself, who forsook a golden crown for a paper one (his artistic kingdom), putting on plays before his queen as a paid entertainer:

Why art thou patient, man? Thou should'st be mad;
And I to make thee mad do mock thee thus.
Stamp, rave, and fret, that I may sing and dance.
Thou would'st be fee'd, I see, to make me sport;
York cannot speak unless he wear a crown.
A crown for York! And, lords, bow low to him:
Hold you his hands whilst I do set it on.
          [*Putting a paper crown on his head.*]
Ay, marry, sir, now looks he like a king!

(*3 Henry VI*, I.iv.89–96)

In Holinshed's *Chronicles* there is no paper crown, but there is a garland of rushes, and the parallels with Jesus are brought to the fore:

> Some write that the duke was taken alive, and in derision caused to stand upon a molehill, on whose head they put a garland instead of a crowne, which they had fashioned and made of sedges and bulrushes; and having so crowned him with that garland, they kneeled down afore him (as the Jewes did unto Christ) in scorne, saieng to him, "Haile King without rule, haile, king without heritage! haile duke and prince without people or possessions."[121]

In having York savagely mocked as a monarch without rule, one who has been reduced to playing a king, Shakespeare exposes his own deepest wound. He has become a mock king, one who puts on plays, like the old king of the revels.

For all their bloodiness, there is a strongly cathartic quality to these dramas, which served to heal national trauma by releasing and transforming the past. What gives the histories their extraordinary depth is the way Shakespeare's identity crisis mirrors the national story. Denied the crown, the king loses his identity, England its sovereignty, and both descend into chaos. Yet there is a promise of redemption: the idea of a hidden king returning to restore the sovereignty of the land is kept alive. Thus we come to realize what should have been realized long ago: writing the histories fulfilled a vital emotional need in Shakespeare. In writing to heal the wounds to his own soul, he brought water for his country's stain; and in seeking to understand his own inheritance, he mapped out England's. Ultimately, he wrote the history plays to come to terms with his own thwarted destiny, and in so doing deepened his nation's self-awareness. By this measure, Shakespeare's plays are all history plays. *Lear, Macbeth,* and *Cymbeline* simply intensify and refine the story, bringing the hidden redeemer into sharper relief.[122]

If Richmond, the exiled earl-king, who returns to cut down the tyrant and redeem his ailing nation, embodies that peculiarly Shakespearean pattern of kingship, then Edgar in *King Lear,* another earl-king, confirms it. Having cleansed himself of his personality and earthbound identity through his shamanlike muttering, shivering, dancing, and stamping, Edgar emerges as the savior of his nation: the new man, the self-mastered one, the philosopher king. In him the crown of England, after the blood and damnation of the civil wars, achieves its true luster. *King Lear* is the quintessence of Shakespeare's historical vision, incorporating the personal, political, and providential dimensions of history. In many ways it is a prophetic account of Britain, a distillation and imagination of its story, past, present, and future. Not only in the history plays but throughout the canon, Shakespeare shows himself to have been a conductor of extraordinary sensitivity for the conflicts of his time. If his works are, in the words of Ted Hughes, "England's creation story," then it was in the political and spiritual pressures of the Tudor age that our national poet crafted the epitome of English history—its mythic jewel—*King Lear*.

TUDOR-CELTIC MYTHOLOGY

The fantasy of the redeemer king, who returns from exile or emerges from hiding, galvanizes Shakespeare's historic vision, and has its origin in the mythology of the kings of Britain embraced by the Tudors. At the heart of this mythology is the outcast king, who makes creative use of his alienation through a deepening spiritual awareness or poetic vision. The Grail legends, whose roots lie in Celtic civilization, would seem to bear this out. The king is wounded, the land sickens, yet all the while a new consciousness is ripening. For Shakespeare, the alienated king becomes an artist, instructing his people from the wings.

The Tudor monarchs, then, lived out the profoundest myth of the Celtic imagination, that of the wounded king and his wasteland, healed by a hidden champion raised in ignorance of his greatness. Shakespeare, it seems, was essential to this "living out," as if he were the fulfillment and coming to consciousness of the prophecy Merlin speaks to Britomart in Book 3 of Spenser's *Faerie Queene:*

> Tho when the terme is full accomplished,
> There shall a sparke of fire, which hath long-while
> Been in his ashes raked up, and hid,
> Be freshly kindled in the fruitfull Ile
> Of *Mona,* where it lurked in exile;
> Which shall break forth into bright burning flame,

And reach into the house, that beares the stile
Of royall maiesty and soveraigne name;
So shall Briton bloud their crowne again reclame.

(III.iii.48)

The Tudors were Welsh landowners, who served the kings of England from the time of Edward I. They came to prominence with one Tudor of Penmynydd (d. 1367) who, having knighted himself in order to take part in a tournament at the court of Edward III, declared he would defend his right at the combat. Since no one challenged him, he became known thereafter as "Sir Tudor." His grandson Owen Tudor (d. 1461) served Richard II on Richard's Irish campaign and was the grandfather of Henry VII. Owen married Catherine de Valois, widow of Henry V, and their son Edmund Tudor brought English royal blood into the family by marrying Margaret Beaufort, a great-great-granddaughter of Edward III. Edmund's son, Henry Tudor, Earl of Richmond, later Henry VII, was ultimately descended from a bastard son of John of Gaunt by his mistress Katherine Swynford. Though he was legitimized by Act of Parliament, his line was barred from the succession.

In the Tudors we have a self-consciously created dynasty, aware of their weak claim to the throne, who buttressed their credentials by tracing their line from King Arthur, the once and future king. In naming his firstborn son Arthur and having him christened at Winchester Cathedral, Henry VII was deliberately invoking the chivalry and glamour of Britain's semimythical past, a considerable irony in view of his own grasping, ungenerous nature and his relentless undermining of the old feudal nobility.

Like all the Tudors, Henry VII had a remarkable flair for political mythmaking, or what we would call today public relations. Adopting the Red Dragon standard of the ancient British king Cadwaladr (who may have been Arthur), he fought under it at Bosworth and subsequently used its green-and-white background for the Tudor colors. According to Geoffrey of Monmouth, the exiled Cadwaladr, whose story echoes that of the Grail king, had a vision in which an angel told him that the devastated kingdom of Britain, symbolized by a lance or spear, would one day be restored to his descendants.

Polydore Virgil looked through this providential lens in his *Anglica Historia,* commissioned by the king: "Thus Henry acquired the kingdom, an event of which foreknowledge had been possible both many centuries earlier and also soon after his birth. For 797 years before, there came one night to Cadwallader, last king of the Britons, some sort of an apparition with a heavenly appearance; this foretold how long afterwards it would come to pass that his descendants would recover the land. This prophecy, they say, came true in Henry, who traced his ancestry back to Cadwallader."[123]

The Tudors, in the grandiosity generated by their lineal insecurity, embraced the notion that they were the promised descendants of Arthur, fated after 800 years of Saxon and Norman rule to bring forth a new royal dynasty of ancient British blood. Basing his genealogy on Geoffrey of Monmouth's *Historia Regum Britannia* (c. 1136), which itself drew from an ancient, vanished tome in the Welsh tongue, Edmund Spenser in his *Faerie Queene* championed this idea of a hidden royal line emerging with Henry Tudor, Earl of Richmond, and destined to live on through a child born to Britomart, the knight of chastity (i.e., Queen Elizabeth). John Dee, a renowned mathematician and astrologer, shared Spenser's vision, taking it into the political and philosophical sphere with his *General and Rare Memorials Pertaining to the Perfect Art of Navigation* (1577), in which he set out his idea of a British empire. As for the religious dimension, the Church of England was in many ways a screen for the revival of a Celtic Christian cult with Elizabeth, the Faerie Queen, at the center, her subjects the knights of an ever-expanding Round Table.

Henry Tudor, Earl of Richmond, enduring long years of obscure and penurious exile in Brittany with a price on his head, made several daring forays into Wales to recruit supporters for his subsequent invasion of England. Once on the throne, he played up the romantic image his deeds fostered in people's minds. In truth, the Tudor dynasty was founded upon conquest (and the killing of a king). In his first speech to Parliament, Henry declared that he owed his crown "to the true judgment of God as shown by the sword on the field of battle." Despite his insistence that this was a *re*conquest, which avenged the original Saxon invasion, a deep insecurity accompanied the dynasty through its 118 years of rule. Nervous even about his wife's superior claim to the throne, Henry was careful to deny her a coronation, not wanting it thought that he was claiming the throne through the heiress of York.

Conquest alone, however romanticized, was not enough. Besides, the very idea of kingship was being reformulated in Renaissance Europe. If he was not a king by right, Henry knew he must place the monarchy on a firm practical and philosophical footing. Machiavelli's *The Prince* had yet to be written, but Henry already embodied many of the principles of *realpolitik* that the Italian enunciated. Determined, ruthless and unfailingly shrewd, he never loosened his grip on power. His reign, like Henry IV's, was riddled with sedition, with two serious attempts to resurrect the Plantagenet dynasty through the pretenders Lambert Simnel and Perkin Warbeck. The king raised men of humble or obscure origins to positions of power and trust, but in truth he trusted no one and established a highly effective espionage service at home and abroad. He also created the country's first bureaucratic administration. His own historian Polydore Virgil accused him of avarice, especially in the final years of his reign. Yet Henry was a man of culture, and like his mother, Lady Margaret Beaufort, founder of St. John's College Cambridge, an apt scholar and fosterer of learning. Like all his descendants in the Tudor line, he was particularly fond of music.

In *Cymbeline,* which can be read as a symbolic history of Britain, Shakespeare's special myth of kingship fuses implicitly with the Tudor conception of its rights in the kingdom. The play's hero, Posthumus Leonatus, after a period in exile on the Continent, returns to Britain via Milford Haven in Wales (the place where Henry Tudor landed his invasion force in 1485). There, his heroic deeds against the imperial forces of Augustus Caesar help win the day for the British, and secure their independence. Though not a king himself, Posthumus is described in royal terms; his name "Leonatus" itself means "lionborn." He marries the king's daughter and heir, Imogen, and is granted a vision of Jupiter, the king of the gods.

Until his elder brother, Arthur, died, Prince Henry, Henry VII's younger son, had been destined for a life in the church. A scholar of wide interests, Henry VIII was profoundly versed in music, astronomy, classical literature, theology, and architecture. He also played and composed music to a professional standard, later making his court the wonder of Europe. A published author, whose tutor John Skelton had been poet laureate, the king also wrote verse.

Greedy for glory, Henry VIII lavished the treasure his father had hoarded on all the large effects that troop with majesty. Obsessed with image and perception, the watchwords of our modern political culture, he was a master of projecting the power of monarchy. Life for Henry was theater; his every act invited a fanfare. Yet all this show masked a deep insecurity, which became more conspicuous as his reign ripened. Beneath the hard crust of the warrior king lurked a sensitive soul, whose feelings were easily hurt and as easily camouflaged by a hearty bonhomie. He treated the court as an extended family, and his desire for familial harmony was very strong. Where there was discord, he reacted with rage, even violence.

Henry's sexual nature was perverted, or at the very least primitive, and the questions over Anne Boleyn's paternity would not go away. If she was his daughter and herself of royal blood, it would make sense of her extraordinary ritual killing, which resembled the ancient sacrifice of the king—or substitute king—to ensure the fertility of the land or, in this case, the royal line.[124] The trumped-up charges against her, Henry's employment of the best swordsman in France to perform the execution, and her high spirits in the days leading up to her death all bespeak some form of sacrificial murder. Henry did get his male heir (within a year of Anne's execution), but a curse seems to have descended upon him and his line.

From the time of his fifth marriage to Catherine Howard, in the summer of 1540, when he was forty-nine, Henry, with his running ulcerous leg, which gave off a fetid smell and had to be dressed continually and which, with his vast sedentary bulk, made activity impossible, embodied the figure of the Grail king ruling with his incurable wound over the wasteland. Both Henry's wound and that of the Grail king were made by spears, Henry's during a jousting accident in his youth. As with the legendary Celtic king, one of the few pastimes Henry enjoyed in the extremity of his condition was fishing in the royal fishpond at Hampton Court, from a wheelchair. Henry's heir and successor, Edward VI, also embodied this archetype, dying a slow and painful death at the age of fifteen, as did *his* successor Mary, while the king's ultimate heir, Elizabeth I, inherited her father's ulcerous leg. As legend had it, the king wounded by the spear would be healed

by the spear (of the redeemer), and it is in this tradition of the wasteland and its redemption that Shakespeare seems to have viewed himself. As Hamlet says:

> The time is out of joint. O cursed spite
> That ever I was born to set it right.
> (I.v.196–197)

As *pater patriae* (father of his people) and supreme governor of
the Church of England, Henry VIII invested the monarchy with a
revitalized, almost mystical sense of its sovereignty, yet he was an
imperialist in outlook. The undoubted love he felt for his wives and
children was usurped by sudden eruptions of hate and violence. His
veneration for the traditions, music, and architecture of the Catholic
church sat uncomfortably with his desecration of the monasteries,
and his love of chivalry and the joust contradicted his protracted attacks on the old feudal nobility. He was no friend of the poor, and if
the executions during his reign, which included thousands of vagrants,
are anything to go by (Holinshed estimates 72,000), Henry was the
bloodiest monarch to sit on the English throne. Yet, as Neville Williams writes, Henry was "the miracle-maker who turned the water
of medieval kingship into the heady wine of a personal, national
monarchy, with the court as its chosen vessel."[125]

~ 9 ~

A Life of Exile

Think not the king did banish thee,
But thou the king.
                        (*Richard II*, I.iii.279–280)

MONSTROUS ADVERSARY

Oxford maintained his stream of comedies for court performance
in the late 1570s, producing early versions of *Cymbeline, Love's Labour's
Lost, All's Well, Two Gentlemen of Verona,* and *The Merchant of Venice*.
The queen, as was her wont, did and said just enough to feed his
dreams of royal success, though he had to continue a stranger to their
son, with no say in his upbringing. The queen supported Oxford's
writing, however pungent the satire, in the knowledge that her supremely gifted son was no politician. Living almost entirely in his
imagination, he would, she judged, be satisfied so long as he could
keep petitioning her through his plays. Others, like Burghley and
Leicester, were not so keen on the idea of an enfant terrible having
free rein at court, and would gladly have silenced his bells once and
for all. As Polonius says to Queen Gertrude of Hamlet's antics:

> Tell him his pranks have been too broad to bear with
> And that your Grace hath screen'd and stood between
> Much heat and him.
>
>   (III.iv.2–4)

There was, however, more to Oxford's fooling than met the eye.
Despite his irreverent and incorrigible wit, when it came to the queen

he was in deadly earnest, and had been deeply shocked by her perfidy in the matter of their child. Having always reserved the sharpest lash for his own back, not scrupling to depict himself in such characters as Macbeth, Falstaff, Angelo, Timon, Bertram, and Thersites, he expected Elizabeth to take his physic, if not with a willing heart, then at least with a modicum of good grace. A measure of her resistance can be gauged from Hamlet's injunction to Gertrude in the closet scene: "You go not till I set you up a glass / Where you may see the inmost part of you," to which she replies in horror, "What wilt thou do? Thou wilt not murder me?" For the introspection he demands is a kind of death to her. There was so much Elizabeth had turned her back on, and now feared even to peep at, lest her conscience be overwhelmed at the sight. "O Hamlet," cries Gertrude, "speak no more. / Thou turn'st my eyes into my very soul, / And there I see such black and grained spots / As will not leave their tinct."

By the 1580s the growing Puritanism in the political culture at court, led by Leicester and Burghley, had already taken root in Parliament and the City. It was actively hostile toward Oxford, his literary movement, and theatrical production in general. Stephen Gosson, in his Puritan tract *The School of Abuse, Containing a Pleasant Invective against Poets, Pipers, Players, Jesters, and Such Like Caterpillars of the Commonwealth* (1579), characterized theaters as little better than whorehouses, targeting Ovid, "the high martial of Venus' field," for special opprobrium. Oxford's sympathies at this time were more Catholic, in both senses of the word: he refused to consider dogmatic differences as a test of spiritual truth, and was taken with the profound imaginative and spiritual beauty of Italian Renaissance culture. Nor did he lack Catholic friends and associates to feed his resentment toward Burghley. In particular, Lord Henry Howard, son of the executed poet Surrey and Oxford's aunt Lady Frances Vere, loomed large in his life. A brilliant scholar and inveterate intriguer, as well as a homosexual, the Catholic Howard was in treasonable correspondence with Mary Queen of Scots. Dangerous as friend or enemy, he was an Iago-like figure who may have been the prime mover in driving a wedge between Oxford and his wife, Anne.

As well as being the son of one of his literary heroes and his first cousin, Howard seems to have reflected back to Oxford an image of his own fallen status. The second son of an attainted father, Howard

Mr. WILLIAM

SHAKESPEARES

COMEDIES,
HISTORIES, &
TRAGEDIES.

Published according to the True Originall Copies.

Martin Droeshout sculpsit London.

LONDON
Printed by Isaac Iaggard, and Ed. Blount. 1623.

Engraving of Shakespeare, 1623, by Martin Droeshout the Younger, which appeared as the frontispiece to the First Folio. The only known portrait of Shakespeare that is remotely contemporary, Droeshout's engraving with its clear mask-line down the side of the face, back-to-front doublet and two right eyes, was a joke intended to alert the reader to the image's hidden meaning.

Left. Engraving of the original monument to Shakespeare in the Holy Trinity Church, Stratford, by Sir William Dugdale, 1656, depicting him as a grain dealer.

Right. The monument to Shakespeare in the Holy Trinity Church, Stratford, as it appears today. The quill and cushion were added in 1748 to make it less like the bust of a rural businessman. The work was executed by Gerard Johnson.

Left. Title page of *Shake-speares Sonnets*, 1609. The author's name would normally be placed between the lines two-thirds of the way down the page. The wording of the title is peculiar and suggests that the author is dead and these are his collected sonnets. The name is hyphenated to indicate a pseudonym.

Opposite. Portrait of Princess Elizabeth, c 1549, by William Scrots. This portrait was probably painted shortly after the Seymour scandal of the previous year, and is evidence of Elizabeth's determination to avoid future opprobrium by presenting herself to the world as a model of chastity and temperance.

King Henry VIII, c. 1536, by Hans Holbein the Younger. Painted around the time that Henry executed Elizabeth's mother, Anne.

Above. Thomas Seymour, 1st Baron Sudeley, c. 1545-9, by Nicholas Denizot. Seymour was Elizabeth's stepfather, and her lover.

Left. Anne Boleyn, c. 1533-6, artist unknown. Elizabeth adopted Anne's motto *Semper Eadem* when she became queen.

Edward de Vere, 17th Earl of Oxford, c.1575. This picture, known as the Welbeck portrait, is said to have been painted while Oxford was in Paris in 1575 and sent back to England as a gift for his wife, Anne Cecil, together with a pair of coach horses. The face bears a striking resemblance to the Ashbourne portrait of Shakespeare.

Robert Dudley, 1st Earl of Leicester, c. 1564, Anglo-Netherlandish School. Elizabeth's Master of Horse and longtime lover, Dudley was ennobled in 1564.

Above. William Cecil, Lord Burghley, c. 1572, by or after Arnold van Brounkhorst, pictured here with his Lord Treasurer's staff of office.

Left. Robert Devereux, 2nd Earl of Essex, c. 1596, after Marcus Gheeraerts the Younger. Essex was hailed as a possible successor to Elizabeth.

It is not vnknowne to yo Lo. that I haue entred into a greate nomber of bondes
to suche, as haue purchasd laudes of me, to discharge them of all incombrauncs
ies: And bycause I staude indebtid vnto her Maᵗⁱᵉ as yoʳ Lo knowythe)
many of ẙ said pourchasers do greatly feare some troble likely to fall
vppon them, by reason of her Maᵗⁱᵉˢ said dett, & especially if the Laudes
of ẙ Lo Darcy and Sʳ Willm Walgraue should be extendyd for the same,
who haue two seuerall statutes of greate somes for their discharge
Wherupon many of ẙ said purchasers haue ben suters vnto me
to procure the dischargynge of her Maᵗⁱᵉˢ said rent, and do seme
very willinge to beare the burden therof, yf by my meanes the
same might be stalled paiable at some conuenient dares I haue
therfore thought good to acquaynte yoʳ Lo. wᵗ this their suyte,
requierynge moste earnestly yoʳ Lo. furtherannce in this behalfe,
wherby I shalbe vnburdened of a greate care, Wᶜ I haue for the
sauynge of my honor, And shall by this meanes also vnburden
my wyfes Joincture, of ẙ charge wᶜ might happen herafter to
be ymposyd vppon ẙ same, yf god should call yoʳ Lo. and me
away before her.

Youre Lordships.

[signature]

My lord, the other day youre man Stainner [Amis] telld me,
that yow sent for Amis my man, and yf he were
absent that Lyle should come vnto yow. I sent Amis
for he was in ẙ way. And I thinke very strange yᵗ
youre Lord. should enter into that course towardes me
wherby I must lerne yᵗ I knew not before, bothe of youre
opinion and god will towardes me. But I pray, my Lord, leaue
yᵗ course, for I mean not to be youre ward nor youre
chyld, I serue her magestie and I am that I am and
by allyance neare to youre lordship, but fre, and scorne
to be offred that iniurie, to thinke I am so weake of
gouernment as to be ruled by seruants, or not able to
gouerne my self. If youre Lord. take and ielous this course,
                                                    yow

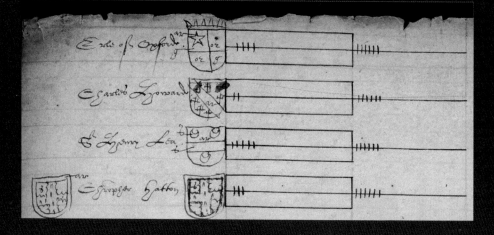

Edward de Vere's distinctive crown signature, which suggests he thought of himself as "Edward VII." This example is taken from Oxford's letter of October 7, 1601, to his brother-in-law Sir Robert Cecil. The line beneath the signature with the seven vertical dashes mimics the "checques" used in jousting tournaments to record the scores of the spear-shaking participants.

An example of scoring "checques" taken from the tournament held in May 1571 at Westminster. The challengers included the Earl of Oxford, who is listed first, Charles Howard, Sir Henry Lee (the Queen's champion), and Christopher Hatton. The prize for the best lance among the tilters fell to Oxford.

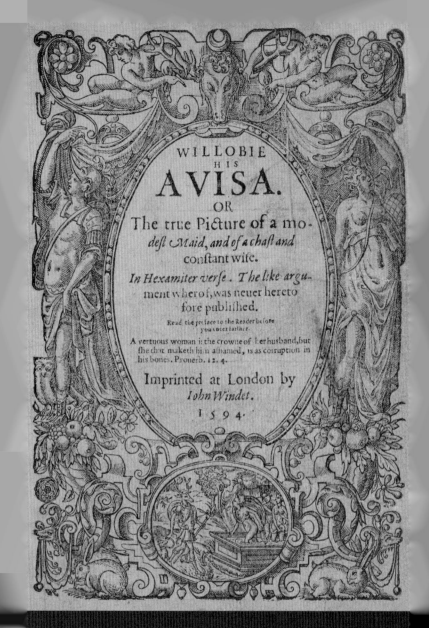

WILLOBIE
HIS
AVISA.
OR
The true Picture of a mo-
dest Maid, and of a chast and
constant wife.

In Hexamiter verse. The like argument wherof, was neuer hereto
fore published.

Read the preface to the Reader before
you enter farther.

A vertuous woman is the crowne of her husband, but
she that maketh him ashamed, is as corruption in
his bones. Prouerb. 12. 4.

Imprinted at London by
Iohn Windet.
1594.

Title page of the anonymous book-length poem, *Willobie His Avisa,* 1594, a work widely regarded as an allegorical account of Queen Elizabeth's love life and its consequences for the succession. At the bottom of the page (above) is a picture of Actaeon surprising the goddess Diana in her bath.

Previous. Portrait of an Unknown Woman (originally identified as Queen Elizabeth I), c. 1594, by Marcus Gheeraerts the Younger. This picture, which shows a pregnant Queen Elizabeth, has had its designation changed at least five times, three of those in the past ten years. When the author saw it at Hampton Court in 2006, it was described as "Shakespeare's Dark Lady."

Left. Venus and Adonis, c. 1555, by Titian. Oxford may have seen Titian's own copy at the artist's studio when he visited Venice in 1575. In it Adonis wears a bonnet, an odd, anachronistic detail that Shakespeare picks up on in his *Venus and Adonis* when he describes Adonis as hiding his angry brow "with his bonnet" (l. 339). The myth of Venus and Adonis provides the psychological framework for much of Shakespeare's work

Below. The Death of Actaeon, c. 1562, by Titian. The tale of Actaeon and Diana is one of Shakespeare's mythic signatures, and reflects the tragedy of his relationship with Elizabeth.

Ditchley Portrait of Queen Elizabeth, c. 1592, by Marcus Gheeraerts the Younger. In this allegorical portrait the Queen stands on the city of Oxford and points toward Southampton. The obscured sonnet on the right begins, "The prince of light. The Sonn by whom . . ." The same veiled story is told in Shakespeare's Sonnet 33.

Robert Cecil, later 1st Earl of Salisbury, known as "Roberto il Diavolo" at court, c. 1602, by John de Critz the Elder.

Above. Henry Howard, Earl of Surrey, c. 1546, artist unknown. A poet and translator, Surrey was the first to write in blank verse.

Left. Henry Howard, later Earl of Northampton, 1594, by a follower of Hieronimo Custodis. Oxford described Howard as "the most arrant villain that lived."

Over. Henry Wriothesley, 3rd Earl of Southampton, "Beauty's Rose" and the "Fair Youth" of Shake-speares Sonnets, c.1600, artist unknown. Southampton was a patron of poets and enthusiast of the theatre.

The allegorical *Rainbow Portrait of Queen Elizabeth I,* c. 1600, by Marcus Gheeraerts the Younger. Although the sun is hidden, the Queen grasps a rainbow in her right hand with the legend, *Non sine sole iris,* implying that there can be no true reign without the son.

Over. Ashbourne Portrait of Shakespeare, date unknown, possibly by Cornelius Ketel. This contested portrait was submitted to x-ray and infrared photography by Charles Wisner Barrell, and his findings reported in the January 1940 edition of *Scientific American.* According to Barrell, it was an overpainted portrait of Edward de Vere.

had grown up in obscurity and without the means to furnish so distinguished and ancient a title. Indulging his passion for scholarship instead, he became a lecturer at Cambridge, the only nobleman of the Elizabethan era to teach at a university. Oxford, too, for reasons of temperament and because of his thwarted political ambition, had made the arts his life. Now he was aligning himself with people who shared the same political foes, and both Howard and his cousin Charles Arundel —who would later flee the country and become a pensioner of the King of Spain—were sworn enemies of the Earl of Leicester, the man who in the words of Hamlet had "kill'd my king and whor'd my mother." It was to prove a catastrophic association for all three men.

One of the things that drew them together in the late 1570s was their support of the queen's proposed marriage to the Duc d'Alençon, a union loudly opposed by Leicester and his nephew Sir Philip Sidney. Oxford was happy to support it because he knew at heart that it was a farce, played out by the queen for her own amusement, vanity, and political advantage. Indeed, from the point of view of his art, Oxford was able to analyze his relationship with Elizabeth through the lens of Alençon's ill-fated courtship, merging himself with the French prince in the character of Bottom. (Anything, too, to keep Leicester in a state of suspended rage.) Oxford's notorious tennis court spat with Sidney in 1579, which prompted the latter to challenge him to a duel, took its life from this rivalry over the queen's matrimonial affairs.

Oxford, who was also friendly with Sir George Howard, master of the queen's armory and a dabbler in the occult, had a highly ambivalent relationship with the Howard family, as did Elizabeth, whose maternal grandmother was a Howard. After all, here was a family that had been intriguing for the throne throughout its titled history, often with disastrous results. Oxford, having fallen out with Henry Howard in 1580, fulminated that the house of Howard was "the most villainous and treacherous race under heaven, and my lord Howard of all the other the most arrant villain that lived." A case, at least in some measure, of the pot calling the kettle black, since the creator of Iago could not have been wholly innocent of intrigue himself.

Any Mozart is bound to have at least one Salieri hovering in the wings, like Vice in the old morality plays; and Howard, a writer himself and immensely proud of his poetic father, played this role in Oxford's life, as did Gabriel Harvey, another Cambridge don, who was also a poet (albeit a plodding and contrived one) and a protégé of the Earl of Leicester. Appointed professor of rhetoric at Cambridge in 1574, Harvey found an early patron in Oxford who, though he valued Harvey's deep learning, was tickled by his pedantry. (Oxford would later satirize him as the schoolmaster Holofernes in *Love's Labour's Lost*.)

Although the poet Fulke Greville was to describe Oxford as "superlative in the Prince's favour" as late as 1579, by December 1577 the Duchess of Suffolk was reporting in a letter to Burghley that Oxford was planning "not to continue a Courtier as he hath done." His ennui with the expensive and time-consuming business of dancing attendance on the queen had deepened. Suddenly he was on a downward spiral. He had been excluded from the Order of the Garter once more, and in the words of Alan Nelson, "Oxford must have felt more than ever like an outsider among insiders"—Hamlet's problem precisely. He was also having an affair with one of the queen's maids of honor, a dark, sultry nineteen-year-old beauty[126] with a taste for literature by the name of Anne Vavasour, who like Oxford was a cousin of Lord Henry Howard. This was poaching right under the queen's nose, and if Oxford was Elizabeth's son, then siring a bastard child, who would itself be of royal blood, was an act of treason. Elizabeth's pride and vanity were sorely affronted.

Their son, Edward Veer, was born in the Maidens' Chamber at Whitehall. Oxford attempted to flee abroad, as he had done in 1574, but the ports were laid for him. Mother, father, and baby were clapped in the Tower under her majesty's severe displeasure. In more carefree days Oxford had written some verses (sometimes attributed to Anne herself), entitled "Vision of a Fair Maid, with Echo Verses," which reveal the ardor and anxiety of Anne's passion for her lover. As can be see in the following extract, much play is made of "Vere" and "Truth":

Three times, with her soft hand, full hard on her left side she knocks,
And sigh'd so sore as might have mov'd some pity in the rocks;
From sighs and shedding amber tears into sweet song she brake,
When thus the echo answered her to every word she spake:
O heavens! who was the first that bred in me this fever?—Vere.

Who was the first that gave the wound whose fear I wear for ever?—Vere.
What tyrant, Cupid, to my harm usurps thy golden quiver?—Vere.
What wight first caught this heart and can from bondage it deliver? — Vere.

Yet who doth most adore this wight, oh hollow caves, tell true?—You.
What nymph deserves his liking best, yet doth in sorrow rue?—You.

The poem displays Oxford's narcissism and his striking ability to dive down into the heart of a young girl while remaining a detached observer. The echoes of the poem in *Romeo and Juliet,* in particular Juliet's speech from her balcony, are telling:

> Bondage is hoarse, and may not speak aloud;
> Else would I tear the cave where Echo lies,
> And make her airy tongue more hoarse than mine,
> With repetition of my Romeo's name.
>
> (II.ii.160–163)

It suggests that Juliet was modeled, at least in part, on Anne Vavasour. Certainly the play gives us a very convincing portrait of the sort of clandestine relationship that Oxford and Anne would have had to conduct at court in order to avoid detection by the queen. There was also the enmity of Anne's family to deal with. Romeo-Oxford's words at the beginning of the balcony scene in which he compares Juliet-Anne to the sun would have infuriated Elizabeth because they struck at the root of her insecurity. Given that Anne was one of the queen's maids of honor, the audacity of the writing sends tingles down the spine:

> Arise fair sun and kill the envious moon
> Who is already sick and pale with grief
> That thou her maid art far more fair than she.
> Be not her maid since she is envious,
> Her vestal livery is but sick and green
> And none but fools do wear it. Cast if off.
>
> (II.ii.4–9)

Edward Veer turned out to be the soldier-scholar that had been his father's youthful ideal. Like many a bastard son of the nobility, he was sent abroad, where he attended the University of Leiden, the first Dutch university, founded by Prince William of Orange in 1575; he then served in the regiment of Oxford's well-loved cousin Sir Francis Vere. A noted scholar, who translated the histories of Polybius from Greek and was a friend of Ben Jonson, Veer may also have been a playwright, and at least one scholar has attributed one of the seminal texts of Jacobean drama, *The Revenger's Tragedy* (1607), to him. It was said that he spent "all summer in the field, all winter in his study." Knighted by King James in 1607, he became a Member of Parliament for Newcastle-under-Lyme. He was killed at the siege of Bois-le-Duc in the Netherlands in 1629.

Anne Vavasour was a manifestation of Anne Cecil's darker, more sensual nature, which rarely, if ever, gets a mention, because she comes to us sweet and compliant, filtered through her father's saccharine condescension. Nevertheless, it was an integral, if suppressed element of that intelligent and passionate woman, whose mother—a forerunner of the bluestockings—was one of the finest Greek scholars in the land and whose father possessed the keenest political brain of a keen bunch. Though Oxford may have had other love affairs during his separation from Anne Cecil, no record of them has come down to us.

More damaging still to Oxford's reputation than the affair with Anne Vavasour was the political scandal that had arisen in December of the previous year when he denounced his former Catholic friends Henry Howard, Charles Arundel, and Francis Southwell before the queen, accusing them of conspiring against the state. It was a risky move that threatened to backfire and expose Oxford himself as a partner in treason. Over the ensuing months the opposing sides traded accusations thick and fast, and all parties, Oxford included, were deprived of their liberty. Oxford's misery was compounded by the Vavasour affair, for which he spent two and a half months in the Tower. When he was finally released in June 1581, he spent at least a further five weeks under house arrest. His banishment from court, moreover, lasted another two years.

Banishment constituted a form of social and political death, and among one's peers it was a mark of public disgrace. Sir Walter Raleigh likened it to being "in a country strange without companion," and Shakespeare wrote of the experience in Sonnet 29:

When, in disgrace with Fortune and men's eyes,
I all alone beweep my outcast state . . .

(lines 1–2)

The queen's disfavor meant no suit at court could prosper, and even a man's political allies turned the other way. For Oxford, it also marked the end of his relationship with Anne Vavasour. He was further held up to public opprobrium when he and his men fought running duels in the streets of London with the Knyvet family, kinsmen of the shamed woman, not unlike the Montagues and Capulets in *Romeo and Juliet*. The feud lasted years, with men killed on both sides. Oxford was seriously wounded in combat with Anne's cousin, Thomas Knyvet. In *Romeo and Juliet*, Romeo is banished from Verona for killing Juliet's cousin, Tybalt, in a duel. His love for Juliet makes banishment seem like death. "Exile," says Romeo, "hath more terror in his look, / Much more than death," and "'banished' is death misterm'd." Banishment and exile are mentioned twenty times in the scene in which Friar Laurence breaks the news of the prince's sentence to the heartstruck Romeo, whose first words after his fatal deed were: "O, I am Fortune's fool."

Knyvet later wrote his adversary a taunting challenge in which he accused Oxford of cowardice and of being "so much *wedded to that shadow of thine* that nothing can have force to awake thy base and sleepy spirits"—a provocative phrase that probably refers to Oxford's writing (i.e., his shadow life as a ghostwriter) or even to a front he was using, possibly John Lyly. Knyvet also refers to the earl's "decayed reputation." That he could write to the premier earl of the realm in such derogatory terms confirms the truth of his gibe. Oxford was lamed for life in the fight, a condition which he laments in the Sonnets, and for which he seems to have held Elizabeth (Fortune) responsible. He refers to this in Sonnet 37, while refuting Knyvet's imputation of baseness by reaffirming the value of his richly creative shadow life. The sonnet is addressed, as the great majority are, to his son by the queen, the 3rd Earl of Southampton, in whose royal promise Oxford takes growing comfort (emphasis mine):

As a decrepit father takes delight
To see his active child do deeds of youth,

So I, *made lame by Fortune's dearest spite,*
Take all my comfort of thy worth and truth. . . .
So then I am not lame, poor, nor despised
Whilst that *this shadow* doth such substance give
That I in thy abundance am sufficed
And by a part of all thy glory live.

(lines 1–4, 9–12)

Howard and Arundel, Oxford's treacherous friends, give the impression of being interchangeable; at least, their accusations against him were very nearly identical. Oxford, however, managed to turn the tables on them, perhaps not as ruthlessly as Hamlet dispatches Rosencrantz and Guildenstern, but certainly with as little compunction. "They are not near my conscience," says Hamlet, "their defeat / Does by their own insinuation grow." The accusations, with their unremittingly vicious tone, have come to be characterized as libels, yet although there is a good deal of projection at work, they are no mere fabrications, but contain a core of emotional truth. Even taking into account the authors' frantic efforts to smear their opponent to save their skins, the libels provide valuable insights into the character and psychology of Edward de Vere.

There are six principal "accusations" against Oxford:

1   *That he told exaggerated or fictitious tales* of his travels and military exploits on the Continent, such as his reconciliation of the two warring parties in the Genoan civil war, and his orations to the state of Venice.

2   *That he railed against the queen,* protesting by the blood of God "that she had the worst voice, and did every•thing with the worst grace that ever any woman did." (One is reminded of Shakespeare's Sonnet 133, "My mistress's eyes are nothing like the sun.") He cast aspersions on her beauty and manner of attire, saying that the meanest shoemaker's wife in Milan was more gallant and delicately suited every day than the queen at Whitsuntide; nor did he spare her integrity, wit, and trustworthiness. He even claimed that he had enjoyed her sexual favors. Two elements in particular are noteworthy: Arundel reports that Oxford declared "that the Queen said he was a bastard for which cause he would never love her and leave

her in the lurch one day"; he also claimed that "the Queen would challenge the primacy which Christ would never give unto his own mother."

3   *That he made fun of Christian dogma and theology.* Charles Arundel put on record that Oxford claimed "the glorious Trinity was an old wives' tale and void of reason, that he could make a better and more orderly scripture in six days." Oxford further stated that scripture was used for political purposes to defend anything, including bawdry, and had been devised to make people afraid of their own shadows. Furthermore, Arundel chronicles Oxford's "most horrible and detestable blasphemy in denial of the divinity of Christ our Saviour, terming . . . Joseph a wittol, and the Blessed Virgin a whore."

4   *That he practiced necromancy,* it being alleged that he copulated with a female spirit, was himself a conjurer, and often had conference with Satan. It was further said that he had written a book of prophecies by demonic inspiration, sometimes referred to as the "Book of Babies." This was considered treasonous, and one picture pointedly "resembled a crowned son to the Queen."

5   *That he was a drunkard and a sodomite.*

6   *That he was a man of violence* who plotted to kill his enemies, among them the Earls of Leicester and Worcester.

It is fascinating to note the nature of Oxford's alleged invective against the queen, his strong feelings of resentment toward her being reflected in his inflammatory declarations about religion and her status as the head of the church. In stating that the queen challenged the primacy which Christ would not give his own mother, Oxford is deliberately comparing Elizabeth to the Virgin Mary, but in the queen's case she would not take second place to her son. Furthermore, when Oxford denies the divinity of Jesus and calls Joseph a compliant cuckold and the Virgin Mary a whore, he is projecting his anger at *his* virgin mother onto the Mother of Christ, as well as betraying his despair in the face of Elizabeth's constant betrayals.

Equally striking is the reference to the book of prophecies, with its figure of a crowned child, for it serves to remind us of Oxford's mystical obsession with the throne and succession, and indeed his ambition for his own royal child, the changeling Earl of Southampton. The third apparition that appears to Macbeth when he consults the witches for the final time is "a child crowned, with a tree in his hand," at which he cries out:

> What is this,
> That rises like the issue of a king;
> And wears upon his baby brow the round
> And top of sovereignty?
>
> (IV.i.86–89)

Oxford's book of prophecy was doubtless interpreted as foretelling the queen's death and the identity of her successor; hence the space devoted to it in the libels—it was the stuff of treason. If he is to be believed, Arundel tried to save his former friend from the danger of being associated with such a book. At the time Arundel wrote the following passage, Oxford was under house arrest, in the care of Sir Thomas Heneage, for certain libels made against the Earl of Leicester:

> I declared to my Lord Harry [Henry Howard] that such a toy [i.e., the "Book of Babies"] Oxford laid up in his desk, which some man of his (as I conceived) thrust upon him under colour of a prophecy, to cozen him of crowns—as indeed it was not rare to pick his purse with pretence of novelties and future accidents—adding further that I feared lest Sir Thomas Heneage, who had the keeping of the fool at that time, lighting on the same, might willfully pervert it to his [i.e., Oxford's] hurt, and give a greater opportunity to those that had a mind to temper or to work against him.[127]

The "fool" in this passage can only mean Oxford, who, with his penchant for blurting out the truth under the guise of folly, was perceived by his peers as the queen's licensed jester. Heneage himself was the treasurer of the queen's chamber, in which capacity he was responsible for the accounts of court theatricals. He later married the widowed Countess of Southampton.

The portrait of Oxford that emerges from the libels is that of a man who, like Dickens, lived on the edge, in a state of perpetual creative excitement. In Oxford's case, this tension led him into bi-

zarre and desperate scrapes, usually involving wildly unguarded statements about himself and others. It was not simply that his tales were
inflated to compensate for an enforced obscurity; he was an iconoclast who delighted in shocking his more pious contemporaries. His
spiraling exaggerations and irreverent wit—which could use anything
to dramatic advantage—bespeak a real-life Falstaff, who all too often
let his invention run away with him. (The core accusations made
against Oxford in 1581, including atheism, blasphemy, bisexuality,
and reckless iconoclasm, foreshadow those made against Marlowe in
1593, only Marlowe was never censured for insulting the queen.)

Oxford's strong rebellious streak comes out in his railing against
Elizabeth and her ministers. That he should have boiled over in private is a measure of his deep frustration with the queen; and the fact
that he would not brook any praise of her wit or person suggests a
certain soured possessiveness. There are many railers in Shakespeare,
some blisteringly effective, others more bombastic—Timon, Thersites,
Philip the Bastard, Parolles, Lucio, and Feste spring to mind—all testimony to their creator's incorrigible tongue. But "railing," which
comes from the Provençal *ralhar*, "to jest," is not the same as libel-
ing. It has a quality of fooling to it. As Olivia says in reply to Malvolio's
criticism of Feste, "There is no slander in an allow'd fool, though he
do nothing but rail." According to Arundel, Oxford could not be
restrained from his "liberty of railing."

As the libels against Oxford suggest, he did not so much lift the
veil of the goddess as rip it from her face. Yet Oxford was a divided
man—part rebel, part pillar of the establishment—and the libels grew
from his attempt to expose his former friends as traitors to their queen
and country. He was divided, too, between feudal lord and bohemian.
Acutely conscious of the impinging power of democratic forces both
in the state, through the dissolution of the old feudal power bases, and
in himself, through the impetus of his literary ambitions (which were
professional ambitions), he attacks the status quo, the queen, the church,
the state, and those in authority over him. Yet by blood and upbringing he is wedded to this very establishment.

The deeper significance of the libels emerges in the phrase "monstrous adversary," which Arundel applies at least twice to Oxford,
and in terms luridly appropriate to such a phrase. For instance, in a
letter to Sir Christopher Hatton, Arundel refers to "my monstrous

adversary Oxford who would drink my blood rather than wine (as well as he loves it)." In a jocular reference to this passage Shakespeare has Hamlet say, "Now could I drink hot blood, / And do such bitter business as the day / Would quake to look on." *Monstrous adversary*: what better phrase to describe what Jung called the shadow, those darker elements of human nature that the ego demonizes?

Oxford wasn't simply Arundel's shadow; he was the *national* shadow, and that is why he was forced to live in obscurity. Not only did he articulate what everyone else exiled from consciousness; *as the sacrificed son of the goddess, he embodied it.* Shakespeare did not create the fairy-tale kingdom of Elizabethan England, as so many commentators have claimed; rather, he exposed it for what it was—a dangerous illusion—and supplanted it with his own profound vision of reality.

Even so, Oxford never abandoned the private mythology he shared with the queen, their own symbolic language that transcended the world of mundane politics. On New Year's Day, 1581, he presented Elizabeth with a gift of a jeweled unicorn of opals, diamonds, pearls, and rubies. Given the insults toward her alleged in the libels, which were no doubt the talk of court society, it was a bold move, intended to cut through the verbiage and rumor with a striking symbol of their shared vision. If Elizabeth was the lion, the overt symbol of royalty, then Oxford was the unicorn, its hidden and mysterious face. It was said that the unicorn, an animal of irreclaimably independent and wayward spirit, could be tamed only by a virgin. Catholic writers saw the virgin and the unicorn as an allegory of Christ's relationship with the Virgin Mary; and in Cathar lore the unicorn was a symbol of the resurrected Christ. Oxford's gift, then, was a highly complex appeal to the queen, casting himself as Christ to her Virgin Mary, i.e., a betrayed figure, yet holding within him the seeds of his own—and his nation's—resurrection. It was an ingenious and wordless reversal of his religious "libels."

KNIGHT OF THE TREE OF THE SUN

Later that same month, at liberty once more, Oxford was one of three challengers in the tournament held at Whitehall to celebrate Philip Howard's elevation to the earldom of Arundel. (Howard was the eldest son of the executed Duke of Norfolk.) Competing as the Knight of the Tree of the Sun, Oxford was once again victorious. He wrote a speech for the occasion, which was delivered to the queen by his page, possibly the seven-year-old Henry Wriothesley, and later published. The opening of the printed account sets the stage:

> By the tilt stood a stately tent of orange tawny taffeta, curiously embroidered with silver, and pendents on the pinnacles very sightly to behold. From forth this tent came the noble Earl of Oxenford in right gilt armor, and sat down under a great high bay tree, the whole stock, branches and leaves whereof, were all gilded over, that nothing but gold could be discerned. By the tree stood twelve tilting staves, all which likewise were gilded clean over. After a solemn sound of most sweet music, he mounted on his courser, very richly caparisoned, when his page ascending the stairs where her Highness stood in the window, delivered to her by speech this oration following.

The major jousting tournaments of Elizabeth's reign, of which this was one, were vast spectacles attended by up to 12,000 people, and lasting several days. A tournament was a chance for the monarch to present herself to the people in a magnificent display of power and prestige. It was also a theater for her nobility, in which they could vie with each other in demonstrations of loyalty. Oxford, an accomplished actor, took full advantage of these opportunities, spending huge sums on props and playing his role to the hilt. On this occasion he put on the sort of show reserved for royalty. Pavilions, for instance, were used by the monarch or his sons for privacy and to make a dramatic appearance "in the field," and had hardly been seen since Henry VIII himself took to the lists half a century earlier. As for the soaring golden tree and gilded staves, what a defiant assertion of privilege for a man who was still officially in disgrace! This was a drama in miniature—a "device" or masque—written, directed, and acted by the Earl of Oxford.

The speech presented by Oxford's page tells of a knight who, finding the grove he inhabits blasted, wanders out onto the open plain, where he finds no respite from his suffering until he spies "a tree so beautiful, that his eyes are dazzled with the brightness."

Approaching it, he meets a hermit who explains to him the nature of the unique tree, which provides relief and nourishment to those who seek its aid. The knight's solemn vow on experiencing the marvelous comfort and protection of the sun tree sounds like Shakespeare explaining the meaning of his assumed name (emphasis mine):

> At the last, resting under the shadow, he [the Knight] felt such content, as nothing could be more comfortable. The days he spent in virtuous delights, the night slipped away in golden dreams, he was never annoyed with venomous enemies, nor disquieted with idle cogitations.
>
> In so much, that finding all felicity in that shade, and all security in that Sun: *he made a solemn vow, to incorporate his harte into that Tree, and engraft his thoughts upon those virtues, swearing that as there is but one Sun to shine over it, one root to give life unto it, one top to maintain Majesty: so there should be but one Knight either to live or die for the defense thereof.*
>
> *Whereupon, he swore himself only to be the Knight of the Tree of the Sun, whose life should end before his loyalty.*

What follows is a clear allegory of Oxford's predicament at the time of the libels:

> Thus cloyed with content, he fell into a sweet slumber, whose smiling countenance showed him void of all care. But his eyes were scarce closed, when he seemed to see diggers undermining the Tree behind him, that Sun-Tree suspecting the Knight to give the diggers aid, might have punished him in her prison, but failing of their pretence, and seeing every blow they struck to light upon their own brains, they threatened him by violence, whom they could not match in virtue.
>
> But he clasping the Tree, as the only anchor of his trust, they could not so much as move him from his cause, whom they determined to martyr without color. Whereupon, they made a challenge to win the Tree by right, and to make it good by arms. At which saying, the Knight being glad to have his truth tried with his valor, for joy awaked.

This is why Oxford was taking part in the tournament: to try his truth with valor and, if necessary, his blood. The bay tree erected

outside his pavilion was a common symbol of constancy in marriage
in the portraits of the time. Here it also represents the tree of the
laureate, whose leaves were worn by the chief poet; this suggests that
the knight is also competing as a poet of great renown, who can match
the violence of his opponents with his exquisitely pointed wit. The
oration ends with this vow of loyalty:

> And now (most virtuous and excellent Princess) seeing such tu-
> mults toward for his Tree, such an honorable presence to judge,
> such worthy knights to joust: I cannot tell whether his perplexity
> or his pleasure be the greater. But this he will avouch at all assays,
> himself to be the most loyal Knight of the Sun-Tree, which who
> so gainsayeth, he is here pressed, either to make him recant it be-
> fore he run, or repent it after. Offering rather to die upon the points
> of a thousand lances, than to yield a jot in constant loyalty.

The tree of the sun stands for Queen Elizabeth, the diggers for
Howard, Arundel, Southwell, and their cynical abettors in the Puritan party, who saw an opportunity to put the knife in when their
adversary was down. The Knight himself is Oxford, the spear-
shaker, who pledges his life to the true spirit of sovereignty embodied by his queen, entering the tournament to prove his love
for his mistress. (There are the predictable puns on Vere: the knight
is "always ripe, yet *ever green*" and "continueth all the year as it were
Ver [i.e., spring].") The fact that Elizabeth did not live up to this
lofty image is neither here nor there; Oxford would continue to
speak to the higher truth in her as long as his quill had ink to bathe
its point in.

Oxford was going to great lengths to reassure the queen of his
loyalty. But he was more than just loyal subject and lover to his
sovereign; he was her son, hence the appellation "Knight of the
Tree of the Sun," which meant the knight of the genealogical tree
of the *son*—he who represented the royal line of his mistress-mother.
Significantly, the sun tree is a potent symbol in alchemy for the
"greater work" of transformation, and it appears from poems such
as *Venus and Adonis,* "The Phoenix and the Turtle," and the Sonnets that Oxford-Shakespeare saw his relationship with Elizabeth
in alchemical terms. Purged in the flames of their transgressive love,

they had produced a new prince (the Fair Youth) with a new vision stamped in his brow. In his oration, Oxford created an allegory of great pith and beauty out of his immediate life circumstances and addressed it to the queen: Shakespeare's exact *modus operandi* in his plays.

In a coda to the oration, we are told that the knight performed "with great honor" and "valiantly brake all the twelve staves." When the tournament was over, the spectators tore the gilt bay tree outside Oxford's tent, as well as the richly embroidered tent itself, into countless fragments, which they carried off as souvenirs. One is reminded of the treatment meted out to Henry VIII after one of his more extravagant entertainments. It was a way for everyone to share in the sovereignty of the king.

THE LOST SON

Oxford's banishment from court following the libels and his affair with Anne Vavasour was not all gloom. For one thing, it gave him time and solitude to commune with his country muses at Wivenhoe and Earl's Colne. In an early poem, "Care and Disappointment," he had written of climbing "the worn and withered tree":

> To entertain my thoughts, and there my hap to moan,
> That never am less idle, lo! than when I am alone.

Benvolio identifies the same solitary habits in Romeo, who gave his friend the slip:

> And stole into the covert of the wood;
> I, measuring his affections by my own,
> That most are busied when they're most alone.
> (I.i.123–125)

The forest to which the exiled lords repair in *As You Like It* is a creative place of music, song, and poetry, where Nature holds sway over Fortune. Even Orlando turns poet there. The same thing happens to the banished Valentine in *Two Gentlemen,* and in his plaint one hears the voice of the author who made such fruitful use of his own exile:

This shadowy desert, unfrequented woods,
I better brook than flourishing peopled towns:
Here can I sit alone, unseen of any,
And to the nightingale's complaining notes
Tune my distresses, and record my woes.

(V.iv.2–6)

It could be said that the English literary Renaissance grew out of the disaffection of banished courtiers. Their sense of alienation led to a more subjective poetry, which ultimately flowered in the superbly self-conscious characters of Shakespeare's maturity, such as Richard III, Hamlet, Othello, and Prospero. In Shakespeare's case, exile both from court and from the queen's love was, one senses, the impetus for this new consciousness. A class of dispossessed noblemen, intent on preserving the mystery of sovereignty, ended up creating a new language—modern English—and did so in the teeth of a burgeoning mercantile and bureaucratic culture.

Banishment was also the ground for Oxford's reconciliation with Anne Cecil, who had been living a cloistered life at her father's Hertfordshire estate, Theobalds. They were reunited in December 1581, though Oxford continued in the bohemian life that allowed his genius greatest rein. Burghley as ever played the meddler in the affairs of his daughter and son-in-law, and there is evidence that he composed many of the letters that arrived at Oxford's door from Anne in the time preceding their reunion, as we have drafts in his own hand, such as these lines written from Cecil House:

As for my father I do assure you, whatsoever hath been reported of him, I know no man can wish better to you than he doth, and yet the practices in Court I fear do seek to make contrary shows.

Burghley, it seems, like his literary double Polonius, *had play'd the desk or table-book.*[128]

Anne, however, was more than capable if not of speaking, then of writing for herself. By August 1582 she had conceived a child by Oxford, a boy born in May the following year, the heir to the Oxford earldom that she and her father had longed for, the latter keenly aware that something might be made of the boy's royal blood. But, alas, the child died in infancy, and Anne expressed her grief in a series of four sonnets and two quatrains, which the author and academic Ellen Moody has described as possibly "the first sonnet sequence in English written by an Englishwoman."[129] For all their wealth of classical allusion and euphuistic coloring, these poems possess a reality and poignancy that are deeply moving. Thematically, they are eerily reminiscent of Shakespeare's sonnets: the adored son distilled into a rose or the marble of monuments; devouring time; the womb as tomb; the vanity of worldly things. The first one begins:

> Had with the morning the Gods left their wills undone
> They had not so soon 'herited such a soul:
> Or if the mouth, time, did not glutton up all,
> Nor I, nor the world, were depriv'd of my Son.

In the second comes this arresting stanza:

> With my Son, my Gold, my Nightingale, and Rose,
> Is gone: for 'twas in him and no other where:
> And well though mine eyes run down like fountains here
> The stone will not speak yet, that doth it inclose.

Her husband is everywhere influential, and this is acknowledged by Anne in her reference to him as Amphion, the unsurpassable poet-musician, and herself as Niobe, his lamenting wife:

> Amphion's wife was turned to a rock. O
> How well I had been, had I had such adventure,
> For then I might again have been the Sepulchre
> Of him that I bare in me, so long ago.

Niobe "all tears," as Hamlet has it, is the pattern of the grieving female for Anne, just as for Shakespeare. In the same volume in which Anne's poems appeared (*Pandora*, 1584) there was an ode by John Soothern taken from Ronsard and turned into a panegyric to Oxford ("Dever"), who is described as a unique talent and the cherisher of all the Muses, an office for which he has won "eternal Fame." Aside from praising his bewitching horsemanship, Soothern focuses on the earl's literary talent:

> Amongst our well renowned men,
> *Dever* merits a silver pen,

Eternally to write his honour,
And I in well polisht verse,
Can set up in our Universe,
A Fame, to endure forever. . . .

For who marketh better than he,
The seven turning flames of the Sky:
Or hath read more of the antique,
Hath greater knowledge in the tongues:
Or understands sooner the sounds,
Of the learner to love Music.

Oxford and Anne would have no more sons together, but between 1584 and 1587 they did produce another three daughters: Bridget, Frances, and Susan. (Frances died in infancy.) The relationship, however, continued to be thorny and triangular, impeded at every turn by the overbearing Burghley. Oxford's resentment at his father-in-law erupted periodically, yet the old man held fast to his mask of self-sacrificing piety. On May 5, 1587, in a letter to Sir Francis Walsingham, Burghley wrote:

> I was so vexed yesternight very late by some grievous sight of my poor daughter's affliction, whom her husband had in the afternoon so troubled with words of reproach of me to her . . . as she spent all the evening in dolour and weeping.
>
> No enemy I have can envy this match, for thereby neither honour nor land nor goodes shall come to their children for whom being 3 already to be kept, and a 4th like to follow, I am only at charge even with sundry families in sundry places for their sustentation [*sic*]. But if their father were of that good nature, as to be thankful for the same, I would be less grieved with the burden. And so I will end an uncomfortable matter.

Oxford was no doubt difficult to live with, but one can't help feeling that the old fox was writing for the gallery of posterity, pleading his own case and subtly demonizing those who got in his way.

Having exploited Oxford financially during his minority, Burghley was now anxious and irritated by his son-in-law's utter inability to deal with money matters. Predictably for one who wrote, "That gentleman who sells an acre of land sells an ounce of credit, for gentility is nothing else but ancient riches," Burghley construed Oxford's worsening poverty as depleted nobility. He complained of the Earl's "lewd servants who . . . undo him with flatteries"—i.e., the hard-up writers that Oxford took under his wing—yet was not above suborning them to spy on their master.

A fly in the Cecilian web his whole life, Oxford was frequently driven to distraction by the intrusions on his privacy and liberty from Burghley's constant espionage. In a postscript to a letter he wrote his father-in-law on October 30, 1584, Oxford expressed his displeasure with icy condescension (emphasis mine):

> My Lord, this other day your man Stainner told me that you sent for Amis, my man, and if he were absent that Lyly [John Lyly, the playwright] should come unto you. I sent Amis, for he was in the way. And I think very strange that your Lordship should enter into that course towards me whereby I must learn that I knew not before, both of your opinion and goodwill towards me. But, I pray, my Lord, leave that course, for I mean not to be your ward nor your child. I serve her Majesty, and *I am that I am,* and by alliance near to your Lordship, but free, and scorn to be offered that injury to think I am so weak of government as to be ruled by servants, or not able to govern myself. If your Lordship take and follow this course you deceive yourself, and make me take another course than yet I have not thought of.

Oxford's haughty declaration of identity, "I am that I am," which is also a declaration of royalty, echoes God's words to Moses in the Book of Exodus, and is to my knowledge to be found in only one other place in the secular literature of Elizabethan England, and that is in Shakespeare's Sonnet 121, in which, moreover, it occurs in an identical context (emphasis mine):

> For why should others' false adulterate eyes
> Give salutation to my sportive blood?
> Or on my frailties why are frailer spies,
> Which in their wills count bad what I think good?
> No, *I am that I am;* and they that level
> At my abuses reckon up their own.

> (lines 5–10)

Still fascinated by Oxford's royal blood and the idea of mingling it with his own to produce a viable royal heir, Burghley seems to have struck a deal whereby Oxford would reconcile with his wife, Anne, and acknowledge their five-year-old daughter, Elizabeth, in return for permission to see his seven-year-old son, Henry Wriothesley, who with the death of his foster father, Thomas, 2nd Earl of Southampton, was made a royal ward of court and moved to Cecil House. (As Oxford had been Burghley's first royal ward, Southampton was to be the last.) At the same time, it is possible that a future contract of marriage was agreed upon for the two children, Elizabeth and Henry, one that would later be urged by Oxford in the first seventeen sonnets of his enigmatic 1609 collection, *Shake-speares Sonnets*.[130] Oxford may have lost a son in the death of his child by Anne, but he gained one in the young Southampton's arrival at Cecil House. This royal son was to be the beacon that lit the darkening path through his final twenty years, inspiring some of his finest work.

FISHER'S FOLLY

Though Oxford resumed some sort of family life with Anne, literature remained his focus. In 1579, he had acquired a splendid mansion with pleasure gardens and bowling alleys on the site of what is now Devonshire Square. The house was called Fisher's Folly because the man who built it with such heedless extravagance, Jasper Fisher, did so in defiance of his debts and modest income. For the better part of a decade Oxford used this princely establishment as headquarters for his literary operations, maintaining Vere House (Oxford Court) as his official London residence. Those whom Burghley excoriated as Oxford's hangers-on and "lewd friends" were in fact serious poets and dramatists committed to their master's artistic enterprise of creating a new literary language, one that could accommodate a more philosophic and poetic kingship. Such men included John Lyly, Robert Greene, Thomas Watson, Thomas Lodge, Thomas Kyd, Anthony Munday, Angel Day, Thomas Churchyard, Thomas Nashe, Abraham Fleming, and even—for a while, it seems—Edmund Spenser. There were also musicians, including the composers William Byrd, John Farmer, and Henry Lichfield; the physician George Baker (who introduced the work of Galen into England); the scientist

Nicholas Hill, who championed the atomic theory; and numerous actors, alchemists, and philosophers. In *Strange News,* published in 1592, Nashe sketches the sort of place that Fisher's Folly might have been for him and the others, and fires a volley in defense of his magnanimous patron, who had been attacked by Gabriel Harvey for harboring lowlifes:

> For the order of my life, it is as civil as a civil orange. I lurk in no corners but converse in a house of credit, as well governed as any college, where there be more rare qualified men and selected good scholars than in any nobleman's house that I know in England.
>
> If I had committed such abominable villainies, or were a base shifting companion, it stood not with my Lord's honour to keep me, but if thou hast said it and canst not prove it, what slanderous dishonour hast thou done him, to give it out that he keeps the committers of abominable villainies and base shifting companions, when they are far honester than thyself.

One is reminded of Goneril's accusation of debauchery leveled at her father's men (his "insolent retinue"), and Lear's indignant reply:

> GONERIL:
> Here do you keep a hundred knights and squires;
> Men so disorder'd, so debosh'd, and bold,
> That this our court, infected with their manners,
> Shows like a riotous inn: epicurism and lust
> Makes it more like a tavern or a brothel
> Than a grac'd palace.
>
> LEAR:
> My train are men of choice and rarest parts,
> That all particulars of duty know,
> And in the most exact regard support
> The worships of their name.
>   (I.iv.238–243, 261–264)

Oxford appeared to be outdoing the profligate Jasper Fisher, but in truth he was pursuing the feudal and princely ideals that flowed in his blood. For the old nobility, no less than the monarchy, expenditure was the acid test of rank, and many families during Elizabeth's reign overreached themselves in their efforts to maintain their status. Acquisition (or commodity) was the new watchword, and those unsuited by temperament or heredity to such a pursuit stretched their means dangerously thin. Many put themselves in the hands of usurers. In 1583 Burghley reported that his son-in-law was "ruined and in adversity" and that his household had been reduced to a handful of servants. Oxford's shame, however, lay less in his financial ruin than in his hobnobbing with bohemians and other social inferiors. He was a down-at-the-heels nobleman, a sort of Robin Hood of the literary world, who was prodigal of his fortune with those who shared his passion for poetry and theater. It was out of his social humiliations that his sharp understanding of character evolved, as well as his ability to become a vessel for the myriad selves that clamored to mask his shame.

Oxford's enemies took advantage of his prolonged exile to put the boot in. Even Burghley conceded that "whilst we seek for favour [for Oxford], all crosses are laid against him, and by untruths sought to be kept in disgrace." He mentions Oxford's fall in Elizabeth's court, "which is now twice yeared, and he punished as far or farther than any like crime hath been, first by her Majesty, and then by the drab's friend in revenge to the peril of his life." In the end, owing to the offices of Sir Walter Raleigh, Elizabeth relented, though Raleigh himself seems to have been nervous about the consequences of Oxford's reinstatement, writing to Burghley: "I am content for your sake to lay the serpent before the fire, as much as in me lieth, that having recovered strength my self may be most in danger of his poison and sting."

In *Henry VI, Part 2,* the Duke of York, that inveterate schemer for the throne, says of the rival lords who have sent him to Ireland: "I fear me you but warm the starvèd snake / Who, cherished in your breasts, will sting your hearts," a passage Raleigh may have had in mind. But how, one might ask, could Raleigh possibly fear the fallen Oxford, who had been stripped of wealth and political influence?

Evidently, Raleigh was aware of Oxford's genius for caricaturing his enemies onstage, his "sting" being in his nib. One is reminded of the words of the Clown in *Antony and Cleopatra,* who in the final scene brings the asp to Cleopatra so she can die before Caesar captures her. When she asks him if he has "the pretty worm of Nilus" with him, he replies:

Truly I have him: but I would not be the party that should desire
you to touch him, for his biting is immortal: those that do die of
it, do seldom or never recover.

(V.ii.244–247)

"Worm" in French is *ver,* and there was only one Vere in the time
of Elizabeth whose bite or sting was "immortal"—i.e., compounded
of great poetry—and that was Oxford-Shakespeare. In the end
Oxford "came to [the Queen's] presence," wrote Sir Roger Manners
at the end of May 1583, "and after some bitter words and speeches,
in the end all sins are forgiven and he may repair to the court at his
pleasure." Emotionally, however, Oxford never truly returned. The
feeling of having been abandoned by the queen and his friends cut
like iron into his soul, and—like Falstaff—he became a sort of perpetual exile at heart. His rage at his dependence on the queen was
building, too, and would eventually lead to the homeless king cursing on the heath in Shakespeare's most heartrending tragedy, and to
Timon's black misanthropy.

The Queen's Men were formed earlier that spring on the initia-
tive of Elizabeth's spymaster Sir Francis Walsingham, who wanted a
company under royal patronage that would produce Protestant propaganda plays. It was composed of the best actors from the other
companies, and several of Oxford's men joined, including Lawrence
and John Dutton. Dramatically, Oxford was working on several
fronts, through his adult and boy companies at the Blackfriars, and
possibly at the Theatre and Curtain as well. (The Blackfriars was a
precursor of Restoration theatre, both culturally—it gave birth to
the "gallant"—and in its design.)

Exile had spurred Oxford's creativity, and 1583 was the year
when he produced the first version of *Hamlet.* The queen and her
courtiers had witnessed his ability to expose the tragicomedy of their
lives with depth and clarity, and had noted his command of political and historical detail. Now that war with Spain was brewing,
the government sought to harness his creative energy in service to
the state, for the theater could be used to whip up patriotic feeling
and give Englishmen a sense of pride and participation in their history. It could also inspire loyalty to the monarch, and faith in the
necessity of war. As Nashe wrote in *Pierce Penniless,* "In plays . . . all

stratagems of war, all the cankerworms that breed on the rust of peace, are most lively anatomized. They show the ill success of treason, the fall of hasty climbers, the wretched end of usurpers, the misery of civil dissension."

Working with the Queen's Men, Oxford was commandeered as the poet-playwright of the fledgling British empire, producing a series of history plays that, on the surface at least, extolled the virtues of national unity and foreign conquest. In 1586 Elizabeth recognized Oxford's service to the state by granting him an annuity of £1,000, which continued for life.[131] It was also by way of compensating him for all he had spent on court theatricals over the previous two decades. Given that the government's average annual expenditure on civil and court affairs at that time was just over £100,000, this was a very large stipend (or bribe), part of which was no doubt earmarked for combatting the Puritan pamphleteers. In return, Oxford probably had to promise the queen that he would not break cover as the author of the plays; hence Hamlet's cry of "I'll take the ghost's word for a thousand pound," i.e., he will become a ghostwriter for £1,000 a year (the very sum Falstaff seeks in *Henry IV, Part 2*). Elizabeth may also have sought assurances from Oxford that his more turbulent days were behind him.

Act III, scene ii, of *Henry IV, Part 1,* in which Prince Hal meets with his father the king and pledges his allegiance, illuminates the relationship between Oxford and Elizabeth at the time of the grant. The king chastises Hal for living degenerately, keeping poor company, and sullying his royal name with "vile participation." Shaping his tirade throughout is an unfavorable comparison of Hal with the rebel hero, Hotspur,[132] who "leads ancient lords and reverend bishops on to bloody battles." To lamenting King Henry, it is his own son who is the rebel, his "nearest and dearest enemy," as he calls Hal, and he is forced to conclude that God has bred for him "revengement and a scourge" out of his own blood:

> Tell me else
> Could such inordinate and low desires,
> Such poor, such bare, such lewd, such mean attempts,
> Such barren pleasures, rude society,
> As thou art match'd withal, and grafted to,

Accompany the greatness of thy blood,
And hold their level with thy princely heart?

(III.ii.11–17)

To Henry, Hal is an anomaly in the royal line, a new and dis-turbing force. Moreover, he is "an alien to the hearts / Of all the court and princes of [the] blood." For his part, Hal vows to be more himself, and to redeem his faults "on Percy's head." He will crush the rebel in single combat. The king, pleased with his response, gives him "charge and sovereign trust" therein. Hal's greatest declaration to his father, however, is one of simple identity, vowing that "in the closing of some glorious day" he will be bold to tell him that he is his son. This does not mean worthy to be his son by mere butchery, for Hal's vision of kingship is very different from his father's; rather, it is a statement of consanguinity—"for good or ill, I am of your blood"—"the closing of some glorious" day being the Day of Judg-ment, when what is true can no longer be hidden.

So, too, Elizabeth gave Oxford "charge and sovereign trust" in 1586, but his service was literary, not martial, his pen his spear. It was a bold move, for like Hal's, Oxford's loyalty strove constantly with feelings of revolt.

When Elizabeth learned of the execution of Mary Queen of Scots in February 1587 (having signed the death warrant with great heavi-ness of heart), she suffered prolonged attacks of hysteria, lashing out at her councillors in her desperation to deflect the intolerable bur-den of guilt. The specter of her executed mother rose before her. Anne, like Mary, accused of treason and denounced as an adulteress, had been condemned to death by a prejudiced jury of English peers. Now Elizabeth was an accomplice to murder, and she had, in a sense, destroyed the sanctity of her office. The execution had also exposed the Achilles' heal of Elizabeth's government—its failure to settle the succession. It was a weak spot that Oxford-Shakespeare preyed upon remorselessly in his history plays. Until the question was settled, the country would remain vulnerable to rebellion, as the 1590s and early 1600s were to prove.

Oxford's wife, Anne, "the sweet little countess of Oxford," died in June 1588 at Greenwich Palace, of a burning fever. She was just thirty-three. We don't know where Oxford was at the time, but he may have been fitting out his ship, the *Edward Bonaventure,* for action against the Armada, which had first sailed for the Channel on May 20 but was now refitting at Corunna in northwest Spain. In a ballad written to celebrate the victory of 1588 over the Armada, Oxford stands "like warlike Mars upon the hatches" of his ship, England's spear-shaker:

> His tusked Boar 'gan foam for inward ire,
> While Pallas filled his breast with warlike fire.[133]

He is not listed among those who attended Anne's funeral, and no doubt he felt crushed by the weight of conflicting emotions. Many at the funeral would have held him responsible for her death. Maybe, like Hamlet, he returned just in time to see her burial rites, observing the ceremony from afar.

Anne's death ushered in a bleak chapter in Oxford's life, a period of withdrawal, during which he was racked with remorse for his harsh treatment of her. It was a time of hardship, too, with the Cecils withdrawing their support, and the Puritans turning the screws on the theaters. Some have conjectured that Oxford suffered a nervous collapse, opening the door to the mad ravings of Timon and King Lear.

Oxford's pain at Anne's death was intensified by his strong identification with her as a victim of Burghley's manipulations and the queen's selfish indifference. Indeed, in the form of Ophelia singing her "mad" songs or weaving her garlands of flowers, she becomes a symbol of the poet himself. Gertrude's strangely detached relationship with Ophelia, which reaches its apex at the scene of the latter's death, could indicate Elizabeth's attitude to both Anne and Oxford around the time of Anne's death. Gertrude watches Ophelia weaving her garlands on the riverbank and is close enough to name each particular flower that she uses in composing them. She continues to observe as the girl engages in the perilous activity of hanging her wreaths on the willow, but does nothing to save her when a bough suddenly breaks and she falls into the water, unless we can imagine the queen running along the bank as Ophelia is swept downstream. Ophelia hanging her garlands on the willow tree is the poet dedicating his works to Queen Elizabeth, and the "envious sliver" that breaks, throwing her to her death, is once again the queen (described as "the envious moon" in *Romeo and Juliet*) who instead of supporting the poet as he had expected, maliciously breaks her bond. Here we have not only a depiction of the queen's jealousy of Oxford's wife, Anne Cecil, but also an evocation of Elizabeth watching Oxford-Shakespeare slip beyond her grasp into the world of his art. From now on their relationship will be lived out principally upon the literary plane.

Ironically, with the death of Anne, a vital thread joining Oxford to the queen was cut.

Part Four

Outcast King

The Very Pattern of Woe

O! how this mother swells up toward my heart;
Hysterica passio! down, thou climbing sorrow!
(*King Lear,* II.iv.54–55)

AS YOU LIKE IT MARKS a turning point in the canon, for Shakespeare—in the guise of Jaques—decides not to return to court but keeps to the wood, leading a removed life. The exiled poet and erstwhile traveler shuns the festivities at the end of the play to guide us into the realm of Shakespeare's tragic vision. He is a threshold character, harbinger of a new energy striving for expression in the poet. This removal from court may not be reflected literally in subsequent plays (Hamlet's milieu, for instance, is undeniably the court), but it registers powerfully in the hero's alienation from society and his realization that he must turn his back on the old model of monarchy with its destructive use of power. He himself cannot hope to share in the old power, which no longer serves the world; instead, he must create a new idea of kingship. He may not be fully aware of this impulse; nevertheless, strong revolutionary forces seek expression through him. Because Shakespeare was deeply conservative by nature, the revolutionary and anarchic powers that seized his soul in middle age created an inner conflict so intense as to threaten his very sanity. The identity crisis he'd kept at bay while in the glow of the queen's love and approval erupted into the open with his banishment from court, and if Elizabeth was his parent, the sense of rejection and betrayal necessarily cut deeper. The resultant chaos and madness are depicted with brutal clarity in Hamlet, Lear, Edgar, Timon, Othello, and Antony.

The traditional way of looking at the plays, which assumes that Shakespeare was driven by impersonal, literary impulses, attributes this sudden darkening of mood to a desire to experiment with tragedy —in order, no doubt, to make himself more complete as an artist. (He'd written successful comedies and histories, so why not branch out into tragedy?) As the professor of English Jonathan Bate writes of Shakespeare's first tragedy:

> Given the vogue for blood-and-guts revenge drama in the later 1580s and early 1590s, how could an aspiring young dramatist like Shakespeare have made his mark without contributing to the genre? If Shakespeare did not write *Titus Andronicus,* we had better quickly find another revenge drama to attribute to him.[134]

With the Stratford man as author, one is continually confronted with this sort of motivational vacuum. Art and life never intersect, let alone engender each other.

When the pain of what he describes is very great, it is tempting to take refuge in the notion that Shakespeare's works are literary exercises, much as the parent of an abused child might prefer to believe his son or daughter has made things up, rather than face a messy and harrowing truth. It is easy to take this route with Shakespeare's tragic debut, *Titus Andronicus,* because the events it describes are so excessively horrific. But to do this is to miss the psychological truth of the piece, its essential realism as a reflection of the author's inner landscape. Marjorie Garber writes that *Titus* "is in a way the radical —the root—of Shakespearean tragedy, the dreamscape or nightmare world laid out for all to see, not disguised by a retreat into metaphor."[135] This undisguised reality must be confronted if we are to penetrate to the heart of Shakespeare's mystery.

One cannot help feeling, in the case of *Titus,* that in the horror of the events he describes Shakespeare finds an effective camouflage for the dangerous political truths he is revealing. We can see the same dynamics in *A Midsummer Night's Dream,* where the more Shakespeare appears to drift off into fantasy, the more frank he is being. One wonders how many at the public theaters would have been able to relate the lurid Roman drama to contemporary political events. Shakespeare's fellow courtiers would have seen the connections instantly.

Just as *King John* in its isolation functions as a key to the history plays, so *Titus Andronicus* unlocks the tragedies, and once again the original source has been "reorganized" by Shakespeare to suit his contemporary agenda. The extraordinary thing about Shakespeare's revenge tragedy is that it does not just enact the vengeance that the story demands; *it is itself an act of vengeance.* One of its most persistent images is writing or literature as a weapon, indeed the only effective weapon in an authoritarian state. Titus, for instance, gives young Lucius weapons wrapped in verse to take to the emperor, and he and his family shoot arrows into the court, bearing veiled messages for the imperial family.

This is a play about disempowerment and the brutal silencing of political adversaries. Titus loses a hand; his daughter Lavinia, a victim of rape, has both her hands and her tongue amputated. At the heart of the play is the myth of Tereus and Philomel as told by Ovid in Book 6 of the *Metamorphoses.* Tereus rapes his sister-in-law Philomel, then cuts out her tongue to prevent her from speaking of his crime. She, however, weaves a tapestry picturing the story of her rape, and has it delivered to her sister Procne, Tereus's wife. In revenge, Procne, with the help of Philomel, kills her son by Tereus, and having roasted his flesh serves it up to the father. When he learns that he has eaten his own son he pursues the two sisters with his sword; but before he can reach them, all three are turned into birds, Philomel herself becoming a nightingale.

For Titus Andronicus and his family, mutilated by the state and denied all means of political redress, the question becomes, "How does one express one's opposition to tyranny?" Titus's answer is to resort to violence. Shakespeare's response, by contrast, can be understood through the actions of Titus's daughter Lavinia, whose brutal rape at the hands of the empress Tamora's sons has left her with no tongue to cry for justice and no hands to weave her tale upon a loom. In a heart-wrenching scene, we find her chasing her young nephew around the room because she wants him to fetch a book for her, which turns out to be Ovid's *Metamorphoses.* She "tosses" the leaves with her stumps until she finds the story that best reflects her own plight, the tragic tale of Philomel's rape. Titus immediately understands what has happened to her. Thus through literature the truth is told; and what better redress could there be? "Literature here comes to the rescue," writes Marjorie Garber, "replacing speech with writing, and telling the truth across the ages." The literary text—not just Ovid's *Metamorphoses,* but Shakespeare's *Titus*—becomes the means by which political crimes are exposed in an authoritarian state.

Next, Titus and his brother Marcus have Lavinia put a staff in her mouth and, guiding it with her stumps, she writes in the sand the names of those who raped and mutilated her. Yet Titus reminds us how easily the written word can be erased when the "angry northern wind" blows, i.e., when tyrants are riled:

> And come, I will get a leaf of brass,
> And with a gad of steel will write these words,
> And lay it by: the angry northern wind
> Will blow these sands like Sibyl's leaves abroad,
> And where's our lesson then?
>
> (IV.i.102–106)

Even Titus's grotesque revenge, in which he serves the empress's sons to her in a pie, if taken metaphorically, conforms to the idea of literature as revenge. The image of the cook preparing a sumptuous feast was not infrequently used in Elizabethan times for a writer composing a work of literature. Anthony Munday, for instance, entitled his 1588 collection of poems *A Banquet of Dainty Conceits.* Titus serving up the empress's sons to their mother in a pie is Shakespeare presenting Elizabeth's unacknowledged children to her, albeit under an enticing crust. He makes a real meal of it, as we would say today.

Whereas Philomel was transformed into a nightingale in Ovid's tale, Lavinia has no such release. She must endure her silence and live with her shame, for she is Shakespeare's image for the poet silenced by the state. To this end he deliberately compares her to Orpheus, the Thracian bard, who was himself dismembered. As Marcus Andronicus says when he comes upon the mutilated Lavinia wandering in the woods:

> O, had the monster seen those lily hands
> Tremble like aspen leaves upon a lute

And make the silken strings delight to kiss them,
He would not have touched them for his life.
Or, had he heard the heavenly harmony
Which that sweet tongue hath made,
He would have dropped his knife and fell asleep,
As Cerberus at the Thracian poet's feet.

(II.iv.44–51)

The rape, silencing, and dismemberment of Lavinia are a metaphor for the mutilation, alienation, and distortion of Shakespeare's works during his lifetime. Owing to state censorship and the efforts of his enemies to neutralize his works or completely silence him, Shakespeare was, in effect, reduced to speaking through signs or gestures (like Lavinia with her stumps)—through allegory, puns, innuendo, metaphor, equivocation, and all the elaborate arts of literary subterfuge. He was also chopped up or fragmented by having to hide behind a variety of pen names. The one became the many. Thus, Lavinia comes to stand for both Shakespeare himself, the silenced poet, and his butchered and pirated works. Titus is determined to understand his daughter's dumb communings, and in these emotional words we can hear Shakespeare's appeal to us to learn to read his works with sufficient depth and application to understand the tragedy of his life:

Speechless complainer, I will learn thy thought;
In thy dumb action will I be as perfect
As begging hermits in their holy prayers:
Thou shalt not sigh, nor hold thy stumps to heaven,
Nor wink, nor nod, nor kneel, nor make a sign,
But I of these will wrest an alphabet,
And by still practice learn to know thy meaning.

(III.ii.39–45)

Extremity of grief leads to a new language, one that must be interpreted as much through the heart as the head. Through his compassion and determination to understand, Titus—metaphorically—becomes the ideal reader of Shakespeare. As Jonathan Bate writes:

Titus wants desperately to empathize with his daughter's pain, to try to understand its cause. Titus here, and Marcus in his monologue, figure forth the process that is at the very core of tragedy. Their words mark out this play, crude as it may sometimes be, as Shakespeare's paradigmatic tragedy. For what is tragedy but the restitution of *lingua* [language] to suffering, the wresting of an alphabet out of woe?[136]

The irony of this insightful remark is that Bate, a dyed-in-the-wool Stratfordian, cannot grasp that the pain Shakespeare evokes in the play is *real* and the tragedy *his own*. The play is brimful of grief, tears (the word occurs forty-two times), and images of overwhelming emotion; and one in particular sticks in the mind: Titus's exhortation to Lavinia to take a knife between her teeth and make a hole to her heart so she can weep into it and "drown the lamenting fool [her heart] in salt-sea tears."

Just as the passage Lavinia "quotes" in Ovid turns out to be a true reflection of her own tragedy, so Shakespeare's text—*Titus Andronicus* itself—is a valid description of his. He, like Lavinia, must resort to myths and ancient tales to tell his story. Through them he is able to create a deeper history of his times, for the tragedy he describes goes beyond the personal to the national, with images of dismemberment and severed body parts feeding into the central metaphor of the breakdown of the body politic. As ever, Shakespeare has his mind on the head of that body, the queen, and the chaos caused by the dissolution of her integrity. The play addresses her with a view to restoring the harmony and unity of the state. As Marcus says to the people of Rome:

> O, let me teach you how to knit again
> This scattered corn into one mutual sheaf,
> These broken limbs again into one body;
> Lest Rome herself be bane unto herself.
>   (V.iii.70–73)

One contemporary Elizabethan event reverberates through the play like an executioner's knell, and that is the amputation of the lawyer John Stubbs's right hand for his *Gaping Gulf*, a tract of 1579 in which he warned Elizabeth about the dangers of marrying the French prince, the duc d'Alençon. The punishment was a brutal act that must have sent shivers down Shakespeare's spine. The word "hand," symbol of both power (through action) and creativity (through writing, weaving, or playing an instrument), occurs seventy-two times in *Titus Andronicus*. The handless arm, by contrast, symbolizes disempowerment and loss of creative expression. The strong arm of the state is set against the severed arm of the artist.

The language Stubbs uses in his tract to portray the threat to national security is that of dissolving boundaries and surreptitious entry. "I would be loath that either France or Spain should have such a porter here to let them in at a postern gate as Monsieur is," writes Stubbs, implying that Elizabeth, in forsaking the chastity that has kept her country intact, is laying it open to invasion. This is analogous to the situation in the opening scene of *Titus,* where the emperor of Rome, Saturninus, stirred by lust, marries Tamora, queen of the Goths, unaware that she is plotting to bring down his government. He has, in effect, given the country into the hands of a foreign power. Rome is quite literally swallowed by a gaping gulf, when the heir to the throne, Bassianus, is murdered and thrown into a pit, which also claims the lives of two of Titus's sons. (The pit is described as a "subtle hole / whose mouth is covered with rude-growing briers" and "upon whose leaves are drops of new-shed blood," because in Shakespeare's mind it is associated with his own queen's devastating promiscuity.)

Tamora, a composite of Queen Elizabeth and Mary Queen of Scots, is ruled by her passions, creating chaos in government and devouring her own children. Her affair with Aaron the Moor threatens to become a national scandal when she is delivered of a child by him. Bearing in mind that the Queen of England used to call the Earl of Leicester her "Moor," we can conclude that the incident is clearly meant to reveal one of the darker secrets of the Elizabethan state. In another extraordinary resurfacing of the Actaeon myth, Tamora is compared to Diana, the moon goddess. When Lavinia and her husband, Bassianus, come upon Tamora in the woods, the empress tells Bassianus that had she Diana's power she would mete out the same punishment to him that Actaeon suffered at the hands of the goddess. In the end, it is Lavinia who is fated to drink from this bitter cup, for like Actaeon transformed into a stag she loses the power of speech, and her delicate hands are turned into hooflike stumps. For Shakespeare, Actaeon was a powerful metaphor for the persecuted artist, and his application of the tale to Lavinia confirms her metaphorical identity with the Bard himself.

As *Titus* makes plain, the tragedies witness the powerful force of vengeance working itself out in Shakespeare's soul, marking his journey from rage to understanding. The great virtue of *Titus*, for all its crudeness and violence, is that it convinces us that Shakespeare's desire for vengeance was real and one of the great motivating forces of the canon. Writing of the *Oresteia*, which, like *Titus*, has at its core the theme of vengeance, Paul Roche notes:

> The blood feud [of the house of Atreus] can end only by total self-destruction, or by giving way to a divinely established justice which is itself evolving—evolving from primitive concepts of retribution into a higher order of compassion, enlightenment, and peace.[137]

This is Shakespeare's journey from *Titus* and *Timon* to *King Lear* and *The Tempest*. On a conscious level, he wrote to instruct and warn the queen, acting as a spiritual mentor of sorts. Subconsciously, however, he could not prevent his rage at his dispossession from rising to the surface. The peculiar gift of *Titus* is that it lights up Shakespeare's emotional landscape in bold outline, providing us with a road map for his subsequent tragedies.

HAMLET OUT OF COURT

Having identified Hamlet as Shakespeare, we can trace his spiritual journey, from exuberant Renaissance prince to alienated courtier to political dissident and beyond. As the histories and tragedies reveal, the journey did not end there: the worst and best were yet to come. *Hamlet* itself functions as a microcosm of the entire process, for not only do we get hints of the more carefree prince of the comedies in Hamlet's dealings with the players, but the events following his banishment from Elsinore are indicative of the rigors and emotional extremes that characterize the tragedies. In a kind of ritual catharsis, of the sort shared by Lear, Edgar, and Timon, Hamlet is stripped by pirates and left naked on the shore of Denmark. From the graveyard scene to his death, he lives as a ghost in his own kingdom. He has become the philosopher king, and there is no place for such a monarch at Elsinore. The sustaining image throughout the work is that of the outcast king, a theme first sounded *sotto voce* in the comedies through the figure of the fool, then building to a crescendo in the histories with the fall of Richard II. It is in the tragedies, however, that the figure takes center stage.

Through it, we realize to what extent Shakespeare was rewriting the history of his time. Even when we take into account the modern misconception "art for art's sake," it is astonishing that no one has understood the reality of this central Shakespearean archetype or sought to discover how it manifested in the politics of the time. Once one sees Hamlet as a real protagonist in Elizabethan politics, and Shakespeare's works as profound chronicles of their time, it is not hard to recognize that the silence surrounding the playwright in his lifetime (and since) has to do with the fact that he himself was the outlawed king of the late Tudor age—or else identified so strongly with the archetype that it amounted to a psychological complex with him. Either we take these extraordinary works as real, or we concede that Shakespeare was of the delusional, schizophrenic type.

If Hamlet had not been killed, and Claudius survived to continue his usurping reign, the unhappy prince might have shared the fate of Timon, ending up as a misanthropic sage on the Danish coast, or the image of poor mad Tom. Only when we traverse the dark landscapes of *Timon* and *Lear* do we realize how full of gall Hamlet was and how his "madness," real or feigned, was caused by the sheer effort of keeping his alienated emotions at bay. The palliative bitterness of his wit was all that shielded him from committing the most heinous of crimes.

From Court to Cave

Timon of Athens, never a popular play, is raw Shakespeare, a *cri de coeur* rather than a fully deliberated work of art, and in its final form may not have been intended for publication. Thus, it provides invaluable insights into the poet's soul-life. Frank Harris wrote that this play marked "the extremity of Shakespeare's suffering," adding, "It's not to be called a work of art, it is hardly even a tragedy; it is the causeless ruin of a soul."[138]

Timon of Athens, the darling of Fortune, knows all the pleasures of the cultured capital. A wealthy aristocrat, he entertains on a princely scale, embellishing his banquets with masques and gifts of jewels. His is the "magic of bounty." Presiding over a court of joy, he cherishes a lofty vision of society, with beauty at its heart. His trust in the goodwill and generosity of his friends is boundless, and he pays bitterly for this trust. Timon, like Hamlet, is both a patron of artists and an artist himself, who writes masques for private performance. He is a prodigal, whose "unmatched mind" and "plenteous bosom" win the allegiance of countless admirers. He is, in a word, Shakespeare.

Timon's admirers prove to be no more than "mouth-friends" who devour him, dipping their meat in his blood, and flattering him as they feed. Having exhausted both his estate and his credit, he turns to his friends for help, and is denied. A switch flips in his brain, from love to hate. The Renaissance prince becomes a vagabond. Exiling himself, Timon leaves Athens empty-handed and heads for the woods overlooking the Aegean. Turning back to take one last look at the great center of civilization that was his home, he cries out, like Lear unbuttoning on the heath:

> Nothing I'll bear from thee
> But nakedness, thou detestable town!
> Take thou that too, with multiplying bans!
> (IV.i.32–34)

It is a heartbreaking image: Timon, rejected by Fortune, cursing from outside the walls of his mother city with all the rage of an abandoned child.

Timon is an anagram of "I'm not," and when he deserts his Athenian mansion to live in a cave by the sea, he loses his identity, becoming "misanthropos" or man-hater. Outside the walls of Fortune's city, he seeks one thing alone: roots. "Earth, yield me roots!" he cries, and "Roots, you clear heavens!" In other words, Timon seeks his lineage, his name. He wants to banish the terrible feeling of nothingness at his core, the feeling of *I'm not*. This namelessness is behind his wish that all distinction between things should dissolve. King or beggar, all or nothing, Timon is an extremist. As the cynical philosopher Apemantus says to him, "The middle of humanity thou never knewest, but the extremity of both ends. When thou wast in thy gilt and perfume, they mock'd thee for too much curiosity; in thy rags thou know'st none, but art despis'd for the contrary."

The imagery used of Timon—sun, phoenix, oak tree—bespeaks a kingly status. But the sun is dimmed, the phoenix transformed to a "naked gull," and the oak tree stripped of its leaves, as he is reduced to nothing. Like the Oak King of Nemi (the sovereign priest of Diana), who was ritually killed on Midsummer Day, Timon is the royal scapegoat driven out, then sacrificed to renew the kingdom.

His final words are, "Sun, hide thy beams, Timon hath done his reign."

Timon divides into the loving philanthropist of Acts I to III and the furious misanthrope of Acts IV and V, and no commentator seems able to reconcile the two. Timon's friends abandon him in his hour of need, and a gentle, civilized man is transformed into a monster. "Know you the quality of Lord Timon's fury?" asks the Second Lord in fear and bewilderment. The First Lord replies, "He's but a mad lord, and nought but humours sways him." Seven lines later the Second Lord himself says gravely, "Lord Timon's mad." What is the cause of this transformation? Why should loss of fortune and the ingratitude of friends drive him mad?

Timon's wealth, scattered so liberally among his friends, is more than mere money—he also gives of himself. Numerous images show him dismembered and consumed by flatterers. He is no ordinary philanthropist, but an artist and patron of artists, whose mind is praised as much as his purse. In addressing him before the masque, which Timon describes as his own, Cupid says, "Hail to thee, worthy Timon, and to all that of his bounties taste! The five best senses acknowledge thee their patron, and come freely to gratulate thy plenteous bosom." What is this plenteous bosom but the source of Timon's genius? It is not unlike Falstaff's "womb" or "belly," with the school of tongues in it, that proves the fat knight's undoing. Timon's genius is both the essence of his bounty and the cause of his downfall.

Gold is used as an image of Timon's genius throughout the play so that, in giving gold, he is sharing the gifts of his mind, which are limitless. Moreover, he is able to turn what others bring him into gold—a suggestion that Shakespeare transformed the work of others. "If I want gold," says the Senator at the beginning of Act II, "steal

but a beggar's dog / And give it Timon—why, the dog coins gold."
Magical bounty, wealth flowing from an inexhaustible source: these
images are more appropriate to intellectual gifts than physical resources. As the critic Leo Alvarez perceptively asks, "Is the play saying that Timon in some way is a poet?"[139] In poetic terms, Timon's
journey takes him from high-flown lyricism in his philanthropic days,
when he gives with an open and loving heart, to bitterest satire when
he exiles himself from Athens, hurling gold and curses at those who
seek him out.

Timon's gift of himself evokes the image of Christian commun-
ion; his friends drink of his blood and eat of his flesh. Bearing in mind
the artistic dimension of his giving, there is a pun both on "corpus"
meaning "body of work" and "talent," the unit of currency used in
the play. (Timon shares his talents with his friends.) Thus, the nour-
ishing power of Timon's body is the imaginative power of Shakespeare's corpus, a body of poetry that has been feeding the world
ever since. In the first banquet scene, Timon weeps for joy as he
addresses his friends, like another Christ addressing his disciples. The
speech wonderfully illustrates Timon's perfect idealism and sensitivity. Can there be anything more gracious or more expressive of a
natural aristocracy and boundlessness of spirit than the following?
"Why, I have often wish'd myself poorer that I might come nearer
to you. We are born to do benefits; and what better or properer can
we call our own than the riches of our friends?" In these words we
hear the alienation of the great artist, separated from ordinary men
by his genius. They also remind us of Karl Marx's piercing insight,
that "money is the alienated ability of mankind." The crux here, in
terms of Shakespeare's life and the despair that fuels *Timon,* is the
appropriation or loss of his literary kingdom. This is what strips him
of his identity, and finally tips him over the edge.

Timon's reckless bounty cannot be understood in terms of poetic genius alone; there is another vital component, which constitutes the hidden core of the work. In the very first scene the Poet of
the play, in describing his latest work—an allegory of Fortune—reveals the mythic heart of Shakespeare's play, the *subjective correlative*
or hidden, unconscious coordinates by which we can make sense of
Timon's subsequent rage.

The Poet describes Fortune as a "sovereign lady" enthroned "upon a high and pleasant hill," beckoning to Lord Timon out of the crowd of suitors with "her ivory hand." The language describing the relationship of the suitors to Fortune is overtly sexual, employing terms such as "mount," "bosom," and "propagate." Timon himself is presented as Fortune's child or minion "bowing his head against the steepy mount" whereon she sits. She is the sole and dominant female presence in the play—goddess of complete being, giver and taker of life. Timon's court is Fortune's court, and Timon her chief suitor. Enthroned upon her hill, she not only looks down on the action but also directs it. Her power over Timon is arbitrary and absolute, and his reversal of fortune is caused by her withdrawal of favor. Fortune not only feeds Timon but *feeds off* him, pursuing him as Venus pursues Adonis, and it is Fortune who turns into a raging boar and brings him down. Above all, it is Fortune, not the perfidy of false friends, who provokes Timon's curses in the final two acts. All that Timon says and does arises from his relationship to omnipresent Fortune. The more he tries to run from her, as when he flees from Athens, the more he falls into her power. Once again the specter of Actaeon hovers over "transformed Timon," as one senator calls him.

Another side to Timon's identification with Fortune is his emotional dependence. There is a pathological quality to his generosity, as when he says, "Methinks I could deal kingdoms to my friends, / And ne'er be weary." This is a form of megalomania, born of an infantile identification with Fortune, the obverse of such outrageous liberality being extreme emotional neediness. Timon's heart, described by his steward as a "beggar," can never receive enough love. His giving reflects a desperate desire to receive what he gives: a flow of never-ending largess and nourishment. He expects Fortune to be an all-nurturing mother, not a fickle mistress. This is why it is appropriate to talk of Timon as the son of Fortune: there are no boundaries between him and the goddess. Like a small child with its mother, there is a complete sense of unity. It is hardly surprising, then, that he should lose his sanity and identity when Fortune withdraws her favor, the all-bounteous parent becoming the devouring mother.

At the beginning of Act IV, when Timon the cave dweller appears for the first time, we hear him deliver a furious and sustained imprecation, his once genial and magnanimous nature swept away on a tide of wrath. Far from railing on about the ingratitude of friends, however, Timon, like Lear in the fields outside Dover, is fiercely erotic in his diatribe, which bears no obvious connection to the plot. Nor are there any female characters who might have inspired such rage and revulsion. This is very much Shakespeare's "trip."

If we are sensitive to the ulterior or mythic plot of the play, and factor in Timon's relationship with Fortune, then his sexual neurosis finds a context. Even the images of Timon being eaten by his flatterers or "mouth-friends" can be seen as a displacement of his (and Shakespeare's) anxiety about being devoured by a mother figure.

In Shakespeare's case, Fortune could mean only one figure, the Tudor monarch, for whom this was a frequent trope. The Roman goddess Fortuna steered the course of people's mundane lives, conferring and denying wealth, raising men up and dashing them down. Often depicted wearing a blindfold and standing on a ball, which might at any moment roll this way or that, Fortune was perceived as arbitrary, enriching and destroying without regard to desert, and creating rivalry among men (in contrast to the artistic brotherhood that is Timon's ideal). Fortune in her fickleness was also presented as a whore. "Thou art a slave, whom Fortune's tender arm / With favour never clasp'd," says Timon to Apemantus, speaking as one who was Fortune's lover before being cast down and transformed.

By the same token, Queen Elizabeth's capriciousness was the despair of those who sued for her favor. Her power to make and unmake careers was beyond question, as was her wantonness. Alvarez de Quadra described her as a "passionate ill-advised woman" with "a hundred thousand devils in her body." That Shakespeare has the queen in mind is clear from the way Timon harps upon the whore masquerading as a virgin:

> Strike me the counterfeit matron:
> It is her habit only that is honest,
> Herself's a bawd. Let not the virgin's cheek
> Make soft thy trenchant sword: for those milk-paps,

That through the window-bars bore at men's eyes,
Are not within the leaf of pity writ,
But set them down horrible traitors.

(IV.iii.114–120)

Most commentators ignore Timon's sexual ranting or consider it irrelevant. Frank Harris, who identifies Timon with Shakespeare, writes, "We must not leave this play before noticing the overpowering erotic strain in Shakespeare which suits Timon as little as it suited Lear." He goes on to marvel that "Shakespeare-Timon eases himself in pages of erotic raving."[140] This erotomania *appears* not to suit Timon or Lear unless one can see the myths that underlie the respective plays: the story of Fortune in one and Oedipus in the other. Whether this venereal vein in Shakespeare fits his characters or not, it is a burden many of them bear. Timon and Lear are not the only ones who rage against the "indistinguishable will" of woman; so do Hamlet, Othello, Troilus, Leontes, and Posthumus, while hardly a play in the canon does not touch on the power of the feminine to unmake man and deprive him of his identity. Herein lies the crux of *Timon of Athens:* it is Fortune's transformation from mother to strumpet that causes Timon's loss of identity. This is the hidden core of the play, and makes sense of Timon's erotic raving, just as Hamlet's inability to kill Claudius is explained by his incestuous feeling for his mother.

Coriolanus's relationship with his mother, Volumnia, illuminates Timon's relationship with Fortune, since Coriolanus's rage at Rome (like Timon's rage at Athens) is displaced anger at his mother. As Menenius says:

Now the gods forbid
That our renowned Rome, whose gratitude
Towards her deserved children is enroll'd
In Jove's own book, like an unnatural dam
Should now eat up her own!

(III.i.287–291)

Caius Martius, having been rebaptized by the Roman state after his victory at Corioli, from which he takes his cognomen Coriolanus, seeks to carve out his own identity in defiance of his mother, and is punished by death. Joining his country's enemies to bend his force against Rome, Coriolanus is unmoved by the entreaties of former friends. As Cominius reports it:

> "Coriolanus"
> He would not answer to; forbad all names:
> He was a kind of nothing, titleless,
> Till he had forg'd himself a name o'th'fire
> Of burning Rome.
>
> (V.i.11–15)

Coriolanus is prepared to destroy Rome in order to create an identity for himself. The above description of him as a titleless man who must make a name for himself conforms to the status in Elizabethan times of the bastard, who was known as *filius nullius* or "son of nobody." The bastard could only gain a surname through outstanding deeds. Timon, by contrast, wills the destruction of Athens by bankrolling Alcibiades's campaign. Yet he, like Coriolanus, loses his identity in the struggle with his all-powerful mother, Fortune. That Shakespeare himself is behind the rebellious forces of Alicibiades is clear from the description of the general's vengeful fury, who "like a boar too savage doth root up / His country's peace" and "*shakes* his threat'ning *sword* / Against the walls of Athens."

Coriolanus and Timon are both idealists incapable of compromising their vision. For all their courage and high-mindedness, both men are emotionally dependent upon their mothers. When the Volscian general Aufidius calls Coriolanus a "boy of tears," Coriolanus is stung to the quick and keeps repeating the word "boy," as if unable to encompass its truth. Moreover, Aufidius tells the Volscian lords that it was not Coriolanus who defeated them, but blind Fortune.

Whereas Coriolanus is assassinated by those same Volscian lords, Timon cheats death by transcending identity itself. Having created his own monument, he quite simply vanishes. His epitaph gives two contradictory statements, "Seek not my name" and "Here lie I, Timon," which can be reconciled only by assuming that Timon was not his real name. In the end, Timon accepts that having no identity is the true source of bounty:

My long sickness
Of health and living now begins to mend,
And nothing brings me all things.
(V.i.185–187)

One is reminded of Cleopatra's words shortly before her death:

My desolation does begin to make
A better life: 'tis paltry to be Caesar:
Not being Fortune, he's but Fortune's knave,
A minister of her will.
(*Antony and Cleopatra*, V.ii.1–4)

Oxford's own fall is reflected in Timon's. For much of the 1570s Oxford was in the highest favor with the queen, and it was bruited that they were lovers. As late as 1579 we are told that no man lived "more gallantly" in the court than he. In other words, he was a more glamorous figure than Leicester, Hatton, or the up-and-coming Raleigh, and according to Gabriel Harvey was the most accomplished of courtiers: "For gallants a brave mirror, a primrose of honor . . . a fellow peerless in England." One is reminded of Ophelia's description of Hamlet as "th'expectancy and rose of the fair state, / The glass of fashion and the mould of form, / Th'observed of all observers." Only three years later, however, Oxford was in exile and so reduced in circumstances that he had but four servants, and one of them "a kind of tumbling boy." Abandoned by his friends at court, he retired to his literary haunts. As he wrote in his early poem "Fortune and Love":

Fortune should ever dwell
In court, where wits excel,
    Love keep the wood.

So to the wood went I,
With love to live and lie,
    Fortune's forlorn.
Experience my youth,
Made me think humble Truth
    In deserts born.

At times Shakespeare clearly felt that exile suited his artistic purposes, allowing him to create a bohemian court away from court that promised a much-needed counterpoise to the increasingly Machiavellian polity of the Cecils. Such is the vision reflected in *As You Like It,* when the banished Duke Senior is able to ask:

> Now my co-mates and brothers in exile,
> Hath not old custom made this life more sweet
> Than that of painted pomp? Are not these woods
> More free from peril than the envious court?
>
> (II.i.1–4)

Amiens replies, "Happy is your Grace, / That can translate the stubbornness of Fortune / Into so quiet and sweet a style."

It is because Shakespeare failed to do this in *Timon of Athens* that it becomes an invaluable document, a sudden shaft leading down into the author's unconscious and revealing the primary myths that shaped his work. Ultimately, Timon's relationship with Fortune illuminates Shakespeare's relationship with Elizabeth. It is the story of one man's struggle to liberate himself from the binding power of an omnipotent queen, bent on destroying his very identity.

SHAKESPEARE THE WALKER

Who has read *King Lear* and not been stirred to the depths by the feeling that the terrible journey its hero takes across the heath and the suffering he endures are Shakespeare's own? One only has to open the book for the storm that blasts through its middle acts to gust into one's heart and home. How could such searing passions, which in the play tear apart a whole culture, *not* have their genesis in the soul life of the author? How could such violent emotions move *us* if they never moved *him*?

Opening one's heart to a great work of literature of the intensity of *King Lear* is like setting forth on a pilgrimage toward an inner realm on the horizon of one's being. Reading and walking, if undertaken in the spirit of wonder and intrepidity that transforms them into a way of life, refresh the soul in profound and allied ways. Thoreau's advice to walkers would be my advice to Shakespeare's readers: "We should go forth on the shortest walk, perchance, in the spirit of undying adventure, never to return—prepared to send back our embalmed hearts only as relics to our desolate kingdoms."[141] As a work that shakes the foundations of western culture, *King Lear* demands this sort of self-abandonment. We never quite return from the journey.

Lear, Gloucester, Edgar, Kent, and the Fool all make the harrowing journey that the play asks of its readers: all are profoundly transformed. All become members of the "Order of Walkers," which, in Thoreau's dispensation, is "a sort of fourth estate, outside of Church and State and People." If these characters are members, then Shakespeare himself is knight commander of the order.

Society cannot tell you what you are, Shakespeare seems to say; you have to move beyond the collective into your own hinterland, where the hawthorn hugs the cold wind and the stars hammer out the unmetalled path of the seeker. "This cold night will turn us all to fools and madmen," says the Fool. But in Shakespeare, it is the fools and madmen who inherit the earth, for wisdom has plucked them by the heels.

> Burning burning burning burning
> O Lord Thou pluckest me out
> O Lord Thou pluckest
>
> burning[142]

Edgar's Story

A nobleman in flight from his bastard brother and a wicked, self-serving court; his picture sent out far and wide; all ports laid for him; a price upon his head: England's most wanted. His heart pounding, he crouches in the hollow trunk of a tree. Armed guards come flying by. He waits till their cries are distant echoes before emerging.

> I heard myself proclaim'd;
> And by the happy hollow of a tree
> Escap'd the hunt.
> (*King Lear,* II.iii.1–3)

This proclamation, at the heart of *King Lear,* reverberates back through Shakespeare's whole corpus. A secret king is proclaimed—

a royal scapegoat—but instead of an entire nation raising a shout of "God save the king!" the words are whispered by the king himself, through the chattering teeth of a fugitive. Edgar—for such is his name—is both king and traitor, savior and pariah. He is in every sense a proclaimed man: chosen by fate, yet rejected by society. It is a vital moment, one on which the play itself—perhaps all the plays of Shakespeare—turn. Edgar, outcast heir to the earldom of Gloucester, godson to the king, and himself the future king, gives up his great name and title to become "Poor Tom," a Bedlam beggar, striking nails and sprigs of rosemary into his bare arms. His moment of proclamation is also a moment of renunciation or self-sacrifice. The perpetual action and velocity of the play are, for the space of twenty-one lines, quieted. His pursuers having rushed past, Edgar steps forth from the hollow of the tree. Divesting himself of his past, the king becomes a vagrant. For a brief moment we are at the still center of the Shakespearean universe, the heart of his mythic world.

These two and a half lines at the center of Shakespeare's most emotionally charged work tell the story of the author in miniature, rather like the posy of a ring. Two figures from classical mythology jump out of that ring. The first is Actaeon, the huntsman who was turned into a stag by the virgin goddess Diana and pursued to death by his own hounds. In the fullest account of the myth, Ovid's *Metamorphoses,* Actaeon is *proclaimed* by those pursuing him. (Edgar, too, is hunted across the land like a wild animal, and wears a horn, but manages to escape the hunt.)

The second figure is Adonis. Edgar escapes the hunt by hiding in the hollow of a tree, and on emerging from the tree decides to assume a new identity. We have here an echo of the myth of Adonis, the son of King Cinyras of Cyprus and his daughter Myrrha, who was turned into a tree, and from whose trunk—as it split open—the beautiful boy was born. Because he was born of an incestuous union, Adonis was hidden in the underworld and brought up in secrecy by Persephone. Edgar's emergence or rebirth from the tree links him with Adonis, another hunted huntsman, mangled by the goddess in the form of a boar.

Shakespeare, it seems, like Edgar, was a proclaimed man, both king and pariah, a fugitive from the wrath of the goddess who silenced him, and whose own birth had somehow been "miraculous" or Adonis-like, a sort of virgin birth. Certainly, the suffering of Edgar in *King Lear* presents us with a deep mystery, which can be solved only with reference to Shakespeare's own experience.

Edgar has been deceived and betrayed by his half brother, the bastard Edmund, who, having convinced their father of his brother's murderous intentions, urges Edgar to flee. And yet, what does Edgar do? Does he seek justice or retribution? Steal abroad to raise an avenging power? No. Rather, he chooses to undergo a brutal penance, though it is he who has been abused. Changing his name, disguising himself, and feigning madness, he follows and comforts first the outcast king, Lear, and second the father who has wronged him. This radical camouflage allows him to "outface / The winds and persecutions of the sky." Edgar, the erstwhile darling of the court, abandons the court to become "a comrade with the wolf and owl." Undergoing a sort of self-crucifixion, he strikes nails and wooden skewers into his arms, and roars his way through "poor pelting villages." But why? Why does Edgar crucify himself?

This question penetrates to the core of Shakespeare's psyche and releases two other mythical figures, who seem to inspire Edgar's sufferings: Oedipus and Jesus. The imagery associated with Jesus is too familiar to require rehearsal here. Oedipus's story is less well known, but no less dramatic. He was exposed on Mount Cithaeron as a baby, his ankles bound and pierced by a skewer, for the oracle of Apollo had warned his father Laius, King of Thebes, that the son born to him by Jocasta would kill him. Oedipus was rescued by a shepherd and brought up by Polybus, King of Corinth, as his son. Told by the oracle that he would kill his father and marry his mother, Oedipus left home. His wanderings took him to Thebes, where he rid the land of the Sphinx, a winged monster with the face of a woman. Nothing could prevent him, however, from fulfilling the grisly terms of the oracle, and Oedipus did indeed end up killing his father and marrying his mother, Jocasta, by whom he had several children. When he learned the truth, Oedipus blinded himself, and was led into exile by his youngest daughter, Antigone.

Could it be that Edgar is attempting to expiate the sin of incest, either in himself or his house, or more accurately that Shakespeare is? For, on the surface, incest has nothing to do with Edgar's story.

THIS COLD NIGHT

Witnessing the meeting of his blinded father, the Earl of Gloucester, with the mad King Lear in the fields outside Dover, Edgar, even after all he has seen, is incredulous:

> I would not take this from report; it is,
> And my heart breaks at it.
>
> (IV.vi.139–140)

His words perfectly express our feelings as readers and spectators when we realize that the story told by Shakespeare in *King Lear* is true. However extreme or bizarre some scenes appear to us, they convey an emotional authenticity born of deep feeling. Either we experience this emotional truth and our hearts "break," opening us up to a new dimension of consciousness, or we remain in the old, hidebound mentality of viewing the plays as entertaining abstractions. Our very incredulity should shock us into awareness. Nor should we forget, as Shakespeare is at constant pains to remind us, that where tyranny prevails truth must go disguised. Kent and Edgar, both forced to adopt aliases, are literal examples. (Shakespeare himself, transformed into the Stratford man, is another.) As the Fool tartly observes, "Truth's a dog must to kennel." Cordelia, first and purest of truth tellers, is banished, returning only at the end of the action to heal her father's torn kingdom. Her final words before leaving England are, "Time shall unfold what plighted cunning hides." As so often, Shakespeare has us poised for the return of truth, like the phoenix rising from its ashes. But what began as a literary game of hide-and-seek, a stretching of his poetic wings, is now a deadly fight for survival, and the social and political devastation of *King Lear* speaks to this in potent fashion.

Beyond all disguise, there is a naked truth in *King Lear* that is the cause of all the upheavals visited upon the kingdom, and compels us to look at Elizabethan history with new eyes. This is Lear himself as the embodiment of the outcast king: Lear on the heath, and in the storm that invades him to the skin. So contrary to nature is this weird asocial phenomenon of the homeless king that the very bonds holding the manifested world together seem on the

point of giving. Even before it happens, Gloucester senses the up-
heaval Lear's tragedy portends:

> Love cools, friendship falls off, brothers divide: in cities, muti-
> nies; in countries, discord; in palaces, treason; and the bond crack'd
> 'twixt son and father. This villain of mine [i.e., Edgar] comes under
> the prediction; there's son against father: the King falls from bias
> of nature; there's father against child. We have seen the best of
> our time: machinations, hollowness, treachery, and all ruinous
> disorders follow us disquietly to our graves.
>
> (I.ii.103–111)

One essential power of the court was to control the presentation
of kingship through its patronage of art. An example is Charles I's patronage of Van Dyck, who presented the diminutive, stammering king
as a heroic figure mounted on a fiery steed. It is inconceivable that the
Stratford man, if he was the author, could have presented such a stark
picture of ruined kingship and gotten away with it.

Lear is his kingdom, and his breakdown means the shattering
of the realm. Its eventual return to order and sanity is stimulated
by the king's newfound compassion for his homeless subjects, of
whom he is now one. Because of its dreamlike quality, the play
reveals Shakespeare's inner landscape with peculiar candor and com-
pleteness, as if his whole psychology has been condensed into a single
drama. It has that strange swiftness of action characteristic of the
dream narrative, and its characters often seem more symbolic than
real. The king alone has full human depth. In a way, he comprises
all the other characters; they are merely figures in the drama of his
soul. Their sufferings and transformations are in some way his own,
for this is Lear's dream—and Shakespeare's—a dream of initiation,
or shamanic vision, that transforms our awareness as fully as his. As
Jung wrote, "The dream is the theater where the dreamer is at once
scene, actor, prompter, stage manager, author, audience, and critic."

Of *Hamlet,* James Kirsch writes, "We can dare the hypothesis that
by writing this play Shakespeare may have freed himself from an illness and was thus able to continue more than ever to be himself. In
Lear he struck the same note."[143] This is the illness of the shaman,
whose "breakdown" is a *breakthrough* to other realms of perception

and spiritual experience. When he "returns," he brings with him an undying vision of personal and communal renewal, which it is his task to communicate. Black Elk's great vision of 1872, during which he fell into a coma for twelve days, "lying like dead all the while," belongs to this tradition.

Whereas *Timon* is relentlessly personal in its focus, *Lear* is much broader in scope, encompassing deep social and political concerns. In many ways, it is a work of political and spiritual prophecy, which telescopes English history into a series of dreamlike images. The play can, for instance, be said to foretell the Civil War that tore England apart in the 1640s, with King Charles I as Lear, the high-handed king driven from his palaces out onto the blustery fields of Nottingham, where he raised his standard; and his son Charles II as Edgar, hunted through the land like an animal, hiding in trees and hedges, picking berries for his food. Disguised as a peasant, his feet bleeding from ill-fitting shoes, the vagabond king went by the name of Will Jones. Yet through his years of exile and privation, Charles learned the art of self-mastery, as his first letter as king to the Speaker of the Commons reveals: "And we hope that we have made that right Christian use of our afflictions, and that the observations and experience we have had hath been such as that we, and we hope all our subjects, shall be the better for what we have seen and suffered."

On this more personal level, *King Lear* explains why Shakespeare suffered so deeply and, because of its national sweep and commanding insights into the mystery of sovereignty, places him at the very heart of state. He, like Lear, is the outcast king, the "angler in the Lake of Darkness," or fisher king, who embodies the Christ archetype that was struggling even then to be incorporated into English political life. For what is the gift of the outcast king, if not true democracy, and what is his lost kingdom, when finally restored, if not the dominion of the free?

If *Lear* is the buried history of England erupting into life, the hidden kingdom of a hidden king, it is reasonable to ask how this submerged realm, no less real for its imaginative life, manifested in the public affairs of the time, and what pressures it created in the body politic. It certainly showed itself in the queen's paranoia over the succession, and her terrible indecision, for she never quite knew whether to turn her back on the shadow kingdom her sexual dysfunction had created, or whether to honor it. Her obsession with her virginity was the other side of the coin. ("God save me, even from thy virtue," says Angelo of Isabella in *Measure for Measure*.) We see it in the extraordinary power accrued by Lord Burghley, the official guardian of state secrets, whose hold over the queen and her government was based on the myths that were created and the laws that were bypassed to protect Elizabeth's reputation.

It was also manifested in the rise of the public theater, which was Shakespeare's way of gathering a constituency about him—of raising his standard. This "wooden O," as he called the public theater, was a radical court where whatever was taboo at Whitehall—e.g., the succession—could find a forum for dramatic expression. The first public theater to be built in Elizabeth's reign, called simply the Theatre, appeared in 1576, when the queen was forty-three and the question of succession had reached boiling point. Thus Elizabeth's court, with its divisive political secrets and bottled-up feelings, its accumulation of broken dreams, unwittingly engendered a compensating culture of unity and revelation in the public theaters springing up on the fringes of the capital. Through them people began to comprehend that alternative political models could be realized. Burghley, Walsingham, and their henchmen were understandably wary of the power the theater gave certain individuals, not least Shakespeare himself, and would no doubt have heeded Hamlet's grim warning to Polonius about the players, "After your death you were better have a bad epitaph than their ill report while you live." (Theater had the power to destroy the reputation of Denmark's chief minister.) They were also keenly aware of the theater's function as a social crucible, where court writers rubbed shoulders with the rougher, more radical elements of London's artistic community. The latter were frequently suborned to spy on the likes of Oxford and Southampton and report back to the government.

During the "wasteland" of the 1590s, with crops failing and rebellion stalking the land, one can almost smell the lost kingdom, with its buried son rotting like a corpse in the cellar of the house of state. But not all was darkness and want. The first glimmers of democracy showed through, both in the determination of certain members of Parliament to curb the power of a sinful sovereign and in Shakespeare's creative vision of the philosopher king lighting others to a sense of their own power. As his Henry V says, "Every subject's duty is the king's, but every subject's soul is his own."

Shakespeare is Britain's national poet because when he fishes in the depths of his soul he is, by some uncanny twist of fate, fishing in the deepest waters of the national soul. In the tragedies, he is also fishing in the dark waters of the Tudor soul, probing its psychic wounds to the quick. If, as Freud claimed, the repressed conflicts of parents appear in the dreams of their offspring, then *King Lear,* as Shakespeare's shamanic dream, illuminates like a flash of lightning the repressed conflicts of the Tudors. In the opening scene, when the enraged Lear cries out to Kent, "Come not between the dragon and his wrath," he could be talking about the ancestral rage of the Tudors (with their red dragon badge), a sort of trapped vital energy, which created ferocious storms in the body politic and could be seen most clearly in the thorny problem of succession.

As the 1590s wore on, Shakespeare could see the seeds of civil war in the factions gathering to wrangle over the succession to the Virgin Queen. The crisis was made more fraught by Elizabeth's retreating farther into fantasy and denial. Her flesh had rebelled; now the fruit of that rebellion stirred in the land. Besieged and bullied by those jockeying for power in a post-Elizabethan age, the queen was shoved out into the political wilderness—like Lear onto the heath—while the dogs had their day. The complex bureaucracy of deceit required to manage the skeletons in the royal cupboard had dimmed the luster of the throne; and Elizabeth herself was blackmailed by the Cecils, who, more than anyone else, protected the lie at the heart of government. Their growing disrespect filtered down through the court. "Little man, little man, the word *must* is not used to Princes," the queen is reputed to have said to Robert Cecil when he tried to order her to bed. She was old, too (Lear's age is stressed repeatedly), and her mental and physical powers were failing.

The nobility had dwindled under Elizabeth's paranoid eye, leaving the monarchy vulnerable to the ambitions of "new men," entrepreneurs who no longer relied on the queen's patronage for wealth and position. As Philip the Bastard says on discovering the body of young Prince Arthur:

> The life, the right, and truth of all this realm
> Is fled to heaven: and England now is left

> To tug and scamble, and to part by th'teeth
> The un-owed interest of proud-swelling state.
> *(King John,* IV.iii.144–147)

As the spirit of capitalism yoked itself to the politics of imperialism, sovereignty and the sanctity of the monarch took a backseat. With the new ethos of "each man for himself," the throne itself was not safe. In Shakespeare, the Machiavel, a common type in the political culture of the age, is often a bastard, who by reason of his illegitimacy stands outside family and society, pledging allegiance to himself alone. He is a calculating observer, a rationalist who sees nature as extraneous to his own inner workings, and therefore to be exploited. The bankruptcy of the old order is clear to him, and he is ready to make capital out of it. As Philip the Bastard says: "Since kings break faith upon commodity, / Gain, be my lord, for I will worship thee!"

Edmund in *King Lear,* another bastard, is essentially an actor, who uses the language of the old order—that of piety and responsibility— as a stalking horse for his political ambitions. Conscious that the life is draining out of the old concepts of sovereignty and society, he is equipped to exploit the new uncertainty, the principal arrows in his quiver being a sharp mind and an absence of natural feeling. Aware that he can become someone else simply by acting the part, he cuts across generations of custom, obligation, and social responsibility, mimicking to perfection the "offices of nature, bond of childhood, effects of courtesy [and] dues of gratitude" that Lear holds precious. This lack of scruples makes Edmund a true man in the eyes of Goneril and Regan. The world is his stage, and he alone of the characters parades his vices. He is conscious in a way his father, the Earl of Gloucester, is not; nor is he bound by collective values as his parent is. Having usurped the earldom from father and brother, Edmund sets his sights on the throne, basing his claim not on blood, but on appetite.

This new opportunism, bringing as it did a new individualism in its wake, was not despised by Shakespeare. Indeed, he was the son of two highly opportunistic parents and wise enough to recognize it as an essential element of his own ambition. He and Elizabeth, both stigmatized as bastards, could relate to Philip the Bastard's defiant assertion, "I am I, how e'er I was begot." What we now call realpolitik was essential to the Tudor doctrine of order at any price, though it is difficult to know whether the Tudors were the old order or the new, or the new dressed up as the old. Determined to create an impregnable dynasty to maintain power through the ages, they had certainly learned the lessons of the Wars of the Roses. In many ways, *King Lear* is a parable of the fall of the House of Tudor, shot through with the author's redemptive fantasy.

After the defeat of the Spanish Armada in 1588, the imperialists dictated English policy at home and abroad. Their far-flung interests demanded a mushrooming bureaucracy, which in the end obscured the meaning and influence of the crown. Sovereignty was now a romantic concept. England's economic and social problems were solved by plundering and "planting" in other parts of the world. Ruthless enterprise took hold, as conditions worsened for the majority of the English. It was only a matter of time (another fifty years, in fact) before the state would kill the king.

Too great a gap between appearance and reality can lead to breakdown or madness. Elizabeth in the 1590s was known for her rages, which could last for days. Goneril and Regan represent the dark face of Elizabeth, which was hidden from her adoring people, whereas Cordelia is the monarch's virginal aspect. If this same dichotomy exists in King Lear, then we would expect to find that he is concealing a dark secret, which triggers his loss of control in the opening scene. Correct identification of this secret should explain many motivational anomalies in the play, and lead us to the heart of Shakespeare's identity crisis.

Like Lear, the queen was both cause and victim of the political storms that blew up in the last decade of her long life. All she'd kept hidden and repressed both before she ascended the throne and during her reign returned in one last storm of passion—but the passion was no longer hers, rearing itself instead in the mutinous impulses of her offspring. Shakespeare mastered his passions through his art; Elizabeth had no such outlet. The demons racking the body natural of the queen played havoc with the body politic, just as the storm that rages inside Lear's head disturbs the world around him. Elizabeth's political identification with her kingdom was matched by Shakespeare's mystical identification with it: no one dreamed of its mysteries as deeply as he. Where she was blind, he brought a new quality of seeing or awareness to the business of being king. As James Kirsch says of Hamlet and his father, so might we say of Shakespeare and Elizabeth: his kingdom was the inner world, hers the political realm. Not only did he not deny the queen; he empathized so strongly with her that it is impossible to contemplate Lear without seeing the countenances of these two great Tudor geniuses flickering in his face. Shakespeare lived out the mythic archetype of the son-consort to Elizabeth's goddess, his life interpenetrating the queen's at every point to yield a spiritual unity that is expressed with peerless aplomb in "The Phoenix and the Turtle":

> So between them Love did shine,
> That the *Turtle* saw his right,
> Flaming in the *Phoenix* sight;
> Either was the other's mine.
>
> Property was thus appalled,
> That the self was not the same;
> Single Natures double name,
> Neither two nor one was called.
>
> Reason in itself confounded,
> Saw division grow together,
> To themselves yet either neither,
> Simple were so well compounded.
>
> That it cried, how true a twain,
> Seemeth this concordant one,
> Love hath Reason, Reason none,
> If what parts can so remain.
>
> (Stanzas 9–12)

On the level of day-to-day exchanges, their relationship was riven with desire, anger, betrayal, and despair; but on the mythic plane to which Shakespeare's imagination raised it, these feelings became the alchemical flame that transformed their union into a spiritual and dynastic consummation. It seems the more Shakespeare tried to rationalize, through literary sleight of hand, what had happened between him and Elizabeth, the more his rage and despair at the taboo they had transgressed welled up from within. Elizabeth was "the guilty goddess of [his] harmful deeds," and he with Hamlet "could accuse himself of such things that it were better his mother had not borne him." *King Lear* is an expression both of that rage and of the ideal vision he pitted against it, he and Elizabeth becoming "one flesh" in the figure of the old, mad king.

Shakespeare's transgression acted as a spur to his art, a dynamic that is beautifully evoked in Coleridge's narrative poem, *The Rime of the Ancient Mariner*. Having shot the sacred albatross, the Mariner is shattered within and becomes a vessel for spiritual forces. He crosses over into the realm of the unconscious with its terrifying, sometimes beautiful images of decay and redemption. He also becomes the scapegoat of his fellow sailors, who fasten the dead bird about his neck. Angelic visions sustain him in the wilderness as he submits to a living death. When he finally returns to shore, the sole survivor of the voyage, he feels impelled to tell the story of his transgression over and over to soothe his fevered soul. Shakespeare's plays constituted a similar act of atonement.

Wrestling with the dark power of the goddess was an intrinsic part of Shakespeare's creative process. It was his attempt to retrieve his name, and free the feminine from the blacker face of nature. Whether he was the queen's son or not, his early experience of mother left him deeply vulnerable to female power and harboring a sense of rage. She appears to have been a woman of terrifying power. Emotionally, there was no rite of separation: her rage was his rage. When he was a young man and she first wooed him, he bathed awhile in the bliss of her approval. Before long, however, she turned her destructive face to him, and he was cast into the dust. Out of his experience came a deep revulsion toward female sexuality and womankind's procreative power ("But to the girdle do the gods inherit. / Beneath is all the fiend's"), and a stinging awareness that through his bastardy he bore the mark of the dark mother. Lear even calls upon the storm to make Nature—depicted as a pregnant woman—miscarry. "And thou, all-shaking thunder, / Smite flat the thick rotundity o' the world! / Crack nature's moulds, all germins spill at once." Behind this terrifying image we can see the specter of Shakespeare himself in the shape of a murderous giant, ransacking the world for his lost identity.

The primary iconoclastic force tearing Lear's England apart is the alienated-son energy engendered by Elizabeth's denial of her offspring, as well as the Tudor dynasty's long legacy of dispossession and paternal failure—of failed succession. In *King Lear,* as in *Hamlet,* paternal power is weak despite the conspicuous presence of fathers. Inheritance is impeded at every turn, and with it the concept of legitimacy. Not only does the son fail to inherit the father's name (and crown), but even the word of the father—or Logos—is swallowed up by the mother. Thus there is no viable path for the succession to follow, no means by which the son might protest or assert his independence. This blocked paternal inheritance forced Shakespeare, like so many of his characters, into the realm of the unconscious, where language resides in its formless state. Here, through a sort of divine dyslexia, he forged for himself a mighty array of brand-new words, which he tipped with chastening fire and shot, Titus-like, into the very citadel of government.

The effect of this energy in *King Lear* is to turn society on its head. Not only is the king driven out onto the heath, but members of the nobility erase their identities and are banished, mutilated, or forced to become servants and beggars. The Earl of Kent is put into the stocks, which for Lear is "worse than murder / To do upon respect such violent outrage." Servants defy and kill their masters, children their parents. As the Fool remarks, in a bitter premonition of the closing years of Elizabeth's reign, "This cold night will turn us all to fools and madmen."

~ *11* ~

Redeeming the Wasteland

Let not the royal bed of Denmark be
A couch for luxury and damned incest.
(*Hamlet,* I.v.82–83)

ALTHOUGH *KING LEAR* IS a tragedy, it has much in common with Shakespeare's finest romance, *The Winter's Tale.* Both treat of the waning years of Elizabeth's reign and take as their theme the loss and retrieval of the kingdom, which in literal terms signifies the fate of England, but metaphorically points to Shakespeare's literary kingdom —his canon. The succession, which is blocked or thwarted until the true heir returns as if from the dead, is central to each.

King Lear begins with talk of a succession crisis. Significantly, the opening dialogue between Kent and Gloucester on the division of the kingdom is interrupted by Kent's glancing over at the latter's bastard issue and asking, "Is that not your son, my Lord?" Thus, within the first seven lines, the themes of succession and bastardy are firmly joined. But the question itself is rather extraordinary, as one would expect two courtiers well known to each other to have knowledge of their respective offspring. Shakespeare tidies up the anomaly by letting slip that Edmund has been abroad nine years, yet the impression lingers that here is a man whose parentage at court is in doubt.

Gloucester professes himself ashamed of the lad's bastardy, but concedes that "the whoreson must be acknowledged." There was, he tells us, good sport at his making. At the same time, he manages to disown Edmund, for though the mother is out of the picture, Gloucester does not hesitate to describe Edmund as born *of her fault.*

As a bastard, then, Edmund stands outside the patriarchal structure of society, bound instead to the mother's avenging power. "Thou, Nature, art my goddess; to thy law / My services are bound." Edgar, the legitimate son, is described by contrast as born "by order of law," revealing himself to his brother at the end of the play with, "My name is Edgar, and *thy father's son*." Thus the bastard belongs to the mother; the legitimate to the father. Similarly, when Edgar confronts his brother in the same scene, he does not blame the loss of his father's eyes on Cornwall, who performed the horrid deed, nor does he blame Edmund; instead he lays the charge at the door of his brother's *mother*. "The dark and vicious place where thee he got / Cost him his eyes." It is an extraordinary assertion, which says much about Shakespeare's psychopathology.

That Edgar turns out to be the heir to the throne makes his conflict with Edmund a wrangle over the succession. The half-blood heir convinces the true heir that their father is against him. This may refer to some misunderstanding or deceit over the succession between the Earls of Essex and Southampton, both likely progeny of Elizabeth. Maybe Essex had cunningly pursuaded the younger man to back his claim.

Either way, Shakespeare and Elizabeth are likely models for the blinded Earl of Gloucester, an Oedipus figure put on the rack for his sexual sin. If his works are any guide, Shakespeare felt ambivalent about his own legitimacy and identified strongly with Philip the Bastard in *King John*. Thus the struggle between Edmund and Edgar symbolizes his own identity crisis. Was he trueborn or a bastard? On the other hand, he seems to have had little doubt that his son by Elizabeth, the Fair Youth of the Sonnets, was legitimate, or in the words of Sonnet 67, that his "Rose" was true. The implied rebuke to Elizabeth ("beauty") is clear:

> Why should poor beauty indirectly seek
> Roses of shadow, since his Rose is true?
> (lines 7–8)

Why should Elizabeth toy with Essex or James of Scotland as her successor when she has a legitimate heir in her son by Shakespeare?

If we understand Goneril and Regan as avenging agents of violated nature, then Gloucester's deoculation fastens him further to the image of Oedipus, the blinded king who unwittingly slept with his mother. Lear, too, is an elderly Adonis pursued across the heath by the agents of affronted nature, while in Gloucester's terrorized imagination, Goneril rends Lear's anointed flesh with "boarish fangs." If Gloucester is punished for trusting his son too far, the punishment far outstrips the crime; if, however, he has transgressed the taboo of incest, poetic justice appears to be at work. In the words of the mad Lear, with his sharpened intuition, Gloucester is "blind Cupid" and "Goneril with a white beard."

The opening exchange between Kent and Gloucester is followed by the entry of Lear and his court. The king, having summoned his family to witness his abdication, kicks off by announcing that he will express his "darker purpose," which remains unstated, casting its shadow over the whole play. Nevertheless, Lear's secret is soon hinted at. In explaining his decision to relinquish power, and later in chastising his youngest daughter, Lear uses the image of a baby for himself: he hopes to set his rest on Cordelia's "kind nursery" and will "crawl toward death." The grotesque notion of this proud and manly king nursing at the breast of his daughter alerts us to the generational confusion surrounding Lear's throne.

In dividing his kingdom, Lear indulges in an extraordinary charade—an act of emotional blackmail—making his gifts of property dependent upon his daughters' professions of love. This is redolent of Elizabeth's well-known weakness for conferring honors on those who flattered her most shamelessly or were susceptible to her sexual charms. Both Goneril and Regan use sexual imagery in their assertions of love for their father, Goneril confessing that her love "makes breath poor and speech unable," while her sister declares herself "an enemy to all other joys / Which the most precious square of sense possesses." Cordelia, understanding the purport of their language, says: "Sure, I shall never marry like my sisters, / To love my father all."

When it is Cordelia's turn to declare her love, her response lets the cat out of the bag, for with the use of a single word she sends Lear into a towering rage. The word "nothing," repeated five times in ten words (and a full thirty times in the play), is a harmless disyllable until one remembers a brief exchange in *Hamlet* between Ophelia and the Danish Prince, in which the hero embarrasses his fiancée with a series of suggestive remarks:

HAMLET: Do you think I meant country matters?"
OPHELIA: I think nothing, my lord.
HAMLET: That's a fair thought to lie between maids' legs.
OPHELIA: What is, my lord?
HAMLET: Nothing.

(III.ii.115–119)

"Nothing" or "no-thing" signified the female genitals. Cordelia, it seems, has unwittingly confronted Lear with the nature of his sin. Certainly his desire to give his kingdom to his daughters, in particular Cordelia, has sexual connotations, because the kingdom symbolized the body of the king in medieval and Renaissance texts.

Just as Gloucester's wife is never mentioned in the play, so Lear has no queen. In dispensing with the mother, Shakespeare reveals Lear's quasi-incestuous, emotionally infantile relationship with his daughters. The Fool perceives this immediately. When Lear asks, "When were you wont to be so full of songs, sirrah?" he replies, "E'er since thou mad'st thy daughters thy mothers," going on to taunt him with putting down his breeches and giving them the rod. When Cordelia refuses to "love him all," Lear throws the tantrum of a small child demanding its mother's exclusive affection. This suppression of the mother releases a more sinister force that suffocates Lear from inside. "O! how this mother swells up toward my heart," he cries. "*Hysterica passio!* Down, thou climbing sorrow! / Thy element's below." His very next words—"Where is this daughter?"—suggest that mother and daughter have fused in his mind. Later, he says to Goneril: "But yet thou art my flesh, my blood, my daughter; / Or rather a disease that's in my flesh, / Which I must needs call mine."

Curiously, Lear begins dividing his kingdom as soon as the first daughter has spoken, instead of waiting until all three have said their piece, so he cannot possibly keep his word to give the largest principality to the most deserving. Equally, his question to Cordelia— "What can you say to draw / A third more opulent than your sisters?"—is absurd, unless he has already divided the kingdom prior to the love contest, with the greatest share reserved for his youngest daughter. Shakespeare is keen to give Cordelia a truth and legitimacy that her older sisters lack, and the penitent Lear will later refer to his youngest daughter's "dear rights." Given that such love contests in mythology invariably involved the choice of a wife, one should understand that, on the symbolic level, Goneril and Regan are Lear's mistresses while Cordelia has the role of spouse. After all, Cordelia loves him "according to [her] bond; no more nor less," as in the word "hus-bond" (husband). No legal bond exists between father and daughter, who are bound by blood; but there is a legal bond between husband and wife. Cordelia goes on to say: "Good my Lord, / You have begot me, bred me, lov'd me: I / Return those duties back as are right fit." Begetting, breeding, and loving are the duties of a wife and mother.

To reinforce the point, one could refer to Lilian Winstanley's book *Macbeth, King Lear, and Contemporary History,* which draws detailed and compelling parallels between Goneril and Regan's savage behavior toward Lear and Mary Queen of Scots' treatment of her husband Lord Darnley, whose murder was described in contemporary accounts as "parricide." The role of Mary's lover, the Earl of Bothwell, in the murder is echoed in Edmund's plan to kill Goneril's husband, the Duke of Albany, in his bid for the throne. (Darnley had been created Duke of Albany in 1565.) Thus, the vicious relationship between a husband and wife seems to underlie *King Lear's* tale of father-daughter strife.

In his speech cursing Cordelia, Lear makes an interesting slip, using the image of child-devourer instead of parent-devourer to describe his daughter's cruelty:

> The barbarous Scythian
> Or he that makes his generation messes
> To gorge his appetite, shall to my bosom
> Be as well neighbour'd, pitied and relieved,
> As thou, my sometime daughter.
>
> (I.i.115–119)

Feeding on the flesh of one's children is a good image for incest, which makes a mess of the generations in a family, confounding the very notion of succession. (Later on Lear will call Goneril a "degenerate bastard," "de-generate" suggesting a regression of the generations.) As the passage makes clear, Lear is disposed to think of Cordelia as a parent figure, with whom he seeks fusion, a return to the womb which is finally achieved at the end of the play when they are together in prison, a place evoked in terms of the garden of paradise.

From the language Lear uses against Cordelia in the first scene, one might suppose he is projecting his own guilt at some heinous offense they share. His accusations of unnatural behavior—he calls her "a wretch whom nature is ashamed / Almost to acknowledge hers"—lead France to suppose she must have committed a monstrous crime. Yet all she has done is refuse to take part in her father's love charade. The Duke of Burgundy, meanwhile, hints at the true source of Lear's fury when he says to Cordelia: "I am sorry that you have so lost a father / That you must lose a husband." Cordelia's refusal to respond to her father except through the word "nothing" implies that the secret she carries is incommunicable or taboo. Like many a victim of incest, she falls silent.

Incest, then, is the elephant in the room in the opening scene, and only when he has finally lost his wits in the third act does Lear speak openly of it: "hide thee, thou bloody hand; / Thou perjured, and thou simular of virtue / That art incestuous." The simular of virtue, like the "most seeming-virtuous queen," is a reference to the Virgin Queen, whose pretended chastity has hoodwinked posterity. At the end of this same speech Lear utters his most celebrated lines in the play—"I am a man / More sinn'd against than sinning"—surely a heartfelt lament from Shakespeare himself.

How does one explain Goneril and Regan's abominable treatment of the father who has given them everything? Can it really be attributed to political ambition alone? To shut the door against an old man in such a fearful storm? According to Gloucester, "his daughters seek his death," but why? Having handed them the reins of power, Lear shows no sign of revoking his decision. His hunting and carousing may be a nuisance to the sisters, his companions expensive to maintain, but this hardly amounts to a political threat. If, however, he is being punished for a transgression that has defiled his daughters, causing them to feel revulsion toward him, the punishment fits the crime, making sense of why they scapegoat the king and drive him out into the wilderness. Regan's part in the ritual emasculation of Gloucester also suggests a vicarious revenge upon the father. One wonders why Lear was not content to live out his retirement in his own palace, tended in comfort by his servants, instead of giving himself over to the mercy of his dog-hearted daughters.

What is clear from the opening scene of the play is that the succession to the throne has been thwarted, and bastardy and incest have played a powerful, if subliminal, role. Lear's love contest and carefully choreographed abdication become a shambles, as his unnatural feelings towards his daughters play havoc with the royal will. The play within the play that he stages does indeed catch the conscience of the king—his own—creating inner chaos that spills out beyond the palace walls. Suddenly the lawlessness beneath the ordered panoply of government rears its head. Dividing his kingdom into two instead of three, with Albany and Cornwall digesting Cordelia's third, Lear gives his sons-in-law a *coronet* to part between them, instead of a crown. Albany and Cornwall already hold the highest title in the English peerage, that of duke, so Lear's gesture could be construed as an insult, or perhaps a joke—Shakespeare's joke at the expense of the royal bastards vying for the throne who, for all their ambition, are destined to wear an earl's coronet rather than the crown royal. Ultimately, their bastardy entails on them the inferior status of daughters.

The dark forces of tyranny and self-interest take over, and the kingdom is plunged into anarchy. This begins the alchemical process by which Lear and the nation he governs are transformed. Cordelia remains pure despite the fault she shares with Lear; her union with her father is presented in terms of the alchemical marriage of brother and sister. In medieval texts this is depicted as the sun and moon embracing, and is an image of the soul infused by the spirit. According to Jung, incest symbolizes the longing for union with the essence of oneself. (The gods of antiquity, who possessed that absolute selfhood, typically contracted incestuous marriages.) Having married the King of France, Cordelia, alone of the sisters, has the title of queen. At the end of the play, therefore, Lear and she are king and queen, an image fastened in our minds by his coming onstage carrying his dying daughter in his arms, like a bridegroom carrying his bride across the threshold.

★ ★ ★

The loss of Lear's kingdom and his harrowing journey across the heath can be understood as a metaphor for Shakespeare's forfeiture of his works (which were attributed to another) and the terrible sense of annihilation into which this tragedy plunged him. For at the heart of his work is the playwright's titanic struggle with the dragon of nothingness. *King Lear,* though charged with terrific energy and volume, draws us irresistibly toward silence, the culminating point of the entire canon. No one who had not wrestled with the likelihood of annihilation could have written this play, more desperate perhaps than anything in English literature. "Never, never, never, never, never!" cries Lear in the extremity of his suffering, a nihilistic dirge echoed in the dying Hamlet's last words: "The rest is silence. O, o, o, o."[144]

Shakespeare's works are his surrogate kingdom, created by way of compensation for the political kingdom he lost through bastardy, incest, political machination, and the official virginity of his royal mother. Yet even this second kingdom, created not only to assert his royal right but to redeem the sovereignty of the nation, was threatened by the same forces that opposed his dynastic ambitions. For the works mined from the imaginative depths of his soul were far more dangerous to the politicians controlling the throne than the impotent scheming of a royal bastard, who could easily be dismissed as mad.

If Cordelia represents the soul of the works, their incorruptible spirit of poetic truth, then her banishment symbolizes the beginning of a process of demoralization, whereby the works are exploited for political and commercial purposes, losing much of their original force and meaning. Goneril and Regan stand for these mercenary forces, as does the bastard Edmund, who, like Iago, another cunning plotter, represents the part of Shakespeare that excelled in weaving the plots of his plays, irrespective of their deeper content—in other words, Shakespeare the theater man (as opposed to Shakespeare the poet), a quasi-professional role, which, as the Sonnets reveal, caused him deep shame. Like a kingdom divided and overrun by opportunists and politicians, the canon was carved up and pirated by unscrupulous brokers and "poet-apes." The First Quarto of *Hamlet* is a stark example.

Another vivid portrayal of this dynamic comes in *Pericles,* when Marina, the lost princess, is sold into prostitution and forced to live among bawds and pimps before being reunited with her father. Even when she escapes from the brothel, she still has to give her earnings to the bawd (i.e., Shakespeare's royalties were enjoyed by the middle-men). That she stands for the works is apparent from Gower's description of her creative skill:

> She sings like one immortal, and she dances
> As goddess-like to her admired lays.
> Deep clerks she dumbs, and with her neele composes
> Nature's own shape, of bud, bird, branch, or berry,
> That even her art sisters the natural roses;
> Her inkle, silk, twin with the rubied cherry:
> That pupils lacks she none of noble race,
> Who pour their bounty on her . . .
>
> (Act V, Chorus, lines 3–10)

Shakespeare, being subject to the aristocratic "prohibition" regarding publication, had no recourse to law, but had to stand back while theatrical entrepreneurs and agents butchered his works and obscured their message. The suffering this caused him as the father of those works forced him into a deeper relationship with himself and led to some of the most inspired poetry in the canon. Thus Edgar and eventually Lear himself, with his crown of weeds, symbolize the new sense of selfhood induced in Shakespeare by the stripping away of all he owned and thought of as his.

Shakespeare's works truly come into being only when he loses his mundane kingdom, or becomes conscious of the impossibility of inheriting it. As with Lear, his "abdication" or loss of royalty leads to his madness or poetic inspiration. Thus one could say that the motive force of Shakespeare's genius is his alienated royalty. The late plays bear this out in particularly deep fashion. The transformation of king into poet is given vivid expression in Cordelia's description of her father singing his way across the fields, crowned with wildflowers.

At the onset of his agony, Lear made this defiant prediction to Goneril:

> Thou shalt find
> That I'll resume the shape which thou dost think
> I have cast off for ever.
>
> (I.iv.306–308)

At the time, he cannot have envisaged retrieving his kingship at the level of poetry rather than politics, for only when he is out on the heath does he start voicing the language of healing and redemption, which is the essence of the new kingdom. This language of compassion, in which the sovereign recognizes his kinship with his poorest and most dejected subjects, proclaims a new social order founded on the politics of love, the love that, according to the Sonnets, "fears not Policy, that heretic / Which works on leases of short-numb'red hours / But all alone stands hugely politic." If, as John Weir Perry claims in his study of schizophrenics, new social myths bubble up from the depths of the psychotic mind, then Lear's myth, that of the living king within each and every individual—a democracy of illumined souls—is startlingly valid. Needless to say, this message would not have been welcomed by the oligarchs of Queen Elizabeth's government.

Lear is also the aged and tyrannical Elizabeth banishing her truth-telling child. Cordelia is art made tongue-tied by authority, and her silence—like the hush before the storm or the wings of the Holy Ghost—hovers over the play until her return in Act IV. Hers is that still-contemplative space in which the old king's conscience can grow. At no point does Cordelia condemn Lear; instead, she holds up a mirror to her tormented parent. Kent is blunter and more outspoken, yet his devotion to his monarch (and the truth) is as unquestionable as hers. When Lear charges him on his life to hold his tongue, Kent cries:

> My life I never held but as a pawn
> To wage against thine enemies; nor fear to lose it,
> Thy safety being motive.
>
> (I.i.154–156)

This is a beautiful description of Shakespeare's devotion to Elizabeth, and his habit of using his works to point out the dangers besetting her throne. Kent further admonishes the king to "see better" and to let him, Kent, remain "the true blank of [his] eye." Kent, like Cordelia, is banished for telling the truth; but instead of going abroad as ordered, he adopts a lowly disguise, camouflaging his speech, changing his name, then offering his services to the beleaguered king.

Again, Shakespeare's own story—that of the banished courtier who disappears into the theater world, adopting a pseudonym to avoid the stigma attached to that profession and continuing to serve his queen by means of his art—lurks beneath the surface of this tale.

Kent describes himself as Lear's "physician," which in a spiritual sense he is. The Fool also speaks the healing language that will re-make the kingdom and, like Kent, follows his tormented master onto the heath, where he speaks to the king's deeper self through proverbs, parables, and snatches of song. He uses gibberish to make the bitterness of the truth bearable, for the reality of Lear's situation is so shocking that even the Fool is tempted to gloss over it. Talking of Lear's folly in forsaking his kingdom, he suddenly breaks into song:

> Then they for sudden joy did weep,
> And I for sorrow sung,
> That such a king should play bo-peep,
> And go the fools among.
> Prithee, Nuncle, keep a schoolmaster that can teach thy Fool to lie;
> I would fain learn to lie.
>
> (I.iv.171–176)

As for Edgar, his artful gobbledygook ("matter and impertinency mixed") helps awaken the king from his dream of false rule. Shakespeare, too, in his portrait of Lear and his three daughters, spoke with great profundity to the unconscious of the queen he served, in particular to the element of her nature that had shut itself off from compassion and motherly feeling. Through *King Lear,* he warns Elizabeth that the price of abandoning her true child is spiritual destitution. If, however, she is prepared to turn and embrace her own humanity, then there is still a chance that their son—like Edgar, a discarded child—will be named king.

THE REDEEMER

Edgar, like Kent before him, assumes an alias, that of Poor Tom. A shivering orphan of the storm, he keeps repeating the words "Poor Tom's a cold!" and "Still through the hawthorn blows the cold wind." He is the shadow of Edgar the nobleman (whose name means "royal warrior"), and talks of coursing "his own shadow for a traitor," his "shadow" being the ghostly author who writes seditious plays. It is poignant to realize that despite his high birth and royal connections, Shakespeare always maintained this image of himself as a child left out in the cold, a marked man condemned to wander in the wilderness, an outlaw "whipp'd from tithing to tithing."

The point at which Lear meets Poor Tom is crucial, for it marks the moment when he feels his own humanity for the first time. As Lear stands outside the hovel in the raging storm, Edgar is concealed within, like the spirit of the chastened king inside the womb of rebirth. "Come not in here, Nuncle; here's a spirit!" cries the terrified Fool. But a sort of baton change has already taken place during the fool's brief foray into the hovel, and when Edgar comes running out, pursued by the "foul fiend," it is to take on the role of guide or psychopomp to the mad king. From now on, the Fool gradually fades from the action, his place taken by the disguised Edgar.

Edgar does more than remind Lear of his folly; he furthers the alchemical process by leading him down into the underworld. His catalog of devils foretokens Lear's descent into hell, symbolized in alchemical writings by a king sealed in a coffin. Edgar is the shaman who, in his self-induced madness, exorcises the demons of his class, just as Shakespeare in his poetic fury exorcised the bloody and incestuous demons of the Tudor dynasty. As nameless ones, both were channels for bringing these devils into consciousness. "Fraterretto calls me, and tells me Nero is an angler in the lake of darkness. Pray, innocent, and beware the foul fiend," cries Poor Tom. It is not difficult to construe the "lake of darkness" when one remembers that Nero committed incest with his mother, Agrippina.

The Dark Lady looms large in Poor Tom's mind. Flibbertigibbet, who "gives the web and the pin" and "squinies the eye," distorting a man's sight, puts him in mind of a witch he once thought to marry:

> Swithold footed thrice the wold;
> He met the night-mare, and her nine-fold;
> Bid her alight,
> And her troth plight,
> And aroint thee, witch, aroint thee!

(III.iv.117–121)

As the itinerant Saxon saint, Swithold, Poor Tom has indeed walked three times across the heath, once as Edgar fleeing from his father, once as Poor Tom guiding the mad king, and once more leading his father to Dover. The night-mare is the troth-breaking Elizabeth with her hidden brood (nine-fold), and Shakespeare curses her—aroint thee, witch!—for her faithlessness. (In *Macbeth* one of the ingredients of the witches' cauldron is the blood of a sow "that hath eaten her nine farrow.") After the words "aroint thee, witch, aroint thee," Kent says to Lear, "How fares your Grace?"—thus linking witch and monarch. This witch-queen or "black angel" is also Shakespeare's muse, haunting Poor Tom "in the voice of a nightingale."

To Lear, Poor Tom is a "noble philosopher," whom he keeps by his side. When he asks what the poor vagrant's study is, he receives the reply, "To prevent the foul fiend and to kill vermin," i.e., to keep out oppressive thoughts. And when Gloucester says to Lear on seeing Poor Tom, "What! Hath your Grace no better company?" Poor Tom interjects, "The Prince of Darkness is a gentleman." In other words, he is fit company for a king because he is a hidden prince, or a prince in darkness—a typically Shakespearean jest! There is also the implication that the fallen Shakespeare, though a prince, can only lay claim to the status of gentleman.

Poor Tom tells us he was once a gentleman, who "curl'd his hair and wore gloves in [his] cap" and "betrayed [his] poor heart to woman," but is now determined to hold fast and "defy the foul fiend." No sooner does he mention the foul fiend than he goes pirouetting off into his own secret language: "Still through the hawthorn blows the cold wind; says suum, mun hey no nonny. Dolphin my boy, boy; sessa! Let him trot by."

As always in Shakespeare, the gibberish is rich in meaning, masking a deeper truth. The hawthorn, sacred to the Greek goddess Maia, mother of Hermes, was the tree of enforced chastity; yet when it was in flower in May, it was used in orgiastic rites. Either way, it was inauspicious for marriage. Maia, though represented in poetry as ever fair and young, was, according to Robert Graves, "a malevolent beldame whose son Hermes conducted souls to Hell."[145] "Says suum, mun hey no nonny": in the Arden Shakespeare "suum" is glossed as the noise of the wind, and certainly the evil winds that blow through the middle acts, like "the rain that raineth every day," are the harsh conditions imposed upon the people by the state. Thus the government decrees that Poor Tom "mun hey no nonny"— "must have no name"—because his boy (son) is the dolphin or Dauphin, the heir to the throne. But Poor Tom feels uneasy blabbing about such a secret, even in code, and shuts himself up with the word "sessa!" (an echo of Cecil?) before asking that the boy be allowed to pass freely.

Edgar transfers his guiding duties from his godfather, Lear, to his father, Gloucester, without missing a beat, as if they were one and the same person, which on a metaphorical level they are. Gloucester, too, is a deceived parent who has rejected a true child in favor of a corrupt one. Once blinded, he is forced into the deep relationship with himself—the inner unity—that is the "incestuous marriage" at the heart of alchemy. Resting on the arm of his wronged son, now a naked beggar, he and Edgar make their way to Dover, toward which the whole action of the play has shifted, as if Shakespeare's characters are all returning to their source before his great book is shut for the final time. ("Dover"—echoing "De Vere"—rings like a judgment bell through the previous scene.)

Leading his father across a level field near Dover, Edgar persuades him that the ground is "horrible steep," and that they are approaching the top of a cliff. He even manages to convince Gloucester that the waves below are audible, though he cannot disguise the fact that his own voice has changed: the young champion is coming into his own. There is no cliff, of course, but ask people who have read or seen *King Lear* to relate the action of the play, and they will tell you of the moment when Edgar leads his father to the edge of the cliff and lets him jump to what the old man believes will be his death. Edgar manages to draw us into his imaginative world so thoroughly that we "see" the cliff through Gloucester's blind eyes. It is all part of the drama he is staging to dispel his father's illusions and reconnect him with the power of life. "Thy life's a miracle!" he cries, running up to his fallen and redeemed father. This act of ritual healing is a microcosm of the entire canon, for Shakespeare himself sought to heal his erring parent through theater. Gloucester's metamorphosis from ruler to seer (which is Lear's metamorphosis, and Edgar's) is a story Shakespeare told over and over: the noble man blind from very nobility, and the empty man who thrust him from his place and saw all that could be seen from very emptiness.[146]

The last battle is fought at Dover. The "new men" appear to have won: Lear and Cordelia are taken prisoner, leaving Regan and Edmund free to marry and become the power in the land. But Edgar has not been through hell for nothing; he is ready to face his dark adversary, his own clear chivalry forged in the flames of suffering. His initiation is over, and when the trumpet sounds the challenge for the third time, he is ready. The herald asks his name and quality, and he replies: "Know my name is lost, / By treason's tooth bare-gnawn and canker-bit / Yet am I noble as the adversary / I come to cope." If Edgar's name is canker-bit, then his name is the "Rose," and if bitten by treason's tooth, he must be royal, for treason can be committed only against the sovereign and the sovereign's immediate family. Having defeated his brother in single combat, Edgar is embraced by the Duke of Albany with the words: "Methought thy very gait did prophesy / A royal nobleness."

Edgar is the vagabond heir, the concealed prince, the champion bred apart, that mysterious element of the alchemical process set aside for use at the end. He is the prophesied heir—in Shakespeare's mythology, the Fair Youth—the brilliant young man who will repair his shattered nation. He is Shakespeare's answer to the question, "What can be opposed to the all-embracing power of the mother?" In other words, he is an immaculately conceived child, who will save the world because he is free of the mother's taint. As Edgar says to Edmund upon revealing himself after the duel: "My name is Edgar, and thy father's son." Lear and Cordelia, united in prison, in the deathless space that Lear always sought, have in effect brought forth a child. This is the final stage of the alchemical process, and is depicted as a son emerging from the mouth of the king, i.e., the king reborn. Edgar, who assumes the throne at the end of the play, is the reborn Lear, and his first words as king announce that his reign will be based not on artifice but on truth: "The weight of this sad time we must obey, / Speak what we feel, not what we ought to say."

In sum, *King Lear* is about the disintegration of a king and his kingdom, leading to a new and vigorous reign under a chastened monarch, one who has achieved self-mastery through intense suffering. This happens only because a strange vagabond earl, whose "roguish madness allows itself to any thing," appears out of left field as the final trumpet sounds. He may have no name but, by heaven, he knows who he is, and he knows his time has come.

Despite this new dawn, we cannot help feeling, on closing the book, that something has been destroyed forever, that one of the pillars of western culture, perhaps even monarchy itself, has crumbled. D. H. Lawrence, talking of *Hamlet,* says much the same thing:

> Henry VIII simply said: "There is no Church, there is only the State." But with Shakespeare the transformation had reached the State also. The King, the Father, the representative of the Consummate Self, the maximum of all life, the symbol of the consummate being, the becoming Supreme, Godlike, Infinite, he must perish and pass away. The Infinite was not infinite, this consummation was not consummated, all this was fallible, false. It was rotten, corrupt. It must go. But Shakespeare was also the thing itself. Hence his horror, his frenzy, his self-loathing. The King, the Emperor is killed in the soul of man, the old order of life is over, the old tree is dead at the root. So said Shakespeare.[147]

But Shakespeare was also the thing itself. The whole canon dramatizes his profound sense of loss and disinheritance, and his search for a deeper source of power. At the heart of his wisdom is the idea of renunciation: giving up one form of identity or power for another. "And you may marvel why I obscur'd myself, / Labouring to save his life," Duke Vincentio says to Isabella of her brother Claudio in *Measure for Measure.* This was the task of salvation Shakespeare set himself through theater: to return his queen and countrymen to the source of good government—compassion. In so doing, he wore a crown far richer than that of monarchs.

Given Edgar's redemptive journey, it is little wonder Shakespeare revived chivalric romance in English, with the aid of his learned cohorts Lyly, Lodge, Watson, Munday, and Greene, for he quickly realized he could make creative use of his alienation by becoming the hero of the genre. Thus he presented himself as the fair unknown, or exiled king, who reappears at the eleventh hour to unite his divided nation and defend the principle of sovereignty.

A crux of the exile-and-return motif is the notion that the king-in-waiting must prove his fitness to rule during a period of exile or foreign adventure by cultivating virtue. This self-mastery then becomes the basis for his government and the renewal of the kingdom. The idea that the prince should not rely solely on his royal blood but should *prove* his worthiness to rule is bound up with the relinquishment of name and identity, for his period of exile is undergone incognito. Only when he returns home and vanquishes the usurper in single combat is his true identity established.

The core myth of chivalric romance is the mythic core of Shakespeare's work. It is also the story of his life, for he used the idealism of chivalric romance to camouflage the realism of his plays. If one remembers that romance was a form of escapism, one begins to see the deep irony at work. The strange and improbable events it depicts are in Shakespeare's case all too real. ("If I should tell my history," says Marina to her father, Pericles, "'twould seem / Like lies, disdain'd in the reporting.") "*The Complete Works of William Shakespeare,*" writes Harold Bloom, "could as soon be called *The Book of Reality,* fantastic as so much of Shakespeare deliberately intends to be."[148] Certainly, no writer ever made more creative use of his identity crisis.

SHAKESPEARE'S ORACLE

The Winter's Tale portrays with the depth and naïve clarity of a fairy tale the drama of the lost heir. It is Shakespeare's most exalted vision of the restoration of the kingdom. Its core theme is revealed in a much earlier play, *Richard II,* when Richard bids farewell to his wife for what he knows will be the last time:

> Think I am dead, and that even here thou takest,
> As from my death-bed, thy last living leave.
> In winter's tedious nights sit by the fire
> With good old folks, and let them tell thee tales
> Of woeful ages long ago betid;
> And ere thou bid good night, to quite their griefs
> Tell thou the lamentable tale of me,
> And send the hearers weeping to their beds;
> For why, the senseless brands will sympathize
> The heavy accent of thy moving tongue,

And in commission weep the fire out,
And some will mourn in ashes, some coal-black,
For the deposing of a rightful king.

(V.i.38–50)

King Richard's winter's tale is about "the deposing of a rightful king," and this idea is at the bottom of Shakespeare's romance. It is the story the doomed prince Mamillius starts to tell his mother, Hermione, before he is interrupted by his enraged father and forcibly separated from her. It is the tale of a young prince doomed never to inherit the throne. As Mamillius says, "A sad tale's best for winter."

In *The Winter's Tale,* Shakespeare evokes the sterile, wintry atmosphere enveloping the court in the final years of Elizabeth. Winter is a time of darkness and gestation, of death before the rebirth of spring, and Shakespeare hints in his play that we must endure the wasteland until winter is over, when his works will flower in their true glory. This political winter is also a premonition of the Puritanism and materialism of subsequent years, when Shakespeare's works were "frozen" by people's ignorance of their origin. Thus, *The Winter's Tale,* no less than *Lear,* is a work of faith, depicting the reinstatement or coming to life of the true author and his works after many years' passing.

As the action opens, Leontes, King of Sicilia, is trying to persuade a boyhood friend and fellow monarch, Polixenes, to prolong his stay at the Sicilian court. Polixenes, having been there nine months already, and with pressing matters of state at home, not unreasonably refuses. Leontes then turns to his heavily pregnant wife, Hermione, and appeals to her to win over their guest. His first words in their exchange—"Tongue-tied our queen?"— immediately ally her with Cordelia, another truth teller silenced by authority, for the pregnant Hermione (whose name derives from "Hermes," the Greek god of literature and inventor of the lyre) represents the author's fertile genius. When she succeeds in persuading Polixenes to stay, Leontes is consumed with jealousy and convinces himself that his wife has been unfaithful. Significantly, Leontes describes Hermione's act of hospitality, which he himself urged on her, as an "entertainment," as if she had put on a little play for the benefit of their guest.

As so often with key episodes in Shakespeare, Leontes's outburst has no objective correlative, i.e., no plausible context in the play, thus compelling us to look to the author's personal story for an explanation, and to the court of Elizabeth for a context. With Leontes as the paranoid Queen Elizabeth and Hermione as her court entertainer, William Shakespeare, everything falls into place. Although she has commissioned Shakespeare's "entertainment," the jealous tyrant misconstrues it, feeling betrayed in some way, as if the playwright were disloyal or had made a fool of her. One thinks of a court masque put on to entertain a visiting dignitary, with Elizabeth scrutinizing every word and gesture for some hidden political message.

Sometimes a character will shadow more than one person, as the dramatist explores different facets of their psychology, so that the pregnant Hermione will suddenly stand for the wanton Elizabeth, and the maddened King Leontes for Shakespeare. The appalling sense of nothingness or loss of identity that Hermione's apparent infidelity engenders in Leontes demands this sort of role reversal. Speaking of his suspicions to Camillo, who believes in Hermione's innocence, Leontes is swallowed up by an impending sense of oblivion:

> Is whispering nothing?
> Is leaning cheek to cheek? is meeting noses?
> . . . . is this nothing?
> Why then the world, and all that's in't, is nothing,
> The covering sky is nothing, Bohemia nothing,
> My wife is nothing, nor nothing have these nothings,
> If this be nothing.
>
> (I.ii.284–285, 292–296)

The thought of the queen's promiscuity drags him into the void.

Having imprisoned Hermione, Leontes sends to the oracle of Apollo to confirm her guilt. In prison her child is born, a girl whom the king instantly brands a bastard, ordering the baby princess to be taken to "some remote and desert place, quite out of our dominions," and abandoned to the crows. Hermione's maid of honor, Paulina, intercedes for her, removing the child from prison by stealth and presenting it to the king, only to have Leontes furiously reject it with the words, "This brat is none of mine; / It is the issue of Polixenes." There are echoes here of Oxford's rejection of his newborn daughter, Elizabeth, when he returned from Italy in 1576, and the subsequent intercession of Katherine, Duchess of Suffolk, which proved no more effective than Paulina's mediation.

After the preliminary statements at her trial, Hermione herself cries out, "I do refer me to the Oracle: Apollo be my judge!" Hermione's standing for Shakespeare gives this statement deep significance, for the dramatist is announcing to the queen and court that he is subject not to their law but to the dictates of Apollo, god of music, poetry, and prophecy. The two envoys from the Oracle duly enter, and an officer reads out Apollo's judgment vindicating Hermione, confirming her daughter to be "truly begotten," and predicting that "the king shall live without an heir, if that which is lost be not found."

No sooner has Leontes dismissed the divine word as false than a servant brings news that his son, Mamillius, is dead, leaving him with no heir. Hermione faints and is taken for dead, but Paulina, who knows better, offers her home as sanctuary. So begins a period of seclusion for Hermione lasting sixteen years. This death in life was also suffered by Shakespeare, who was forced to hide behind pseudonyms and employ a front man. Thus it can be said of him, as of Hermione, that he was struck dead by the judgment of Apollo; i.e., his commitment to the poetic life imposed a sort of death sentence, whereby he could compose only anonymously—as if dead.

The words of the Oracle in *The Winter's Tale* apply with pitiful urgency to Elizabeth's heirless reign, especially its latter half. Elizabeth, like Leontes, was consumed with the rage of all she had denied in life. England, like Sicilia in the play, became a sterile wasteland, with Elizabeth as the wounded Grail king. There may well be a pun on "Sicilia" in the name given to England by Continental observers in the 1590s, *regnum Cecilianum* (i.e., the increasingly bureaucratic kingdom of the Cecils—pronounced "Sicils"—William and Robert). The energy Elizabeth expended protecting her secrets and repressing her natural instincts created an atmosphere of paranoia and claustrophobia at court, and for the first half of *The Winter's Tale* we feel trapped, like helpless subjects, in the delusional mind of Leontes.

Once again Shakespeare burrows deep into the Tudor psyche. When Leontes says to Hermione, "Your actions are my dreams," we can hear Elizabeth conceding to Shakespeare that his acts (plays) resonate in the deepest layers of her unconscious. Through Leontes we sense the violent passions that shook Elizabeth's father, Henry VIII, not least in his brutal condemnation of an innocent wife (and Hermione's "trial" mirrors the impeachment of Anne Boleyn). Elizabeth's fury was no less violent than that of Leontes, as when a maid of honor became pregnant or was secretly married. She clapped the poor girl in the Tower, not out of jealousy at her own inability to marry or have children (as some historians suggest), but from intense guilt at being reminded of her own transgressions.

Like Elizabeth, Leontes lives in a fantasy world, where his every wish and prejudice can be enforced by will. He succeeds in imposing his reality on others until the power of art, symbolized by the Oracle of Apollo, breaks through his illusion. So it was with Elizabeth's delusion; the more her actions exposed the myth of the Virgin Queen for what it was, the more furiously and arbitrarily she sought to impose its "truth." Yet in rejecting true love for the sake of a vacuous fantasy, she was doomed to live under the Oracle of Apollo. In other words, in denying the truth of Shakespeare's art, Elizabeth was condemned to live through it, becoming an involuntary actor in its drama.

Hermione's daughter by Leontes is given the name Perdita, meaning "lost one" or "things lost," and is left on the coast of Bohemia, the kingdom ruled by Polixenes. Antigonus, given the unenviable task of abandoning the baby, leaves her with a casket containing gold, letters, and a mantle and jewel belonging to her mother the queen, marks of royalty by which she can be identified in the future. She represents not only Shakespeare's lost child by Queen Elizabeth, but his *brainchild,* the plays. Interestingly, she is "cast forth to crows," birds sacred to Apollo. Alienated from her royal inheritance, Perdita is brought up in obscurity by a shepherd and his son (described as a "clown"). Bohemia, in contrast to Sicilia, is a land of shepherds, fertility, and seasonal joy: a realm of art, far from the bureaucracy and realpolitik of Leontes's court.

Elizabeth, of course, like Perdita, had been deprived of her mother by the brutality of her father, stripped of her legitimacy and royal status, and banished from court, living for many years in rustic obscurity (Cheshunt, Hatfield, Woodstock). Through *The Winter's Tale* Oxford-Shakespeare is reminding the queen that she was once an outcast and pleading with her not to reject their royal son, Southampton, in the same manner.

★ ★ ★

In describing the shepherd and his son, Shakespeare has a lot of fun lampooning William Shakspere and his father, John, and with them the whole Stratfordian tradition. With the very first words of the shepherd, he mocks the idea of what we call today "the lost years" of William Shakspere (the pre-London years), which, because we have no record of his education or doings, are filled for the most part with legends of his poaching exploits. In particular, he is supposed to have broken into Sir Thomas Lucy's deer park, later aggravating the offense by writing a ballad upon the aggrieved squire. He also got Anne Hathaway pregnant and ended up marrying her. "I would there were no age between ten and three-and-twenty," exclaims the shepherd, "or that youth would sleep out the rest; for there is nothing in the between but getting wenches with child, wronging the ancientry, stealing, fighting—" Like the Shakspere, father and son deal in wool. Their sudden, inexplicable wealth and the extraordinary beauty and virtue of their child become the subject of incredulous gossip. Talking of his son, Prince Florizel, Polixenes remarks:

> I have this intelligence, that he is seldom from the house of a most homely shepherd; a man, they say, that from very nothing, and beyond the imagination of his neighbours, is grown into an unspeakable estate.

To which Camillo adds:

> I have heard, sir, of such a man, who hath a daughter of most rare note: the report of her is extended more than can be thought to begin from such a cottage.
>
> (IV.ii.38–45)

Shakespeareans have been wondering all along how works which evince such a profound knowledge of the court and the life of royalty could have originated from a dealer in wool and other bagged commodities who, having grown up illiterate and in poverty, suddenly came into a great fortune around 1597. Perdita is obviously of royal parentage; it shines through in her beauty, nobility of spirit, and graceful manner of expression. As a gentleman of the court observes when her true birth is discovered, "the majesty of the creature in resemblance of the mother, the affection of nobleness which nature shows above her breeding, and many other evidences proclaim her, with all certainty, to be the king's daughter."

In Act V, scene ii, Shakespeare mocks the pretensions to gentility of the shepherd and his son in a hilarious dialogue between the two newly rewarded yokels and the rogue Autolycus, during which they refer to themselves almost every other line as "gentlemen born." One is reminded of the Stratford man's repeated applications for a coat of arms, which resulted in his being able to style himself "William Shakspere, gentleman," as well as Jonson's swipe at him in *Every Man Out of His Humour* in the character of Sogliardo, a simple country fellow who buys himself a coat of arms with the crest of a boar without a head, rampant. The jester, Carlo Buffone, takes this crest as a fitting description of Sogliardo himself, whom he characterizes as "a swine without a head, without brain, wit, anything indeed, ramping to gentility."

Perdita, raised among shepherds and clowns in the wilds of Bohemia, is Shakespeare's poetry having to make its way in the crude, rough-and-ready world of the theater, where concerns of day-to-day performance take precedence over the lofty designs of the poet. To the outside observer, in this case Polixenes, it is clear that this is not the girl's natural milieu:

> This is the prettiest low-born lass that ever
> Ran on the green-sward: nothing she does or seems
> But smacks of something greater than herself,
> Too noble for this place.
>
> (IV.iv.156–159)

She might have remained in rustic obscurity forever, had not her natural royalty of spirit attracted to itself the selfsame quality in Florizel, Prince of Bohemia, who encounters her when his hawk—another bird sacred to Apollo—flies across the shepherd's land. Like Perdita, Florizel assumes the mantle of the lost heir, playing truant from his father's court. Forced by his enraged parent to make a choice, he announces that he would rather be "heir to [his] affection" than to the throne of Bohemia. At the sheepshearing festival in Act IV, he dresses himself in humble clothes, thus conforming to the archetype of hidden royalty embodied by Perdita. She, on the other hand, is tricked up as the goddess Flora. As she remarks to Florizel:

> Your high self,
> The gracious mark o' th' land, you have obscur'd
> With a swain's wearing, and me, poor lowly maid,
> Most goddess-like prank'd up.
>
> (IV.iv.7–10)

In truth, the two are interchangeable. Even the names Flora and Florizel are virtually identical: Florizel means "little flower," as in the "little western flower" of *A Midsummer Night's Dream.* Together they represent Shakespeare's corpus, suffused as it is with his royalty of nature. Florizel, like Ferdinand in *The Tempest,* is the Fair Youth, and Perdita his Miranda. When Perdita imagines Florizel's father, the King, happening upon his son in such a lowly condition, she blushes for shame: "O the Fates! / How would he look, to see his work, so noble, / Vilely bound up?" (It is an apt description of Shakespeare's plays fronted by the Stratfordian.) Polixenes himself, on piercing his son's disguise, shows himself in agreement with Perdita's sentiment: "Thou art too base / To be acknowledg'd," he thunders. "Thou a sceptre's heir, / That thus affects a sheep-hook!" But Florizel is unabashed by his transformation, and in his justification we can hear Shakespeare's reason for hiding his own royalty:

> The gods themselves,
> Humbling their deities to love, have taken
> The shapes of beasts upon them: Jupiter
> Became a bull, and bellow'd; the green Neptune
> A ram, and bleated; and the fire-rob'd god,
> Golden Apollo, a poor humble swain,
> As I seem now. Their transformations
> Were never for a piece of beauty rarer.
>
> (IV.iv.25–32)

It is to preserve this rarest piece of beauty—his works— that the true author has obscured himself.

At the sheepshearing festival, Perdita distributes flowers to the shepherds and other guests. If the flowers, as so often in Elizabethan literature, symbolize poetry, then Shakespeare is indicating that it is he who gives to other writers, not the other way around, as the Stratford theory requires. Handing them around, Perdita calls upon the goddess Proserpina for the flowers she dropped from the infernal chariot when Pluto abducted her. It is a deeply significant reference, which resonates with the central theme of the play: the death and resurrection of the author and his works. Perdita, like Proserpina, has been snatched from her mother and taken to the wilderness (the underworld). *The Winter's Tale* is the story of her restoration, and that of the kingdom. Like Proserpina, she finds love and marriage in the underworld, and eventually is able to return to her grieving parents. On a metaphorical level this is Shakespeare's wish for himself and his works: that through our understanding he will be recognized for who he was and his plays revealed in their true colors.

The myth of Pluto and Proserpina is the psychic substance out of which the twin fates of Elizabeth and Shakespeare were woven. Therefore, each can be closely identified with Perdita. The outcast Elizabeth was violated by her "uncle," Seymour (Pluto was Proserpina's uncle), and Shakespeare, it seems, was the fruit of that trespass. With his birth the cycle began again: abandonment, loss of status, obscurity, the longing for redemption. Proserpina's marriage to Pluto, king of the underworld, can symbolize the marriage of Elizabeth to the buried king, Shakespeare. The myth also attaches itself to Hermione, who "dies" to be reborn at the end of the play.

Before proceeding to the final scene, we must quickly open the door to that picturesque rogue Autolycus, a threshold figure like Bottom or Jaques, who enchants and repels in equal measure, acting as a bridge between the worlds of courtier and artisan. In mythology Autolycus was the son of the god Hermes, which links him with Hermione and literature, and therefore with Shakespeare. Peddler and thief, he sings his way through the countryside with a stock of fantastical ballads, and fabrics of every color and description. (As with Bottom the weaver, cloth is used as a metaphor for story.) He is no ordinary peddler, having been one of the prince's followers, who wore costly velvet before being "whipped out of the court," not for his vices but—as he says—for one of his virtues. This was the typical punishment for the court jester who had gone too far, so no doubt the virtue that caused Autolycus's sudden departure from the upper echelons of society was telling the truth.

Eventually, toward the end of the play, he exchanges garments with Prince Florizel, a playful image for the restoration of Shakespeare's lost status. Ultimately, Autolycus is a self-deprecating portrait of the author, an aristocratic poet of the highest order who, having dirtied his hands in the commercial world of the public theaters, saw himself in his darker hours as a jobbing writer with all the tricks of the trade up his sleeve. Autolycus is Shakespeare's acknowledgment that he has in part resigned himself to the rather crude persona he has had to assume in order to survive. It is almost as if Shakespeare merged himself with his new alter ego, Mr. Shakspere of Stratford, and found the experience strangely liberating, not unlike Prince Hal hamming it up at the Boar's Head.

Defying his father's will, Florizel flees with Perdita to Sicilia, where they present themselves at the court of Leontes. Polixenes follows, as do Perdita's surrogate father and brother (the shepherd and clown), together with Autolycus, thus setting the stage for the final revelations and reunions. In the penultimate scene, these disclosures are reported through the conversation of certain gentlemen of the court; we do not witness them directly. Those relating the events speak of them in wondrous terms, as if they have witnessed a miracle; and the participants themselves, we learn, were speechless with amazement. The Oracle has been fulfilled: Leontes has found his lost heir, and the kingdom is restored. The proof of Perdita's identity, the mantle of Queen Hermione, is produced by the shepherd and his son, who, fearing the consequences of maintaining the fiction that Perdita is theirs, have come clean and thrown themselves on the mercy of the king. Just as it becomes clear to the court that Perdita, far from being a shepherd's daughter, is the child of royalty, so it dawns on us that Shakespeare's plays, far from being created by a simple Stratford farmer, were of royal origin. Other gentlemen at court compare the events to "an old tale" of doubtful veracity, which is Shakespeare's way of suggesting that his plays will be dismissed as fiction because the events they potray, though real, appear fantastic. And so it has proved.

This reported wonder puts us in the right frame of mind to witness the final scene of revelation, in which Paulina leads the assembled company, chief among them Perdita, Florizel, and the two kings, to a chapel in her house to show them a statue of Hermione she has had made, fashioned by "that rare Italian master, Julio Romano." The scene is a sort of play within the play, artfully directed by Paulina, who has given refuge to the "dead" Hermione for sixteen years. Once the company is gathered, Paulina pulls back a curtain to reveal the queen, standing on a raised platform. Everyone takes her to be a statue of the rarest artistry. In its verisimilitude the piece appears to outdo nature, which in Shakespeare's book is the highest praise for a work of art. "The fixure of her eye has motion in't, / As we are mock'd with art," cries Leontes, whose conscience has been struck by the figure before him:

> I am asham'd: does not the stone rebuke me
> For being more stone than it? O royal piece!
> There's magic in thy majesty, which has
> My evils conjur'd to remembrance.
>
> (V.iii.37–40)

Can one think of a better way to praise Shakespeare than by exclaiming, "There's magic in thy majesty"? And was he not always trying to get Elizabeth to call her evils to mind, and so become a better monarch? Perdita, Hermione's daughter, kneels before the "statue," addressing it as "Dear queen, that ended when I but began," which beyond its literal meaning signifies that Shakespeare "died" to society—or was forced to diguise himself—when his plays were first made public.

When it becomes clear that Leontes is desperate to touch the "statue," Paulina unleashes the deus ex machina of her little production and calls upon the royal company to awaken their faith. Then, as music sounds, she beckons to Hermione with the words, "'Tis time; descend; be stone no more; approach; / Strike all that look upon with marvel. Come!" And Hermione descends. It is a deeply moving moment, not only in the play's immediate context of the redemption of Leontes and the reunion of Hermione and her lost daughter, but in the wider context of Shakespeare's hope that one day he will live again and be reunited with the works he fathered. Just as Hermione is canonized by her saintly forbearance, so Shakespeare—perceived more as a body of work than a human being—has been turned into his canon.[149] Hermione's descent is also Shakespeare's invitation to Queen Elizabeth to discard the myth of virginity that has turned her to stone, and so acknowledge her child.

Today, what we have is a Stratford icon, a two-dimensional figure with no soul and no plausible life. Nevertheless, as Oxford is slowly released from the skeleton cupboard of history, the icon is beginning to crack and take on a more human form. That said, the truth is so wondrous and so powerful that even today, we are disinclined to believe it. As Paulina says of Hermione,

> That she is living,
> Were it but told you, should be hooted at
> Like an old tale.
>
> (V.iii.115–117)

The metamorphosis of art into life, signified by the coming to life of the statue, not only looks forward to the day when knowledge of the true author will bring the works fully to life, but also marks out an essential quality of the plays themselves: the fact that *they are the life,* not only of the dramatist, but of the times in which he lived. Their fabulousness is their reality. The final scene of *The Winter's Tale* takes place in a chapel, and when Paulina draws the curtain to reveal Hermione, it is as if the veil of the temple has been rent and we are finally free to make our own relationship with Shakespeare, without the mediation of the academic establishment. We can reach out and touch him for ourselves.

The Winter's Tale, then, is an allegory of mistaken authorship and its consequences, with parentage used as a metaphor for authorship. The revelation of Perdita's true parentage, and with it her royal status, and her reunion with her lost mother (or creator) is Shakespeare's abiding dream of his own restoration, both as author and as royal prince. For this he must trust to time with the unshakable faith that Hermione places in the eventual triumph of truth. As he wrote in *The Rape of Lucrece*:

> Time's glory is to calm contending kings,
> To unmask falsehood and bring truth to light.
>
> (lines 939–940)

~ 12 ~

Family of the Rose

From fairest creatures we desire increase
That thereby beauty's *Rose* might never die.
(Sonnet 1, lines 1–2)

A Tainted Wether of the Flock

The writers Oxford gathered about him at Fisher's Folly were like a quasi-feudal retinue, and are reflected in Falstaff's bibulous crew of Bardolph, Nym, and Pistol.[150] Having lost the extensive estates that would have allowed him to live like his fellow peers of the old nobility, Oxford bound his "band of brothers" by the force of his artistic vision. Quite apart from the gifts of lands and money he made to many of his followers, even to the detriment of his own family, Oxford, by dint of his openhearted generosity and the magnanimity of his genius, won the devotion of those who served his cause. Thomas Churchyard referred to Oxford quite typically as "a noble man of such worth, as I will employ all I have to honour his worthiness." John Farmer, dedicating his *Plainsong* (1591) to Oxford, wrote, "Not only myself am vowed to your commandment, but all that is in me is dedicated to your Lordship's service." Nashe was less formal, declaring, "I love and admire thy pleasant witty humour, which no care or cross can make unconversable."

The warmth of the dedications, nearly all with tributes to his prodigious talent, is a good index of the feelings Oxford inspired in those who shared his objectives. There was a real sense of camaraderie among his followers, fostered by their shared mission and the very real dangers they worked under. As Anthony Munday wrote to Oxford at the end of *The Mirror of Mutability* (1579):

> My noble master, farewell. May your desires which are dear to us all prevail. Earnestly do I pray for your welfare and success in the struggle. To the guardianship of Christ I commit you and yours, till the day when as conquerors we may peacefully resume our literary discussions.

It is certainly remarkable, and unique in the annals of the Elizabethan age, that someone so impoverished should continue to be honored with offerings by the artists of the time, whose first concern quite naturally had to be the shilling in their pockets. The convivial gatherings at the Mermaid Tavern and other "ordinaries"—inspiration and hilarity flowing in equal measure with Rhenish wine—were compensation enough, it seems, especially if the man at the head of the table could ensure publication of your works. Nashe wrote to Oxford in his dedication of *Strange News* (1592):

> By whatsoever thy visage holdeth most precious I beseech thee, by . . . the blue boar in the spittle, I conjure thee to draw out thy purse and give me nothing for the dedication of my pamphlet. Thou art a good fellow I know, and hadst rather spend jests than money. Let it be the task of thy best terms to safe-conduct this book through the enemies' country.

When one studies the other dedications of the time, to Leicester, Walsingham, Essex, and the queen herself, one is struck by the tortuous formality. Here, by contrast, Nashe and Oxford are on refreshingly debonair terms, which make for a humorous and heartfelt address.

The devotion Oxford excited in his men, and they in him, is best reflected in Henry V's stirring speech to his motley troops as they prepare to pit themselves against the full might of the French cavalry at Agincourt. Warfare, as we've seen, was often used as a metaphor for literature by this author:

> We few, we happy few, we band of brothers;
> For he to-day that sheds his blood with me

Shall be my brother; be he ne'er so vile
This day shall gentle his condition:
And gentlemen in England now a-bed
Shall think themselves accurs'd they were not here,
And hold their manhoods cheap whiles any speaks
That fought with us upon Saint Crispin's day.[151]

(IV.iii.60–67)

And yet to Elizabeth and her government, Fisher's Folly, that unorthodox college with its eccentric Dionysian king, could not have boded well, any more than the self-banished Lear and his riotous knights were a sight to cheer the eye of Goneril and her sister. He may have been a poor mad king, but by heaven he could speak to the point.

In Elizabeth's reign, feudalism was giving way to a mercantile, capitalistic world, which was quite alien to Oxford. His was the world of noblesse oblige, in which good name was the "immediate jewel" of a man's soul and money followed generosity of spirit, not the other way around. Oxford's chief substance, of which he gave unstintingly, was his literary genius, which blazed a trail for his fellow writers. He encouraged them, read and criticized their works, offered suggestions, and apparently even rewrote passages from works submitted to him. As Nashe says to Oxford ("his *very* friend, Master Apis Lapis") in his dedication of *Strange News* (1592):

Yea, you are such an infinite Maecenas to learned men, that there is not that morsel of meat they can carve you, but you will eat for their sakes, and accept very thankfully. . . . *Verily, verily,* all poor scholars acknowledge you as their patron, providitore and supporter, for there cannot a threadbare cloak sooner peep forth but you straight press it to be an outbrother of your bounty.

He also poured out his worldly substance in a flow of bounty which was truly kingly, and which constituted a sort of spiritual largess. Even today, it falls to the Prince of Wales to embody the profound and spontaneous spirit of liberality that the monarch, hamstrung by political concerns, cannot publicly evince. Generosity on the scale of Oxford's did not come without a price, however. By 1591 he was £11,000 in debt (£1 million in today's money), £4,445 of it in accumulated interest,[152] and if one counts the punitive bonds he was forced to sign against the debt, the figure rises to £23,000. His debt was to the crown, and in Oxford's case that meant the court of wards, of which his father-in-law was master, so one can be sure that the great bulk of the interest on the debt found its way into Burghley's purse. Oxford's fall was dramatic. According to Daphne Pearson "[his] personal annual income fell from some estimated £3,500 in 1562 to between £20 and £70 on his death in 1604."[153] Hopeless as ever with money, Oxford tried to commute his annuity of £1,000 to a onetime payment of £5,000. Even such a princely stipend did not cover the costs of mounting lavish productions at court, at Blackfriars, and elsewhere. In a letter of February 1601 to Sir Robert Cecil, suing for the Presidency of Wales, Oxford suggested that the post might be granted him "in regard of my youth, time and fortune spent in her Court, adding thereto Her Majesty's favours and promises, which drew me on without any mistrust the more to presume in mine own expenses." But it was to no avail. Oxford was no longer a member of the inner circle. As his £1,000 stipend bore witness, he was little more than a hired entertainer.

It was not uncommon for members of the old nobility to put themselves in the hands of usurers; the difference in Oxford's case was that the chief usurer was his own father-in-law, who had been castigated as such in various antigovernment tracts. In *A Declaration of the True Causes* (1592), for instance, Burghley's greed is seen in the context of his overweening ambition:

> And he that (as is said before) was far inferior to be matched in rank with the nobility of the realm, hath in a few years so over-matched them all, and either by feigned crimes cut them off, or by one means or other so maimed them of their due honour and authority that he hath now made himself *Dictator perpetuus*.
>
> There is no subject in England of more opulence, none of more authority, nor none of more power, than himself: and there-fore none to withstand his intended match between the Lady Arbella Stuart [a claimant to the throne] and his grandchild [one of the sons of his elder son, Thomas Cecil]. Whereby England may happen to have a King Cecil the first, that is suddenly meta-morphosed from a groom of the wardrobe to the wearing of the best robe within the wardrobe.

But most infortunate is it, that he . . . is yet permitted to plunge the realm into what further calamities himself listeth, and to hazard the shedding of the best blood of the nobility and people, for the only establishing of his own house and posterity: to make the ruinated families of the one and the dead bodies of the other the steps to mount unto his intended height.[154]

Having drained Oxford dry through the control he exercised over his estates in the court of wards, Burghley proceeded to take his children from him and publicly humiliate him as a deadbeat father. On the death of his wife, Mildred, in April 1589, Burghley had a joint tomb erected for her and their daughter Anne, on which he brazenly published his own view of the plight of his surviving granddaughters—Oxford's daughters. His entry for Susan Vere, the youngest, in its flourish of naked self-justification, is typical of the man:

Lady Susan, born 26th May 1587, who was too young to recognize either her mother or her grandmother, but is beginning to recognize her most loving grandfather, who has the care of all these children, so that they may not be deprived either of a pious education or of a suitable upbringing.

No mention of her father, who has been erased from the record. According to the Shakespeare scholar Dorothy Ogburn, "'The great Lord Burghley's whole policy and practice are revealed in this memorial."[155]

Then in December 1591, as part of a deal that never materialized, Oxford surrendered the heart of his de Vere inheritance by alienating Hedingham Castle to Burghley in trust for his three daughters, Elizabeth, Bridget, and Susan. It was an abdication with rich consequences for literature, if *King Lear* is anything to judge by. The Fool's punning taunt to Lear on the loss of his palaces bears witness to Oxford's bitter self-reproach over the forfeit of Hedingham (emphasis mine):

He that has a house to put's *head in has* a good head-piece.

(III.ii.25–26)

When Oxford had originally proposed the move, it was, he imagined, in return for the demesne of Denbigh in North Wales, which might have proved a congenial retreat for the aging writer, now forty-three years old. His main concern, however, was for the provision of his family. As he wrote to Burghley:

> So shall my children be provided for, myself at length settled in quiet, and I hope your lordship, remaining no cause for you to think me an evil father, nor any doubt in me, but that I may enjoy that friendship from your lordship that so near a match, and not fruitless, may lawfully expect. Good my lord, think of this, and let me have both your furtherance and counsel in this cause. For to tell troth I am weary of an unsettled life, which is the very pestilence that happens unto courtiers, that propound to themselves no end of their time, therein bestowed.

Oxford was in no doubt that Burghley considered him a bad father; and his broken family was a source of anxiety and regret. It is true he had made many sacrifices, some of them reckless, in his pursuit of the artistic life, but the financial and emotional pressure placed upon him by his father-in-law cut deep. *The Merchant of Venice* casts light on our understanding of their fateful relationship. Burghley had Oxford on the hip, as Shylock has Antonio, and was ruthless in pursuing his pound of flesh. Everything, to his mind, was subject to the market; hence his chilling advice to his son Robert on choosing a wife: "Let her not be poor, how generous soever. For a man can buy nothing in the market with gentility." Antonio's profound sadness of spirit, which comes from beyond the play, has its origin in Oxford's exile from his name and family. Like Hamlet enjoining Horatio, Antonio is concerned that his young friend should set the record straight:

> I am a tainted wether of the flock,
> Meetest for death . . .
> You cannot better be employ'd Bassanio,
> Than to live still and write mine epitaph.
>   (IV.i.114–115, 117–118)

Here is a man whose only hope for justice is posthumous, and who feels emasculated (a "wether" being a castrated ram) by the rigors of a state in which "malice bears down truth." The pound of Antonio's flesh sought by Shylock has many meanings, including his manhood, but when one considers that the forfeit is further defined by Shylock as to be cut "nearest the merchant's heart," then the true meaning of this violation impresses itself on our consciousness. For in the case of the hidden author, what could be nearer the heart than his own works? And what is that body which Burghley-Shylock intends to mutilate, but the author's literary corpus, written on parchment, which in those days was made from the skins of sheep, cows, or goats? ("A pound of man's flesh taken from a man," cries Shylock in impish humor, "is not so estimable, profitable neither, / As flesh of muttons, beefs, or goats.") Bassanio makes the connection between body and parchment overt when, on receiving Antonio's letter declaring the forfeiture of his bond, he says to Portia:

> Here is a letter lady,
> The paper as the body of my friend,
> And every word in it a gaping wound
> Issuing life-blood.
>   (III.ii.262–265)

One is reminded of the passage in the New Testament in which St. Paul tells the Corinthians that *they are* his epistle, "written not with ink, but with the Spirit of the living God; not in tables of stone, but in fleshy tables of the heart."[156] In Shakespeare's Sonnets, too, there are many passages in which the Fair Youth is transformed by the poet into a book, his body drained of blood, that he might survive, "confounding Age's cruel knife" ("Age" is capitalized in Sonnet 63 to represent the septuagenarian Burghley).

Burghley may have taken Oxford's flesh in the sense of his family, and even his works—by insisting on anonymity—but he could not take that which he desired above all: the royal blood to which Oxford's drama so eloquently speaks. That Oxford is Antonio is put beyond doubt by Bassanio's praise of his friend as "one in whom / The ancient Roman honour more appears / Than any that draws breath in Italy," a phrase echoed in Chapman's eulogy of Oxford in *The Revenge of Bussy D'Ambois:* "he had a face / Like one of the most ancient honour'd Romans / From whence his noblest family was deriv'd."

At several points Burghley touches the life of Shylock, a character who shares many traits with Polonius, not least his portentously repetitious speech. Quite apart from his obsession with money and his daughter and his lexical idiosyncrasies, there are his puritanical dislike of plays and masques; his usury; his plain black dress, which included skullcap and gabardine (a garment, incidentally, not worn by the Jews of Venice); and his sanctimoniousness, which provokes Antonio to declare, "The devil can cite Scripture for his purpose." Shylock swears by "Jacob's staff"; Burghley was never seen without the lord treasurer's long white staff of office. Moreover, Shylock's hero is clearly Jacob, who stole his brother's birthright and usurped his blessing, and Burghley can be said to have stolen Oxford's birthright as well as the blessing due from his royal parent. Shakespeare, then, is using the Jewishness of Shylock to convey the Puritanism of Burghley, as was often done by those who wanted to take a swipe at the more extreme manifestations of Protestantism. For instance, in one Catholic tract Burghley is accused of fortifying what is described as "this new erected synagogue," meaning the Protestant church.

In the end, Antonio is reprieved through the good offices of Portia ("this mortal breathing saint," i.e., Queen Elizabeth), but there is still a price to pay, and his penultimate utterance in the play is "I am dumb!"

THE BROKEN FAMILY

There is a strong connection between Oxford's ruined finances and his defective family life. It is not simply that his money problems put pressure on his relationship with his wife and children, and with his wife's father and brother; there was something deeper at work, which can be traced back to his childhood, and birth. Because he had no blood father and family to give him a sense of responsibility or allegiance to those closest to him, nor a mother who could provide even the most basic sense of love and security—indeed, his mother shamelessly violated those things—family itself became a sort of taboo, a feeling reinforced by his guardian's persistent exploitation of him. Oxford tended to look beyond his immediate circle for emotional sustenance, finding his earliest consolation in books, then reaching out to those who could assist him in bringing his creative dreams to life: the actors and artists who became his friends and protégés and who were free from the taint of family bonds. For him, theater really was the proverbial home for orphans. Historians have condemned Oxford for what they describe as his cold and ruthless treatment of his family without taking the time to understand that the conventional matrix of parent–child and husband–wife relationships might have been an emotional minefield for him. Let us not forget that Henry Howard, who for all his enmity knew Oxford well, described him as a "wandering and wasteful child . . . that had no playfellows but kings and queens to sport withal."

The lost, idealized father—a figure we see at work in the psyche of Hamlet, Bertram, Orlando, and Richard II—and the omnipotent mother, an equally forceful presence in Shakespeare, constitute what can loosely be called a mother complex. This was a particularly potent distillation in Oxford's case, if, as the evidence suggests, his mother was the most powerful woman in the land, his blood father executed before he was born, and his surrogate father quite possibly murdered in order to keep his royal parentage a secret. The mother complex, in its devouring, incestuous form, dissolves the usual bonds of family, creating a severely dysfunctional detachment in the subject, which might be described as narcissistic. (An extreme example would be Oedipus, who killed his father and married his mother.) The boundaries between self and other are often fragile in such cases, and bestow a wonderfully porous, art-engendering sensibility, yet leave the subject vulnerable to emotional exploitation. The effect of such dynamics can be equally disastrous in the financial realm, with the subject having little or no concept of what is his and what belongs to others. This can lead to callous theft on the one hand and inordinate generosity or extravagance on the other.

An example of reckless bounty is Antonio's "sacrifice" for his dear friend Bassanio. Their friendship, one of the most affecting in all of Shakespeare, has the feel of a father-son relationship (in Shakespeare's source, Fiorentino's *Il Pecarone,* the relationship is godfather to godson), and it may be that their close friendship is a mask for a blood bond that they are not at liberty to profess. Yet there is clearly something ulterior about this bond, something both magical and tragic that is intrinsic to Antonio's sacrifice. Antonio's love for Bassanio might almost be described as narcissistic, for in spite of—or perhaps because of—his sacrifice, there seems to be more self-love than love-of-other in his heart, as if the youth is a mirror in which he sees himself reflected with uncommon clarity. There is certainly an exorbitance to his generosity that connotes a barely sustainable sense of separation between himself and his young friend. Antonio assures Bassanio that his purse, his person, and his "extremest means" lie all unlocked to his occasions, and that his credit in Venice "shall be rack'd even to the uttermost" in order to furnish the necessary funds for his courtship of Portia! For Bassanio to have doubted him for even one moment is perceived as a crime:

> And out of doubt you do me now more wrong
> In making question of my uttermost
> Than if you had made waste of all I have.
>
> (I.i.155–157)

This is no ordinary relationship, even if it is one of father and hidden son, a supposition that is supported by young Launcelet Gobbo's extraodinary assertion, "Truth will come to light, murder cannot be hid long, *a man's son may,* but in the end truth will out." (For why has Shakespeare introduced the Gobbos into the play except as a comic mirror of the Antonio-Bassanio relationship?) The sacrifice Antonio is prepared to make could only be for the very highest aim. Proponents of the Earl of Oxford have long recognized that Bassanio—base son (of) E.O.—is in fact the Fair Youth of the Sonnets, Oxford's son by Queen Elizabeth, the 3rd Earl of Southampton. As Salanio says of Antonio's affection for Bassanio ("I think he only loves the world for him"), so Shakespeare says to the Fair Youth,

> For nothing this wide universe I call
> Save thou, my Rose; in it thou art my all.
>
> (Sonnet 109, lines 13–14)

This unique relationship becomes Oxford-Shakespeare's retreat from the pressures and anxieties of family life. As for Bassanio's courtship of Portia, it seems to be a metaphor for Southampton's suing for the throne. In this context, Antonio's funding of his friend's marital campaign, even down to pawning his life for him, reflects Oxford's literary crusade on behalf of his son's royal claim. His wealth, then, is the poetic talent that he employs in service to the true heir.

Certainly, it is hard to deny that family life in Shakespeare is what we might now call a train wreck: broken, dysfunctional, divisive, alienating. This is true whether one is talking of husband–wife or parent–child relationships. In the entire canon, the word "family" occurs only seven times, three of them, ironically, in *Titus Andronicus*. The next word in the concordance is "famine," which seems sadly apposite as a term to qualify the poet's concept of family. Shakespeare's greatest lovers, Antony and Cleopatra, are adulterers; and the nearest he gets to a happy married couple are the psychopathic Macbeths, for Juliet's parents, the Capulets, have no real intimacy, and Othello ends up murdering Desdemona. Many of the most hopeful characters in the plays—Juliet herself being one good example, and Bertram another—are coerced into marriage. Many of these are political unions, such as Antony's shameful marriage to Caesar's sister Octavia. As the Shakespeare scholar Ann Jennalie Cook writes of the plays, "Marriage as a purely private affair simply does not exist."[157]

But even these broken unions are exceptional, because for the most part spouses simply aren't there. Lear, Gloucester, Shylock, Duncan, Prospero, Leonato, Bolingbroke, Polonius, Polixenes, and Egeon—to name ten—all have children, but no wife. And when both partners are present, the result is more often than not, in the words of Stephen Greenblatt, "mutual isolation." As the devoted Portia complains to her husband, Brutus, from whose inner life she finds herself excluded: "Dwell I but in the suburbs of your good pleasure?" Greenblatt, who is clearly puzzled by the poet's strange bias, declares with admirable reserve, "Shakespeare was curiously restrained in his depictions of what it is actually like to be married."[158]

He was also curiously restrained in his depictions of what it is actually like to be the son or daughter of parents or vice versa, i.e., to live within a family structure. One only has to think of Lear and his daughters, Gloucester and Edgar, Hamlet and his mother, Polonius and Ophelia, Henry IV and Prince Hal, Capulet and Juliet, Shylock and Jessica, the Countess and Bertram, Constance and her young son Arthur, and Coriolanus and his mother Volumnia to realize just how unusual Shakespeare's experience of family was. The parents in each case abuse their power; they are suffocating figures who force their children into some form of rebellion or flight, and for whom ambition is an essential element of their love. Lady Macbeth, putting ambition above family feeling, offers to rip the baby from her breast and dash its brains out, so long as she can be queen. But where is the child she talks of? When women are parents, as in the case of Gertrude, Volumnia, Constance, and the Countess in *All's Well,* the fatherless son must arm himself against the power of the mother and find a way to be reborn from the depths of his own soul, just as Coriolanus seeks to forge himself a new name in the fires of his native Rome. As Janet Adelman so insightfully puts it, "Both plays [*Macbeth* and *Coriolanus*] construct the exaggerated masculinity of their heroes simultaneously as an attempt to separate from the mother and as the playing out of her bloodthirsty will; both enact the paradox through which the son is never more the mother's creature than when he attempts to escape her."[159]

When fathers are parents, on the other hand, they either long for their children's death (Lear, Henry IV, Leontes, Shylock), exploit them (Polonius, Capulet, Prospero), or are mere ghosts, like Pericles or the Ghost in *Hamlet.* Fathers have little authority in Shakespeare, and hardly ever confer legitimacy. Rather, the hero seeks a surrogate father: Hamlet in Yorick, Hal in Falstaff, Arthur in Hubert. A jester, an anarchist, and a jailer: these are Shakespeare's fathers. In this great gap of male authority stand the witches of *Macbeth,* unstitching the sanctity of kings. Duncan is murdered, his "gash'd stabs look[ing] like a breach in nature / For ruin's wasteful entrance," while Macduff, the avenging hero, is only worthy to be Shakespeare's redeemer because he is not born of woman.

The parent, either mother or father, will often live as an idealized vision in the mind of their offspring. Hamlet's father is an obvious example, but there are also Bertram's father in *All's Well,* Perdita's mother (Hermione) in *Winter's Tale* and Marina's mother (Thaisa) in *Pericles.* Daughters in Shakespeare often act as his escape route from the family by serving as symbols of his works—or brainchildren. As such, they are wholly under the dramatist's control, and can be used to purge the darker aspects of the mother. Sons, by contrast, are more often than not son-lovers or son-consorts, the most famous being Bertram, Hamlet, Troilus, Antony, Timon, Macbeth, and Coriolanus. (Even when the mother is not literally there, she is psychologically present through the spouse or some other dominant female presence, such as Fortune.) These figures necessarily short-circuit family life through their warped experience of the feminine.

Shakespeare's perception of courtship as an exhilarating and sometimes dangerous linguistic game, which is nevertheless doomed to disillusionment, and his disgusted rejection of marriage as something unnatural, stem no doubt from his forbidden relationship with Elizabeth. After all, hers was hardly a straight rudder to steer by. To her, both marriage and motherhood appeared taboo, except perhaps in the imaginatively incestuous sense of being both wife and mother to her people. Maybe she felt safe only in committing herself on this abstract, political level, true intimacy being too painful.

THE NAME OF THE ROSE

Shakespeare's idealism in love is celebrated the world over, yet that love, far from being a means to married bliss or intimate friendship, is rather an escape from the family as most mortals understand and experience it. It has the same mystical, self-centered quality apparent in Elizabeth's professions of love for her people; and if a family is involved, then it is removed from mundane concerns, like a heraldic carving high on a castle wall. The sonnets are the purest expression of this, for even when the poet is urging the Fair Youth to marry and beget an heir, it is done in the name of a spiritual-dynastic end, as his opening words aver:

> From fairest creatures we desire increase,
> That thereby beauty's Rose might never die.
>> (Sonnet 1)

It is a love, moreover, that can be perfected only in death, its consequences in life being almost wholly tragic. Its goal, though highly aesthetic, is yet strongly political. Shakespeare's idealistic relationship to the mysterious Fair Youth is a key to the meaning of his works. So it was with the Earl of Oxford. The burdens and crosses, often self-inflicted, that he bore in his family life were redeemed by his relationship with his royal son, Henry Wriothesley, generally agreed by scholars to have been Shakespeare's Fair Youth. The unorthodox relationship between Oxford and his concealed son and sovereign lord, Southampton, best account for the deeply idiosyncratic tenor of the Sonnets.

The records, carefully weeded by Burghley, do not reveal what kind of intimacy existed between Oxford and Southampton while the latter was under his guardianship at Cecil House between 1582 and his coming-of-age in 1594. Not that he would have spent all his time at Burghley's establishment; far from it, and then only until the age of eighteen. The young earl would also have whiled away many an hour attending the queen at court. Southampton had pronounced literary and dramatic tastes, and in his twenties would become addicted to theater, spending his afternoons at the playhouse. It is not unreasonable to assume that if, like Oberon, Oxford managed to persuade the Fairy Queen to allow him to have the changeling child as his "henchman" in Fairyland (the theater world), then he would have introduced his boy to the stage—most likely at Blackfriars—and written parts for him, such as Puck, Falstaff's page, Moth, Ariel, and Mamillius. The boy would also have played female roles, such as Viola in *Twelfth Night*. In his *Portrait of Mr. W.H.*, Oscar Wilde surmises that the Fair Youth was a boy actor by the name of Willie Hughes, for whom Shakespeare created roles such as Viola, Imogen, Juliet, Rosalind (herself called "fair youth"), and Portia. Much of the imagery of the Sonnets gives credence to such a theory. Here is the opening of Sonnet 38:

> How can my Muse want subject to invent,
> While thou dost breathe, that pour'st into my verse
> Thine own sweet argument, too excellent
> For every vulgar paper to rehearse?
>
> (lines 1–4)

Unorthodox scholars have suggested that Southampton used the name Will or Will Shakespeare when acting, and that this is borne out by the virtual unity of identity between him and the poet of the Sonnets. "My friend and I are one," writes Shakespeare in Sonnet 42, and in 62 he addresses the friend directly with the words, "'Tis thee, myself, that for myself I praise." In Sonnet 62 he even indicts himself of self-love for loving the youth with such fervor, a trope that emphasizes the strong narcissism of his affection. In his comedy *Cynthia's Revels or The Fountain of Self-Love,* Ben Jonson satirizes Oxford and Southampton as Amorphus and Asotus, "a pair of butterflies," with Amorphus-Oxford fastidiously coaching his young charge in the actor's art. Rehearsing what sounds like *Romeo and Juliet,* he instructs the young lover in how to approach his sweetheart:

> First, you present yourself, thus: and spying her, you fall off, and walk some two turns; in which time, it is to be supposed, your passion hath sufficiently whited your face, then stifling a sigh or two, and closing your lips, with a trembling boldness, and bold terror, you advance yourself forward.
>
> (III.iii.6–11)

In 1594 *Willobie His Avisa,* a long cryptic poem of well over 3,000 lines, was published and then quickly suppressed. Treating allegorically of the queen's love life (she being the chaste Avisa), it opened up the forbidden question of the succession. Avisa, who bears Elizabeth's motto "Always the Same" and is married to her country, has five suitors—five claimants to her throne, so to speak—the fifth going by the name "Henrico Willobego, Italo-Hispalensis." This H.W. is described as a "new actor"; his friend and mentor W.S. is termed "the old player." Apart from the obvious pun on actor-pretender, as in pretender to the throne, there is clearly a personal reference here to Southampton's and Oxford's love of theater. The section on Henrico Willobego opens with the following:

> H.W. being suddenly infected with the contagion of a fantastical fit, at the first sight of *A[visa],* pineth a while in secret grief, at length not able any longer to endure the burning heat of so fervent a humour, bewrayeth the secrecy of his disease unto his familiar friend W.S. who not long before had tried the courtesy of the like passion, and was now newly recovered of the like infection.

Owing to his keen imagination and a strong bohemian streak, the young Southampton was often described as "fantastical," his early life following the pattern of Oxford's to an uncanny degree. He was a royal ward under the care of Cecil; went to Cecil's old Cambridge college, St. John's, where the queen attended his graduation; and from there went to Gray's Inn. He too made a profound impression on the queen when he first appeared at court, and efforts were made to marry him into the Cecil family. That 1590 ushered in such a harsh and desperate decade ensured that Essex and Southampton, the brightest stars in the firmament, were greeted with an almost messianic fervor.

At the start of the 1590s, Oxford realized that he himself had no chance of inheriting his mother's throne, disgraced as he was in the eyes of his peers. The only hope of keeping alive his dream of a new royalty—that of "beauty's rose"—was to plow his efforts into glorifying Southampton's claim. With this in mind, he took up the Sonnets, which tell the "golden story" of the youth's sovereignty, and at the same time revised his old plays for publication. As he wrote in Sonnet 76:

> O, know, sweet love, I always write of you,
> And you and love are still my argument;
> So all my best is dressing old words new,
> Spending again what is already spent:
>> For as the sun is daily new and old,
>> So is my love still telling what is told.
>
> (lines 9–14)

The sun (son) being daily new and old echoes the idea of the new actor and the old player in *Willobie His Avisa*. Similarly, the suit to the queen undertaken by H.W. is not a love suit but a plea (camouflaged by words of love) to be recognized as her heir. W.S.'s advice to him must be understood in the same terms:

> Well, say no more: I know thy grief,
> And face from whence these flames arise,
> It is not hard to find relief,
> If thou wilt follow good advice:
>> She is no Saint, She is no Nun,
>> I think in time she may be won.

Little wonder the book was suppressed! When W.S. talks of Avisa-Elizabeth being no saint, his meaning is political. That is, he is suggesting that Elizabeth has amply demonstrated that she is not truly wedded to her kingdom, and therefore she won't necessarily maintain forever the pretence that she is the Virgin Queen, a guise that prevents her from naming a successor of her blood. The verse from Proverbs that appears on the title page of *Avisa* was a bitter reflection upon Elizabeth's broken troth with England: "A virtuous woman is the crown of her husband, but she that maketh him ashamed, is as corruption in his bones."

At the bottom of the title page is a drawing of Actaeon surprising the goddess Diana, bathing naked. Actaeon has already sprouted his antlered head, which appears again at the top of the page, crowned with a crescent moon, while the rest of his body remains human, suggesting perhaps that this very book will take the queen unawares. H.W., having been rejected by Avisa, compares himself to the "wounded deer, whose tender sides are bathed in blood" (i.e., Actaeon savaged by his own hounds). Thus the illustration on the title page points to the supremacy of H.W.'s suit, or rather that of the duo, H.W. and W.S. The transformed Actaeon is also a good example of a symbol once applied to Oxford now reassigned to Southampton.

Much has been made of the sensation that the seventeen-year-old Southampton created when he first arrived at court, with his long hair, red-and-white complexion, and perfect manners. He was mildly effeminate, too, just enough to set off his manly graces, and his royalty of bearing was delightfully unaffected. Both men and women were drawn to him, and, as had happened with the young Oxford, it was whispered in certain circles that he was of royal blood. Rumors even leaked from the court; hence Nashe's audacity in dedicating his poem "The Choice of Valentines" to Southampton in these thinly veiled lines:

> Pardon, sweet flower of matchless poetry,
> And fairest bud the red rose ever bare . . .
> Ne blame my verse of loose unchastity
> For painting forth the things that hidden are.

In other words, Southampton is the fairest child that the "red rose" (Elizabeth) bore E. Ver (Oxford). He is also the child of "matchless poetry" (Shakespeare). It is obvious why Nashe is apologizing for broaching a taboo!

Southampton's charm seems to have been of a mercurial kind, and to begin with he had a reputation for flightiness and self-will. Bridget

Manners, sister of the Earl of Rutland, found him altogether too young and quixotic—inclined to get carried away. Stephanie Hopkins Hughes notes that Southampton's unusually long hair was "a trait symbolic of the Merovingian kings," said to be the royal descendants of Jesus and Mary Magdalene, and that he may have been perceived "by some of the more romantic aristocratic elements of court society" as a potential redeemer figure, come to sit upon the throne of his ancestor David.[160] "Describe Adonis," wrote Shakespeare to Southampton in Sonnet 53, "and the counterfeit / Is poorly imitated after you," again identifying the addressee with his own youthful self, the beloved of the mortal Venus. The difference now was that the queen was almost sixty years of age.

Southampton was not only beautiful and ingenious but also very wealthy and highly cultured (he was, for instance, fluent in Italian). Poets and scholars were soon dedicating their works to him in the most profuse terms, as if he were a kind of sovereign. Thomas Nashe, one of Oxford's literary satellites, dedicated *The Unfortunate Traveller,* his thinly veiled allegory of Oxford's Continental adventures, to Southampton, declaring, "A dear lover and cherisher you are, as well of the lovers of poets, as of poets themselves." Before long, he had become part of the Essex House circle of scholars, poets, and statesmen, heirs to the star-studded Leicester-Sidney coterie that had met under the same roof in the 1570s and early 1580s. Sir John Harington, Barnabe Barnes, Michael Drayton, Fulke Greville, Edward Dyer, George Chapman, Samuel Daniel, John Florio, Henry Cuffe, Jean Hotman, the Killigrews, Anthony and Francis Bacon, Henry Savile, the Earls of Rutland and Bedford, Henry Wotton, and William Temple were some of the luminaries who graced the halls of Essex House. Its leader, Robert Devereux, Earl of Essex, had inherited Sidney's sword and married his widow, Frances Walsingham. He had also captured the heart and allegiance of Southampton, six years his junior and his sworn companion in all things perilous. The two earls had first met when they were wards of the crown at Cecil House, and although Southampton lacked his friend's inexorable ambition, the pair were bound by common cause and mutual loyalty.

Oxford's surviving letters of the 1590s and beyond reveal very little about his relations with his daughters, and other records are silent on how they perceived their brilliant, high-strung, eccentric father, who was no doubt quite a disturbing presence in their lives. Elizabeth Vere, in particular, might have felt ambivalent about the father who for the first six years of her life had refused to acknowledge that she was his. There may have been tremendous anger, too, and this could have communicated itself to the younger sisters, both of whom had good reason to feel abandoned by Oxford. Even after Burghley's death, Oxford had no formal care of his children; their uncle Robert Cecil was made guardian, and they were sent to live with Lucy, Countess of Bedford, at Chenies in Buckinghamshire. If we make *King Lear* our guide, then beneath the outward forms of love and devotion a destructive fury simmered in the daughters. If, as was rumored, Elizabeth Vere had an affair with the Earl of Essex, who may in part have inspired the character of Edmund, then she assumes the lineaments of Goneril with more certainty. The exception would be the youngest, Susan, who became a devotee of theater and acted in court masques. She also had a hand in protecting her father's literary legacy.

If the daughters felt a sense of awe and pride at their father's achievement, it was more than likely traversed by a deep vein of shame at being the offspring of a figure who was largely ostracized in the circles in which they moved. As an aging bohemian who liked to carouse with the quick-witted and leave a trail of tailors' bills across London, Oxford may have thought of himself with self-deprecating exaggeration as a kind of Falstaff, a slightly disgraceful figure presiding over a riotous ad hoc school of literati, a court of misrule, either at the Steelyard[161] or at the Boar's Head tavern in Eastcheap (which would become a favorite performance space for his players). A sudden shaft of light into a corner of Oxford's life in 1590 lends credence to his quasi-Falstaffian existence at this time. He had rented rooms for his cronies near St. Paul's from Mistress Julia Penn, and one of the oldest of them, the poet Thomas Churchyard, had taken up residence there. Oxford, however, had been backward in paying the rent and other expenses. It was Churchyard who replied to Mistress Penn's demand for satisfaction:

> I stand to that bargain, knowing my good lord so noble (and of such great consideration) that he will perform what I promised in the highest degree of his bounty. . . . I absolutely here, for the love

and honour I bear my lord, bind myself and all I have in the world unto you for the satisfying of you for the first quarter's rent of the rooms my lord did take, and further for the coals, billets, faggots, beer, wine, and any other thing spent by his honourable means.

Mistress Penn decided to take legal action to recover the sum that was owed her, and Churchyard took sanctuary, possibly at the nearby Church of St. Benet's at Paul's Wharf. The case dragged on. In the meantime Mistress Penn communicated with Oxford directly, and wrote to him of the great grief and sorrow she had suffered for his "unkind dealing" with her, adding:

You know, my Lord, you had anything in my house whatsoever you or your men would demand, if it were in my house. If it had been a thousand times more I would have been glad to pleasure your Lordship withal. Therefore, good my Lord, deal with me in courtesy, for that you and I shall come at that dreadful day and give account for all your doing.

In *Henry IV, Part 2,* Mistress Quickly appoints two officers to arrest Falstaff for debt. Standing with them outside the Boar's Head tavern, she enlarges on his crimes:

I am undone by his going [Falstaff is going to the wars], I warrant you, he's an infinitive thing upon my score. . . . I pray you, since my exion [action] is entered, and my case so openly known to the world, let him be brought to his answer. A hundred mark is a long one for a poor lone woman to bear, and I have borne, and borne, and borne, and have been fubbed off, and fubbed off, and fubbed off, from this day to that day, and it is a shame to be thought on. There is no honesty in such dealing . . .

(II.i.22–23, 28–35)

The Lord Chief Justice arrives with his men, and having heard both sides of the case, says to Falstaff: "You have, as it appears to me, practised upon the easy-yielding spirit of this woman, and made her serve your uses both in purse and in person." Falstaff, having taken Mistress Quickly aside, tells her to wash her face and withdraw her action, adding: "Come, thou must not be in this humour with me, dost not know me? Come, come, I know thou wast set on to this." When one discovers that Mistress Penn was the mother-in-law of Burghley's private secretary Michael Hicks, these words become understandable. The old fox had been up to his tricks again.

We do not know when Oxford first revealed his true identity to his young protégé, nor is it known whether Southampton's deep admiration for this mysterious foster father, Shake-speare, became tempered with shame the more he was lionized by the smart young men at court, who pandered to his vanity and flattered his dreams of royal success. The relationship between Falstaff and Prince Hal, no less than that between Antonio and Bassanio, seems to speak eloquently of this touching friendship between a fallen man and his prodigal son, one that is both highly idealistic—platonic even—and at the same time fraught with feelings of shame and rejection. That they cannot acknowledge each other openly is a constant source of sorrow, as is the poet's shame at his compromised status, which he feels could harm the Fair Youth's chances of succeeding to the throne. Sonnet 36 captures all these ideas beautifully:

> Let me confess that we two must be twain
> Although our undivided loves are one:
> So shall those blots that do with me remain,
> Without thy help by me be borne alone.
> In our two loves there is but one respect,
> Though in our lives a separable spite,
> Which though it alter not love's sole effect,
> Yet doth it steal sweet hours from love's delight.
> I may not evermore acknowledge thee,
> Lest my bewailed guilt should do thee shame;
> Nor thou with public kindness honour me
> Unless thou take that honour from thy name:
>   But do not so; I love thee in such sort
>   As, thou being mine, mine is thy good report.

The poet's guilt is further defined in Sonnet 88 by the legal term "attainted," which connoted the "corruption of blood" imposed upon one condemned of treason, whereby he could neither inherit nor transmit property or titles by descent:

Upon thy part I can set down a story
Of faults concealed wherein I am attainted,
That thou, in losing me, shall win much glory.

(lines 6–8)

On the basis of the poet's declaration in Sonnet 42 that he and the Fair Youth are one, it is easy to accept that Prince Hal can stand for both Oxford and Southampton, according to which way one turns the lens. Falstaff is the Oxford who has given up hope of the throne for himself in order to raise up his royal son. He must rest content with a surrogate kingdom, that of language, in which his supremacy is unchallenged. The tavern is his theater, and the theater his court, and there no one can best him, especially when it comes to playing the king. Falstaff *is* the playwright who creates hilarious scenes from his experiences, as witness his intended skits against Justice Shallow: "I will devise matter enough out of this Shallow to keep Prince Henry in continual laughter the wearing out of six fashions." Indeed, he threatens to drive Hal out of his kingdom "with a dagger of lath" (a theater prop), and later on uses the same object for his scepter when he plays the part of the prince's father during their tavern burlesque. Yet beneath the unconquerable, some would say implacable, wit lies the fear that the prince will spurn him. Why, then, does Prince Hal have such power over old Jack Falstaff? Harold Bloom has the answer:

> Hal's displaced paternal love is Falstaff's vulnerability, his one weakness, and the origin of his destruction. Time annihilates other Shakespearean protagonists, but not Falstaff, who dies for love. . . . The greatest of all fictive wits dies the death of a rejected father-substitute, and also of a dishonored mentor.[162]

It is significant that Falstaff should mention the story of Dives and Lazarus (the rich man and the beggar) three times in his bibulous disquisitions, leaving us with the powerful image of the rich man in his purple robes, "burning, burning," for this is surely the king being purged from Falstaff's soul, while Lazarus, bearing the name of the resurrected one, ascends to heaven in his rags. Falstaff has unwittingly painted himself into the picture as royal scapegoat. Oxford, who was notorious not only among the nobility but in literary circles for having become a "beggar" of the queen's favor, was given the name Pierce Penniless by Nashe. In *Summer's Last Will and Testament,* Nashe's only extant drama, Ver or Spring, in rendering an account of his spending to Summer, declares unashamedly:

> What I had, I have spent on good fellows; in these sports you have
> seen, which are proper to the spring, and others of like sort . . . have
> I bestowed all my flowery treasure and flower of my youth.

In other words, Oxford has spent his fortune putting on plays. Ver goes on to praise beggary, arguing with great panache that all poets, philosophers, and alchemists are beggars. The Summer of the title, who is also the play's hero, is none other than Henry VIII's old jester, Will Somer, who was famous for improvising verses. Robert Armin, a fool under the patronage of Oxford, wrote of him:

> When he was sad, the King and he would rime:
> Thus Will exiled sadness many a time.

Somer died during the reign of Elizabeth, in 1560, and Eva Turner Clark conjectures that he sometimes accompanied the 16th Earl of Oxford's players when they wintered at Hedingham Castle.[163] (The earl had been lord great chamberlain to Somer's late master, Henry VIII, and knew the jester well.) If this is the case, then the young Oxford would have found in this "fellow of infinite jest" an unusual and possibly Falstaffian mentor, recalling him in later years with the same fondness that Hamlet evinces toward (in Bloom's words) his "foster father" Yorick. And later, when he came to choose his pen name, Oxford may well have been drawn to the Christian name of the man who had been able to charm a bilious old king with his irreverent verse.

Ultimately, Falstaff is imprisoned in his own kingdom of language, where wit takes precedence over feeling. When he says that his womb undoes him, it is his womb of wit—his invention—rather than his great belly. Though wondrously humorous, the fat knight seems to have almost no feeling toward others; he is too wrapped up in the great adventure on which his great wit is willy-nilly leading him. He is indeed a kind of autocrat, albeit of conceit (as the Elizabethans called it), who overbears any attempt by others to encompass him. We see this same dissociation of feeling in Hal, who, as he lets us know in his opening soliloquy in *Henry IV, Part 1,* is merely playing along with his tavern companions as part of his grand plan of political and spiritual self-transformation. When the time comes to reject Falstaff, he will have no compunction. As Warwick tells the king not long before the latter dies:

> The Prince but studies his companions
> Like a strange tongue, wherein, to gain the language,
> 'Tis needful that the most immodest word
> Be look'd upon and learnt; which once attain'd,
> Your Highness knows, comes to no further use
> But to be known and hated.
>
> (*2 Henry IV,* IV.iv.68–73)

In confidently predicting that Hal will, "in the perfectness of time, cast off his followers," Warwick uses the telling image of an experiment in language to describe the prince's attitude toward his friends. This objectivity of feeling, for want of a better phrase, appears to be a strong element in Oxford-Shakespeare's nature. We see it not just in Falstaff and Hal, but in Betram, Adonis, and Hamlet. Even the great lovers such as Romeo and Antony lose their feelings in an excess of self-dramatization. This inability to love is particularly pronounced in Hamlet, who sees not only others but also himself as objects in the drama of his life. As he says to Ophelia: "I could interpret between you and your love if I could see the puppets dallying." "Your love" is, of course, Hamlet himself. With so many of Shakespeare's characters the mind is on tiptoe, as if it were on the verge of mania. If Shakespeare did indeed invent human personality as we know it today, as Harold Bloom has claimed, it says much about the narcissism and self-alienation of modern man.

All this is germane to the life of Oxford, whose feelings were driven down to a mythic stratum of his soul by the deep, unhealable wound he sustained to his sense of family, both by virtue of his transgressive birth and the subsequent fostering from men such as Sir Thomas Smith and Sir William Cecil (Lord Burghley), stern men with little talent for affection. Oxford learned to shape his feeling responses along mythic lines, according to the characters and stories of ancient Greek and Roman literature, as well as the heroes of English history, whose soaring emotions and high-hearted exploits provided a delightful escape from his gnawing sense of nobodiness. Thus whenever he expresses personal feelings, they are highly colored, overwhelmed even, by the archetypal energies that flowed from his original soul-wound. Experience for him possessed a mythic charge, which is why he frequently used dreams to give a realistic context to the extravagant imagery with which he instinctively evokes strong feeling (Cleopatra's description of her love for the departed Antony being an excellent example).

It is as if Shakespeare's feelings are projected onto the world. At her death, Ophelia sings like the swan that has remained mute all its life, but does not weep; the Queen, who observes it, does not weep; but nature weeps, by means of the willow and the brook. Drama provided Shakespeare with a medium for evoking feeling in others without having to connect directly with his own painful emotions. While he remained trapped behind a veil of tears, unable to reach through it to those around him, the world was flooded with his emotions. His personal lack became literature's infinite gain.[164]

Hal and Falstaff (or Hamlet and Falstaff) seem to represent an inner battle in Shakespeare between king and rebel. In his case this was not just an interior spiritual dilemma but a real political conflict enacted in the everyday world. Just as Falstaff clings to Hal in order to hold on to the last vestiges of his own ravaged kingliness, and thus save himself from falling irrevocably into the role of jester, so Oxford clung to Southampton to maintain a sense of his own royalty as his dreams of kingship faded.

So often when Oxford-Shakespeare addresses Southampton in the Sonnets, one gets the impression that the younger man has become a symbol or cipher for the poet's own royalty. This symbol, "beauty's rose," is the consummation of the royal line that both men represent, as well as the perfection of Shake-speare's art. His lofty, philosophical love for Southampton is not only an expression of his artistic ideal but also an escape from the pressures and suffering of traditional family life. He feels he must reach beyond this at all costs. Ultimately, however, the Sonnets are about Shakespeare's obsession with his own thwarted royalty (his "cause"); and the redemption that he seeks in the Fair Youth is really the resurrection of his own brilliant promise. The final couplet of Sonnet 112, far from being an expression of unconditional love, is a statement of the poet's absolute dedication to his own cause:

> You are so strongly in my purpose bred
> That all the world besides methinks are dead.
>
> (lines 13–14)

The poet and the Fair Youth have become indistinguishable, merged in the mystic-dynastic rose, which "all alone stands hugely politic." In another sonnet he talks of his mind being crowned with the young man. Again, the archetypal core breaks through the shell of personality. That others perceived this extraordinary relationship as one of vanity on the poet's part is borne out by these lines from Chapman, spoken by his Hamlet-like protagonist Clermont:

> And as the foolish poet that still writ
> All his most self-loved verse in paper royal,
> Of parchment ruled with lead, smoothed with the pumice,
> Bound richly up, and strung with crimson strings;
> Never so blest as when he writ and read
> The ape-loved issue of his brain, and never
> But joying in himself, admiring ever.
>
> (*The Revenge of Bussy D'Ambois*, II.i.186–192)

The book with crimson strings is the book of the Sonnets that the sitter is holding in the highly contested Ashbourne portrait of Shakespeare, which was discovered by X-ray to be an overpainting of the Earl of Oxford.[165] He is painted as Hamlet in black, with a skull beneath his right arm. The "ever" and "never" in Chapman's verses make the familiar pun on Oxford's name, E. Vere.

Ultimately, the Sonnets tell the tragedy of a dying dynasty, and its struggle to keep the vision of its royalty alive despite the opposition of its head, the Dark Lady (Queen Elizabeth), who is determined that the story of her unacknowledged heirs—the poet himself (Oxford) and the Fair Youth (Southampton)—should remain forever in the shadows, despite the fact that the child, unlike Elizabeth's other progeny, had been planned, as Sonnet 124 makes clear (emphasis mine):

> If my dear love were but the child of state,
> It might for Fortune's bastard be unfathered,
> As subject to Time's love or to Time's hate,
> Weeds among weeds, or flowers with flowers gathered.
> *No, it was builded far from accident . . .*
> It fears not Policy, that heretic
> Which works on leases of short-numb'red hours,
> But all alone stands hugely politic.
>
> (lines 1–5, 9–11)

The poet is almost driven to distraction by her stubborn refusal to countenance the truth, and even warns her that he might reveal what has so far been kept hidden, both by her princely decree and by the masking subtlety of his poetry:

> Be wise as thou art cruel: do not press
> My tongue-tied patience with too much disdain,
> Lest sorrow lend me words, and words express
> The manner of my pity-wanting pain . . .
> For if I should despair, I should grow mad,
> And in my madness might speak ill of thee.
>
> (Sonnet 140, lines 1–4, 9–10)

This hidden family of Oxford's, which bore the highest name in the land, that of the "Rose," was kept pure by the flame of his imagination, despite the gnawing sense of shame he felt at his own life-long involvement with the theater. In it no less than in his art, his identity was supremely vested. His nominal family, that of Vere, was by contrast a mere shadow, though to the world it has been the other way around. Even when his dream was in tatters, and he cried from the lungs of the mad Lear, "Never, never, never, never, never!" he imagined that he or his son would yet rise phoenix-like from the ashes of the queen's honor.

~ *13* ~

Final Sacrifice

So shall she leave her blessedness to one . . .
Who from the sacred ashes of her honour
Shall star-like rise.
               (*Henry VIII*, V.iv.43, 45–46)

AGING ROYAL SUITOR

It was not just Oxford's purse that was empty as England entered the 1590s; with war against Spain dragging on, both in the Netherlands and on the high seas, the national purse itself was looking distinctly threadbare. Mismanagement of the country's finances—principally through the crown's sale of monopolies—and a series of disastrous harvests had sent inflation rocketing. There was famine in the countryside, and a series of epidemics devastated the cities. The government responded with greater repression. The Puritans, interpreting the miserable state of affairs as God's judgment upon a sinful nation, grew in influence. The theaters were closed for long periods, and stricter censorship was imposed.

The queen was increasingly capricious, as she tried with ever more grotesque results to shore up her Fairy Queen image against the ravages of time. Her tremendous vanity, privately a source of ridicule among her maids of honor, was bolstered by the swashbuckling attentions of the young Earl of Essex, who wrote to her, "I do confess that as a man I have been more subject to your natural beauty, than as a subject to the power of a king." Essex certainly knew which strings to pluck. As Laertes in *Hamlet* and the blustering Hotspur in *Henry IV, Part 1,* he was perceived by Oxford as the chief threat to his own son's succession. In a letter to Robert Cecil in October 1595, Oxford objects to the suggestion that he should seek Essex's help in a suit to the queen, declaring it "a thing I cannot do in honour, sith I have already received diverse injuries and wrongs from him, which bar me from all such base courses."

It is an enormous shame, as well as an incalculable loss to literature that the Cecils made it their business to destroy so many of Oxford's letters, not just to themselves, but to his literary friends, who were constantly monitored by the secret service, and whose lodgings could be raided at any time and their papers destroyed. Anything that might readily betray the Shake-speare secret was, one feels, consigned to oblivion. And given that the great "poetomachia," or war of the poets, that raged through the 1590s and beyond concerned the succession to the throne, and how much could or could not be revealed about Shakespeare's true identity and that of his theater-loving son, the correspondence of other writers may also have been consigned to the fire. The Cecils were scrupulous in preserving the records of their time in government, so long as these records reflected favorably on themselves. Many of Oxford's replies to Burghley's letters have vanished, together no doubt with much correspondence that he initiated. Yet even with this level of censorship, the letters that remain, though largely business communications, reveal the essential patterns of Shakespeare's thought and diction. Oxford cannot put pen to paper, however mundane the subject, without creating beauty in sound and image. Rich pearls are scattered through the letters.

Throughout the 1590s, and until his death in 1604, Oxford was a suitor, both to Queen Elizabeth and to her successor, King James, for an array of posts and grants, from the governorship of Jersey to the presidency of Wales. It was a slow, frustrating, and costly business, with the queen maddeningly resourceful in finding pretexts for delay or, failing that, declaring the sudden termination of the suit. As ever, Oxford's channel of influence, now that his own star had waned, was the Cecils. A few of the letters we have were written directly to the queen, as when Oxford sought a licence to import oils, wools, and fruits, only to have Elizabeth change her mind at the last moment. "But having drawn my books," writes Oxford, "Your

Majesty resisted the signing of them, that so I was put to a great charge thereby and my suit overthrown." Threatened as she was by the notion of empowering her heirs in any way, Elizabeth could be outright abusive. When Oxford suggested to the queen that he be allowed to try his title to the Forest of Essex in the courts, he was strongly rebuffed. "But I found that so displeasing unto her," he wrote, "that in place of receiving that ordinary favour which is of course granted to the meanest subject, I was brow-beaten and had many bitter speeches given me." Oxford is writing to Burghley, and goes on: "She had done me more favour if she had suffered me to try my title at law than this arbitrament under pretence of expedition and grace. The extremity had been far more safe than the remedy, which I was persuaded to accept."

With Elizabeth's own fickle nature as the final arbiter, the suitor often found himself in a hall of smoke and mirrors, the prize held tantalizingly close, yet with no reasonable hope of grasping it. In the end, many had to abandon their suits for lack of funds. Oxford puts it memorably in his June 25, 1585 letter to Burghley, in which he asks his father-in-law for a loan in order to continue his petitioning:

> For, being now almost at a point to taste that good which Her Majesty shall determine, yet am I as one that hath long besieged a fort and [is] not able to compass the end or reap the fruit of his travail, being forced to levy his siege for want of munition. Being therefore thus disfurnished and unprovided for to follow Her Majesty, as I perceive she will look for, I most earnestly desire your Lordship that you will lend me £200 till Her Majesty performeth her promise.

One of Oxford's most persistent suits, spanning the entire 1590s, concerned the farming of her Majesty's tin in Devon and Cornwall. The title of the office, lord warden of the stannaries, was relinquished by Sir Walter Raleigh in 1594–1595, by which time Oxford had, in his own words, "consumed four or five years in a flattering hope of idle words." The office was a royal one, traditionally held by the Prince of Wales, and the tinners had their own parliament or stannary court, which held session on the open moor. In 1337 Edward III had granted the stannaries to his eldest son, the Black Prince, who was also Duke of Cornwall. Maybe this was why it appealed to Oxford's imagination and spurred his doggedness in a decade-long suit that was to prove futile.

Oxford was not slow to register his frustration, as when he wrote to Cecil regarding his claim for the forfeited lands of Sir Charles Danvers, who had been executed for taking part in Essex's rebellion: "Howsoever, an answer shall be most welcome unto me, now being the best expectation of my tedious suit, thinking therein my time lost more precious than the suit itself." His tone was often resigned, as when he wrote laconically at the end of a postscript, "If Her Majesty's affections be forfeits of men's estates, we must endure it." Oxford could also lose his temper; for instance, he wrote to her Majesty that he would not be rewarded for his labor "with a mock," and expressed his feeling that he had been "rejected and neglected." Yet he was always prepared to believe in the queen, whatever her former abuses, and this faith calls forth some of his finest prose. As he writes to Robert Cecil regarding the governorship of the Isle of Jersey:

> Although my bad success in former suits to Her Majesty have given me cause to bury my hopes in the deep and bottom of despair, rather than now to attempt, after so many trials made in vain and so many opportunities escaped, the effects of fair words or fruits of golden promises, yet for that, I cannot believe but that there hath been always a true correspondence of word and intention in Her Majesty. I do conjecture that with a little help, that which of itself hath brought forth so fair blossoms will also yield fruit.

At the end of the letter he is even able to summon a little morbid humor on the subject:

> If she [the queen] shall not deign me this in an opportunity of time so fitting, what time shall I attend, which is uncertain to all men, unless in the graves of men there were a time to receive benefits and good turns from princes?

What a thrill to realize we are reading the personal correspondence of William Shake-speare!

In a letter of January 1602, once again concerning the Danvers escheat, which became a virtual saga, Oxford expressed his hope that the queen "after so many gracious words which she gave me at Greenwich upon her departure, exceeding this which I expect, will not now draw in the beams of her princely grace to my discouragement and her own detriment." This letter is particularly fascinating because of the tide of unease and mistrust that runs through it and because the language makes one feel that, beneath the surface worries of his flagging suit, Oxford is anxious about his personal reputation and the posthumous fate of his writings, no doubt dreading the final annihilation of his name and achievement. Talking about the deceits practiced by those attempting to wrest the suit from him, he writes that "time and truth have unmasked all difficulties," yet "the truth, much oppressed by the friends of the contrary part, is likely, if not wholly to be defaced, yet so extenuated as the virtue thereof will be of little effect." (One thinks of the botched texts of pirated plays.) His faith in humanity has been eroded, and he does not exclude Robert Cecil from this general suspicion, for at the end of the letter he has to assure himself that his brother-in-law's "words and deeds dwell not asunder." In the end, however, he must simply trust to time:

> Another confidence I had in yourself, in whom, without offence let me speak it, I am to cast some doubt, by reason, as in your last letters I found a wavering style much differing from your former assurances, I fear now to be left *in medio rerum omnium certamine et discrimine* [i.e., left hanging at the critical moment of the contentious suit], which if it so fall out I shall bear it by the grace of God with an equal mind, sith time and experience have given me sufficient understanding of worldly frailty. But I hope better, though I cast the worst, howsoever, for *finis coronat opus* [the end crowns the work], and then everything will be laid open, every doubt resolved into a plain sense.

Writing again to Cecil, with James now on the throne, this time regarding his suit for the keepership of Waltham Forest and Havering Park, Oxford once more, albeit unwittingly, sounds the note of the hidden author estranged from his works:

> So that by this and the former means, I have been thus long dispossessed; but I hope truth is subject to no prescription, for truth

is truth though never so old, and time cannot make that false which was once true.

Oxford's relationship with Robert Cecil was superficially more cordial than his dealings with Burghley had been—his teeth were more firmly gritted—and in his letters to Robert he describes him as his only friend and supporter at court except for the queen herself. Oxford and Cecil had been brought up in the same household, the humanist academy for young aristocrats that was Cecil House; and Cecil, Oxford's junior by fourteen years, was in awe of his dazzling foster brother. Robert, who had been born with curvature of the spine, had grown up as a bookish youth, puny, sickly, diffident, and so diminutive that the queen would later nickname him her "Pigmy," a sobriquet he detested, and—only slightly more palatably—her "Elf." His sharp intellect, wide reading, and European travels would have recommended him to Oxford, who no doubt looked on with compassion at the precocious hunchback's absolute subjection to the will of his father, who bound him more as political disciple than son. Oxford knew well enough what it was to be fettered by such a controlling and manipulative figure. Both men, too, were outsiders and scapegoats, albeit of a very different kind. Robert, who was known by his fellow courtiers as "Roberto il Diavolo" and whose physical deformities made life uncomfortable in a court dominated by warriors, athletes, and beautiful dancers, carried the shadow or unacknowledged ugliness of this vainglorious society.

Oxford found Robert Cecil more flexible and far subtler than his father, and could relate to him on the level of music and literature, yet he had to tread carefully, for he knew that his reputation and the fate of his works were to a large extent in the hands of a man who bore the world a terrific grudge. After all, had he not lampooned this man as Richard III in his great historical tragedy? And had not their cousin Francis Bacon written his essay "Of Deformity" with Cecil in mind, setting the tone with these plainspoken lines: "Deformed persons are commonly even with nature: for as nature hath done ill by them, so do they by nature; being for the most part (as the Scripture saith) *void of natural affection;* and so they have their revenge of nature"? For all this, many of Oxford's letters mention his kinship with Robert and demonstrate, if not actual warmth, then a certain remembered affection. The thanks he offers Cecil over the Danvers suit are, he writes, "to be sealed up in an eternal remembrance to yourself." In March 1601, he writes regarding the presidency of Wales and ends the letter "in all kindness and kindred," echoing Hamlet's pairing of these concepts ("a little more than kin and less than kind").

If all the glory of literature and all the praise of all the Muses were due to the queen, as Oxford had declared in 1573, then he proved to be a poor suitor in the early 1590s, laying few offerings at her Majesty's feet. The truth was that Oxford had withdrawn somewhat from the literary and theatrical fray following the Marprelate controversy, and was busy revising his plays for publication. The Paul's Boys, one of the companies Oxford had fostered, had been suspended for lampooning Martin Marprelate as an ape, and none of the companies, not even the Queen's Men, was licensed to play in London. It seems that Gabriel Harvey and his Puritan backers were hell-bent on exposing Oxford and letting the country know that the lord great chamberlain of England was a playwright, who consorted with actors and other denizens of the South Bank. References to him in their tirades were becoming bolder, and he himself had been too frank in his dramas, making, as he writes in Sonnet 110, "old offences of affections new." Consequently, Oxford went to ground for a time.

As it was, this fantastical nobleman was but dimly known by certain percipient folk to be the mysterious playwright whose works were delighting Londoners, and his reddish beard, melancholy, piercing eyes and high-strung features were barely perceptible as he limped along the street (a high-brow Oedipus), his signature toothpick in his mouth and a large hat pulled deep over his brow. Had he been stopped and felt compelled to remove his hat, his interlocutor would have gazed upon a face that was, like Amorphus's, another "volume of essays," and heard a diction that, according to Jonson, was all skimmed cream. He could not be too careful. Were his true identity to be discovered, and with it his concealed profession, the monarchy itself could feel the heat. This ultimate disgrace is hinted at in Thomas Edwards's *Narcissus* (1595), which evokes Shakespeare by the name Adonis. Having told us that Shakespeare masks himself behind his characters of high rank, Edwards makes this extraordinary tribute:

> Eke in purple robes destain'd.
> Amid'st the centre of this clime,
> I have heard say doth remain,
>   One whose power floweth far,
> That should have been of our rhyme
>   The only object and the star.
>
> (L'Envoy, lines 49–54)

Shake-speare's purple robes are his royal robes, stained by association with the stage, and the "star" is a reference to Oxford's family badge: the "mollet" or five-pointed star. The same year that *Narcissus* appeared, Rowland White wrote to Sir Robert Sidney, "Some say my Lord of Oxford is dead"—a startling indication of his growing obscurity, at least to those not in the know. As ever, he was passed over in the Garter elections, sometimes failing to pick up a single vote from his fellow peers.

In his *Fate of the Butterfly* (1590), Edmund Spenser had already told how the malicious spider Aragnoll (Burghley), "his false heart fraught with all treason's store," had entrapped the beautiful butterfly Clarion (Oxford), thus depriving the world of "all happiness." The following year, in his *Tears of the Muses,* one of a series of poems entitled *Complaints,* which chronicled in allegorical terms the bitter opposition of the government to the flowering of the liberal arts in late Elizabethan England, Spenser bewailed the decline of poetry and the dramatic arts through the spread of what he termed "ugly Barbarism," by which he meant the Puritan values espoused by Burghley and others. Referring, presumably, to the court comedies of Lyly and Oxford-Shakespeare, he lamented the end of true laughter and delight, rooted in learning and understanding. Each of the nine Muses takes a turn giving plaint to this loss of quality. Thalia, Muse of comedy, after a general lament for "the sweet delights of learning's treasure / That wont with Comick sock to beautify / The painted Theaters," goes on to mourn the loss of a dramatic art of such finespun discrimination that "man's life in his likest image / Was limned forth." Then come the passages that scholars have rightly sensed refer to Shakespeare, but which cannot by any stretch of the imagination be brought within the context of the life of William of Stratford. As descriptive of Oxford's removed and tongue-tied state at the beginning of the 1590s, on the other hand, they are perfectly apt:

> And he the man, whom Nature selfe had made
> To mock her selfe, and Truth to imitate,
> With kindly counter under Mimick shade,
> Our pleasant *Willy,* ah is dead of late:
> With whom all joy and jolly merriment
> Is also deaded, and in dolour drent.
>
> But that same gentle Spirit, from whose pen
> Large streames of honnie and sweete Nectar flowe,
> Scorning the boldnes of such base-borne men,
> Which dare their follies forth so rashlie throwe;
> Doth rather choose to sit in idle Cell,
> Than so himselfe to mockerie to sell.
>
> (lines 205–210, 217–222)

As J. T. Looney convincingly demonstrated, Oxford had already been identified as "Willie," the shepherd who takes part in a rhyming contest with Perigot (Sidney) in the August eclogue of Spenser's *Shepheardes Calendar* (1579). This "death" of Oxford's that Spenser refers to is the same death that casts a pall over Antonio at the opening of *The Merchant of Venice,* a morbid sadness brought on by an unnamed loss, a renunciation of something so precious that his very identity is threatened. Jaques, the self-exiled courtier in *As You Like It,* is another channel for this deep pathos.

Ironically, part of this loss of self was expressed in exterior events in Oxford's life that would normally be construed as moments of singular happiness, but that for him were necessarily tinged with self-sacrificial melancholy. For instance, at the end of December 1591 Oxford married one of the queen's maids of honor, with—for once—her Majesty's wholehearted approval. Indeed, it may even be that the queen herself had appointed the match in order to provide Oxford with some much-needed stability and support in his declining years. Known for her beauty and clarity of mind, Elizabeth Trentham was about thirty years of age at the time of the wedding. She and her brother Francis immediately took control of Oxford's ruinous finances in order to stop the rot and ensure that there would be some patrimony, however diminished, for his heir. That heir, Henry de Vere, later 18th Earl of Oxford, and no doubt named for Henry Wriothesley, was born to the couple at their home in Stoke Newington on February 24, 1593. (Henry was not a de Vere name, just as Edward had not been; nor was it a Wriothesley name.) Stoke Newington, known for its "connections with Dissent and literature," was a small village three miles north of London proper. It was outside the jurisdiction of the City fathers, and within easy distance of the theaters in Shoreditch, which had been running for more than twenty-five years. And even in the sixteenth century it played a vital role in supplying the fast-growing capital with water. It sounds very much like Shakespeare territory.

In 1590, with the publication of the first three books of the *Faerie Queene,* Spenser wrote a dedicatory sonnet to Oxford, in which he emphasized the earl's special bond with the Muses (the Heliconian imps), as well as the peculiar quality of narcissism that was a hallmark of his plays. He also hints that he knows of Oxford's relationship with "love," i.e., Queen Elizabeth. Spenser is dedicating the work to him both for his noble ancestry (spelling modernized):

> And also for the love, which thou dost bear
> To th'*Heliconian* imps, and they to thee,
> They unto thee, and thou to them most dear:
> Dear as thou art unto thy self, so love
> That loves and honors thee, as doth behove.
>
> (lines 10–14)

Oxford was memorialized in the *Faerie Queene* through a number of characters, though perhaps most prominently through Sir Calidore, the Knight of Courtesy and hero of Book VI, who in Canto IX exchanges his spear for a shepherd's hook.

For the last eleven years of his life, from 1593, Oxford would attend Parliament only once, having little faith in the political machine. If, however, he was to make one last bid to change the course of history, he would have to turn his idle cell into a hive of activity.

Becoming Shake-speare

Barred from political and military affairs, denied the visible marks of royal favor, his suits constantly baffled by the queen, looked down upon by his peers, his plays an object of shame, Oxford made the Fair Youth the refuge and glory of his art.

There is no doubt that the beautiful young Earl of Southampton—Shakespeare's patron, as history has it—was susceptible to flattery, and he received it in spades from the poets of the time. George Peele, for instance, addressed him as "the young Prince of Hampshire." Even his peers seemed fascinated, and in 1592, at the age of eighteen, he was proposed as a knight of the Garter, a singular honor for one so young. As the historian Charlotte Stopes writes:

> He was not appointed, but the fact of his name having been proposed was in itself an honour so great at his early age that it had never before been paid to any one not of Royal Blood.[166]

It turned his head and, much to the queen's annoyance, he began to give himself airs. Predictably, he attracted the wrong sort of company. Oxford rebuked him in a fatherly fashion in the Sonnets, even to the point of telling him that he was growing common. "Lilies that fester," he wrote in Sonnet 94, using the symbol of the heir to the throne, "smell far worse than weeds."

It seems that the truth of Southampton's birth had begun to leak out in certain literary and political circles, and Burghley saw an opportunity to quash the rumors by advertising a marriage between his young ward and his eldest granddaughter, Elizabeth Vere. After all, it was hardly likely that he would encourage the son and daughter of the Earl of Oxford to marry each other. Burghley, as ever, was killing two birds with one stone. He knew very well that Southampton was of royal blood twice over, through the queen *and* Oxford, and was tantalized by the idea that this elusive substance might flow in the veins of his descendants. As Hank Whittemore suggests, however, it may be that Burghley was simply following through on an agreement, made with Oxford in 1581 at the time of the reconciliation with Anne, that he would work behind the scenes for Southampton's succession so long as the youth married Burghley's granddaughter upon coming of age.[167] Like his alter ego Polonius, Burghley "went round to work," yet even with both potential spouses under one roof, his campaign was soon faltering, for Southampton refused to fall in. And here the young man's vanity may have saved him, for the last thing he wanted was to mingle his blood with that of the parvenus Cecils. But there were grounds more relevant than this for abjuring the match. First, he would be committing incest; second, he would be bending his neck to the Cecil yoke, an act of submission that he refused to countenance, both for itself and also because he had seen the effects of that family's stifling political control on his father.

Burghley, knowing the young man's fascination with literature, commissioned one of his secretaries, John Clapham, to write a Latin poem, *Narcissus* (1591), which warned Southampton of the danger of falling too deeply in love with himself. In other words, the poem was urging him to set aside his scruples regarding marriage and embrace Burghley's choice. There was also a sly dig or two at Oxford, as when Narcissus is said to have been nurtured "with the warm milk of Error." The match was also Oxford's choice, for he was too seasoned an observer not to know that, in turning his back on the Cecils, Southampton would be excluding himself from the throne. Just as Antonio does his utmost to see his young friend Bassanio married, even to the extent of pawning his life to Shylock, so Oxford was prepared to facilitate this royal union, though it meant giving up the title to his works. The first seventeen Sonnets of the sequence of 154 published in 1609, sometimes known as the "procreation sonnets," urge Southampton to marry and beget an heir to save the Tudor dynasty from extinction ("that beauty's *Rose* might never die"). Oxford is bold in his appeal to Southampton's royal instincts; nor is he afraid to acknowledge his own interest:

> Be as thy presence is, gracious and kind,
> Or to thyself at least kind-hearted prove:
> Make thee another self for love of me,
> That beauty still may live in thine or thee.
> (Sonnet 10, lines 11–14)

If the young man cannot bring himself to yield, then the poet gloomily prognosticates that his end will be "truth's and beauty's doom and date." The language of the Sonnets, in stark contrast to the plays, has been deliberately restricted. Nearly all the words are key words that reverberate with great connotative depth as they fashion a private symbolic world, designed to keep the royal mysteries of which they treat veiled from prying eyes. Yet the right people could understand them if they put their minds to it.

An excellent example is Sonnet 105, which in simple, almost liturgical language states the theme of the sacred trinity—Elizabeth, Southampton, Oxford (fair, kind, and true)—while acknowledging the infinite variety that these three concepts, or figures, are made to engender. Nothing expresses more clearly the notion that the Sonnets are allegorical and deeply secretive than these mysterious lines:

> Let not my love be called idolatry,
> Nor my beloved as an idol show,
> Since all alike my songs and praises be
> To one, of one, still such, and ever so.[168]
> Kind is my love to-day, to-morrow kind,
> Still constant in a wondrous excellence;
> Therefore my verse, to constancy confined,
> One thing expressing, leaves out difference.
> "Fair, kind, and true" is all my argument,
> "Fair, kind, and true," varying to other words;
> And in this change is my invention spent,
> Three themes in one, which wondrous scope affords.
> Fair, kind, and true have often lived alone,
> Which three till now never kept seat in one.

To suggest that these are love poems in the conventional sense, as scholars do, is preposterous. Rather, they are the hymns of a mystery religion, wherein Shakespeare has winnowed his words with such scrupulousness that the verse stands as pure as the mystery he is describing—a mystery both sacred and profane, private and political.

Southampton's bullheaded refusal to marry his half-sister (and collude in the incestuous kingmaking of his parents) cost him a fine of £5,000, levied by his guardian Burghley. It was a punitive tax for frustrating the old man's dynastic ambitions. What Oxford made of his son's defiant gesture is harder to assess, but there was no doubt a fair admixture of pride mingled with his disappointment. Describing Southampton as a humanist who was "deeply committed not only to learning but also to the developing national identity in the arts, including poetry and drama," Hank Whittemore makes the telling observation that "by turning his back on the political advice urged upon him by the Earl of Oxford, his father [i.e., to secure the throne by allying himself with the Cecils], Southampton ironically shows himself, above all, to be Shakespearean."[169] Subsequent publications reveal that others had seen through Burghley's political matchmaking. In 1597, for instance, William Burton dedicated his *Most Delectable History of Clitophon and Leucippe* (a free translation from the Greek of Achilles Tatius) to Southampton. The romance tells how the hero Clitophon defies the strict injunction of his father to marry his half-sister Calligone, eloping instead with his true love, Leucippe. After many trials and separations, the two lovers are finally reunited—as in *Pericles*—at the temple of Diana at Ephesus, whither Leucippe's reconciled father is guided by a vision of the goddess. Southampton's biographer, G. P. V. Akrigg, writes of one of the more lurid passages of the tale:

> This is strong stuff and one scholar has surmised that the reason why only one copy of *Clitophon and Leucippe* survived into our century could be that the book may have been one of those burned by order of the Archbishop of Canterbury. What is interesting is that Burton chose Southampton as the dedicatee for his work. Presumably he thought the Earl would like it.[170]

The reason that Burton chose Southampton as the dedicatee is that the romance tells the earl's story with remarkable fidelity, for not long after he had evaded his foster father's plan to marry him to his half-sister, it was noticed that he was paying court to one of the queen's maids of honor, Elizabeth Vernon, whose name quite literally spelled out his rejection of Elizabeth Vere, and whom he would one day secretly marry. Before this, Southampton had seemed in high favor with the queen, but suddenly the case was altered. As one court observer put it:

> My Lord of Southampton offering to help the Queen to her horse, was refused, he is gone from the Court, and not yet returned.

Though dismayed by Southampton's blunders, which he too had committed in youth, Oxford took up his spear-pen (the term, incidentally, from which Nashe derived the name "Pears Peniless") on behalf of his son's royal right. In this he seems to have had the queen's tacit support, though to satisfy her Privy Council she was forced to impose a new and permanent anonymity on him, backed by the shady presence of that poor poet-ape, William Shakspere of Stratford. In 1593 Gabriel Harvey wrote a cryptic poem, *Gorgon, or the Wonderfull Yeare,* full of references to Oxford's transformation, which includes this stanza under its own private heading, "A Stanza Declarative: to the Lovers of Admirable Workes":

> Pleased it hath, a *Gentlewoman rare,*
>> With Phoenix quill in diamond hand of Art,
>> To muzzle the redoubtable Bull-bare,
>> And play the galiard Championess's part.
> Though miracles surcease, yet Wonder see
>> *The mightiest miracle of Ninety Three.*

The rare Gentlewoman with the phoenix quill can only be Queen Elizabeth, who has silenced or tongue-tied the formidable Oxford. (Here Harvey shows off his knowledge of languages, for "bare" or "bear," as in "carry," ultimately derives from the Latin *ferre,* as does the word "ford." Thus Bull-bare yields Ox-ford.) Yet at the same time the lady has proved his staunch champion—for instance, by granting him the £1,000 annuity. As for the mightiest miracle of 1593, it was the first appearance of the name William Shakespeare in print, appended to the dedication of *Venus and Adonis* published that summer.

The publication of this highly mannered *poème à clef* stunned the literary world of London, following as it did upon the heels of a vicious Puritan clampdown on the theater, which led to the "deaths" of Greene, Marlowe, Lyly, Kyd, and Watson, all of whom were removed from the literary fray. From the ashes of these fellow artists, Shake-speare rose up, phoenix-like. If he had a spear in one hand, then in the other he clutched a little book, which told the true story of the birth of his royal son, the Earl of Southampton. The term "Shakespeare," did not of course designate a new writer—though it was intended to seem so—but rather the reinvention of an old one, indeed the oldest, in the sense that he was the fountainhead from which the others had drawn their life. As he wrote in the dedication to Southampton:

> But if the first heir of my invention prove deformed, I shall be sorry it had so noble a godfather, and never after ear so barren a land, for fear it yield me still so bad a harvest. I leave it to your honourable survey, and your Honour to your heart's content; which I wish may always answer your own wish and the world's hopeful expectation.

The "invention" mentioned is Oxford's invented name, William Shake-speare, and its first heir is of course *Venus and Adonis*. Southampton's "own wish" is his aspiration to the throne, and "the world's hopeful expectation"—echoed in "the world's due" of Sonnet 1—is, in his father's eyes at least, the same thing. When, six years later, Sir John Hayward dedicated his *First Part of the Life and Reign of Henry IV* to the Earl of Essex, he addressed him in equally unequivocal terms, only he ended up in the Tower for his pains, under sentence of death. "Great thou art in hope," he wrote, "greater in the expectation of future time." Earing "so barren a land" is, of course, a bold swipe at the Virgin Queen, the mother of the dedicatee.

It is not known whether Elizabeth connived at the publication of the poem, and if so for what reason, but the scandalous little book did remarkably well to pass the censors. Perhaps she thought it better to let Oxford have his say allegorically, in feigning poetry, than to risk driving his frustration into more open channels. As for Southampton, one wonders whether he took offense at the suggestive work, which soon had the whole of London gossiping, or blushed as deeply as the hotly pursued Adonis to hear of his mother's immodesty. One man who would have been grievously nettled was Burghley, who, while it suited him, tried all he could to camouflage Southampton's parentage. Oxford, he must have known, would not go gentle into that good night. Out of a very private family tragedy, one obsessively rehearsed in the Sonnets, emerged the phenomenon we know today as Shake-speare, just as the Church of England grew out of Henry VIII's turbulent love for Anne Boleyn.

Having repudiated the Cecils and lost the favor of the queen, Southampton began to see Essex as the only path to the throne, or at least the only means of creating a non-Cecilian monarchy. Thus he decided in favor of the sword rather than the pen, though the works of his father have kept the dream of enlightened kingship alive even today, with a new William and a new Henry biding the nod of history.[171]

IMMORTAL LONGINGS

In 1593 Oxford, like the most famous of all spear-shakers, Pallas Athena, sprang fully armed from the brow of Zeus. Reborn from the depths of his being, he now bore the pen name William Shakespeare. Whatever deals were struck with the establishment, be it the Cecils or Elizabeth, this is still the name by which we know the great poet-playwright. With the plays now in the public domain, it was deemed essential to mask their true nature as court dramas. Oxford, on the other hand, may have realized that this was his chance to advertise his cause to the people.

In Sonnets 135 and 136 he makes considerable play of the fact that in subjugating himself to the royal will he was transformed into a man called Will—was in effect annihilated. One might wonder what would have happened if, instead, the queen had subjugated herself to the power of Shake-speare's creative will, and made it the presiding genius of the late Tudor dynasty. Would her own royal will (the monarchy) have been enlightened as a result? These questions seem to hover between the lines of the two "Will" Sonnets. Unmistakable, however, is the poet's sense that he is finally little more than a name:

> Make but my name thy love, and love that still,
> And then thou lovest me, for my name is Will.
> (Sonnet 136, lines 13–14)

The bitter irony of these last five words has been missed by those eager to use them as a trite assertion of identity on the part of William Shakspere of Stratford.

One of the premises of this book has been that we should trust Hamlet's injunction to Polonius to respect the players as "the abstract and brief chronicles of the time," for this is Shakespeare's instruction to us to read his plays as histories. He knew that little of what really went on at the court of Elizabeth would find its way into the official records and be handed down to future generations. A principal function of his plays, therefore, was to reinsert himself into the history of his age, for though he could not contradict his official annihilation through open political dissent, he could defy it by means of his art. Even here, however, as we saw in *The Winter's Tale,* he could not be sure that his account would be believed. When he talks of the Fair Youth's royalty, he is expressing the highest truth of his art, and by reflection that means his own sovereign claim. Sonnet 17 expresses his anxiety with all the grace that he attributes to his royal son (emphasis mine):

> Who will believe my verse in time to come
> If it were filled with your most high deserts?
> Though yet, heaven knows, it is but as a tomb
> Which hides your life and shows not half your parts.
> If I could write the beauty of your eyes
> And in fresh numbers number all your graces,
> The age to come would say, "This poet lies—
> Such heavenly touches ne'er touched earthly faces."
> So should my papers, yellowed with their age,
> Be scorned, like old men of less truth than tongue,
> *And your true rights be termed a poet's rage*
> *And stretched metre of an antique song.*
> But were some child of yours alive that time,
> You should live twice—in it and in my rhyme.

From the time that the name Shake-speare breaks cover and appears publicly and unequivocally in print as that of the great poet of the age, Oxford largely disappears from view, or as B. M. Ward puts it, "a veil seems to descend over his life."[172] We know that he remarried and had a son by his second wife, and that he was carrying out some sort of office on behalf of the queen, for he refers to it in a letter to Burghley in July, 1594. We also know that he was in some way physically incapacitated after his duel with Thomas Knyvet in 1582. In a letter of 1597 to Burghley, for instance, he writes, "I have not an able body which might have served to attend on Her Majesty." Six years later we find him informing Robert Cecil that "by reason of my infirmity, I cannot come among you so often as I wish." So what was he doing?

It is clear that Oxford was spending his time revising his stock of plays composed over the previous two decades, with a view to publication. He was continually bringing these "abstract and brief chronicles of the age" up to date by adding topical references. Now, however, he did more. He refurbished his works, conscientious poet that he was, to champion the Fair Youth, the redeemer born of the father (like Edgar and Macduff), and therefore free from the power of the mother to confound succession. His old hopes and dreams of a new sovereignty were scoured and refashioned.

The plays do indeed show signs of thorough revision, as if they were living creatures that the author was continually feeding and watering. As he grows, so do they. What was originally an entirely dramatic piece (or "device," as it was called at court)—a thing of the moment created under pressure of a particular time and for a particular purpose—was gradually infused with a deeper poetry while losing none of its topicality and power to influence political thought. It became, in other words, an enduring work of literature. A good example is *Antony and Cleopatra,* which he transformed into a monument to his relationship with the queen. As Elizabeth's power waned, and Oxford felt relegated to the outskirts of political life, he began to look back with nostalgia at what might have been, and this in turn spurred him to immortalize their union. All his hopes had been vested in her:

> Alack, our terrene moon
> Is now eclips'd, and it portends alone
> The fall of Antony!
>
> (III.xiii.152–154)

The play is a tremendous indictment of imperialism, the universal wolf that swallows up sovereignty, identity, and truth. And what does Shakespeare hold up against this vast impersonal power, but the breath of poetry? *How with this rage shall beauty hold a plea, whose action is no stronger than a flower?* It is nobler in his eyes, as in Antony's, to have been a soldier (i.e., a spear-shaker) than an emperor, arms as so often in Shakespeare standing duty for letters. His has always been Hamlet's aim of transforming the queen rather than killing the king—raising her to the loftiest poetry of her nature. Yet even to attempt such a thing is to wrestle with the regressive demons of the goddess. Into Cleopatra, that serpent of old Nile, Oxford crammed all Elizabeth's maddening contradictions, then had her transcend them.

The moon had ruled Elizabeth during her arbitrary, willful reign; her *son* had not been allowed to shine. This vital part of her had been consigned to the underworld, and become in its own eyes little more than a worm. When Gloucester sees a beggar in the storm, he thinks a man a worm, and at that moment his son Edgar comes into his mind. Edgar, the outcast son, is the worm (worm in French being *ver*). When Cleopatra arranges to die in her monument, a clown enters with an asp—or worm, as he calls it—hidden in a basket of figs. If the clown, as so often, represents the unacknowledged son, i.e., Shake-speare himself, then the asp or worm is his pen, which has the power both to kill and to make immortal. (This is the asp-quill that makes up the name Pasquill, a persona that Oxford adopted to combat the puritan writer, Martin Marprelate.) When the clown exits, wishing Cleopatra "joy o' the worm," she puts the asp to her bosom, as if it were her child. As she exclaims to Charmian:

> Peace, peace!
> Dost thou not see my baby at my breast,
> That sucks the nurse asleep?
> (V.ii.307–309)

This is no innocent babe, but one who has the power to call Caesar "ass unpolicied," and whose "biting is immortal." We die by what we reject or cast out, and so Cleopatra-Elizabeth meets her end through the sweet poison of her outcast son.

Kingdom's Loss

As the 1590s advanced, Shakespeare the political agitator (or dramatist) yielded ground to Shakespeare the seer (or poet), a tension held in nice balance by his adopted name, William Shake-speare.[173] Quarto editions of the plays began appearing in 1594 with *Titus Andronicus*, though as yet no name was affixed to the title pages, and no fewer than fifteen new titles appeared in print over the next ten years. It was an exceptional rate of publication by any standards. There were clearly other titles in private circulation as well. In 1598, the year when the name William Shakespeare first appeared on the title page of a play, Francis Meres listed in his *Palladis Tamia* twelve Shakespearean plays, including four that were not published until the First Folio of 1623. Evidently, the works had been stockpiled over a considerable period, with many unpublished titles known only to a cultured elite. All that was to change in the late 1590s and early 1600s.

The year 1594 was also when the Lord Chamberlain's Men were established under the nominal patronage of the lord chamberlain, Henry Carey, 1st Baron Hunsdon. Hunsdon was the son of Anne Boleyn's sister Mary, making him a first cousin of the queen. He was also rumored to be the secret son of Henry VIII, who had a much publicized affair with Mary Boleyn during the 1520s. A brusque, soldierly man, plainspoken to a fault, who had no obvious interest in literature and spent much of his time a long way from court, Hunsdon may have been a front for the other lord chamberlain of the time, the lord *great* chamberlain, Edward de Vere, Earl of Oxford. With his residence in London and his lifelong passion for the theater, Oxford makes a much more plausible impresario for Shakespeare's company, as the Lord Chamberlain's Men have since become known. Indeed, the company may have been founded as part of the muzzling of Oxford in 1593. For its first four years, the company performed in Shoreditch, at the Theatre and Curtain playhouses, both of them in Oxford's backyard, and Shakespeare's plays quickly became their staple stock.

In April 1594 Ferdinando, Lord Strange—Earl of Derby since the previous September—died in suspicious circumstances, at age thirty-five. As a potential heir to the throne (he was the great-great-grandson of Henry VII, through Henry's younger daughter Mary), with Catholic sympathies and an acting company known for its seditious repertory, Strange was perceived as a threat to the Cecils' plans for a Protestant succession controlled by the Privy Council. In London it was rumored that Burghley had had the young nobleman poisoned. Later that same year, the Jesuit priest Robert Persons raised the succession ante by pseudonymously publishing *A Conference about the Next Succession to the Crown of England,* in which he openly discussed the rival claimants to Elizabeth's throne. Though he ostensibly maintained a stance of neutrality, it was common knowledge that he supported the claim of the Infanta Isabella of Spain, who was descended from John of Gaunt. The work was pointedly dedicated to the Earl of Essex, one of Elizabeth's hidden heirs. Shakespeare, meanwhile, had cast his vote with *Venus and Adonis* (1593) and *The Rape of Lucrece* (1594).

The Cecils were still said to favor the claim of Edward Seymour, Lord Beauchamp, Katherine Grey's elder son, though he had sullied his chances somewhat with a poor marriage. His younger brother, Thomas, was also in the running and had appealed the declaration of illegitimacy against his parents' marriage made by Archbishop Parker's commission in 1562. Another Protestant contender, still just in the running, was the Puritan Earl of Huntingdon who, like the infanta, traced his claim back to the warring sons of Edward III. Then there was the Stuart line, descended from Henry VII's elder daughter, Margaret Tudor. The senior representative of this line was James of Scotland, who evinced a steely determination to succeed his godmother on the throne of England, keeping a weather eye on all his rivals. The weakness of his claim lay both in his foreign birth and in the fact that Henry VIII had excluded the Stuarts from the succession. His cousin Arbella Stuart, the daughter of James's uncle Charles Stuart, Earl of Lennox, had been born in England, however, and was looked upon by many as a desirable alternative to the mildly repulsive James.

In 1597 Oxford and his countess moved to King's Place in Hackney, a former royal residence, where three Tudor monarchs, including Elizabeth and her father, Henry, had held their courts. With Oxford himself broke, it was purchased by a syndicate comprising his wife, his brother-in-law Francis, and two other friends of the Trentham family. The house possessed a "fair long gallery" 160 feet in length, a chapel, a magnificent great hall, two studies, and "a proper library to lay books in." Its gardens were extensive and of great variety, the whole estate comprising some 270 acres of woods and meadows. Oxford may well have adapted one of the larger rooms as a private theater, where he could try out scenes and plays before an invited audience of friends and literary colleagues, and indulge his own enthusiasm for acting. Women's parts, contrary to the convention of the time, were probably played by cultured women from his own social circle, rather than boys. Indeed, it may have been at King's Place that his youngest daughter, Susan, who was only ten years old in 1597, developed her love of acting. She would later play in the masques of Ben Jonson and Inigo Jones at the court of James I.[174]

The year he moved into King's Place, Oxford wrote to Lord Burghley to support a proposed match between his middle daughter, Bridget Vere, and William Herbert, the elder son of the 2nd Earl of Pembroke and his wife, Mary Sidney. As the 3rd Earl of Pembroke, William Herbert, was destined be one of the "incomparable pair of brethren" to whom the First Folio was dedicated in 1623. His father, the 2nd Earl, was well known to Oxford as the patron of a company of players, Pembroke's Men, which had been in existence since the 1570s and which in the 1590s performed certain Shakespeare plays including *Titus Andronicus* and *Henry VI, Part 3*. That same year, 1597, the company had caused a scandal by performing a highly seditious play by Thomas Nashe and Ben Jonson, *The Isle of Dogs,* a satirical comedy that seems to have been less than delicate in exposing the vital links between the queen, a certain playwright, and the succession. A taboo had clearly been violated, as the words of their contemporaray Francis Meres attest: "As Actaeon was worried by his own hounds, so is Tom Nashe of his Isle of Dogs." The play was called in and destroyed, warrants were issued for the authors' arrest, and the public theaters were ordered closed. In the end, Bridget Vere did not marry William Herbert, but her younger sister Susan did eventually marry his brother Philip, later Earl of Montgomery, the other half of "the incomparable pair of brethren." The eldest sister, Elizabeth, over whose legitimacy there had been such a coil, had married another man with a deep interest in theater, William Stanley, 6th Earl of Derby, patron of his brother's old company Lord Strange's Men—now Derby's Men—which put on the first recorded performance of Shakespeare's *Richard III*. In June 1599 it was reported in a private letter between two friends that "the Earl of Derby is busied only in penning comedies for the common players."

Under the will of Henry VIII, Derby, like his brother before him, had a claim to the throne through his mother, Lady Margaret Clifford, heiress presumptive to Elizabeth from 1578 until her own death in 1596. He was also the titular King of the Isle of Man. Through the marriage of Stanley to his granddaughter, Burghley was once again bringing a royal claimant within his sphere of control. The wedding was celebrated at Greenwich in the presence of the queen in January 1595, and it is thought that one of Shake-speare's plays, probably *A Midsummer Night's Dream,* was performed by the Lord Chamberlain's Men as part of the festivities. Oxford would most likely have directed the play, and if his skit on himself in the figure of Don Adriano de Armado in *Love's Labour's Lost* is to be taken seriously, he may even have acted in it. Not everyone would have approved, of course, and in a letter written to Burghley five days after the wedding, John Carey, Lord Hunsdon's second son, flattered the old man by saying that his sterling presence in his granddaughter's life meant that "the imperfections of her father [i.e., Oxford] shall be no blemish to her honour." Oxford, then, was intimately connected with all the major acting companies of the time (Charles Howard, patron of the Lord Admiral's Men and a cousin of Anne Boleyn, was also well known to him) and, crucially, with those who would shepherd the publication of the First Folio in the twilight of James's reign.

Lord Burghley died in August 1598, leaving the royal treasury bare. In his final illness he was visited by the queen, who fed him soup with her own hand. Despite a painful swelling in his hands, he managed to take up his pen and write to his son Robert to record this signal act of royal favor. As ever, nothing that shed a benevolent or sympathetic light over him or his would be omitted from the painstaking record that he was leaving for posterity. Yet, as these remarkable lines attest, Burghley let his guard slip just a little:

> I pray you diligently and effectually to let Her Majesty understand
> how her singular kindness doth overcome my power to acquit it,
> who, though she will not be a mother, yet she showeth herself, by
> feeding me with her own princely hand, as a careful norice [nurse].

"Who, though she will not be a mother" can hardly mean "the queen will not have a child now that she is sixty-five years old," for that would be to state the blindingly obvious. Rather, it means Elizabeth was determined not to acknowledge that she was a mother, preferring to maintain the fiction of her virginity.

Burghley left nothing to Oxford in his will, nor did he mention his name. His political legacy he entrusted to his son Robert, whom he had trained up from an early age. The decade since his daughter Anne's death had not been a happy one for his relations with Oxford, though he had continued to "support" his son-in-law in his peerlessly equivocal manner, alienating Oxford's children as thoroughly as he had his property. In a letter to Robert Cecil on her grandfather's death, Bridget Vere wrote, "And now that he [Burghley] is gone that was so dear unto you and me, you are unto me as a father in his stead, and in having you I shall think the want of him to be the less." This attitude must have been a bitter pill for Oxford.

The year of Burghley's death was also the year when Oxford was dug deeper beneath his fictive name, as witness the publication of Francis Meres's *Palladis Tamia,* praising Shakespeare for his supremacy in both comedy and tragedy. There were those, however, who were not prepared to see Oxford obliterated without offering some tribute to his genius. Richard Barnefield smuggled this eulogy into *The Encomium of Lady Pecunia* (1598), with the usual puns on Oxford's family name, Vere (emphasis mine):

> And Shakespeare then, whose honey-flowing vain
> (Pleasing the world) thy praises doth obtain,
> Whose *Venus* and whose *Lucrece* (sweet and chaste)
> Thy name in fame's immortal book have plac'd.
> Live *ever* thou, at least in fame live *ever.*
> Well may the body die, but fame dies *never.*

Both Southampton and Essex remained in disgrace after returning from the war in Ireland without the queen's leave in September 1599; and Essex, chafing under his restraint and denied access to the queen, began to foment rebellion. He was bent on ousting his arch-enemy Robert Cecil, by force of arms if necessary, though he was accused by some—and not without cause—of desiring the throne for himself. In order to spread insurgency and educate the populace of London as to their real agenda, Essex and Southampton had Shakespeare's *Richard II* played at venues throughout the capital, with an abdication scene, absent in the quarto of 1597, specially added by the author. In this now infamous scene, King Richard takes the crown and hands it to his successor, the rebel Henry Bolingbroke.

This would suggest that the earls were hoping to persuade the decrepit Elizabeth to abdicate, but in favor of whom? Essex or Southampton? The play also condemns those "caterpillars of the commonwealth" who lead the monarch astray with flattery and false counsel. In Sonnet 35 Oxford admits to Southampton that he has "authoriz[ed] thy trespass with compare," i.e., given him precedents for rebellion in his plays. Provoked by Cecil's cunning, Essex finally rode out of his house at the head of a company of men on February 8, 1601, and went careering through the City shouting, "For the Queen! For the Queen! A plot is laid for my life!" Southampton, as ever, was with him. Had they gone in the opposite direction, westward to Whitehall, they may well have succeeded in taking the palace. As it was, the armed support they had been promised by Sheriff Smyth did not materialize, and the rebellion petered out. After a skirmish on Ludgate Hill, in which Essex was shot through the hat, the leaders returned to their base, where later that evening they surrendered to Lord Admiral Howard, who had come to arrest them in the name of the queen. That night the two earls were conveyed to the Tower.

In eleven days they were standing trial at Westminster Hall before a tribunal of twenty-five peers, chief among them Edward de Vere, Earl of Oxford. For most of the proceedings, Robert Cecil was concealed (like Polonius) behind an arras, but he came out to deny Essex's accusation that he had supported the claim to the English throne of the Infanta of Spain. Both Essex and Southampton defended themselves with eloquence and dignity, but Essex's plea that his primary aim had been to rescue the queen from her enemies was trumped by the crown prosecutor, Edward Coke, who asserted that the earl had coveted the title King Robert I. (Coke was Robert Cecil's nephew.) According to the historian Lucy Aikin, Southampton "behaved throughout with a mildness and an ingenuous modesty which moved all hearts in his favour." Yet the verdict was a foregone conclusion, and when the prisoners were led away the ax was turned toward them, as men condemned to die. What must it have cost Oxford to rise with his fellow peers and, looking upon his beloved son, pronounce the word "aye" to the charge of "guilty"? Essex was beheaded two days later, on Ash Wednesday, after fully confessing his fault upon the scaffold. Executed in the heart of winter, Essex was the god-king of the dying year, sacrificed to ensure the fertility of the famine-struck kingdom and the continuing vigor of its sixty-seven-year-old monarch. He had been Elizabeth's final mask of youth. Southampton's sentence was commuted to life imprisonment. It is likely that the condition of this reprieve was a full renunciation of his claim to the throne, and for Oxford his oath that he would never reveal his relationship to Southampton, nor promote his royal claim.

Essex's rebellion had been created as much by Oxford-Shakespeare's writing as anything, for his plays had been the vortex of alienated-son energy that drew in the rebellious earls. Both Essex and Southampton had in a sense become actors in the Shakespearean drama of succession; but then, so had all the great figures of the time, including Elizabeth.

The failure of the rebellion in 1601 marked to all intents and purposes the end of Elizabeth's reign. The execution of Essex was the ultimate crime, the murder of a son, a chilling reminder to Oxford of what he could expect—if not literally, then figuratively. Of course, it could be argued that Elizabeth had no choice; her hand was forced by Robert Cecil, the worm in the rose. Whatever the truth, the execution turned her wits. Guilt deprived her of sleep (as it deprives Lady Macbeth); and, according to her godson Sir John Harington, she would pace up and down her privy chamber, stamping her feet and thrusting her rusty sword into the arras. He interpreted her actions as a sign that she was riven with fear at the thought of further insurrection, but this hardly seems plausible. The "thick-coming fancies" that kept her from her rest were rather the phantoms of her victims. Like a senile, epicene Hamlet, she was haunted—though in her case not by the ghost of a dead father, but by the wraith of a murdered son. "I did her wrong," mutters Lear, in thinking about his banished child. Maybe old Queen Margaret's curse to Queen Elizabeth, Edward IV's wife, in *Richard III* rang in her head—"Die neither mother, wife, nor England's Queen!" —for in executing Essex she had broken her bond with the people.

The fall of Essex was simply another mirror in which Oxford, artist that he was, reviewed his own ruin. As he revised *Richard III* to immortalize the hunchbacked Cecil as one of the world's Machiavels, he added a passage depicting the grief-stricken Queen Elizabeth, mourning the death of her husband Edward.[175] The tears were his, but he gave them to Elizabeth, for it comforted him to think of her mourning his loss:

> Give me no help in lamentation:
> I am not barren to bring forth complaints:
> All springs reduce their currents to mine eyes,
> That I, being govern'd by the watery moon,
> May send forth plenteous tears to drown the world.
> Ah, for my husband, for my dear lord Edward!
>
> (II.ii.66–71)

With Southampton now condemned to rot in the Tower, "a jewel hung in ghastly night," as he puts it in Sonnet 27, and his own life buried forever beneath the rubble of political falsehood, Oxford may have contemplated suicide, as his forlorn plaints in Sonnet 66 suggest he did:

> Tired with all these for restful death I cry:
> As to behold desert a beggar born,
> And needy nothing trimmed in jollity,
> And purest faith unhappily forsworn,
> And gilded honour shamefully misplaced,
> And maiden virtue rudely strumpeted,
> And right perfection wrongfully disgraced,
> And strength by limping sway disabled,
> And art made tongue-tied by authority,
> And folly, doctor-like, controlling skill,
> And simple truth miscalled simplicity,
> And captive good attending captain ill:
>> Tired with all these, from these would I be gone,
>> Save that to die I leave my love alone.

He was indeed a deserving man who had been born a beggar; he, too, had dressed himself in gay apparel, though at heart a nobody, without heirs or antecedents; and he had pledged himself in deepest love to his sovereign, only to be shamefully betrayed. It is a moving enumeration of the broken troth at the heart of his relationship with Elizabeth, and the effect it had on his art and freedom, to say nothing of the liberty of their son.

Elizabeth died on March 24, 1603, in her seventieth year, leaving no will and without having designated a successor. But Cecil and the Privy Council had long been paving the way for James of Scotland, son of the executed Mary Queen of Scots, to step into her shoes, and an envoy was sent to invite him into his new kingdom. A month after the queen's death, Oxford wrote in a letter to Robert Cecil:

> I cannot but find a great grief in myself to remember the mistress which we have lost, under whom both you and myself from our greenest years have been in a manner brought up; and although it hath pleased God after an earthly kingdom to take her up into a more permanent and heavenly state, wherein I do not doubt but she is crowned with glory, and to give us a prince wise, learned, and enriched with all virtues, yet the long time which we spent in her service, we cannot look for so much left of our days as to bestow upon another, neither the long acquaintance and kind familiarities wherewith she did use us, we are not ever to expect from another prince, as denied by the infirmity of age and common course of reason. In this common shipwreck, mine is above all the rest, who least regarded, though often comforted of all her followers, she hath left to try my fortune among the alterations of time and chance, either without sail whereby to take the advantage of any prosperous gale, or with anchor to ride till the storm be overpast. There is nothing therefore left to my comfort but the excellent virtues and deep wisdom wherewith God hath endued our new Master and Sovereign Lord, who doth not come amongst us as a stranger but as a natural prince, succeeding by right of blood and inheritance, not as a conqueror, but as the true shepherd of Christ's flock to cherish and comfort them.

In the rush to eulogize the departed queen there was no elegy to Elizabeth from the pen of Shakespeare, a conspicuous omission until one realizes that he could hardly have done such a thing without revealing his true feelings, and therefore his identity. His silence, however, did not go unnoticed. Henry Chettle, in *England's Mourning Garment* (1603), wrote:

> Nor doth the silver-tongued Melicert
> Drop from his honied muse one sable tear
> To mourn her death that graced his desert,

And to his lays opened her royal ear.
Shepherd, remember our Elizabeth,
And sing her rape, done by that Tarquin, death.

One could argue that Oxford-Shakespeare had already written his lamentation for Elizabeth in "The Phoenix and the Turtle," a haunting, almost religious poem in which he mourns the death of their clandestine royal line. The *threnos* that ends the poem speaks of their esoteric union, and how it—together with the poet's works (i.e., truth)—must finally be consigned to the realm of those things that can only "seem, but cannot be":

> Beauty, Truth, and Rarity,
> Grace in all simplicity,
> Here enclosed, in cinders lie.
>
> Death is now the *Phoenix* nest,
> And the *Turtles* loyal breast,
> To eternity doth rest.
>
> Leaving no posterity,
> 'Twas not their infirmity,
> It was married Chastity.
>
> Truth may seem, but cannot be,
> Beauty brag, but tis not she,
> Truth and Beauty buried be.
>
> (lines 53–64)

The paradox of "married chastity" would have pointed Shakespeare's readers in the right direction. Had they turned to *Macbeth*, they would have read a bitterer version:

> Upon my head they plac'd a fruitless crown,
> And put a barren scepter in my gripe,
> Thence to be wrench'd with an unlineal hand,
> No son of mine succeeding.
>
> (III.i.60–63)

Did Elizabeth ever hear these words of Macbeth's and, if so, what thoughts passed through her head?

Although Oxford was careful to assure Cecil of his loyalty to the new sovereign by stressing James's "right of blood and inheritance," only a week before Elizabeth's death he had invited the Earl of Lincoln to supper at King's Place, where after a sumptuous dinner he "inveighed much against the nation of the Scots, and began to enter into question of his Majesty's [i.e. James's] title [to the throne]." Oxford then urged Lincoln to send for his nephew, Lord Hastings (heir to the earldom of Huntingdon), who was of royal blood, and to convey him to France, where he would find friends to back his cause. Oxford was no doubt trying to draw out Lincoln to test the opposition to James, for uppermost in his thoughts was surely not Henry Hastings but Henry Wriothesley, his own son, imprisoned in the Tower. As it was, Lincoln got cold feet and blabbed to Sir John Peyton, the lieutenant of the Tower, who later justified his failure to act on the news by claiming that Oxford was wholly without means "to raise any combustion in the state"—that he was, in the words of Professor Nelson, "a toothless lion." It seems that Oxford's imagination got the better of him on this occasion; he could not resist the hope, however vain, that the Tudor line might still prevail, even at the eleventh hour. The succession never released its hold on his imagination, and in the end Oxford proved "the most active opponent of James among English noblemen at the time of the Queen's death."[176]

Oxford fell into line when he realized that his opposition was unrealistic, and his name, much to Lincoln's astonishment, appeared on the printed proclamation of James's accession as issued by the Privy Council. One of James's first acts was to pardon Southampton, who was released from the Tower in April and was made captain of the Isle of Wight (his own island kingdom). The scholar-king also proved a generous benefactor to the occupant of King's Place, "Great Oxford" as he called him, whom he surely knew as the man behind the name Shake-speare. He renewed Oxford's £1,000 annuity, and granted his long-standing suit for the keepership of the Forest of Essex and also of Havering House, Oxford and Elizabeth's old trysting ground. According to some sources, he also appointed Oxford to the Privy Council. As for the theater, all three companies licensed to perform in London, including the combined company of Oxford's and Worcester's Men, were taken under royal patronage. As lord great chamberlain, Oxford carried the basin and ewer at James's coronation, so that the king of the political realm was offered purificatory water by the man who would become king over the imagination of an entire nation. What wouldn't one give to know what words were exchanged between these two monarchs? Only two months before the ceremony, Oxford had written to Cecil:

> Nothing adorns a king more than justice, nor in anything doth a king more resemble God than in justice, which is the head of all virtue, and he that is endued therewith hath all the rest.

James, well aware of the danger posed by the popular and glamorous Southampton, decided to keep him close and shower him with honors, rather than make him a martyr to the disaffected. When Oxford died—on June 24, 1604, less than a year after James's coronation— James had Southampton arrested, and released the next day. Maybe James thought that without Oxford's restraining hand Southampton might try to make good his claim to the throne. A more likely scenario, given the complete absence of notices at his death, the fact that he left no will, and the rich symbolism of the date of his passing —it was the feast of St. John the Baptist, and the day on which the oak-king was sacrificially burned alive—is that Oxford did not die, but went into hiding, quite possibly on the Isle of Man where his son-in-law and fellow playwright, the Earl of Derby, was king. Some remote corner of the Isle of Wight, Southampton's bailiwick, is another possibility. He may even have gone abroad, in which case James's sudden panic and his interrogation of Oxford's royal son make more sense. James was seeking assurances. But why would Oxford disappear when James had shown him such favor, and was the king made a party to the secret? The likely answer is that Oxford still felt threatened by Robert Cecil, now James's first minister, and was concerned that Cecil might yet attempt to seize his manuscripts and have them destroyed. Oxford was, after all, engaged in the formidable task of converting his stage plays into enduring works of literature. Given Cecil's preference for secrecy, it is unlikely that James would have been told the truth of Oxford's Rosicrucian-style "death."

Evidence of James's ignorance on this score is found in the tributes he paid to the dead author, such as the greatly expanded and amended version of *Hamlet* (the Second Quarto) published in 1604 under the royal coat of arms, and the festival of seven Shakespeare plays he put on at court for the Christmas season that same year. The year 1604 is also when the flood of new Shakespearean publications dried up. Between 1603 and 1622 only three new Shakespeare quartos appear: *King Lear, Troilus and Cressida,* and *Othello.* This means that the rate of publication as compared with 1594 to 1603 had slowed down from one quarto every eight months to one quarto every seven years. Then in 1623, with the publication of the First Folio, we get a sudden flux of eighteen new plays all at once. Something clearly happened in 1603–1604 to bring publication of the Shakespeare plays to a halt for two decades—presumably, the deaths of Elizabeth and Shakespeare. Yet the question still remains: why was publication of the First Folio delayed until 1623, toward the end of James's reign? A likely explanation is that the plays staked out an alternative claim to the throne, and their philosophy of enlightened self-determination was a reproach to a king who believed in his own divine right to the exclusion of everyone else's.

If Oxford did disappear, it might explain the strangely removed quality of *The Tempest,* which reads as though Shakespeare was looking at his life from the outside and seeing with objective freshness all the marvelous characters that made up the essential myth of his soul-life and drove his creativity for four decades. The play could also quite literally tell the story of Oxford's removal from London to a deserted spot, and the growing power of his art over his contemporaries. As Alonso says to Prospero:

> I long
> To hear the story of your life, which must
> Take the ear strangely.
>
> (V.i.312–314)

To which the magus replies, "I'll deliver all," which is Shakespeare's usual invitation to his audience to hear the play again.

The entire action of the play leads up to Prospero's great speech of renunciation, in which he vows to break his staff, bury it in the earth, and "deeper than did ever plummet sound" drown his book, a passage that harks back to Alonso's premature lament for his lost heir, prince Ferdinand: "Therefor my son i'th'ooze is bedded; and / I'll seek him deeper than did ever plummet sound, / And with him there lie mudded." Book and prince both sink to the bottom of the ocean, awaiting their day of restoration.

In *Henry VIII,* which was included in the First Folio of 1623, the fallen Wolsey talks of having swum in a sea of glory, buoyed up with pride but far beyond his depth, only to find himself, once his bubble has burst, at the mercy of "a rude stream that must for ever hide me," like Ophelia pulled singing beneath the current. It is significant that in his 1619 dedication of the three books of *Primaleon of Greece,* published as a single volume, Anthony Munday used the image of the sleeping book, because *Primaleon* is recognized by scholars as a primary source for *The Tempest.* The first two books were originally dedicated to Oxford in the 1590s, and even the later dedication to his son Henry de Vere was used by Munday as an opportunity to praise the father:

> Among the embrions of my younger brain, these three several parts of *Primaleon of Greece* were the tribute of my duty and service to him [Oxford]: which books, having long time slept in oblivion, and (in a manner) quite out of memory: by favour of these more friendly times, coming once more to be seen on the world's public theatre.

The Tempest is full of images of drowning, slumbering—and awakening. Although the author has been at such pains to assert his identity through his works, there still remains at the end of the play, in Prospero's parting lines, the fear that it will be swallowed up for good by our ignorance, and that he will lose not one kingdom, but two. That is why he seeks our imaginative participation; without it, his cause is lost and he remains an outcast of the island:

> Gentle breath of yours my sails
> Must fill, or else my project fails.
> (Epilogue, lines 11–12)

In drowning his book, however, and thus returning it to the collective unconscious, Shakespeare ensures that it will work from within us, gradually releasing its truth over time, its magic seeping up into the hearts of an entire civilization.

In his long poem *Sir Philip Sydney's Ourania* (1606), having described Oxford as "Albion's pearl," Nathaniel Baxter pays him this moving tribute:

> Weak are the wits that measure Noble-men,
> By accidental things that ebb and flow;
> His learning made him honourable then,
> As trees their goodness by their fruits do show,
> So we do Princes by their virtues know.
> For riches, if they make a King; tell then;
> What differ poorest Kings from poorest men?
>
> (lines 15–21)

Oxford may have been the poorest king, but the kingdom he created was of the richest sort, and in one way or another we in the English-speaking world have all become his subjects.

Earlier in the book, much was made of Hamlet's cause, and his plea to Horatio to report it and him aright to the unsatisfied. Only one of the Earl of Oxford's books has so far been found, a 1568 Geneva Bible discovered at the Folger Shakespeare Library in 1990 and annotated in the original owner's hand. Oxford's Bible marginalia speak to those themes which were at the heart of his life, and which prove to have been the energy centers of the Shakespeare canon.[177] The one that perhaps stands out above all is the idea that he will be vindicated in heaven, and brought forth to the light. He has, for instance, marked Revelation 3.5, "He that overcometh shall be clothed in white array, and I will not put out his name out of the book of life, but I will confess his name before my Father, and before his Angels," a poignant verse for one whose name had been obliterated on earth. Most moving of all, however, given the kingdom he had lost and the rehabilitation he sought through his works, which were truly his good deeds, is the following gloss on Psalm 37, which he underlined heavily:

> As the hope of the daylight causeth us not to be offended with the darkness of the night, so ought we patiently to trust that God will clear our cause and restore us to our right.

Shine forth, thou star of poets!

Acknowledgments

My interest in the Shakespeare authorship question was sparked when I was a child, by my late grandfather, Charles St. Albans, who was president of the Shakespearean Authorship Society (formerly the Shakespeare Fellowship) and a genial exponent of the case for Edward de Vere. He also owned the Gheeraerts portrait of de Vere, whose probing blue-gray eyes followed me around the room with such intentness. My first thanks go to him for providing a link, in blood and spirit, to our exceptional forebear.

I should also like to thank my South African godmother, Daphne Wray, who sent me a copy of J. Thomas Looney's *Shakespeare Identified* when I was sixteen, as this was the impetus for my own scholarly interest in the subject. Looney was, of course, the first to rescue Edward de Vere from oblivion, and I am greatly in his debt, and in that of those bright, indefatigable scholars, now deceased, who succeeded him, in particular B. M. Ward, Percy Allen, Eva Turner Clark, Dorothy Ogburn, Charles Wisner Barrell, and William Plumer Fowler. Among these, I should like to single out for special mention two exceptional Oxfordians, whom I had the honor of knowing and befriending: Charlton Ogburn Jr., author of *The Mysterious William Shakespeare* (1984); and Ruth Loyd Miller, whose tireless research is still opening up vistas for today's authorship sleuths.

My deep gratitude goes to all those in the Shakespeare Oxford Society (S.O.S.) who made my speaking tour of America (1991–1997) not only possible but pleasurable and meaningful, in particular Isabel Holden, who arranged my very first lecture, at the Folger Shakespeare Library in April 1991; my tour manager, John Louther, and his wife Pat; his successor, Trudy Atkins; John Price, then the president of the S.O.S.; and Elisabeth Sears, another former president. There isn't room to mention all those who sponsored me and were my hosts along the way, so all must accept my heartfelt thanks in the names of Sandy Hochberg, Michael Pisapia, Len Deming, Richard Whalen, Sally Mosher, Randall Sherman, Russ des Cognets, Ron Hess, Carole Sue Lipman, Aaron Tatum, Phil Haldeman, Richard Kennedy, Wayne Shore, Elliott Stone, Lynn Gargill, Warren Wyneken, Morse Johnson, Bill Hunt, Patrick Horsbrugh, Dr. David Goldenberg, Pidge Sexton, Professor Felicia Londré, Larry Wells, Joe Hunter, Bill Allison, Irvin Matus, and the Cheney family of Macungie, Pennsylvania.

Many Oxfordian scholars in the United States have inspired and informed my thinking on Shakespeare, in particular Charles Boyle, who founded and directed the Ever Theatre; Bill Boyle, former editor of the Shakespeare Oxford Newsletter and founder of Shakespeare Online Authorship Resources (SOAR); Hank Whittemore, author of the definitive work on Shakespeare's Sonnets, *The Monument,* and a true pioneer of the new Shakespeare paradigm; plumber of the Tudor soul, Sandy Hochberg; author and researcher Betty Sears; Dr. Roger Stritmatter, whose scholarship is always an inspiration; Stephanie Hopkins Hughes, whose penetrating observations on the age have been of benefit to all Oxfordians; Oxford's finest biographer, Mark Anderson; the author and columnist Joe Sobran, whose *Alias Shakespeare* is as elegant and cogent a statement of the case for de Vere as one is likely to encounter; and Professor Daniel Wright of Concordia University, founding director of the Shakespeare Authorship Studies Conference and head of the Shakespeare Authorship Research Center. Thanks are also due to Simon Simpson, Laura Wilson, Verily Anderson, Mark Rylance, Dr. William Leahy, Dr. John Rollett, Lisa Stephens Immen, Sue Campbell, Adrian and Sally Stott, and John and Valerie Nicholson for many fascinating hours discussing the Shakespeare authorship question.

I want to give special thanks to the author, musician, and composer Sally Mosher for her insightful comments on the first draft of the book, and likewise to the Shakespeare scholar Adam Hall for his sage direction and encouragement. De Vere's descendant Lawrence David Moon, himself a poet, novelist, and composer, was of invaluable assistance in reducing the monstrous first draft to some semblance of a publishable book or, as he put it, "discovering the lotus in the forest." Randall Sherman, former president of the Shakespeare Oxford Society, provided me with a bowered retreat at his home in Nevada City to tackle the bulk of the editing. And more thanks than I can express are due to Simon Horton for his deep counsels.

In addition, I have received kind assistance from the staff of the London Library, in particular Gosia Lawik, the Folger Shakespeare Library, Washington, D.C., the Huntington Library in San Marino, California, and the Classics Department of Uppingham School, ably directed by Will Chuter.

I should like to thank my erstwhile agent Natasha Fairweather and my publisher Morgan Entrekin for their faith in this work; and of course my editor, the unflappable Jamison Stoltz, for his skill and vision in steering me toward a better-written, better-argued book. Even his thundering marginal prohibitions—"No, no, no!" or "Cut, cut, cut!"—began to seem necessary, even welcome restraints upon my more quixotic sallies. My gratitude also goes to the copyeditor Susan Garner, who scoured and polished the text to great effect.

Thanks as ever go to my family and friends for their support, especially to my mother, Rosemary Exmouth, and my grandmother Rose Scoones for their singular generosity, and to my son James for his good-humored forbearance.

Last, but by no means least, I should like to thank the book's dedicatee, Lisa Marie Wilson, for her help, which has been heroic on every conceivable level. Time and again she rescued both book and author from despair, finally guiding them triumphantly home. Her deep insights into the Shakespeare canon, of which I have shamelessly availed myself, often lit the way. From the bottom of my heart, thank you.

Notes

1. It is in fact around four times larger in area (nine inches by seven and a quarter) than the title-page portrait of any other author of the period. See Dr. John M. Rollett, "The Mystery of Shakespeare's Doublet," unpublished article, 2006.

2. They would also have known that the mute swan was given royal status in the twelfth century.

3. Clare Asquith writes: "Reputed scholars such as John [Payne] Collier and James Halliwell-Philips, who dedicated their lives to consolidating the legend of the English Bard, are known to have stolen, forged and destroyed numerous documents as they worked their way unsupervised through various libraries and private collections," *Shadowplay*, Public Affairs, New York, 2005, p. 282.

4. They are Emilia Lanier, Fulke Greville, Henry Neville, Mary Sidney, and the mysterious William Hastings.

5. Frank Harris, *The Man Shakespeare and His Tragic Life Story*, Frank Palmer, London, 1911, p. 18.

6. Looney's publisher begged him to adopt a pseudonym himself, but Looney was not interested in such politic subterfuge.

7. For the full list see J. T. Looney, *Shakespeare Identified*, Cecil Palmer, London, 1920, pp. 118–119 and p. 131.

8. Warren Hope (with Kim Holston), *The Shakespeare Controversy*, McFarland, Jefferson, N.C., 1992, p. 111.

9. All these passages of Crosby's are taken from his essay "Shakespeare's Attitude toward the Working Classes," in Leo Tolstoy, *Tolstoy on Shakespeare*, Funk and Wagnalls, New York, 1907.

10. Gary Taylor, *Reinventing Shakespeare*, Oxford University Press, Oxford, 1989, pp. 114–115.

11. Harris, *The Man Shakespeare and His Tragic Life Story*, p. xi.

12. Stephen Greenblatt, *Will in the World: How Shakespeare Became Shakespeare*, Pimlico, London, 2005, p. 155.

13. In Sonnet 69 Shakespeare tells Southampton, "But why thy odour matcheth not thy show / The soil is this, that thou dost common grow."

14. George Puttenham, *The Arte of English Poesie*, ed. G. D. Willcock and A. Walker, Cambridge University Press, Cambridge, 1936, p. 61.

15. In his Epigram LVI, "On Poet-Ape."

16. Four hundred years later, scholars still don't know the true identity of Martin Mar-prelate.

17. In his *Thesaurus Linguae Graecas* (Geneva, 1572), Henri Estienne refers to Pallas Athena as *hastae vibratrix* ("spear-shaker").

18. *The Sovereign Flower*, Methuen, London, 1958, p.13.

19. *Shylock, The History of a Character*, Benjamin Blom, New York, 1968, p. 22.

20. Stephanie Hopkins Hughes, *Oxford and Byron*, Paradigm Press, Portland, Oreg., 1993, p. 26.

21. In *Gorboduc* by Thomas Norton and Thomas Sackville, Queen Videna describes the king her husband as "In kind a father, not in kindliness" (I.i.18). More famously, Hamlet describes Claudius as "A little more than kin, and less than kind" (I.ii.65), because he is both uncle and father ("more than kin") yet fails to treat Hamlet with the love one might expect from a blood relative ("less than kind").

22. *Hamlet*, II.ii.372.

23. Mortimer Levine, *Tudor Dynastic Problems*, George Allen and Unwin, London, 1973, p. 156.

24. Lytton Strachey, *Elizabeth and Essex*, Chatto and Windus, London, 1928 (reprinted, Penguin, 1971), p. 19.

25. Marc Shell, ed., intr., *Elizabeth's Glass*, University of Nebraska Press, 1993; fol.19r–v.

26. In *Hamlet*, IV.iii., when Gertrude asks her son if he has forgotten her, he replies: "No, by the rood, not so. / You are the Queen, your husband's brother's wife."

27. He also made advances to Elizabeth's half-sister, Princess Mary. In this he was like Edmund in *King Lear*.

28. "Wit" in those days meant intelligence rather than sense of humor.

29. Duchess of Feria (ascribed to Henry Clifford, a member of her household), *Life of Jane Dormer*, London, 1887, p. 86.

30. For a thorough examination of Elizabeth's medical record, see Frederick Chamberlin, *The Private Character of Queen Elizabeth*, Bodley Head, London, 1921. Chamberlin attributes Elizabeth's anemia, bad

heart, and weak constitution to "a diseased father," hinting at con-
genital syphilis as the Tudor curse.

31. Victor von Klarwill, ed., *Queen Elizabeth and Some Foreigners,*
    Brentano's, New York, 1928, pp. 113–115.

32. John Lingard, *History of England* 8 vols., 1819–1830, Vol. 5, p. 258.

33. Carolly Erickson, *The First Elizabeth,* Robson, London, 2001, p. 194
    (originally published 1983).

34. Roy Strong, *Gloriana: The Portraits of Elizabeth I,* Pimlico, London,
    1987, p. 147.

35. James Bennett, ed., *The Works of Roger Ascham,* White, Cochrane, Lon-
    don, 1815, pp. 181, 182.

36. *Shakespeare, Oxford, and Elizabethan Times,* Denis Archer, London,
    1933; p. 70. Admiral Holland's information comes from the so-called
    Scandal Letter written by Mary Queen of Scots to Elizabeth c.1583–
    1584, in which she lists certain charges made against Elizabeth by the
    Countess of Shrewsbury.

37. *Shakespeare After All,* Anchor, New York, 2005, pp. 558–559.

38. Shell, *Elizabeth's Glass,* p. 121: "Alas, yea, for Thou hast broken the
    kindred of my old father, calling me daughter of adoption."

39. The Scandal Letter (see note 36), is reproduced in Chamberlin, *The
    Private Character of Queen Elizabeth,* pp. 166–169. The original is at
    Hatfield House.

40. Philip Morant, *The History and Antiquities of the County of Essex,*
    T. Osborne, London, 1763–1768, vol. 2, p. 293.

41. The legal proceedings, including Golding's statement, are in Latin. I
    have relied on the translation by Louis Thorn Golding in his book *An
    Elizabethan Puritan* (Richard R. Smith, New York, 1937), which is
    quoted in Alan Nelson's *Monstrous Adversary,* pp. 40–41. Other trans-
    lations, however, render the relevant Latin phrase as "under fourteen
    years of age" rather than "a minor of fourteen years." There seems to
    be no authoritative reading as yet.

42. B. M. Ward, *The Seventeenth Earl of Oxford,* John Murray, London,
    1928, p. 8.

43. Lawrence Stone, *The Crisis of the Aristocracy 1558–1641* (abridged ed.),
    Oxford University Press, Oxford, 1967, p. 306.

44. There is also, in the portrait of Thomas Woodstock, an admixture of
    Oxford's other early "protectors," namely William Cecil and Arthur
    Golding.

45. Mary Dewar, *Sir Thomas Smith: A Tudor Intellectual in Office,* Athlone,
    London, 1964, p. 14.

46. For my knowledge of Sir Thomas Smith and his milieu I am indebted to Stephanie Hopkins Hughes, "Shakespeare's Tutors: The Education of Edward de Vere," 2000 (unpublished manuscript).

47. George Puttenham, *The Arte of English Poesie,* London, 1589, book 1, chap. XXXI.

48. "Windsor Forest," lines 291–292.

49. For further details see "Relation made to Sir Francis Englefield by an Englishman named Arthur Dudley, claiming to be the son of Queen Elizabeth," in Dorothy and Charlton Ogburn Sr., *This Star of England,* Coward-McCann, New York, 1952, pp. 1252–1256.

50. Ovid, *Metamorphoses* (trans. Mary M. Innes), Penguin, London, 1984, Book XV, lines 872–879.

51. *Monstrous Adversary*, Liverpool University Press, Liverpool, 2003, p. 46.

52. See Nelson, *Monstrous Adversary,* p. 306 and p. 475, n. 10.

53. "The Political Use of the Stage in Shakspere's Time," *New Shakspere Society Transactions,* July 10, 1874, p. 371.

54. From a letter written by Mendoza to Gabriel de Zayas, secretary to Philip II of Spain, quoted in B. M. Ward, *The Seventeenth Earl of Oxford,* John Murray, London, 1928, pp. 160–162.

55. Cecil Papers, xiii, p.109 (298/2). Fletcher's original text, *In nuptias clarissimi D. Edouardi Vere,* is in Latin hexameters; the translation used here is B. M. Ward's in *The Seventeenth Earl of Oxford,* pp. 60–61.

56. Historical Manuscripts Commission, *Rutland,* i, p. 96.

57. HMC, *Rutland,* i, p. 94.

58. Lodge (1791), ii, pp. 100–101 (from Talbot Papers, vol. F, f. 79).

59. Public Record Office, SP 12/91[/36], f. 64.

60. Cecil Papers 9/1; April 27, 1576.

61. John Nichols, *The Progresses and Public Processions of Queen Elizabeth,* London, 1823, Vol. 2, pp. 388–389.

62. Dorothy Ogburn and Charlton Ogburn Sr., *This Star of England,* Coward-McCann, New York, 1952, p. 837.

63. Thomas Wright, *The History and Topography of the County of Essex,* G. Virtue, London, 1836, Vol. 1, p. 516.

64. Barry Took, *"All's Well that Ends Well,"* in Roger Sales, ed., *Shakespeare in Perspective,* Vol. 1, Ariel, London, 1982.

65. "But your Majesty may think my suit will be very long where I am so long ere I begin it," spouts the troubled Burghley, following it five lines later with this seventeen-line sentence: "My suit therefore shall be presently to your Majesty but in general sort, that whereas I am, by God's visitation with some infirmity and yet not yet great, stayed from

coming to do my duty to your Majesty at this time, and my daughter, the Countess of Oxford, also occasioned to her great grief to be absent from your Majesty's Court, and that the occasion of her absence may be diversely reported to your Majesty, as I said before, by some of ignorance by some percase otherwise, it may please your Majesty—because the ground and working thereupon toucheth me as nearly as any worldly cause in my conceit can do to continue your princely consideration of us both—of me as of an old worn servant that dare compare with the best, the greatest, the oldest and the youngest, for loyalty and devotion, giving place to many others in other worldly qualities, as your Majesty shall prefer any before me; and of my daughter, your Majesty's most humble young servant, as of one that is towards your Majesty in dutiful love and fear, yea, in fervent admiration of your graces to contend with any her equals, and in the cause betwixt my Lord of Oxford and her, whether it be for respect of misliking in me or misdeeming of hers whereof I cannot yet know the certainty, I do avow in the presence of God and of his angels whom I do call as ministers of his ire, if in this I do utter any untruth."

66. Ben Jonson, *Poetaster,* I.i. The original Latin lines are from Ovid's *Amores,* I.xv.

67. Harold Clark Goddard, *The Meaning of Shakespeare*, Chicago University Press, Chicago, Ill., 1951, p. 83.

68. B. M. Ward, *The Seventeenth Earl of Oxford,* p. 83.

69. This translation, apparently by Professor Peter Levi, appears in Richard Malim, ed., *Great Oxford,* Parapress, Tunbridge Wells, 2004, p. 16. Malim is the author of the article in question, "Did Oxford Know Ronsard?"

70. In real life, Surrey never set foot in Italy, though he did employ an Italian jester.

71. Mark Anderson, *Shakespeare by Another Name,* Gotham, New York, 2005, pp. 90–91.

72. I.e., *Dramatic Art by Rote and Extemporaneous.*

73. "Edward de Vere and the Commedia dell'Arte," *Shakespeare Authorship Review,* No. 2, Autumn 1959.

74. *A Hundreth Sundrie Flowres,* ed. G. W. Pigman III, Clarendon Press, Oxford, 2000, p. 341; lines 141–148.

75. Ibid., p. 342; lines 177–178.

76. Ibid., p. 343; lines 213–216.

77. Ibid. pp. 341–342; lines 161–166.

78. Sir Egerton Brydges, ed., *The Paradise of Dainty Devices,* London, 1810, p. 11.

79. Leah Scragg, ed., *Euphues: The Anatomy of Wit* and *Euphues and His England*, Manchester University Press, Manchester, 2003, p. 353.

80. Theodore L. Steinberg, "The Anatomy of *Euphues*," *Studies in English Literature, 1500–1900*, Vol.17, No.1, The English Renaissance (Winter 1977), pp. 27–38.

81. John Lyly, *The Woman in the Moone*, Act I.

82. Scragg, *Euphues*, pp. 336–337.

83. John Lyly, *Love's Metamorphosis*, III.i.

84. John Lyly, *The Woman in the Moone*, Act V.

85. Thomas Watson, *Hekatompathia*, no. VIII.

86. Oxford's letter to the reader that prefaces Bartholomew Clerke's *Courtier* (1571).

87. B. M. Ward, *The Seventeenth Earl of Oxford*, pp. 157–158.

88. Clare Asquith, *Shadowplay*, Public Affairs, New York, 2005, p. 80.

89. *Shakespeare's Imagery*, Cambridge University Press, Cambridge, 1979, p. 4.

90. *Shakespeare's Imagery*, p. 190.

91. *Shakespeare: The Invention of the Human*, Riverhead, New York, 1998, p. 504.

92. *Shakespeare and the Goddess of Complete Being*, Faber and Faber, London, 1992, p. 504.

93. Ibid., pp. 39–40.

94. Or in the words of Professor Don Cameron Allen, "a forty-year-old countess with a taste for Chapel Royal altos."

95. I am indebted to Dr. Roger Stritmatter for this insight. See his "A Law Case in Verse: *Venus and Adonis* and the Authorship Question," *Tennessee Law Review*, Vol. 72, pp. 307–355.

96. Ovid, *Metamorphoses*, Book III, line 198.

97. Lady Macbeth, it will be remembered, says to her husband "look like th'innocent flower, / But be the serpent under't" (I.v.65–66).

98. Katherine Duncan-Jones, "Much Ado with Red and White: The Earliest Readers of Shakespeare's *Venus and Adonis*," *RES New Series*, Vol. XLIV, No. 176, 1993, p. 482.

99. V.ii.13–15.

100. Marguerite Alexander, *Shakespeare and His Contemporaries*, Heinemann, London, 1979, pp. 28–29.

101. Martin Hume, *The Courtships of Queen Elizabeth*, p. 200, quoted in Eva Turner Clark, *Hidden Allusions in Shakespeare's Plays*, Payson, New York, 1931, p. 207.

102. "Of Standins, Pseudonyms, Mummings and Disguisings," *Shakespeare Oxford Newsletter*, Winter 1997, pp. 4–6 and p. 23.

103. Robert Graves in *The White Goddess,* Farrar, Straus, and Giroux, New York, 1948, p. 217, mentions the May Day stag-mummers of Abbot's Bromley in Staffordshire, one of whom would have originally been disguised as a stag, chased, and eaten!

104. *The Man Shakespeare and His Tragic Life-Story,* Frank Palmer, London, 1911, p. 167.

105. A point made by Charles K. Boyle, "Allowed Fools: Notes on an Oxfordian *Twelfth Night,*" unpublished paper, 1992, p. 2.

106. G. G. Gervinus, *Shakespeare Commentaries* (trans. F. E. Bunnett), Smith, Elder and Co., London, 1875, p. 438.

107. According to Hatton's biographer Eric St. John Brooks, *Sir Christopher Hatton,* Cape, London, 1946, this letter was written on June 7, 1573.

108. *The Men Who Would Be King,* Phoenix, London, 2005, p. 161.

109. "I have a device to make all well," says Bottom at the second rehearsal. "Write me a prologue, and let the prologue seem to say we will do no harm with our swords, and that Pyramus is not killed indeed; and for the more better assurance, tell them that I, Pyramus, am not Pyramus, but Bottom the weaver. This will put them out of fear" (III.i.15–21).

110. *Suffocating Mothers,* Routledge, New York and London, 1992, p. 79.

111. These words are spoken by the king in the epilogue to *All's Well That Ends Well.*

112. At the beginning of *Richard II,* when Shakespeare is describing Richard in all his arrogant pride and kingly pomp, the picture he paints is unconvincing. But when, in the second half of the play, he describes the king's gentleness and suffering as the crown slips through his fingers, Richard comes alive.

113. *Shakespeare's History Plays,* Penguin, New York, 1969, p. 147.

114. Ibid., p. 321.

115. Act II, scene i.

116. B. M. Ward, "Shakespeare and the Anglo-Spanish War, 1585–1604," *Revue Anglo-Americaine,* December 1929.

117. Richard Simpson, "The Politics of Shakspere's Historical Plays," *New Shakspere Society Transactions* 1.2 (1874), pp. 413–414.

118. *1 Henry IV,* IV.iii.57–58.

119. *2 Henry VI,* I.iii.59.

120. *The Meaning of Shakespeare,* University of Chicago Press, Chicago, Ill., 1951, p. 386.

121. Raphael Holinshed, *The Third Volume of Chronicles,* London, 1586, p. 659.

122. It is vital to see Shakespeare's other Holinshed kings—Lear, Cymbeline, and Macbeth—as part of a greater historical sequence that
eventually encompasses the entire history of the British race. All the
plays can be fitted into a single cycle or 2,000-year historical sweep
from c. 860 B.C. to the birth of Queen Elizabeth I in A.D. 1533. Yet
if we include the so-called apocryphal plays such as *Locrine* and *The
Birth of Merlin,* it becomes clear that in recording the soul-life of his
nation Shakespeare went right back to the mythic origins of Britain,
beginning with the first king Brutus, from whom the Britons derived
their name. Brutus was the great-grandson of Aeneas, founder of the
Roman state, and was exiled for accidentally killing his father. As
forecast to him by the goddess Diana, his wanderings finally took him
to the island of Albion (the White Land), where he created a new
Troy. He was the father of Locrinus, or Locrine. (It is worth noting that Aeneas was the son of Venus, or Aphrodite, goddess of
beauty and the arts, so that Britain in a sense became a goddess nation.)
Then we have Lear or Llyr who ruled c. 861–801 B.C.; Cymbeline
or Cunobelinus, c. 18 B.C.–A.D. 12; and Vortigern and Aurelius
Ambrosias (who appear in *The Birth of Merlin*), both of whom ruled
in the years before King Arthur and his father Uther Pendragon. These
are followed by Edmund Ironside (A.D. 1000), Macbeth (A.D. 1040),
and the Plantagenet kings John, Edward III and the whole York-
Lancaster crew he spawned, and finally the Tudor king Henry VIII,
father of Shakespeare's own queen, Elizabeth I.

123. *The Anglica Historia of Polydore Virgil* (1534), ed. Denis Hay, Book
XXIV, Royal Historical Society, London, 1950, p. 5.

124. For a full explanation of this theory, see Margaret Murray's extraordinary work *The Divine King in England,* Faber and Faber, London,
1954, pp. 126–144.

125. *Henry VIII and His Court,* Cardinal, London, 1973, p. 260.

126. Charles Wisner Barrell calls her "the Yorkshire Gypsy" in "'Shakespeare's' Own Secret Drama" (Part 6), *Shakespeare Fellowship News-
Letter,* Vol. III, No. 6, October 1942.

127. Passage reproduced in Alan H. Nelson, *Monstrous Adversary: The Life
of Edward de Vere, 17th Earl of Oxford,* Liverpool University Press,
Liverpool, 2003, pp. 218–219.

128. *Hamlet,* II.ii.136.

129. "Six Elegiac Poems, Possibly by Anne Cecil de Vere, Countess of
Oxford," *English Literary Renaissance,* Vol. 19, 1989.

130. I am indebted to Hank Whittemore for this suggestion, which appears in his one-man show *Shake-speares Treason* (2008).

131. The Reverend Dr. John Ward, who became vicar of Stratford-upon-Avon in 1662, wrote in his notebook that Shakespeare "supplied the stage with 2 plays every year, and for that had an allowance so large that he spent at the rate of £1,000 a year, as I have heard." In view of the dialogue between the Archbishop of Canterbury and the Bishop of Ely in Act I Scene i of *Henry V* concerning a payment of £1,000 into the royal coffers, it is interesting to note that Oxford's stipend was paid out of the revenues of the Bishopric of Ely.

132. Hotspur was an ancestor of Margery Wentworth, mother of Lord Admiral Thomas Seymour.

133. From "A song in praise of the English Nobilitie," which appeared in the pamphlet by I.L. [John Lyly?] entitled *An Answer to the untruths, published and printed in Spaine,* 1589.

134. *Shakespeare and Ovid,* Clarendon, Oxford, 1993, p. 101.

135. *Shakespeare After All,* Anchor, New York, 2004, p. 84.

136. *Shakespeare and Ovid,* p. 117.

137. Paul Roche (trans.), *The Orestes Plays of Aeschylus,* New American Library, 1962, p. xiv.

138. Frank Harris, *The Man Shakespeare and His Tragic Life Story,* p. 337.

139. Leo Paul S. Alvarez, "Timon of Athens" in *Shakespeare as Political Thinker,* eds. John Alvis and Thomas G. West, Carolina Academic Press, Durham, N.C., 1981, pp. 157–179.

140. Frank Harris, *The Man Shakespeare and His Tragic Life Story,* p. 339.

141. *Walking,* Beacon, Boston, Mass., 1991, p. 73. Originally published 1862 in *Atlantic* magazine.

142. T. S. Eliot, *The Waste Land and other poems,* Faber and Faber, London, 1940, lines 308–311.

143. James Kirsch, *Shakespeare's Royal Self,* C. G. Jung Foundation, New York, 1966, p. 181.

144. In the First Folio edition of the play.

145. *The White Goddess,* Farrar, Straus, and Giroux, New York, 1948, p. 174.

146. This is John Turner's adaptation of W. B. Yeats's famous saying in *Essays and Introductions,* substituting "nobility" for Yeats's "wisdom." See Graham Holderness, Nick Potter, and John Turner, *Shakespeare Out of Court,* St. Martin's, New York, 1990, pp. 5–6.

147. *Twilight in Italy,* Penguin, London, 1977 (first published by Duckworth, 1916), p. 79.

148. Harold Bloom, *Shakespeare: The Invention of the Human,* Riverhead, New York, 1998, p. 17.

149. In the First Folio Jonson refers to Shakespeare as "a Moniment, without a tombe," "moniment" or "muniment" meaning a document or title deed. It is a particularly well-chosen word, since the plays stake Shakespeare's title to the throne and are, in truth, his title deed.

150. They seem to have stood for Marlowe, Kyd, and Peele, all members of Oxford's circle in the 1580s.

151. It is no coincidence that the twins Crispin and Crispianus, born to a noble Roman family and martyred in A.D. 286, were the patron saints of leatherworkers, a common pun of the time for writers, who traditionally plied the skins of animals with their quills. Nor would Oxford have been ignorant of the fact that the Latin verb *crispare,* from which Crispin derives, means "to shake or brandish" a weapon, as in his adopted name Shake-speare.

152. See Professor Alan Nelson, *Monstrous Adversary,* Liverpool University Press, Liverpool, 2003, p. 334.

153. *Edward de Vere: The Crisis and Consequences of Wardship*, Ashgate, Aldershot, 2005, p. 1.

154. The full title of this anonymous tract published in Cologne in 1592 is *A Declaration of the True Causes of the Great Troubles Presupposed to be Intended against the Realm of England. Wherein the indifferent reader shall manifestly perceive by whom and by what means the realm is brought into these present pretended perils.*

155. "Elizabeth and Shakespeare: England's Power and Glory," unpublished typescript, 1973, p. 524.

156. 2 Corinthians, 3.2–3.

157. *Making a Match: Courtship in Shakespeare and His Society,* Princeton University Press, Princeton, N.J., 1991, p. 240.

158. Stephen Greenblatt, *Will in the World,* p. 127.

159. *Suffocating Mothers,* Routledge, New York and London, 1992, p. 130.

160. "Southampton's Hair," unpublished article, 2002, p. 1.

161. A Rhenish winehouse on the site of the Steelyard complex, owned from medieval times by the Hanseatic merchants, and mentioned several times by Nashe as the venue for many a literary shindig. Inside were two very large paintings by Holbein, *The Triumph of Riches* and *The Triumph of Poverty,* which clearly influenced the author of *Timon of Athens.*

162. *Shakespeare: The Invention of the Human,* Riverhead, New York, 1998, p. 272.

163. *Hidden Allusions in Shakespeare's Plays,* Payson, New York, 1931, p. 488.

164. We would do well to remember James Joyce's words in *Ulysses,* The Bodley Head, London, 1960, (p. 236) during the discussion of

Shakespeare in the Dublin Library: "The supreme question about a work of art is out of how deep a life does it spring?"

165. The Folger Shakespeare Library in Washington, D.C., which owns the portrait, fearful of the implications of the X-ray research, has now declared the portrait to be of Sir Hugh Hamersley, a former lord mayor of London.

166. *The Life of Henry, Third Earl of Southampton, Shakespeare's Patron,* Cambridge University Press, Cambridge, 1922, p. 55. It is surely noteworthy, too, that in the *History of the Order of the Garter* under "Third Earl of Southampton" is written the phrase "Comme son Beau Père" (i.e., like his stepfather), referring to Thomas Wriothesley, the Second Earl of Southampton, suggesting some sort of adoptive relationship.

167. *The Monument,* Meadow Geese, Marshfield Hills, Mass., 2005, p. 55.

168. This line deftly combines all three persons: Southampton's motto was "One for all, all for one" (i.e., "To one, of one"), the queen's "Ever the same" (i.e., "still such" and "ever so"), and Oxford himself was, of course, "ever" or E. Ver.

169. *The Monument,* p. 55.

170. *Shakespeare and the Earl of Southampton,* Hamish Hamilton, London, 1968, p. 55.

171. Princes William and Harry, the two sons of the Prince of Wales, and ultimate heirs of Elizabeth II.

172. B. M. Ward, *The Seventeenth Earl of Oxford,* John Murray, London, 1928, p. 299.

173. Will was the generic name for a shepherd (hence poet). The meanings of Shakespeare have been dealt with in Chapter 1.

174. There is a charming sketch of Susan Vere as Thomyris in Ben Jonson's *The Masque of Queens,* acted at Whitehall, February 2, 1609.

175. King Edward IV, whose wife was Elizabeth Woodville.

176. Alan H. Nelson: *Monstrous Adversary,* Liverpool University Press, Liverpool, 2003, p. 411.

177. Dr Roger Stritmatter's PhD dissertation "Edward de Vere's Geneva Bible," (University of Massachusetts, Amherst, 2000), which analyzes the correspondences between Oxford's marginalia and passages in the Shakespeare canon, cannot be praised too highly.

Bibliography

Adelman, Janet. *Suffocating Mothers: Fantasies of Maternal Origin in Shakespeare's Plays*. Routledge, New York and London, 1992.

Akrigg, G. P. V. *Shakespeare and the Earl of Southampton*. Hamish Hamilton, London, 1968.

Alexander, Marguerite. *Shakespeare and His Contemporaries*. Heinemann, London, 1979.

Alford, Stephen. *Burghley: William Cecil at the Court of Elizabeth I*. Yale University Press, New Haven, Conn., 2008.

Allen, Percy. *The Case for Edward de Vere 17th Earl of Oxford as "Shakespeare."* Cecil Palmer, London, 1930.

——. *The Oxford-Shakespeare Case Corroborated*. Cecil Palmer, London, 1931.

——. *The Plays of Shakespeare and Chapman in Relation to French History*. Denis Archer, London, 1933.

Alvarez, Leo Paul S. "Timon of Athens." In *Shakespeare as Political Thinker,* edited by John Alvis and Thomas G. West, Carolina Academic Press, Durham, N.C., 1981.

Anderson, Mark. *Shakespeare by Another Name*. Gotham, New York, 2005.

Anderson, Verily. *The De Veres of Castle Hedingham*. Terence Dalton, Lavenham, 1993.

Asquith, Clare. *Shadowplay: The Hidden Beliefs and Coded Politics of William Shakespeare*. Public Affairs, New York, 2005.

Bacon, Francis. *Essays*. Dent, London, 1972.

Bate, Jonathan. *Shakespeare and Ovid*. Clarendon, Oxford, 1993.

——. *The Genius of Shakespeare*. Picador, London, 1997.

Beauclerk-Dewar, Peter, and Roger S. Powell. *Right Royal Bastards*. Burke's Peerage and Gentry, London, 2006.

Bennett, James, ed. *The Works of Roger Ascham*. White, Cochrane, London, 1815.

Berry, Wendell. *The Unsettling of America: Culture and Agriculture.* Sierra Club Books, San Francisco, Calif., 1986.

Bloom, Harold. *Shakespeare: The Invention of the Human.* Riverhead, New York, 1998.

———. *Hamlet: Poem Unlimited.* Canongate, Edinburgh, 2003.

Boccaccio, Giovanni. *The Decameron: Selected Tales.* Dover, New York, 2000.

Brandes, George. *William Shakespeare: A Critical Study.* Heinemann, London, 1899.

Braunmuller, A. R., and Michael Hattaway, eds. *The Cambridge Companion to English Renaissance Drama.* Cambridge University Press, Cambridge, 1990.

Brooke, C. F. Tucker. *The Shakespeare Apocrypha.* Oxford University Press, Oxford, 1929.

Brooks, Eric St. John. *Sir Christopher Hatton.* Cape, London, 1946.

Campbell, Lily B. *Tudor Conceptions of History and Tragedy in "A Mirror for Magsitrates."* University of California Press, Berkeley, 1936.

Castiglione, Baldesar. *The Book of the Courtier.* Penguin, London, 1986.

Cecil, David. *The Cecils of Hatfield House.* Houghton Mifflin, Boston, Mass., 1973.

Chamberlin, Frederick. *The Private Character of Queen Elizabeth.* Bodley Head, London, 1921.

———. *The Sayings of Queen Elizabeth.* Bodley Head, London, 1923.

Childs, Jessie. *Henry VIII's Last Victim: The Life and Times of Henry Howard, Earl of Surrey.* Cape, London, 2006.

Chiljan, Katherine, ed. *Letters and Poems of Edward, Earl of Oxford.* Private publication, 1998.

Clark, Eva Turner. *Hidden Allusions in Shakespeare's Plays.* Payson, New York, 1931.

Cook, Ann Jennalie. *The Privileged Playgoers of Shakespeare's London, 1576–1642.* Princeton University Press, Princeton, N.J., 1981.

———. *Making a Match: Courtship in Shakespeare and His Society.* Princeton University Press, Princeton, N.J., 1991.

Crosby, Ernest. "Shakespeare's Attitude toward the Working Classes." In *Tolstoy on Shakespeare,* by Leo Tolstoy. Funk and Wagnalls, New York, 1907.

Danby, John F. *Shakespeare's Doctrine of Nature.* Faber and Faber, London, 1948.

Dawkins, Peter. *Arcadia.* Francis Bacon Research Trust, London, 1988.

De Lisle, Leanda. *After Elizabeth*. HarperCollins, London, 2004.

————. *The Sisters Who Would Be Queen*. Harper, London, 2008.

De Luna, B. N. *The Queen Declined*. Oxford University Press, Oxford, 1970.

Dewar, Mary. *Sir Thomas Smith: A Tudor Intellectual in Office*. Athlone, London, 1964.

Doran, Susan, and Thomas S. Freeman, eds. *The Myth of Elizabeth*. Palgrave Macmillan, New York, 2003.

Dormer, Jane, Duchess of Feria (ascribed to Henry Clifford, a member of her household). *Life of Jane Dormer*. London, 1887.

Edinger, Edward F. *The Eternal Drama: The Inner Meaning of Greek Mythology*. Shambhala, Boston, Mass., 1994.

Eliot, T. S. *The Wasteland and Other Poems*. Faber and Faber, London, 1940.

Erickson, Carolly. *The First Elizabeth*. Robson, London, 1983.

Fowler, William Plumer. *Shakespeare Revealed in Oxford's Letters*. Peter E. Randall, Portsmouth, N.H., 1986.

Fraser, Antonia. *Mary Queen of Scots*. Panther, St. Albans, 1970.

————. *King James I of England*. Weidenfeld and Nicolson, London, 1974.

Frazer, Sir James. *The Golden Bough*. Macmillan, New York, 1963.

Garber, Marjorie. *Shakespeare's Ghost Writers*. Methuen, New York, 1987.

————. *Shakespeare After All*. Anchor, New York, 2004.

Gervinus, G. G., trans. F. E. Bunnett. *Shakespeare Commentaries*. Smith, Elder and Co., London, 1875.

Gillingham, John. *The Wars of the Roses*. Louisiana State University Press, Baton Rouge, 1981.

Given-Wilson, Chris, and Alice Curteis. *The Royal Bastards of Medieval England*. Routledge and Kegan Paul, London, 1984.

Goddard, Harold Clark. *The Meaning of Shakespeare*. University of Chicago Press, Chicago, Ill., 1951.

Golding, Arthur, trans. *Ovid's Metamorphoses*. Paul Dry, Philadelphia, Pa., 2000.

Graves, Robert. *The White Goddess*. Farrar, Straus and Giroux, New York, 1948.

Graves, Robert, trans. *The Golden Ass*. Farrar, Straus and Giroux, New York, 1951.

Green, Martin. *Wriothesley's Roses*. Clevedon, Baltimore, Md., 1993.

Greenblatt, Stephen. *Will in the World: How Shakespeare Became Shakespeare*. Pimlico, London, 2005.

Hackett, Helen. *Virgin Mother, Maiden Queen: Queen Elizabeth and the Cult of the Virgin Mary.* Macmillan, London, 1995.

Hadfield, Andrew. *Shakespeare and Renaissance Politics.* Arden Shakespeare, London, 2004.

Hancox, Joy. *Kingdom for a Stage: Magicians and Aristocrats in the Elizabethan Theatre.* Sutton, Stroud, 2001.

Harris, Frank. *The Man Shakespeare and His Tragic Life Story.* Frank Palmer, London, 1911.

Hartnoll, Phyllis. *A Concise History of the Theatre.* Thames and Hudson, London, 1968.

Haynes, Alan. *Robert Cecil, 1st Earl of Salisbury.* Peter Owen, London, 1989.

———. *The Elizabethan Secret Services.* Sutton, Stroud, 1992.

Hays, Michael L. *Shakespearean Tragedy as Chivalric Romance.* Brewer, Cambridge, 2003.

Hess, W. Ron. *The Dark Side of Shakespeare,* Vol. 1. Writers Club, New York, 2002.

Hibbert, Christopher. *The Virgin Queen: Personal History of Elizabeth I.* Penguin, London, 1992.

Holderness, Graham, Nick Potter, and John Turner. *Shakespeare Out of Court: Dramatizations of Court Society.* St. Martin's, New York, 1990.

Holland, H. H. *Shakespeare, Oxford, and Elizabethan Times.* Denis Archer, London, 1933.

Holmes, Edward. *Discovering Shakespeare.* Mycroft, Chester-le-Street, Co. Durham, 2001.

Holmes, Jeremy. *Narcissism.* Icon, Cambridge, 2001.

Honigmann, E. A. J. *Shakespeare: The "Lost Years."* Manchester University Press, Manchester, 1985.

Hope, Warren (with Kim Holston). *The Shakespeare Controversy.* McFarland, Jefferson, N.C., 1992.

Howarth, David. *Images of Rule: Art and Politics in the English Renaissance.* Macmillan, London, 1997.

Hughes, Stephanie Hopkins. *Oxford and Byron.* Paradigm Press, Portland, Oreg., 1993.

———. *Shakespeare's Tutors: The Education of Edward de Vere.* Unpublished typescript, 2000.

———. "Southampton's Hair," Unpublished article, 2002.

Hughes, Ted. *Shakespeare and the Goddess of Complete Being.* Faber and Faber, London, 1992.

Jones, Ernest. *Hamlet and Oedipus.* Doubleday, New York, 1949.

Jonson, Ben. *Complete Plays.* Dent, London, 1910.

Jung, Emma, and Marie-Louise Von Franz. *The Grail Legend*. Princeton University Press, Princeton, N.J., 1998.

Kerenyi, C. *The Gods of the Greeks*. Thames and Hudson, London, 1951.

Kirsch, James. *Shakespeare's Royal Self*. C. G. Jung Foundation, New York, 1966.

Klarwill, Victor von, ed. *Queen Elizabeth and Some Foreigners*. Brentano's, New York, 1928.

Knight, G. Wilson. *The Crown of Life*. Methuen, London, 1948.

———. *The Mutual Flame*. Methuen, London, 1955.

———. *The Sovereign Flower*. Methuen, London, 1958.

Lacey, Robert. *Sir Walter Ralegh*. Cardinal, London, 1975.

Lawrence, D. H. *Twilight in Italy*. Duckworth, London, 1916; Penguin, London, 1977.

Lemon, Robert, ed. *Calendar of State Papers Domestic, 1547–1625*, 12 vols, London, 1856–1872.

Levine, Mortimer. *Tudor Dynastic Problems, 1460–1571*. George Allen and Unwin, New York, 1973.

Lingard, John. *History of England*, 8 vols. London, 1819–1830.

Lings, Martin. *The Sacred Art of Shakespeare*. Inner Traditions, Rochester, Vt., 1998.

Looney, J. Thomas. *Shakespeare Identified in Edward de Vere, the Seventeenth Earl of Oxford*. Cecil Palmer, London, 1920.

———. *The Poems of Edward de Vere, Seventeenth Earl of Oxford*. Cecil Palmer, London, 1921.

Maclean, John. *The Life of Sir Thomas Seymour, Knight*. John Camden Hotten, London, 1869.

Malim, Richard, ed. *Great Oxford: Essays on the Life and Work of Edward de Vere*. Parapress, Tunbridge Wells, 2004.

Martyn, Trea. *Elizabeth in the Garden*. Faber and Faber, London, 2008.

Masson, David. *Shakespeare Personally*. Smith, Elder, London, 1914.

May, Steven W. *The Poems of Edward de Vere, Seventeenth Earl of Oxford, and of Robert Devereux, Second Earl of Essex*. University of North Carolina Press, Chapel Hill, 1980.

Miller, Ruth Loyd. *Oxfordian Vistas*. Kennikat, Port Washington, N.Y., 1975.

Miller, Ruth Loyd, ed. *A Hundreth Sundrie Flowres*. Kennikat, Port Washington, N.Y., 1975.

Morant, Rev. Philip. *The History and Antiquities of the County of Essex*, 2 Vols., T. Osborne, London, 1768.

Muir, Kenneth, and Sean O'Loughlin. *The Voyage to Illyria: A New Study of Shakespeare*. Methuen, London, 1937.

Murray, Margaret. *The Divine King in England*. Faber and Faber, London, 1954.

Nashe, Thomas. *The Unfortunate Traveller and Other Works*, ed. J. B. Steane. Penguin, London, 1972.

Nelson, Alan H. *Monstrous Adversary: The Life of Edward de Vere, 17th Earl of Oxford*. Liverpool University Press, Liverpool, 2003.

Nicholl, Charles. *The Chemical Theatre*. Routledge & Kegan Paul, London and Boston, 1980.

———. *The Reckoning: The Murder of Christopher Marlowe*. Jonathan Cape, London, 1992.

Nichols, John. *The Progresses and Public Processions of Queen Elizabeth*, 3 vols. London, 1823.

Norton, Elizabeth. *Jane Seymour, Henry VIII's True Love*. Amberley, Stroud, 2009.

Ogburn, Charlton. *The Mysterious William Shakespeare: The Myth and the Reality*. Dodd, Mead, New York, 1984.

Ogburn, Dorothy, and Charlton Ogburn Sr. *This Star of England*. Coward-McCann, New York, 1952.

Ovid (Publius Ovidius Naso), trans. Mary M. Innes. *Metamorphoses*. Penguin, London, 1984.

———, trans. Peter Green. *The Poems of Exile*. University of California Press, Berkeley, 2005.

Patterson, Annabel. *Censorship and Interpretation*. University of Wisconsin Press, Madison, 1984.

Pearson, Daphne. *Edward de Vere: The Crisis and Consequences of Wardship*. Ashgate, Aldershot, Hants., 2005.

Phillips, G. W. *Lord Burghley in Shakespeare*. Thornton Butterworth, London, 1936.

Pigman, G. W. III, ed. *A Hundreth Sundrie Flowers*. Clarendon Press, Oxford, 2000.

Plutarch (Lucius Mestrius Plutarchus), trans. Thomas North. *The Lives of the Noble Grecians and Romans*. Wordsworth, Ware, Herts, 1998.

Powys, John Cowper. *Suspended Judgments: Essays on Books and Sensations*. G. Arnold Shaw, New York, 1916.

Puttenham, George. *The Arte of English Poesie*, ed. Gladys Doidge Willcock and Alice Walker. Cambridge University Press, Cambridge, 1936.

Read, Conyers. *Mr. Secretary Cecil and Queen Elizabeth*. Cape, London, 1955.
————. *Lord Burghley and Queen Elizabeth*. Cape, London, 1960.
Righter, Anne. *Shakespeare and the Idea of the Play*. Chatto and Windus, London, 1962.
Ross, Josephine. *The Men Who Would Be King*. Phoenix, London, 2005.

Sales, Roger, ed. *Shakespeare in Perspective,* Vol. 1. Ariel, London, 1982.
Schmidgall, Gary. *Shakespeare and the Poet's Life*. University Press of Kentucky, Lexington, 1990.
Sears, Elisabeth. *Shakespeare and The Tudor Rose*. Meadow Geese, Marshfield Mills, Mass., 1992.
Shakespeare, William. *The Arden Shakespeare Complete Works*, ed. Richard Proudfoot, Ann Thompson, and David Scott Kastan. Thomson Learning, London, 2002.
Shell, Marc. *The End of Kinship*. Stanford University Press, Stanford, Calif., 1988.
————, ed., intro. *Elizabeth's Glass*. University of Nebraska Press, Lincoln, 1993.
Sidney, Sir Philip. *Defence of Poesy,* ed. Dorothy M. Macardle. St. Martin's, New York, 1966.
————. *The Countess of Pembroke's Arcadia,* ed. Maurice Evans. Penguin, London, 1987.
Simpson, Richard. "The Politics of Shakspeare's Historical Plays," *New Shakespeare Society Transactions*, I. 2(1874), 413–414.
————. *The School of Shakspere*. Chatto and Windus, London, 1878.
Sinsheimer, Hermann. *Shylock: The History of a Character*. Benjamin Blom, New York, 1968.
Smith, Lacey Baldwin. *Treason in Tudor England: Politics and Paranoia*. Cape, London, 1986.
Sophocles, trans. Sir George Young. *Oedipus Rex*. Dover, New York, 1991.
————, trans. Sir George Young. *Oedipus at Colonus*. Dover, New York, 1999.
Southworth, John. *Fools and Jesters at the English Court*. Sutton, Stroud, 1998.
Spenser, Edmund. *The Poetical Works of Edmund Spenser*, ed. J. C. Smith and E. De Selincourt. Oxford University Press, Oxford, 1952.
Spurgeon, Caroline. *Shakespeare's Imagery*. Cambridge University Press, Cambridge, 1979.
Starkey, David. *Elizabeth*. Vintage, London, 2001.
Stone, Lawrence. *The Crisis of the Aristocracy, 1558–1641*. Oxford University Press, Oxford, 1967.
Strachey, Lytton. *Elizabeth and Essex*. Chatto and Windus, London, 1928.
Stritmatter, Roger A. *Edward de Vere's Geneva Bible*. Oxenford Press, Northampton, Mass., 2001.

Strong, Roy. *Gloriana: The Portraits of Elizabeth I.* Pimlico, London, 1987.

Tanner, J. R. *Tudor Constitutional Documents A.D. 1485–1603.* Cambridge University Press, Cambridge, 1922.

Taylor, Gary. *Reinventing Shakespeare.* Oxford University Press, Oxford, 1989.

Thomson, Elizabeth, ed. *The Chamberlain Letters.* John Murray, London, 1966.

Tillyard, E. M. W. *Shakespeare's History Plays.* Penguin, London, 1969.

Tolstoy, Leo. *Tolstoy on Shakespeare.* Funk and Wagnalls, New York, 1907.

Turton, Godfrey. *The Dragon's Breed: The Story of the Tudors.* Peter Davies, London, 1969.

Walker, Julia M, ed. *Dissing Elizabeth: Negative Representations of Gloriana.* Duke University Press, Durham, N.C., and London, 1998.

Ward, B. M. *The Seventeenth Earl of Oxford.* John Murray, London, 1928.

———. "Shakespeare and the Anglo-Spanish War, 1585–1604," *Revue Anglo-Americaine,* December 1929.

Whittemore, Hank. *The Monument.* Meadow Geese, Marshfield Hills, Mass., 2005.

——— with Ted Story. *Shakespeare's Treason.* Private publication, 2008.

Williams, Neville. *Henry VIII and His Court.* Cardinal, London, 1971.

———. *The Life and Times of Elizabeth I.* Weidenfeld and Nicolson, London, 1972.

———. *All the Queen's Men: Elizabeth I and Her Courtiers.* Cardinal, London, 1974.

Wilson, Derek. *The Uncrowned Kings of England.* Constable, London, 2005.

Winstanley, Lilian. *Macbeth, King Lear, and Contemporary History.* Cambridge University Press, Cambridge, 1922.

Wright, Thomas. *The History and Topography of the County of Essex,* 2 vols. G. Virtue, London, 1836.

Yates, Frances A. *Astraea: The Imperial Theme in the Sixteenth Century.* Ark, London, 1975.

———. *The Occult Philosophy in the Elizabethan Age.* Routledge and Kegan Paul, London, 1979.

Young, Alan. *Tudor and Jacobean Tournaments.* George Philip, London, 1987.

Yukteswar, Swami Sri. *The Holy Science.* Self-Realization Fellowship, Los Angeles, Calif., 1990.

William Shakespeare, engraving from the First Folio by Martin Droeshout the Younger. By permission of the Folger Shakespeare Library, Washington D.C. (STC 22273).

Title page of *Shake-speares Sonnets,* 1609. By permission of the Folger Shakespeare Library, Washington D.C. (STC 22353).

Original monument to Shakespeare, Holy Trinity Church, Stratford, engraving by Sir William Dugdale. By permission of the Folger Shakespeare Library, Washington D.C. (D2479 folio).

Monument to Shakespeare as it appears today, Holy Trinity Church, Stratford by Gerard Johnson. Photo: Shakespeare Birthplace Trust, Stratford-upon-Avon.

Elizabeth I when a Princess, by William Scrots. The Royal Collection © 2009 Her Majesty Queen Elizabeth II.

King Henry VIII by Hans Holbein. © National Portrait Gallery, London.

Anne Boleyn, artist unknown. © National Portrait Gallery, London.

Thomas Seymour, 1st Baron Sudeley by Nicholas Denizot. © National Maritime Museum, Greenwich, London.

Edward de Vere, 17th Earl of Oxford, artist unknown. Private collection; on loan to the National Portrait Gallery, London.

Robert Dudley, 1st Earl of Leicester, Anglo-Netherlandish School. Waddesdon, The Rothschild Collection (Rothschild Family Trust). Photo: Mike Fear. © The National Trust, Waddesdon Manor.

Robert Devereux, 2nd Earl of Essex, after Marcus Gheeraerts the Younger. © National Portrait Gallery, London.

William Cecil, Lord Burghley by or after Arnold van Brounkhorst. © National Portrait Gallery, London.

Letter from the 17th Earl of Oxford to Lord Burghley, October 30, 1584. By permission of the British Library (Lansdowne 42, Folio 97).

Edward de Vere's crown signature, taken from his letter of October 7, 1601 to Sir Robert Cecil, in the possession of the Marquis of Salisbury.

"Checques" taken from the jousting tournament held in May, 1571, at Westminster. By permission of the Bodleian Library, Oxford (Ashmolean 845, fol. 164).

Portrait of an Unknown Woman, by Marcus Gheeraerts the Younger. The Royal Collection © 2009 Her Majesty Queen Elizabeth II.

Title page of *Willobie His Avisa,* 1594. By permission of the Folger Shakespeare Library, Washington D.C. (STC 25755 Copy 2).

Venus and Adonis, 1555, by Titian. © The National Gallery, London.

The Death of Actaeon, c.1562, by Titian. © The National Gallery, London.

Ditchley Portrait of Queen Elizabeth I by Marcus Gheeraerts the Younger. © National Portrait Gallery, London.

Robert Cecil, later 1st Earl of Salisbury by John de Critz the Elder. © National Portrait Gallery, London.

Henry Howard, later Earl of Northampton by a follower of Hieronimo Custodis. The Worshipful Company of Mercers in the City of London.

Henry Howard, Earl of Surrey, artist unknown. © National Portrait Gallery, London.

Henry Wriothesley, 3rd Earl of Southampton, artist unknown. Private collection; on loan to the National Portrait Gallery, London.

Rainbow Portrait of Queen Elizabeth I by Marcus Gheeraerts the Younger. Hatfield House, Hertfordshire. By kind permission of the Marquis of Salisbury.

Ashbourne Portrait of Shakespeare, possibly by Cornelius Ketel. By permission of the Folger Shakespeare Library, Washington D.C.

Index